Citizens and the State in Authoritarian Regimes

Citizens and the State
in Authoritarian Regimes

COMPARING CHINA AND RUSSIA

Karrie J. Koesel, Valerie J. Bunce, and
Jessica Chen Weiss

OXFORD
UNIVERSITY PRESS

Oxford University Press is a department of the University of Oxford. It furthers
the University's objective of excellence in research, scholarship, and education
by publishing worldwide. Oxford is a registered trade mark of Oxford University
Press in the UK and certain other countries.

Published in the United States of America by Oxford University Press
198 Madison Avenue, New York, NY 10016, United States of America.

© Oxford University Press 2020

Library of Congress Cataloging-in-Publication Data
Names: Koesel, Karrie J., 1974– editor. | Bunce, Valerie J., 1949– editor. |
Weiss, Jessica Chen, editor.
Title: Citizens and the state in authoritarian regimes : comparing China
and Russia / edited by Karrie J. Koesel, Valerie J. Bunce, and Jessica Chen Weiss.
Description: New York, NY : Oxford University Press, 2020. |
Includes bibliographical references and index.
Identifiers: LCCN 2019040651 (print) | LCCN 2019040652 (ebook) |
ISBN 9780190093488 (hardback) | ISBN 9780190093495 (paperback) |
ISBN9780190093518 (epub) | ISBN 9780190093501 (updf) | ISBN 9780190093525 (online)
Subjects: LCSH: Political participation—China. |
Political participation—Russia (Federation) | Political stability—China. |
Political stability—Russia (Federation) | Authoritarianism—China. |
Authoritarianism—Russia (Federation) | China--Politics and government—2002– |
Russia (Federation)—Politics and government—1991–
Classification: LCC JQ1516 .C55 2020 (print) | LCC JQ1516 (ebook) |
DDC 320.947—dc23
LC record available at https://lccn.loc.gov/2019040651
LC ebook record available at https://lccn.loc.gov/2019040652

9 8 7 6 5 4 3 2 1

Paperback printed by Marquis, Canada
Hardback printed by Bridgeport National Bindery, Inc., United States of America

For our families

CONTENTS

ACKNOWLEDGMENTS

Like so many projects, this one began with a complaint. Why, we asked each other, were there so few examples of articles and books that compared the politics of contemporary Russia and China? As Karrie can readily testify (along with Elizabeth Plantan and Maria Repnikova, two other contributors to this volume), it is not easy for individual scholars to carry out such a comparison, since it depends, for example, on proficiency in both Russian and Chinese. On the other hand, what a useful comparison this would be! These two countries share a communist past; they are the most influential dictatorships in the world today; and yet they represent such different approaches to the authoritarian project. While Russia holds regular, competitive national elections (albeit not on an even playing field), China does not. China is a Communist Party dictatorship—as the Soviet Union was for seventy-three years.

Also like so many projects, this one took some time to develop. We held two conferences, one in September 2016 at Cornell and another in March 2017 at Notre Dame. The purpose of these conferences was to place in the same room scholars who work on Russia, China, or both countries to encourage them to explore together various aspects of regime–society relations in these two states. The goals of these conferences were threefold. One was to help many of us break out of our one-country habit—a habit that is quite ingrained when the country of interest happens to be a major power. Another was to open up the discussion of Russia and China to female scholars and more junior scholars, thereby addressing another pressing problem in the academy—its stubborn reliance on "old-boy networks." A final goal was to move the group toward an edited volume by asking contributors to tackle two overarching questions: What does this comparison tell us about authoritarian politics in general? What does it tell us about the politics of these two regimes in particular?

Many people and programs helped us move from a vague desire to fill in a gaping hole in the literature to finalizing an edited volume. In addition to the contributors to this volume, there were many others who presented and served as discussants in the first and/or second conference—Allen Carlson, Eli Friedman, Haifeng Huang, Victoria Hui, Iain Johnston, Elisabeth Koll, Tina Lee, Jim McAdams, Andy Mertha, Liz Perry, Jessica Pisano, Molly Roberts, Graeme Robertson, Rory Truex, and Susanne Wengle. The chapters benefited enormously from their thoughtful feedback. In addition, we thank the Einaudi Center for International Studies, the East Asia Program, the Department of Government, and the Institute for the Social Sciences at Cornell University for their support of the first conference. We are also grateful to the Nanovic Institute for European Studies, the Liu Institute for Asia and Asian Studies, the Kellogg Institute for International Studies, and the Institute for Scholarship in the Liberal Arts at the University of Notre Dame for their support of the second conference. Special thanks are due to Melanie Webb at the Nanovic Institute for organizing the Notre Dame conference.

We are grateful to Oxford University Press—especially David McBride, Holly Mitchell, and C. Asish Krishna—for guiding this project to completion. The volume was also improved by the careful reading provided by two anonymous reviewers.

Above all, we would like to thank our families—Patrick, Sasha, Addi, Ron, Nick, Jeremy, Rae, and Lee—for enduring our absences, keeping us grounded, and supporting us along the way. It is to them that we dedicate this book.

CONTRIBUTORS

Mark R. Beissinger, Princeton University

Valerie J. Bunce, Cornell University

Greg Distelhorst, University of Toronto

Manfred Elfstrom, University of British Columbia, Okanagan

Diana Fu, University of Toronto

Karrie J. Koesel, University of Notre Dame

Tomila Lankina, London School of Economics

Aleksandar Matovski, Williams College

Yulia Netesova, London School of Economics

Elizabeth Plantan, Harvard University

Maria Repnikova, Georgia State University

Bryn Rosenfeld, Cornell University

Jeremy Wallace, Cornell University

Kohei Watanabe, University of Innsbruck

Jessica Chen Weiss, Cornell University

Introduction

REGIMES AND SOCIETIES IN AUTHORITARIAN STATES

Valerie J. Bunce, Karrie J. Koesel, and Jessica Chen Weiss

Authoritarian leaders need two things from the societies they rule. First, autocrats need their support, or at the very least their acquiescence. If citizens rebel, the leader can lose her job—and sometimes even her life.[1] Authoritarian rulers, like their democratic counterparts, can be held accountable by their citizens, though different mechanisms are at work. In authoritarian states, leaders govern knowing that the public can rise up and depose them at virtually any time (Schedler 2013; Acemoglu and Robinson 2006). To make matters worse for autocrats, popular unrest can serve as a signal to other actors, such as the military, opposition leaders, and even politicians closely tied to the regime, that the leader's hold on power is weakening. When this happens, a dynamic can ensue wherein restive publics feed restive elites—and the reverse. The familiar distinction drawn by students of authoritarian politics between popular and elite challenges to the ruler, therefore, is often blurred in practice.[2]

Second, autocrats depend on the public (and members of the ruling circle) for good information (Dallin and Breslauer 1970; Manion 2015). Bad information means bad decisions, which contribute to a decline over time in the regime's performance. In turn, sliding performance can spark and link the two rebellions that all forward-looking autocrats need to anticipate if they are to maintain their hold on power—uprisings carried out by ordinary citizens and those started by fickle members of the ruling circle.

Authoritarian rulers know that their political future rests on their ability to minimize political unrest and maximize good information. On the face of it, achieving both objectives should be a cinch for vigilant authoritarian leaders. For example, a typical autocrat has lots of money and many attractive jobs to distribute to both her supporters and her would-be challengers.

In addition, authoritarian rulers have a large and usually loyal coercive apparatus, close ties to economic elites (who depend on political leaders for their survival and profits), and control over key political institutions, such as the courts, the police, local governments, the media, the ruling party, and the bureaucracy. Therefore, autocrats have substantial carrots and sticks at their disposal that allow them to collect useful information, prevent their opponents from accessing the information they need to mount credible challenges to the ruler, and convince citizens and members of the ruling circle that rebellion is neither warranted nor wise.

Despite their many assets, however, autocrats still find it devilishly difficult to craft a governing strategy that gives them the political stability and reliable information they seek. In the real world of dictatorship, even seemingly optimal strategies generate costs, both anticipated and unanticipated. These costs, in turn, often translate into painful trade-offs. Pursuing policies that maximize compliance often means forfeiting good information, yet placing a premium on getting good information can work against popular compliance. For all their power and money, autocrats nonetheless confront hard choices.

Trade-offs Between Repression and Liberalization

Consider the difference between a hard-line approach to governing, which in an authoritarian context refers to a regime using extensive repression to control the population, and a softer approach, in which a regime gives the population more leeway to read, say, and do whatever they want (see Gitelman 1970; Przeworski 1991; O'Donnell and Schmitter 1986; Haggard and Kaufman 2018). For authoritarian rulers, reliance on repression has the advantage of keeping publics and elites too afraid to share their concerns with anyone else and, therefore, far less willing and able to come together to mount credible challenges to the ruler. However, repression is costly. Fearful people hide and distort information. Powerful incentives to be quiet or, if pressed, to pass on unrelentingly positive feedback about the leader and her government do not just translate into bad policies and poor feedback in the short term; they also expose the regime to some unexpected and potentially dangerous surprises down the road. For example, bad agricultural policies, if unchecked, can lead to famine; seemingly loyal lieutenants can spend years hatching a secret plot to depose the leader; opposition groups can organize behind the scenes; and docile publics can wait for an opportunity to express their mounting grievances (Kapuscinski 1989). Repression, then, breeds false preferences, which lull autocrats into thinking that they are better informed, more successful, and more powerful than they actually are.

A repressive environment also leads citizens to distrust the regime, which means that the leader is forced to base his claim to rule on their grudging acquiescence (which can easily slide into anger) rather than widespread popular support (which has many advantages for the leader). If an authoritarian ruler is popular, it is much harder for civilian and military elites to stage a coup d'état, and it is far easier for the leader to weather the inevitable political and economic storms that come his way.

Repression is also a problem because it is very hard for leaders (and the scholars who study them) to predict whether it will in fact preempt protest, as intended, or have the opposite effect of sparking unrest (Bellin 2004, 2012; Martin 2016). Moreover, repression is expensive (Greitens 2016; Svolik 2012). It costs a lot of money to police the population, yet efforts to reduce these outlays are hampered by the size and power of the security sector in repressive states and by fears within the leadership stratum that cutbacks will not just exacerbate tensions between the security forces and the military but also increase the likelihood of a military coup. Autocrats who rely on repression for long periods of time, moreover, are trapped in a contradiction. The longer repression lasts, the more its costs mount both to the leader and to the public.[3] The costs to the leader of reducing repression, however, also increase over time, as public and elite grievances against the leader and the regime grow.

By contrast, a more liberalized political atmosphere, where citizens are less afraid of the regime and have more opportunities to do and say what they want, might seem less likely to threaten a leader's tenure. A more open political environment could lead citizens to appreciate their regime and feel comfortable expressing their true preferences. Such an environment might maximize the leader's support and improve the quality of information available to the government.

But a liberalized or liberalizing dictatorship also carries great risks. Most obviously, the state forfeits at least some of its control over the population. Less control can easily slide into little to no control, which can force the leader to respond with a crackdown or result in the collapse of the regime. Less obviously, the tensions between a relatively open politics, combined with the limitations on civil liberties and political rights built into every dictatorship, feed continuing and often acrimonious conflicts between the state and society and within the state itself over where the lines should be drawn between state control and personal freedom, political order and political chaos, and democracy and dictatorship. These conflicts over how to proceed in such a fluid political context are particularly destabilizing because opposition groups and ordinary citizens are also uncertain and divided about goals and strategies. At the extreme, such turbulence can set the stage for revolution—as we saw during the last decades of the tsarist autocracy in Russia, and during the last decades of the Qing Dynasty and continuing through the Republican and warlord periods in China. In this way, an autocrat's strategy of liberalization can be every bit as subversive as a strategy of repression. Liberalization can set the stage for the fall of the leader, the regime, and even the state.

Repressive and Liberalizing Orders: Chinese and Russian Choices

We are not engaging in an abstract exercise when we sketch out these scenarios associated with repressive and liberalized authoritarian orders. It was precisely these dynamics that unfolded in China and the Soviet Union from the mid-1980s to the early 1990s. To provide some background: In the case of China, market-oriented economic reforms in the early 1980s led to growing demands, especially among students, for political reforms, such as an end to corruption, a reduced role for the Chinese Communist Party (CCP) and the state in everyday life, and an expansion of civil liberties and political rights (Calhoun 1993). Despite periodic support for these reforms from some parts of the political leadership, in June 1989 the Chinese government opted to use military force to crack down on protesters who had assembled for more than a month and a half in Beijing's Tiananmen Square and in many other major cities across China. In the months and years that followed, every Chinese leader made it clear that while some economic liberalization was desirable, political liberalization was out of the question. Leaders defended the hegemony of the CCP, used legal and coercive means to set limits on what was politically acceptable, and continued their ambitious and largely successful program of economic reform. While specific Chinese leaders may have differed on how to maximize political stability and economic growth while minimizing corruption, they all converged on the necessity of one-party rule, repression of the opposition, and control over the public (Manion 2004; Shambaugh 2008). While the forms and extent of a market economy were subject to debate and change in the decades that followed the crisis of 1989, the dictatorship of the CCP was not.

While there are some striking commonalities between China and Russia—for instance, long rule by a Communist Party that came to power through revolution and in the context of a world war, and, in the decade or so preceding their major reforms, growing doubts within the highest reaches of the governing Communist Party about the ability of a state-owned, centrally planned, and largely closed economy to generate technological innovation and rapid economic growth—the Russian story of reform is different. Following his rise to power in the Soviet Union in 1985, Mikhail Gorbachev introduced a series of ambitious economic and political reforms at home and abroad that were to serve the purpose of revitalizing Soviet economic, political, and social life. In contrast to the Chinese leadership's approach of liberalizing the economy but keeping the Communist Party dictatorship in place, Gorbachev's vision of reform in the Soviet Union saw economic liberalization and political liberalization as natural, necessary, and equal partners. In Gorbachev's view, just as more competition in the economy would spur technological innovation and economic growth while enhancing the Soviet Union's ability to transition to a consumer society, so a more open media and competitive politics promised to reduce corruption, bring the best and brightest politicians to power, and energize the public (Brown 1996). Political liberalization also had more practical roles to play. It would prevent an entrenched and corrupt Communist Party from blocking economic reform, and it would encourage the West (and opposition groups in Eastern Europe) to support Gorbachev's coalition.

The differences between the Soviet and Chinese approaches to reform, however, were not just a product of how Gorbachev and Deng individually weighed the costs and benefits of economic and political liberalization. They also grew out of contrasting reform traditions—that is, how (and how successfully) Russia and China had carried out reforms in their past—and contrasting threats to the reform project from key political players. Russia has a long history of its leaders responding to domestic and international crises by introducing bold and simultaneous reforms in politics, economics, and international relations (Bunce 1993), an approach that seems to have repeatedly paid off. For example, Russia maintained its sovereignty in the face of powerful and continuing threats from the West beginning in the fourteenth century; Russia succeeded in becoming a major European power in the nineteenth century; and in the twentieth century the Soviet Union emerged from World War II as a superpower.

By contrast, the Chinese responded to the Western threat in a very different way. After resisting the idea of reform, the Chinese state finally began introducing limited economic or political reforms (usually the former) in the nineteenth and early twentieth centuries. These efforts, however, did not stop the West from compromising China's sovereignty and did not save the Qing Dynasty. After the communists came to power in 1949, Mao broke with Chinese tradition and used political mobilization and political conflict to further his economic and political objectives. However, the politics and policies associated with the Great Leap Forward and the Great Proletarian Cultural Revolution had disastrous consequences both for "the masses" and for the CCP. The Chinese leadership learned from these Maoist experiments that having the Party in control was far preferable, for political and economic reasons, to allowing politics to be in command.

If their experiences with political and economic reform before and during Communist Party rule shaped how Gorbachev and Deng approached reform in the 1980s, so did their immediate political and economic contexts. The Soviet experiment began thirty years before the communists won power in China. This meant that, in comparison with China in the 1980s, the Soviet economy at that time was far more developed, the economic drawbacks of the communist model of development were much more in evidence, and the ruling Communist Party, thanks in part to the extraordinary stability of the Brezhnev era (1964–1982), was far more politically secure, corrupt, and hostile to all change. Gorbachev and his allies thus had little choice but to liberalize Soviet politics in order to reduce the obstacles to economic reform. They needed, in effect, to weaken a Communist Party that had grown too strong.

By contrast, the Chinese reformers, also intent on economic reform but fully aware of the damage Mao had done to both Chinese society and the CCP, needed to unite and strengthen their Communist Party.

To a far greater extent than happened in China, in the Soviet Union (which had a larger and more ripened civil society) Gorbachev's reforms led easily and quickly to growing popular protests. Because of Soviet control over Eastern Europe and the political and economic integration among states that were members of the Soviet bloc, protests erupted in Eastern Europe as well, becoming a region-wide dynamic that could not be controlled from Moscow. In both the Soviet Union and Eastern Europe, the protests focused on two sets of demands: more democratic rights (a demand that surfaced in China as well) and more national rights (which did not play a role in the Chinese events of June 1989). The latter set of demands included calls for a Poland independent of Soviet domination and a Latvia, Georgia, and Ukraine with more autonomy within the Soviet federation or possibly independent statehood (Bunce 1999; Beissinger 2002; Brown 2009). Indeed, the demands for national autonomy and democratic rights in the Soviet republics and in Eastern Europe often went hand in hand because democratic rights, the leaders of nationalist movements argued, could be realized only once national rights were established.

The end result in 1990–1991 was the opposite of what was seen in China. Rather than the continuation of Communist Party rule, we saw instead the collapse of Soviet Communist Party hegemony, the Soviet state, the Soviet bloc, and the Cold War international order. The Soviet Union divided into fifteen states whose boundaries corresponded to those of the fifteen republics that had once made up the Soviet federation. The Russian Federation, the core of the old Soviet Union and its largest republic, made a sharp break with communism and launched a simultaneous transition to capitalism and democracy. A decade later, however, under the leadership of Vladimir Putin, Russia began to return to its authoritarian roots even as it continued on its capitalist path (Zimmerman 2014; Gel'man 2015; Greene and Robertson 2019). While the Yeltsin experiment with democracy had elements of authoritarian politics, the transition to authoritarianism in Russia really began in earnest after Putin was reelected president by a landslide in 2004 (Gill 2015; Taylor 2018). Putin waged a war on democracy on multiple fronts—for example, accumulating more power in his own hands (informally and through changes in the constitution); exerting more control over local political officials and the oligarchs that had dominated the Russian economy since the fall of communism; expanding state control over the economy, the media, and civil society; and harassing opposition candidates and parties (Gill 2015; Gel'man 2015; Taylor 2018).

It is this return to dictatorship in Russia and the much more continuous story of dictatorship in China that serve as the major rationale for this book's comparison of these two countries. And the different paths that the Soviet Union and China took in the wake of economic reforms and political unrest from 1985 to 1991, as just outlined, will help us understand the contemporary dynamics of regime-society politics in Russia and China.

Regime-Society Relations in Russia and China

The purpose of this volume is to analyze the strategic interactions between authoritarian regimes and their societies. There is no shortage of works on this subject.[4] However, the approach taken in this volume is distinctive in a number of respects. First, we compare contemporary Russia and China. As we elaborate later in this chapter, such a comparison is both rare and needed. When these two important authoritarian regimes are placed side by side, the similarities and differences between them produce new insights about each country as well as about regime-society interactions in autocratic countries.

This volume is also distinctive in focusing far more attention on *how* each of these states and their societies interact than on the larger question that has received so much attention in the literature on authoritarian politics—that is, the future of the regime itself. Because all of our contributors work on Russia, China, or both countries, we have all learned, often the hard way, about how dangerous it is to speculate about their future. Some of us remember, for example, a popular joke that made the rounds in Eastern Europe during the communist era: "We know what happened in the past and what will happen in the future. The present, however, is a real mystery." But it is the history of Soviet and Chinese studies and of the countries themselves that makes us appreciate the importance (and difficulty) of analyzing the present and the risks associated with making sweeping claims about the future. During the Cold War, many specialists in the Soviet Union and China, working with very little data and facing pressures to inform policymakers (especially in the Soviet case), devoted an enormous amount of time to looking into their crystal balls.

On a more concrete level, we also remember mid-May 1989, when Gorbachev went to China to hold a summit with Deng. While both leaders were facing unprecedented levels of popular unrest at the time, Gorbachev was advancing daring political and economic reforms at home and abroad; he appeared to be secure in power; and the future of the Soviet Union looked bright. The West, it is fair to say, was captivated by the Gorbachev revolution. By contrast, Deng was resisting political liberalization, he appeared (not for the first time) to be losing personal power and political control, and the future of Chinese communism looked cloudy. Needless to say, that evaluation three decades ago of the two leaders and the future of the Chinese and Soviet reform projects, not to mention the two states, did not age very well. The Soviet approach to reform and the subsequent Russian experiment with democracy and capitalism became cautionary tales, whereas the Chinese approach to reform became the model to emulate.

Finally, rather than treat all of society as a single unit of analysis and thereby flatten the political landscape to the point where all variation disappears, the contributors to this volume unpack "society" and address such issues as what various groups want from the state, how they bargain, and what they get. Like other analysts, we are interested in how leaders approach the dilemmas of managing the citizenry and the reactions, in turn, of citizens to the state's strategies; we explore how the regime interacts with labor, journalists, protesters with various agendas, and non-governmental organizations.[5]

Key Questions

Our inquiry into the politics of regime-society relations in Russia and China is guided by five basic questions. First, what do societal groups want, and how have they expressed their preferences? Second, how have authoritarian leaders responded to the concerns of various societal groups, and what strategies have Russian and Chinese rulers used to stay in power while simultaneously forging political stability and gathering information? Third, how have societal groups responded to the initiatives taken by the autocrats—for example, have they resisted them, complied, or responded in a more nuanced manner? Fourth, what are the costs and benefits, anticipated and unexpected, of the bargains political leaders and their societies have struck? Finally, how similar and how different are these dynamics in Russia and China, and how can we account for the patterns in regime-society relations that we have uncovered in this volume?

In the remainder of this chapter, we set the stage for the chapters that follow. We begin by fleshing out the rationale behind our decision to focus on Russia and China. We then turn to a discussion of the literature on authoritarian politics. Our goal is to extract from this very large body of work key terms and findings that can serve as points of departure for our study. We close the chapter with an overview of each essay in this volume and a summary of this volume's contributions to our understanding of authoritarian regimes in general and the Russian and Chinese variants on authoritarian rule in particular.

Why Russia and China?

There are two reasons we focus our study on a comparison of authoritarian politics in contemporary Russia and China. First, we seek to fill a major gap in the literature on authoritarian regimes. While there are many studies of authoritarian rule in each of these countries, there are very few analyses that compare them.[6] This is surprising for at least two reasons. One is the precedent for carrying out such comparisons, albeit between China and the Soviet Union between 1949 and 1991, the period when both states were communist dictatorships.[7] Second is that China and Russia are arguably the most important authoritarian regimes in the world today. They are the most powerful authoritarian states in global politics and to varying degrees serve as models for other authoritarian regimes that want to emulate their successful formula for combining authoritarian rule with economic growth and international prominence.

Methodological Payoffs

There are also excellent methodological reasons for comparing Russia and China. The norm in the study of authoritarian regimes has been to focus on either all authoritarian states (as in some quantitative and deductive studies) or just one country.[8] Our study is designed to hit the sweet spot between these two extremes. This means that we can take advantage of the benefits of a two-case comparison. As Sidney Tarrow (2010) has persuasively argued, a major analytical benefit of this approach is that a helpful balance can be struck between addressing important theoretical concerns while paying sufficient attention to empirics. This balance is particularly welcome when one is interested, as we are, in processes of interaction as well as causes and outcomes; variation over time within countries; the role of political leadership; and the behavior of various subsets of societal actors interacting with the state (also see Slater 2010).

In addition, Russia and China are in many respects optimal countries for carrying out a two-case comparison. Aside from both being prominent authoritarian regimes, China and Russia share long histories of authoritarian politics in general and communist rule in particular. They also share high scores on cross-national measures of corruption. And despite differences in the design and practice of authoritarian politics in Russia and China, as we will discuss later, personalized rule has taken on central importance in both countries. Putin has defined Russian politics since 2000, even when he served as prime minister rather than president for four years (2008–2012) in deference to term limits in the Russian constitution. Xi, who took the reins of the Chinese Communist Party twelve years after Putin, clearly has similar ambitions for China. It is telling that in February 2018, Xi succeeded in convincing the CCP to remove presidential term limits in the Chinese constitution, paving the way for a potential lifetime appointment (Putin still faces term limits, but he has changed the Russian constitution to extend them).

The differences between the two countries are also striking and analytically useful. We have already made note of some differences—for example, with respect to their historical relationship with the West, their experiences with economic and political reforms before and during communism, and the divergent impact of popular uprisings in 1989 on the regime and the state. Perhaps the most important aspect of what happened in that pivotal year is that while the Communist Party stayed in power in China and has been in command since 1949, it formally gave up its political monopoly in Russia in 1990. What then followed, as previously noted, was a decade-long experiment with democracy under Boris Yeltsin that gave way, under Putin's tutelage, to a return to authoritarian rule.[9] While Russia and China have, as a result, converged over the past fifteen years or so, the Communist Party in Russia is a mere shadow of both its former self and the Chinese Communist Party. Moreover, the ruling party in Russia, United Russia (which has had several names over the course of its existence), functions more as a parking lot for ambitious individuals than as a political party that stands for certain ideological principles, actively recruits candidates, structures the preferences of the citizenry, and mobilizes voters in order to win elections and enact policies.

Another contrast between the two countries is their role in the international system. While China has been upwardly mobile in international politics and economics over the past two decades, the collapse of communism in the Soviet Union, the disintegration of the Soviet state in 1990–1991, and the implosion of the Russian economy in the 1990s had the opposite effect. While Putin is intent on restoring Russia's prominence in the international system (and he has been aided in that quest by Russia's nuclear weapons, its important geopolitical location, the size of the Russian military, its assets in oil and gas, and its role as a regional hegemon in the post-Soviet space), the fact remains that there are built-in limits to Russian reassertion of international influence. One is the size of its population, and another is the size of its economy. By contrast, China is becoming what Russia can only spot in its rearview mirror.

We end this discussion with a final difference between China and Russia, which the chapters that follow this introduction repeatedly mine. These two countries represent two very different approaches to authoritarian rule.[10] China is a non-competitive authoritarian regime, which means that elites, not publics, select national political leaders. Competition for power is hidden, taking place within a hegemonic ruling party rather than within a ruling family or among political parties (Landry 2008; Manion 2015). In short, China is a one-party communist dictatorship. By contrast, like most authoritarian regimes in the world, especially since the end of the Cold War, Russia is a competitive authoritarian regime (a type of regime also sometimes described as electoral authoritarian or hybrid). This means that citizens select national political leaders in elections that feature competition among multiple parties and candidates, with at least some of those parties and candidates functioning as authentic opponents to the regime.[11] These elections open up the possibility that authoritarian incumbents or their anointed successors can lose. But they are nonetheless tilted in the direction of sustaining the political status quo for several reasons: state control over much of the media and the economy; electoral rules that work in favor of the regime and against the opposition; harassment of the opposition and the regime's success in compromising it; the long tenure of leaders (which discourages citizens from wasting their votes on the opposition); and in many cases electoral fraud (Levitsky and Way 2010; Hale 2011; Bunce and Wolchik 2011; Rundlett and Svolik 2016). In addition, rational voters will often prefer the devil they know (and the benefits that devil has repeatedly delivered) to the devil they do not know (who may or may not provide comparable benefits) (Blaydes 2011).

It would be wrong to conclude from this discussion that competitive authoritarian regimes, precisely because of electoral competition, are inherently less sustainable than their non-competitive counterparts or, conversely, that elections in the competitive variant on authoritarian politics are mere shams that allow leaders the image but not the reality of facing verdicts from voters.[12] The fact is that both types of authoritarian regimes can be sustainable and elections in hybrid regimes can lead to the defeat of authoritarian incumbents or their anointed successors.

All that recognized, there are two consequences of the contrast between competitive and non-competitive authoritarian regimes that we are secure in drawing. First, while it is hard to predict the outbreak of conflicts between regime and society in China, it is somewhat easier to do so in Russia. This is largely because elections provide regular focal points for publics to express their concerns—at the ballot box and therefore in the streets (Bunce and Wolchik 2011). In this sense, Russia is like many regimes around the world, whether authoritarian or democratic, in that electoral cycles tend to correlate with cycles of contentious politics (Trejo 2012; Tarrow 2011).

Second, the presence or absence of political alternatives in competitive and non-competitive authoritarian regimes has powerful effects on regime-society relations. Borrowing from Adam Przeworski (1982): politics changes if citizens come to see their regime as possibly temporary rather than permanent. Put differently, and borrowing once again from Przeworski (1991): there is a different politics when the regime is widely understood to be the only game in town than when many people begin to wonder whether it in fact is. As we will discover in the chapters that follow, Russia's detour from authoritarianism in the 1990s, coupled with the rise of competitive authoritarianism in the decade that followed, has generated a much more open bargaining dynamic between state and society than what we see in China as a result of continuity in authoritarian rule in China and the absence of competitive elections.

Authoritarian Politics: Strong but Stressed Leaders

The analysis of authoritarian regimes is a growth industry in both the academic and policy worlds.[13] The interest in authoritarian politics reflects a convergence between trends in the real world—including the rise of China and the return of Russia to international prominence, along with democratic backsliding in relatively new democracies such as Poland and Hungary and, surprisingly, in some old ones as well—and trends in the discipline of political science.[14] The latter trends include the growing interest in analyzing politics as a strategic game—an approach that is easier to apply in dictatorships than democracies because of limited information about the internal (and sometimes external) workings of dictatorships, the relative unimportance of institutions in most authoritarian regimes (but see Gandhi 2007), and the bigger imprint of individual political leaders in contemporary authoritarian states. Put simply: once you subtract pluralism, it becomes simpler to map politics. It is also easier to assume that the overarching goal of authoritarian rulers is to stay in power because of the virtual disappearance, since the end of the Cold War, of ideologically based authoritarian regimes. It is fair to say that, as far as trends over the past thirty or so years in the nature of authoritarian regimes are concerned, the cynics have won and the dreamers have lost.

This volume builds on two sets of claims in the recent literature on authoritarian politics. The first focuses on some important implications of the argument, already discussed, that most authoritarian rulers are driven above all by their desire to stay in power. In some ways, that goal is easy to meet. Authoritarian rulers often have access to extensive resources, whether they use them to court or to coerce their citizens; they have learned how to protect themselves from threats, such as military coups d'état; and they often have a say in how citizens are socialized.[15] In addition, civil society is typically weak in authoritarian states (Howard 2003; Beissinger 2017).

While authoritarian rulers are certain about what they want, they nonetheless live in an extraordinarily uncertain world. They cannot be sure that they know what is going on around them, because authoritarian rule generates powerful incentives for people (who are, after all, as self-interested as the leader) to hide what they know and/or to lie. In addition, authoritarian rulers cannot be certain how long they will be in office (Schedler 2013). As a result, for all the power they seem to have, authoritarian rulers are quite insecure. They worry constantly about challenges to their power, and they continually seek ways to protect and expand it.

These considerations lead authoritarian rulers to place a high premium on preemption. It is better to prevent, dilute, or redirect a challenge to their rule than to allow it to form and grow. As a result, the politics of authoritarian rule is in large measure the politics of preemption.[16] In practice, this means that authoritarian rulers rely on negative incentives, such as repression of the public in general and harassment and marginalization of the opposition and civil society groups in particular, or on positive incentives, such as investment in the development and socialization of shared values that can then be repeatedly evoked; the creation of civil society organizations tied to the regime that provide useful benefits to citizens; and the distribution of benefits to the public through, say, economic growth, public works projects, expansion of the government, and targeted allocation of jobs, goods, and money.[17]

The variation in whether authoritarian rulers rely on carrots or sticks (and which carrots and sticks they actually use) should not obscure the fact that authoritarian rulers have a relatively simple formula for ruling. They want to stay in power; they fear instability; and they go to considerable lengths to prevent instability, or, failing that, to stop it.

Types of Authoritarian Regimes

Students of authoritarian politics also devote a lot of attention to variation among authoritarian regimes: the design and importance of political institutions, the methods used to select political leaders and the types of leaders that govern, the rights enjoyed by the citizenry, and the sustainability of the regime. This variation has generated an ongoing discussion among scholars about how to categorize these regimes.[18] In our view, the most useful distinction is the one we drew earlier between Russia and China—that is, between competitive and non-competitive authoritarian regimes. This distinction is simple; it avoids the problem, common to many typologies, of authoritarian regimes belonging to more than one category; and it accounts for all authoritarian regimes in the world.

Most importantly, however, this distinction seems to be politically consequential—a potential that is explored throughout this volume. We can provide five examples of important questions that are brought to the fore by the contrast between competitive and non-competitive authoritarianism. First, because Putin's regime has retained at least some of the institutions of Russia's experiment with democracy in the 1990s, does it follow that competitive authoritarian rule is less repressive than "fully" authoritarian rule in China? And can we assume that Russia, because of its democratic past, has a larger, more contentious, better-organized, and therefore more effective opposition than China?

Second, do democratic institutions in Russia, however hollow, help explain why protests in Russia erupted in response to widespread and quite visible electoral fraud in December 2011?[19] Do those remnants of democratic life from the 1990s also explain why Putin's popular support fell when he as prime minister and Dmitry Medvedev as president cynically announced eight months before the next national presidential election that they had decided once again to exchange offices?

Third, since citizens in Russia choose their presidents and members of parliament through semi-competitive elections, does this mean that ordinary Russians have more influence on public officials and public policy than citizens in China, where political leaders are selected through a hidden process that holds leaders accountable to other elites rather than to the citizenry? Conversely, do competitive elections in authoritarian settings work in some ways against accountable and inclusive governance? For instance, do Russian leaders use elections to give people a sense that they exert political influence, and then, with the public placated, feel freer to govern without further consultation and do whatever they want? By contrast, does the absence of competitive elections at the national level in China give Chinese officials more incentives than Russian officials to find alternative ways to listen to people in society and take their concerns into account? Do Russian officials, in short, have a lesser burden of proof when dealing with their citizens than their Chinese counterparts?

Fourth, while all competitive authoritarian regimes have weak political parties, the non-competitive regimes that are one-party dictatorships, such as China, feature a single, very strong party that rests on a formidable combination of despotism and penetration (Mann 1984). This contrast introduces two interesting and related questions. One is why Putin (and Yeltsin before him) has refused to build a strong, hegemonic party.[20] The other (which provides a clue to the first question) is whether weak party systems tend to be associated with personalized rule in competitive authoritarian systems. The implication here is that dictators have several options when it comes to reducing the likelihood of defections from the ruling circle. They can use a strong ruling party with significant political and economic assets to maintain ruling coalitions, or they themselves can provide the assets to individual elites (Dawisha 2014; Myers 2016; Markus 2015).

Finally, while it is true that all rational authoritarian rulers worry about political stability, it is also the case that they face different kinds of challenges as a result of two factors: how repressive the regime is and whether the regime is competitive or non-competitive (Bunce and Wolchik 2018). Thus, because China is a repressive, non-competitive system, the biggest challenge to its survival is likely to be popular uprisings—as we saw in Tiananmen Square in 1989 and as we have seen in so many other regimes that share the same characteristics, such as the Soviet Union and Eastern Europe from 1989 to 1991. By contrast, when making predictions about what their irate citizens might do, Russian leaders have reasons to fear mass uprisings *and* electoral defeats. Indeed, in other competitive authoritarian regimes, the two have often gone together and led to the empowerment of the opposition, followed by a transition to democracy (Bunce and Wolchik 2011). What is more, even local elections can be a problem for the Russian leadership. The September 2017 municipal elections in Moscow, for example, indicate that the Russian opposition is gaining significant political ground. In every other case in post-communist Europe and Eurasia where authoritarian rulers in competitive authoritarian regimes lost national elections and were replaced by the opposition, the opposition had begun its quest for national power by first scoring important victories in local elections (Gorokhovskaia 2019; Bunce and Wolchik 2011).

All the essays in this volume, therefore, proceed from a shared point of departure: they treat regime-society relations in Russia and China as a strategic game. In keeping with the literature on authoritarian politics yet mindful of our focus on Russia and China, the contributors to this book take seriously the distinction between competitive and non-competitive authoritarian regimes and see it as playing a key role in shaping the details of the regime-society game—who plays, their preferences, and the resources they bring to the table.

These commonalities recognized, however, the innovative essays in this volume focus on different aspects of regime-society relations in Russia and China and unpack both regime and societal actors. Moreover, while they build on the literature, they also challenge and amend it in striking ways.

Organization of the Volume

The organization of this volume is designed to take readers through the strategic interactions between authoritarian regimes and the societies they rule. In the first section, "Preempting Threats," the authors identify the strategies that Putin and Xi have designed and used to preempt popular challenges to their rule. In his contribution, "The New Normal: A Neopolitical Turn in China's Reform Era" (Chapter 2), Jeremy Wallace argues that the Xi regime has shifted away from technocratic rule in favor of more politicized and ideological strategies of control. These include greater centralization of power, a more assertive role for the Party, crackdowns on corruption and regime opponents, and expanded standards of behavior for local officials. Wallace notes that this shift has been a response to the accumulated costs of quantified rule and growing risks to political stability in China. Rather than focus popular attention on a select set of quantifiable targets, such as GDP growth, the "new normal" in Chinese politics has diversified the set of metrics used to evaluate local officials, increased central monitoring of local agents, and emphasized process over outcomes.

In the next essay in this opening section (Chapter 3), Diana Fu and Greg Distelhorst show how the Chinese Communist Party under Xi Jinping has adopted different strategies for dealing with contentious versus institutionalized forms of political participation. Whereas both forms of grassroots participation had flourished under the prior Hu regime, the Xi administration has shown little tolerance for contentious participation and civil society. At the same time, institutionalized avenues of participation have been unaffected by the restricted space for contentious politics. Looking at measures of online appeals (local mayors' mailboxes), freedom-of-information requests, and administrative lawsuits, Fu and Distelhorst show that these forms of institutionalized participation have persisted—and in some cases increased—in the Xi era.

In the final chapter in this section (Chapter 4), "Diffusion-Proofing: Russian and Chinese Responses to Waves of Popular Mobilizations Against

Authoritarian Rulers," Karrie Koesel and Valerie Bunce move the discussion about leadership strategies in three new directions—by evaluating international and not just domestic threats to the tenure of authoritarian rulers, by treating leadership responses to threats as an amalgam of foreign and domestic policy initiatives, and by comparing Russia and China. Koesel and Bunce examine how the Russian and Chinese leadership responded to two cross-national waves of popular challenges to authoritarian rulers—the color revolutions in post-communist Europe and Eurasia (1998–2005) and the Arab Spring (2010–2011). They argue, first, that both regimes felt quite threatened by these waves, even when the protesters used techniques that did not fit Russian or Chinese circumstances and even when the uprisings occurred very far from the borders of China and Russia. Second, they argue that the Chinese and Russian leadership responded to these dangerous international precedents by crafting a remarkably sophisticated and surprisingly similar ensemble of foreign and domestic policy initiatives—what Koesel and Bunce summarize as "diffusion-proofing"—that reduced the likelihood that these waves would engulf China and Russia as well. What the two regimes did in effect was to reduce the incentives and the capacity of their publics to emulate these international precedents of popular uprisings against authoritarian rulers.

The second section of the book, "Media Politics," addresses the related questions of how both regimes control and use state-run media as well as how the media in turn works for and against these regimes. The first essay, "Critical Journalists in China and Russia: Encounters with Ambiguity" (Chapter 5), by Maria Repnikova, compares the relationship between the Chinese and Russian states and what she terms the critical media: journalists who routinely push the boundaries of permissible reporting. She argues that there is a good deal more collaboration between the two players in China than in Russia. Repnikova demonstrates that Chinese journalists receive clear, intense, and preemptive signals from those in power on a "red zone of untouchable topics," whereas their Russian counterparts must navigate a freer but more arbitrary and opaque political environment with few clear red lines. She concludes that the structured ambiguity in China means that journalists engage in a cautious improvisation with the regime, whereas Russian journalists must navigate the gray zone of political sensitivity and adopt a mixed strategy that ranges from defiant opposition to self-censorship.

The second essay in this section, "How Russian Media Control, Manipulate, and Leverage Public Discontent: Framing Protest in Autocracies" (Chapter 6), by Tomila Lankina, Kohei Watanabe, and Yulia Netesova, compares the media reporting and framing of nationalist versus anti-regime protests. Lankina, Watanabe, and Netesova demonstrate that the Russian state-controlled media provided substantial coverage of mass protest events from 2011 to 2013, even when demonstrations openly targeted the regime. However, they note that coverage of popular protests is carefully tailored—that is, the media first places a positive spin on demonstrations as a democratic right, but this framing shifts to one of public disorder as street activism grows. As a point of contrast, they also find that protests with a nationalist agenda seldom elicit a public disorder frame in the media, even when anti-regime demonstrations are occurring around the same time or nearby. This suggests that authoritarian power-holders closely monitor public discontent and tailor media narratives accordingly.

The third section of this volume, "Law and Labor," shifts the focus to some of the key societal actors in both countries. The key question is how Russia and China use legal regulation of civil society and their variable responses to labor unrest to preempt instability and further their authoritarian project. In "A Tale of Two Laws: Managing Foreign Agents and Overseas NGOs in Russia and China" (Chapter 7), Elizabeth Plantan builds on arguments about diffusion-proofing introduced by Koesel and Bunce in Chapter 4 to compare the content and consequences of recent laws enacted in Russia (2012 and 2015) and China (2017) to regulate non-governmental organizations that receive international funding. She argues that in many respects the laws resemble one another (and, likely not coincidentally, laws in many other authoritarian regimes as well). In both countries these legal initiatives are justified on the basis of national security and create an uncertain and chilling environment for civil society groups, and yet they stop short of implementing a fully repressive agenda by banning civil society. There is, however, one contrast that emerges between the Russian and Chinese approach to controlling NGOs—a contrast that we also see in other chapters, such as by Repnikova (Chapter 5). While the state and NGOs in Russia are usually quite separate and often in an adversarial relationship, the relationship between the Chinese state and NGOs is more often characterized as interactive and consultative—though the Chinese state, of course, retains the upper hand, with repression always a possibility.

In "Holding the Government's Attention: State Sector Workers in China" (Chapter 8), Manfred Elfstrom poses a basic question that is usually left unanswered in studies of political unrest in authoritarian regimes: What is it about worker strikes, protests, and riots that threaten the Chinese state? Is the key issue for them that these actions pose problems for economic stability and growth (for instance, the fact that they threaten important economic actors), or is it their threats to social stability (for example, the possibility that "unruly behavior" on the part of labor will spread to other segments of society)? His analysis of the strikes, riots, and protests that took place from 2004 to 2015, and whether officials responded in a coercive manner or offered concessions, suggests that the Chinese regime is most nervous about worker demands that threaten international capital and state-owned enterprises, and more worried about protests that have the potential to spread from workers to other sectors of society than about less visible actions. What is striking is that protests as a form of worker collective action have increased in recent years. As Elfstrom concludes, while the Chinese state, like virtually all states, seeks both political stability and economic growth, it must in practice make some hard choices when confronting unrest and its likely consequences. It must draw a line between unrest that is tolerable and unrest that is dangerous.

The final set of essays in the book, "Building Public Support," addresses the ways in which the Russian and Chinese regimes have built popular support and how successful they have been in that endeavor. In "The Logic of Vladimir Putin's Popular Appeal" (Chapter 9), Aleksandar Matovski argues that Putin's claim to rule and his remarkably strong public support over the past eighteen years are based on his success in providing political order and national and personal security—in direct contrast to the chaos of the 1990s when his predecessor, Boris Yeltsin, was in power. Nonetheless, as Matovski notes, Putin's support is fragile. In Matovski's phrasing: there are limits to how long accountability can be "delayed and suspended." As the turbulent 1990s recede, Russians have begun to use other yardsticks to evaluate Putin. For example, rather than political order as the sole criterion, they are focusing their evaluations on regime performance with respect to corruption, inequality, and economic growth, as well as adherence to certain democratic principles. With his brand increasingly questioned, Putin is under growing pressure to appear as a leader who resolves crises, even if that means exaggerating or even inventing threats to the Russian nation and state. It is precisely this dynamic that we see in the case of Russian interventions in Ukraine from 2014 to the present. Just as the crisis in Ukraine is portrayed by the Russian state-run media as a major threat to Russia and to most Ukrainians, so does the annexation of Crimea in March 2014 play to Russian national pride.

In Chapter 10, "Legitimacy, Resilience, and Political Education in Russia and China: Learning to be Loyal," Karrie Koesel compares the extensive and elaborate traditions of political and patriotic education in Russia and China and how these regimes attempt to socialize students to be supportive of those in power. She argues that political education is a preemptive strategy of authoritarian resilience and aims to cultivate students who are loyal to both the nation and the regime. She suggests that in spite of dramatically different political pathways and distinctive approaches to authoritarian rule, the Russian and Chinese leaderships are socializing students in similar and multidimensional ways. Koesel makes this argument by mining textbooks, teachers' handbooks, and politics examinations to illustrate the values that the CCP and Kremlin deem most important and want to transmit to youth. She demonstrates that political education in China is highly centralized and that strategies of legitimation over the past three decades have expanded beyond Marxist-Leninist ideology to embrace support for Chinese political institutions, laws, and markets. Russian patriotic education, too, has revived under the stewardship of Putin and stresses the importance of "democratic" institutions and laws, but it also gives prominence to patriotism, defense of the motherland, and the necessity of strong, centralized leadership.

The final essay of this section continues the focus on youth and future elites as loyal regime stakeholders. Bryn Rosenfeld's chapter, "Going Public: Choosing to Work for the Russian State," explores the political and career aspirations of Russian young people who intend to join the state sector. Drawing on an original survey from three elite Russian universities, she examines whether and how Russia's future public servants differ from others in their views of the importance of political freedom, order, national security, and strong economic performance. Rosenfeld finds that Russian youth aspire to work for an autocratic state not because they necessarily favor autocratic values nor hope to instill more democratic institutions but because they come from universities with strong alumni networks linked to the state administration or from families with a parent working in the public sector, and in some cases they felt that their families lost out during the post-communist transition. Interestingly, her chapter reveals that when Russian youth initially become public servants their attitudes and political behavior largely mirror those of people who pursue careers in the private sector, yet over time public servants' political attitudes shift, suggesting that Russia's large public sector also plays a vital role in socializing regime support.

The conclusion to the volume, by Mark Beissinger, returns to many of the themes introduced in the chapters that highlight the similarities and distinctive approaches to authoritarian rule, yet brings in a global framing. Beissinger concludes that although authoritarianism has taken divergent forms in Russia and China, both are globalized authoritarian regimes that have developed strikingly similar strategies to minimize the risks and reap the rewards of heightened global exposure.

Contributions: Questioning Assumptions, Critical Periods, and Regime Variation

What lessons can we draw from the twelve chapters in this volume? We highlight two contributions to the study of authoritarian regimes in general and, more specifically, Chinese and Russian politics. First, the essays call into question some of the key assumptions that have served as the foundation for contemporary analyses of authoritarian regimes. In particular, the norm in the field has been to assume that regime-society relations in authoritarian states are purely domestic processes (but see Weiss 2014; Morrison 2015). By contrast, some of the essays in this volume, while recognizing the importance of the domestic arena, situate interactions between the state and the citizenry in Russia and China in an international context (see the chapters by Koesel and Bunce, Plantan, and Matovski). This means that just as authoritarian leaders face international as well as domestic threats to their power, so the actions they take to preempt or eliminate them in either arena often combine by necessity an ensemble of domestic *and* foreign policies. At the same time, international threats (and many domestic threats as well) can be helpful as well as harmful to authoritarian rulers. An international crisis can provide an opportunity for the leader to mobilize popular support, discourage potential challengers to his power from taking action, and divide and demobilize the opposition. Moreover, if the leader came to power with a mandate to deliver the country from crises, as in Putin's case, then real or imagined crises that are successfully addressed may be useful for refreshing the leader's ruling mandate.

The essays also suggest that we need to rethink how we have understood bargaining between authoritarian regimes and the societies they govern. The essays in this volume offer several amendments. One is to recognize that what citizens and ruling elites want and do is shaped not just by their immediate environment but also by longer-term factors, such as historical precedents and political socialization. For example, the Koesel and Rosenfeld chapters remind us that acquiescence is not just a calculation by citizens and elites about the costs associated with challenging the regime; it also underscores the importance of evaluating the regime's success in creating obedient subjects.

At the same time, contrary to the familiar decision tree approach, some chapters in this volume suggest that authoritarian rulers do not have to choose between repression and co-optation when responding to real or potential challenges to their rule; they can do both (see especially the chapters by Fu and Distelhorst, Koesel, Wallace, and Elfstrom). Indeed, why not? A dual strategy of using both carrots and sticks has several benefits—it keeps everyone guessing, and it provides leaders with an insurance policy (for neither political scientists nor authoritarian rulers are very good at predicting whether it is better to punish or reward unruly subjects).

This leads us to a final assumption in the literature on authoritarian rule that is rarely mentioned, largely because it is widely viewed as a tautology— that is, the inverse relationship between political repression and popular influence on political leaders and public policy. Put more concretely, it is often assumed that because the Russian regime is less repressive than its Chinese counterpart, Russian citizens have more influence on politicians and policies. This contrast, moreover, seems to flow directly from the key differences between competitive and non-competitive authoritarian regimes. While Russian politicians face electoral constraints, Chinese politicians do not.

Yet the inverse relationship between repression and influence does not survive the empirical tests provided by the essays in this volume. Again and again, we find that while Chinese leaders regularly consult with or solicit views from society (see the chapter by Fu and Distelhorst), these kinds of contacts are quite uneven and less common in Russia. Moreover, while legal change in China builds on extensive discussion and consultation, in Russia it can be both very elitist and quite rushed (see the chapter by Plantan). As a result, our comparison of Russia and China leads to a counterintuitive finding: the Chinese regime is often more likely to seek citizen input than the Russian regime.

Regime Variation and Critical Periods

A final important contribution of this volume is to explain what difference being different makes; that is, not only how and where the Russian and Chinese practices of authoritarianism diverge so much from each other but also why this is the case. As for the how and where, we refer not just to obvious distinctions between elected rulers in Russia and selected rulers in China but also to four other contrasts. One is that the Putin regime is much less organized and interventionist than the Chinese political leadership, which orchestrates politics and leaves very little to chance or invention at the national and local levels. At the same time, while the Chinese regime is committed to building the rule of law (or rule by law) to create a more predictable and therefore more stable political environment, the Russian regime is best described as preferring rule without law (Gallagher 2017; Lei 2018; Popova 2017; but see Gaaze 2017). Third, while Chinese groups have strong incentives to moderate their demands as a precondition for both their survival and influence, Russian groups operate in a more uncertain environment wherein a broader range of demands can be entertained but where moderating them does not generate either guaranteed or predictable payoffs. Finally, as argued earlier, while the Chinese regime goes to some lengths to consult with societal groups, the Russian regime is far more slapdash.

The question then becomes how we can explain these very different approaches to the conduct of regime-society relations (see Gehlbach, Sonin, and Svolik 2016). The essays in this volume converge on an original answer. While they recognize the important role played by differences between competitive and non-competitive variants on authoritarianism, they drill deeper and look at historical legacies and the powerful impact in particular of the years 1985–1991 on the subsequent development and practices of authoritarian rule in China and Russia. As we argued earlier, popular protests erupted during this time as a result of reform in both China and the Soviet Union. However, differences in their reform traditions, the obstacles to reform the leaders faced, and, therefore, whether the leader chose to liberalize politics and/or economics (Gorbachev did both; Deng did only the latter) led in the Soviet/Russian case to a bold experiment in building capitalism, democracy, and a new state from scratch and in the Chinese case to an even stronger commitment than in the past to the regime, the state, and economic reforms. While pluralist politics flowered in Russia in the 1990s in the aftermath of popular unrest, the Chinese party-state used violence against its people to reassert control and limit further discussions of political liberalization in the 1990s and beyond.

More importantly, this volume allows us to fast-forward twenty-five years and evaluate the longer-term impact of these divergent responses to popular unrest. What we have discovered is that the decade-long experiment with democracy in Russia left important legacies that continue to shape politics under Putin's dictatorship—for instance, the retention of democratic political institutions, such as popularly elected national and local governments, as well as multiple political parties that are a shadow of their former selves but could transition back to forces of democratic change; competitive elections that could in theory lead to turnovers in government; and a liberal opposition (defined here to include political parties, civil society groups, and parts of the media) that is independent of the regime, locked into an adversarial relationship with it, and quite diverse with respect to its goals and strategies.

While these residues have the potential of becoming staging areas for a return to democracy, they also play two other roles. One is that they remind us why Russia is a competitive authoritarian regime (and why China is not). The other is that Putin has no choice but to work with the institutions of the 1990s. While he gains some legitimacy by virtue of Russia retaining some democratic niceties, he also faces more political uncertainty than Xi. It is not just that Putin's tenure is subject to the will of the voters rather than the Communist Party. It is also that China has just abolished a key institutional constraint on its leader—that is, term limits.

In addition, there are a number of less obvious but equally important traces left by the pluralist past. One is that while Russians were deeply disappointed by their experiences with democracy, they nonetheless continue to resist Putin's violations of democratic norms (Chaisty and Whitefield 2013). As we saw in the 2011 parliamentary elections, for example, Russians have taken to the streets when they have good evidence that the regime has committed major electoral fraud. In the same year, moreover, Putin's public support took a hit when he, after serving for three years as prime minister as a result of term limits in the Russian constitution, made it clear to the public that they would play no role in choosing the next president—this was to be a decision that Putin and President Medvedev would make. The 2012 Russian presidential election, in short, was treated as a foregone conclusion.

Another legacy of the democratic experiment is that Putin's power rests in part on his ability to maintain high levels of public support—a source of worry for Putin that is more typical of his democratic counterparts. Finally, in the 1990s Russia broke with the underlying logic of a communist order—that is, the need of the state to orchestrate what societal actors think, say, and do. While the Putin regime can certainly be repressive, its control over society is much less consistent and invasive than what we see in China.

By contrast, the legacy of the crisis of 1989 in China was very different. Because there was no break with authoritarianism and the state used force successfully to defend the regime, Chinese elites have been able to make a convincing case to the citizenry that the regime is here to stay. The regime, in short, achieved what Beatriz Magaloni (2006) has termed an "aura of invincibility." The seeming permanence of the regime was combined with impressive economic performance—a combination that allowed the regime to win some popular support. At the same time, however, relations between the state and members of society were based on a complex calculus. While the regime had to balance its need for information with its fear that the hegemony of the CCP could be challenged once again, societal groups were also engaged in a juggling act. While they needed to avoid any criticisms of the regime that would invite crackdowns, they also wanted to capitalize on the political leverage they enjoyed as a result of the regime's fear of political instability. In the intersection between these calculations the two sides found some common ground. The combative authoritarianism of 1989 gave way to consultative authoritarianism (Truex 2017; He and Warren 2011; Weller 2008; Nathan 2003), though in recent years the regime has become more repressive once again.

The critical period of the mid-1980s to 1991, therefore, led Russia and China to diverge both in the institutional design of the regime and in the way the regime and society bargain with each other. While there are many similarities between these two countries, such as the many decades both devoted to their communist experiments, their role as charter members if not leaders of the authoritarian club, and the overarching commitment of their leaders to defending their power and their regime, it is in fact the differences between them that stand out in this volume.

Notes

1. Acemoglu and Robinson 2006; but see Beissinger 2013 on the changing nature of mass protests and revolution.

2. Svolik 2012. Also see Bueno de Mesquita and Smith 2011; Art 2012.

3. See, for example, Taylor 2011.

4. See, for instance, Kapuscinski 1989; Lhosa 2000; Wintrobe 2001; Acemoglu and Robinson 2006; Robertson 2009; Slater 2010; Bueno de Mesquita and Smith 2011; Art 2012; Chen 2012; Svolik 2012; Schedler 2013; Gabowitsch 2013; Greene 2014; Gehlbach, Sonin, and Svolik 2016; Beissinger 2017.

5. For different approaches to analyzing regime-society relations, see, for instance, Migdal 1998; Pepinsky 2009; O'Brien 2008; Robertson 2009; Wright 2010; Chen 2012; Beissinger 2013; Teets 2014.

6. But see Koesel 2014.

7. See, for instance, Bernstein 1967; Wemheuer 2014; Dimitrov 2013; Bandelj and Solinger 2012.

8. For instance, Wintrobe 2001; Dickson 2011; Svolik 2012; Bueno de Mesquita and Smith 2011; Gill 2015; Gel'man 2015; Wallace 2014; Teets 2014; Wright 2010. But Slater 2010 is a welcome exception.

9. For competing views about how accurate it is to categorize Russia as a democracy in the 1990s, see Gill 2015 versus Rivera and Rivera 2009.

10. And see Gehlbach, Sonin, and Svolik 2016.

11. We are distinguishing, therefore, between regimes that have fake competition—for example, in Uzbekistan, where all the parties and candidates running for office are tied to the regime—and real competition—where at least some of the parties competing for votes are separate from the regime.

12. On the complicated place of elections in competitive authoritarian regimes, see, for instance, Matovski 2018; Bunce and Wolchik 2011; Rundlett and Svolik 2016.

13. Art 2012.

14. See, for instance, Levitsky and Ziblatt 2018; Grzymala-Busse 2017; Berman 2017.

15. See, for instance, Taylor 2011; Greitens 2016; Bellin 2004, 2012; Quinlivan 1999; Schurmann 1968.

16. For a particularly rich discussion of this point, see Kapuscinski 1989; but in a more political science mode, see Silitski 2005; Tsai 2006; Robertson 2009; Wright 2010, 2011; Svolik 2012; Greene 2014; Wallace 2014; Teets 2014; Bunce 2017.

17. See, for example, Gandhi and Lust-Okar 2009; Blaydes 2011; but also Letsa 2017. On repression in particular, see Bellin 2004, 2012; Greitens 2016; Taylor 2011.

18. See, for instance, Geddes, Frantz, and Wright 2014; Kailitz 2013; Weeks 2014.

19. Greene 2014; Gabowitsch 2013; Kara-Murza 2012; Koesel and Bunce 2012.

20. See, for instance, Hale 2006.

References

Acemoglu, Daron, and James A. Robinson. 2006. *Economic Origins of Dictatorship and Democracy*. New York: Cambridge University Press.

Art, David. 2012. "What Do We Know About Authoritarianism After Ten Years?" *Comparative Politics* 44, no. 2: 351–373.

Bandelj, Nina, and Dorothy Solinger, eds. 2012. *Socialism Vanquished, Socialism Challenged: Eastern Europe and China, 1989–2009*. New York: Oxford University Press.

Beissinger, Mark. 2002. *Nationalist Mobilization and the Collapse of the Soviet State*. Cambridge: Cambridge University Press.

Beissinger, Mark. 2013. "The Semblance of Democratic Revolution: Coalitions in Ukraine's Orange Revolution." *American Political Science Review* 107, no. 3: 574–592.

Beissinger, Mark. 2017. "'Conventional' and 'Virtual' Civil Societies in Authoritarian Regimes." *Comparative Politics* 49, no. 3: 351–371.

Bellin, Eva. 2004. "The Robustness of Authoritarianism in the Middle East: Exceptionalism in Comparative Perspective." *Comparative Politics* 36, no. 2: 139–157.

Bellin, Eva. 2012. "Reconsidering the Robustness of Authoritarianism in the Middle East: Lessons of the Arab Spring." *Comparative Politics* 44, no. 2: 127–149.

Berman, Sheri. 2017. "Populism Is a Symptom, Rather than a Cause: The Decline of Center-Left Parties and the Rise of Threats to Democracy." Project on Global Populisms, Freeman Spogli Institute, Stanford University. https://fsi-live.s3.us-west-1.amazonaws.com/s3fs-public/populism_is_a_symptom_rather_than_a_cause_stanford_global_populisms_conference.pdf.

Bernstein, Thomas. 1967. "Leadership and Mobilization in the Soviet and Chinese Collectivization Campaigns of 1929–1930 and 1955–1956." *China Quarterly* 31: 1–47.

Blaydes, Lisa. 2011. *Elections and Distributive Power in Mubarak's Egypt.* New York: Cambridge University Press.

Brown, Archie. 2009. *Seven Years That Changed the World: Perestroika in Perspective.* Oxford: Oxford University Press.

Brown, Archie. 1996. *The Gorbachev Factor.* Oxford: Oxford University Press.

Bueno de Mesquita, Bruce, and Alastair Smith. 2011. *The Dictator's Handbook: Why Bad Behavior Is Almost Always Good Politics.* New York: Public Affairs.

Bunce, Valerie. 1993. "Domestic Reform and International Change: The Gorbachev Reforms in Historical Perspective." International Organization 47, no. 1: 107–138.

Bunce, Valerie. 1999. *Subversive Institutions: The Design and Destruction of Socialism and the State.* Cambridge: Cambridge University Press.

Bunce, Valerie. 2017. "The Prospects for a Color Revolution in Russia." *Daedalus* 146, no. 2: 19–29.

Bunce, Valerie, and Sharon Wolchik. 2011. *Defeating Authoritarian Leaders in Postcommunist Countries.* Cambridge: Cambridge University Press.

Bunce, Valerie, and Sharon Wolchik. 2018. "Modes of Popular Mobilization Against Authoritarian Rulers: A Comparison of 1989, the Color Revolutions and the MENA Uprisings." *Demokratizatsiya* 26, no. 2: 173–194.

Calhoun, Craig. 1993. *Neither Gods Nor Emperors: Students and the Struggle for Democracy in China.* Berkeley: University of California Press.

Chaisty, Paul, and Stephen Whitefield. 2013. "Forward to Democracy or Back to Authoritarianism? The Attitudinal Bases of Mass Support for the Russian Election Protests of 2011–2012." *Post-Soviet Affairs* 29, no. 5: 387–403.

Chen, Xi. 2012. *Social Protest and Contentious Authoritarianism in China.* Cambridge: Cambridge University Press.

Dallin, Alexander, and George Breslauer. 1970. *Political Terror in Communist Systems.* Berkeley: University of California Press.

Dawisha, Karen. 2014. *Putin's Kleptocracy: Who Owns Russia?* New York: Simon and Schuster.

Dickson, Bruce. 2011. "Sustaining Party Rule in China: Coercion, Co-Optation and Their Consequences." In *The Dynamics of Democratization, Dictatorship, Development and Diffusion,* ed. Nathan Brown. Baltimore: Johns Hopkins University Press.

Dimitrov, Martin, ed. 2013. *Why Communism Didn't Collapse.* Cambridge: Cambridge University Press.

Elfstrom, Manfred. 2016. "Resistance, Repression, Responsiveness: Workers and Change in China." Ph.D. dissertation, Cornell University.

Gaaze, Konstantin. 2017. "Taking the Plunge: Russia's New Managerial Class." Carnegie Report, November 15, 2017. http://carnegie.ru/commentary/74578.

Gabowitsch, Mischa. 2013. *Protest in Putin's Russia.* Cambridge: Polity Press.

Gallagher, Mary. 2017. *Authoritarian Legality in China: Law, Workers and the State.* Cambridge: Cambridge University Press.

Gandhi, Jennifer. 2007. "Authoritarian Institutions and the Survival of Autocrats." *Comparative Political Studies* 40, no. 11: 1279–1301.

Gandhi, Jennifer, and Ellen Lust-Okar. 2009. "Elections Under Authoritarianism." *Annual Review of Political Science* 12: 403–422.

Geddes, Barbara, Erica Frantz, and Joseph Wright, eds. 2014. "Autocratic Breakdowns and Regime Transitions: A New Data Set." *Perspectives on Politics* 12, no. 2: 212–331.

Gehlbach, Scott, Konstantin Sonin, and Milan Svolik. 2016. "Formal Models of Authoritarian Politics." *Annual Review of Political Science* 19: 565–584.

Gel'man, Vladimir. 2015. *Authoritarian Russia: Analyzing Post-Soviet Regime Changes.* Pittsburgh: University of Pittsburgh Press.

Gill, Graeme. 2015. *Building an Authoritarian Polity: Russia in Post-Soviet Times.* Cambridge: Cambridge University Press.

Gitelman, Zvi. 1970. "Power and Authority in Eastern Europe." In *Change in Communist Systems*, ed. Chalmers Johnson. Stanford: Stanford University Press.

Gorokhovskaia, Yana. 2019. "What It Takes to Win When the Game Is Rigged: The Evolution of Opposition Electoral Strategies in Moscow, 2012–17." *Democratization* 26, no. 6: 975–992.

Greene, Samuel A. 2014. *Moscow in Movement: Power and Opposition in Putin's Russia.* Stanford: Stanford University Press.

Greene, Samuel A., and Graeme Robertson. 2019. *Putin v. People: The Perilous Politics of a Divided Russia.* New Haven: Yale University Press.

Greitens, Sheena Chestnut. 2016. *Dictators and Their Secret Police: Coercive Institutions and State Violence.* Cambridge: Cambridge University Press.

Grzymala-Busse, Anna. 2017. "Populism and the Erosion of Democracy in Poland and Hungary." Project on Global Populisms, Freeman Spogli Institute, Stanford University. https://fsi-live.s3.us-west-1.amazonaws.com/s3fs-public/grzymala-busse_memo_1_0.pdf.

Haggard, Stephen, and Robert R. Kaufman. 2018. *Dictators and Democrats: Masses, Elites and Regime Change.* Princeton: Princeton University Press.

Hale, Henry. 2006. *Why Not Parties in Russia? Democracy, Federalism and the State.* Cambridge: Cambridge University Press.

Hale, Henry. 2011. "Hybrid Regimes: When Democracy and Autocracy Mix." In *The Dynamics of Democratization, Dictatorship, Development and Diffusion*, ed. Nathan Brown, 23–45. Baltimore: Johns Hopkins University Press.

He, Baogang, and Mark E. Warren. 2011. "Authoritarian Deliberation: The Deliberative Turn in Chinese Political Development." *Perspectives on Politics* 9, no. 2: 269–289.

Howard, Marc. 2003. *The Weakness of Civil Society in Postcommunist Europe.* Cambridge: Cambridge University Press.

Kailitz, Steffen. 2013. "Classifying Political Regimes Revisited: Legitimation and Durability." *Democratization* 20, no. 1: 39–60.

Kapuscinski, Ryszard. 1989. *The Emperor: Downfall of an Autocrat.* New York: Vintage.

Kara-Murza, Vladimir. 2012. "Russia's Local Elections: Politics in Spite of Putin." *World Affairs* 175, no 3: 53–60.

Koesel, Karrie J. 2014. *Religion and Authoritarianism: Cooperation, Conflict, and the Consequences.* New York: Cambridge University Press.

Koesel, Karrie J., and Valerie J. Bunce. 2012. "Putin, Popular Protests and Political Trajectories in Russia: A Comparative Perspective." *Post-Soviet Affairs* 28, no. 4: 403–423.

Landry, Pierre. 2008. *Decentralization and Authoritarianism in China: The Communist Party's Control of Local Elites in the Post-Mao Era.* Cambridge: Cambridge University Press.

Lei, Ya-Wen. 2018. *The Contentious Public Sphere: Law, Media and Authoritarian Rule in China.* Princeton: Princeton University Press.

Letsa, Natalie. 2017. "'The People's Choice': Popular (Il)legitimacy in Autocratic Cameroon." *Journal of Modern African Studies* 55, no. 4: 647–679.

Levitsky, Steven, and Lucan Way. 2010. *Competitive Authoritarianism: Hybrid Regimes After the Cold War.* Cambridge: Cambridge University Press.

Levitsky, Steven, and David Ziblatt. 2018. *How Democracies Die*. New York: Penguin Random House.

Lhosa, Maria Vargas. 2000. *Feast of the Goat*. New York: Farrar, Straus and Giroux.

Magaloni, Beatriz. 2006. *Voting for Autocracy: Hegemonic Party Survival and Its Demise in Mexico*. Cambridge: Cambridge University Press.

Mann, Michael. 1984. "The Autonomous Power of the State: Its Origins, Mechanisms and Results." *European Journal of Sociology* 25, no. 2: 185–211.

Manion, Melanie. 2004. *Corruption by Design: Building Clean Government in Mainland China and Hong Kong*. Cambridge, MA: Harvard University Press.

Manion, Melanie. 2015. *Information for Autocrats: Representation in Chinese Local Congresses*. Cambridge: Cambridge University Press.

Markus, Stanislav. 2015. *Property, Predation and Protection: Piranha Capitalism in Russia and Ukraine*. Cambridge: Cambridge University Press.

Martin, Brian. 2016. "From Political Jiu-jitsu to the Backfire Dynamic: How Repression Can Promote Mobilization." In *Civil Resistance: Comparative Perspectives on Non-Violent Struggle*, ed. Kurt Schock. Minneapolis: University of Minnesota Press.

Matovski, Aleksandar. 2018. "Popular Dictatorships: Crises, Mass Opinion and the Rise of Electoral Authoritarianism." Unpublished manuscript.

Migdal, Joel. 1998. *Strong Societies and Weak States: State-Society Relations and State Capabilities in the Third World*. Princeton: Princeton University Press.

Morrison, Kevin. 2015. *Non-Taxation and Representation: The Fiscal Foundations of Political Stability*. Cambridge: Cambridge University Press.

Nathan, Andrew. 2003. "Authoritarian Resilience." *Journal of Democracy* 14, no. 1: 6–17.

Myers, Steven Lee. 2016. *The New Tsar: The Rise and Reign of Vladimir Putin*. New York: Alfred A. Knopf.

O'Brien, Kevin, ed. 2008. *Popular Protest in China*. Cambridge, MA: Harvard University Press.

O'Donnell, Guillermo, and Philippe C. Schmitter. 1986. *Transitions from Authoritarian Rule: Tentative Conclusions About Uncertain Democracies*. Baltimore: Johns Hopkins University Press.

Pepinsky, Tom. 2009. *Economic Crises and the Breakdown of Authoritarian Regimes: Indonesia and Malaysia in Comparative Perspective*. Cambridge: Cambridge University Press.

Popova, Maria. 2017. "Putin-Style 'Rule of Law' and the Prospects for Change." *Daedalus* 146, no. 2: 64–73.

Przeworski, Adam. 1982. "'The Man of Iron' and Men of Iron in Poland." *PS: Political Science and Politics* 15, no. 1: 18–31.

Przeworski, Adam. 1991. *Democracy and the Market*. Cambridge: Cambridge University Press.

Quinlivan, James T. 1999. "Coup-Proofing: Its Practice and Consequences in the Middle East." *International Security* 24, no. 2: 131–165.

Rivera, David, and Sharon Rivera. 2009. "Yeltsin, Putin, and Clinton: Presidential Leadership and Russian Democratization in Comparative Perspective." *Perspectives on Politics* 7, no. 3: 591–610.

Robertson, Graeme. 2009. "Managing Society: Protest, Civil Society and Regime in Putin's Russia." *Slavic Review* 68, no. 3: 528–547.

Rundlett, Ashlea, and Milan Svolik. 2016. "Deliver the Vote! Micromotives and Macrobehavior in Electoral Fraud." *American Political Science Review* 110, no. 1: 180–197.

Schedler, Andreas. 2013. *The Politics of Uncertainty: Sustaining and Subverting Electoral Authoritarianism.* Oxford: Oxford University Press.

Schurmann, Franz. 1968. *Ideology and Organization in Communist China.* Berkeley: University of California Press.

Shambaugh, David. 2008. *China's Communist Party: Atrophy and Adaptation.* Berkeley: University of California Press.

Silitski, Vitali. 2005. "Preempting Democracy: The Case of Belarus." *Journal of Democracy* 16, no. 4: 83–97.

Slater, Dan. 2010. *Ordering Power: Contentious Politics and Authoritarian Leviathans in Southeast Asia.* Cambridge: Cambridge University Press.

Svolik, Milan. 2012. *The Politics of Authoritarian Rule.* Cambridge: Cambridge University Press.

Tarrow, Sidney. 2010. "The Strategy of Paired Comparison: Toward a Theory of Practice." *Comparative Political Studies* 43, no. 2: 230–259.

Tarrow, Sidney. 2011. *Contentious Politics and Social Movements.* Cambridge: Cambridge University Press.

Taylor, Brian. 2011. *State-Building in Putin's Russia: Policing and Coercion After Communism.* New York: Cambridge University Press.

Taylor, Brian. 2018. *The Code of Putinism.* New York: Oxford University Press.

Teets, Jessica. 2014. *Civil Society Under Authoritarianism: The China Model.* New York: Cambridge University Press.

Trejo, Guillermo. 2012. *Popular Movements in Autocracies: Religion, Repression and Indigenous Collective Action in Mexico.* Cambridge: Cambridge University Press.

Truex, Rory. 2017. "Consultative Authoritarianism and Its Limits." *Comparative Political Studies* 50, no. 3: 329–361.

Tsai, Kellee. 2006. "Adaptive Informal Institutions and Endogenous Institutional Change in China." *World Politics* 59, no. 1: 116–141.

Wallace, Jeremy. 2014. *Cities and Stability: Urbanization, Redistribution and Regime Survival in China.* New York: Oxford University Press.

Weeks, Jessica. 2014. *Dictators at War and Peace.* Ithaca, NY: Cornell University Press.

Weller, Robert. 2008. "Responsive Authoritarianism." In *Political Change in China*, ed. G. Bruce and L. Diamond, 117–143. Boulder, CO: Lynne Rienner Publishers.

Weiss, Jessica Chen. 2014. *Powerful Patriots: Nationalist Protest in China's Foreign Relations.* New York: Oxford University Press.

Wemheuer, Felix. 2014. *Famine Politics in Maoist China and the Soviet Union.* New Haven: Yale University Press.

Wintrobe, Ronald. 2001. "How to Understand and Deal with Dictatorship: An Economist's View." *Economics of Governance* 2, no. 1: 35–58

Wright, Teresa. 2010. *Accepting Authoritarianism: State-Society Relations in China's Reform Era.* Stanford: Stanford University Press.

Wright, Teresa. 2011. "Perpetuating Communist Party Rule in China." *Journal of International Affairs* 65, no. 1: 31–45.

Zimmerman, William. 2014. *Ruling Russia: Authoritarianism from the Revolution to Putin.* Princeton: Princeton University Press.

SECTION } I

Preempting Threats

2 }

The New Normal

A NEOPOLITICAL TURN IN CHINA'S REFORM ERA

Jeremy Wallace

The drama was high and the tension thick when President Xi Jinping visited Hebei to attend what became four marathon "democratic life meetings" over two days following months of preparation. On the verge of tears, officials admitted their failings to Xi and the country's people via Chinese Central Television (CCTV).[1] Zhou Benshun, the province's Party secretary, stated, "I cared very much about development speed and economic volumes but not as much about people's own interests."[2] This emotional display of political conflict—explicitly attacking the value of quantitative metrics of performance—is but one example introducing a new normal in Chinese politics.

In the past few years, politics in the People's Republic of China (PRC) has been remade. Both institutional and rhetorical changes characterize this neopolitical "new normal" (新常态), which coincides with Xi Jinping's rise to the top of the party-state hierarchy.[3] Xi has been described as the most powerful Chinese leader since Mao Zedong, but these changes extend well beyond Xi himself.[4] Political authority has been centralized in the anti-corruption unit of the Chinese Communist Party (CCP), the Central Commission on Discipline Inspection (CCDI), while complaints against officials have begun to air publicly, commercial and state-run media broadcast cadres' self-criticisms, and leaders push to imbue officialdom with traditional morals.[5] The public airing of criticisms and self-criticisms has not been limited to officials. Repression and humiliation have been used against critics as wide-ranging as Hong Kong booksellers, feminist activists, and rights lawyers, among others.[6] Most ominously, the government has embarked on a massive detention and reeducation scheme in Xinjiang, with the number of those interned estimated to be in the hundreds of thousands or even surpassing a million.[7]

How do we understand political change inside non-democratic polities? Over the past two decades, a spate of new research on authoritarianism has emerged, focusing on regime survival and the institutions inside these regimes; however, works that distinguish between more subtle shifts remain rare.[8] Similarly, the Polity data series and other continuous measures of democracy rarely capture such moves in their scores, as they are more focused on the democracy-dictatorship divide.[9] New multidimensional measures of authoritarian rule can capture some aspects of change (namely, shifts in personalism and institutionalization of power), but even they overlook policy and rhetorical adjustments.[10] I argue that scholars of authoritarianism should push to understand the who, how, and why of authoritarian regimes, and should use this framework to analyze developments in contemporary Chinese politics.[11]

The remaking of Chinese politics over the past half decade has led some watchers of its politics to claim that the reform era is ending.[12] Instead, I argue that the Chinese regime is shifting its mix of strategies away from a technocratic rule, where numbers dominate and the institutions of control attempt to be invisible, and toward a new and more politicized environment.[13] These changes are not so radical as to signal the end of the reform era, let alone the end of the regime itself.[14] Instead, they can be thought of as adjustments to the regime's size, form, and purpose. Centralization decreases the effective size of the regime, and rhetorical and bureaucratic changes reflect modifications to its form and purpose. To demonstrate this claim's validity requires detailing both how these changes differ from prior reform era governance and how they still remain fruitfully rooted in this period rather than the beginning of some new era of Chinese politics.[15] That is, this chapter's framework shows this new normal as occupying a middle ground between those who argue nothing has changed and those who say everything has.

The political transformation at the start of the reform era engendered difficulties that were in part solved by central leaders choosing to limit their ability to monitor local governments. This limited vision focused on a few quantified outcomes (most notably GDP, fiscal revenue, population control, and social stability) and produced strong results on these metrics but simultaneously generated substantial negative externalities in other dimensions (corruption, pollution, hidden local debt, and falsified statistics). This institutional schema helps account for China's rapid economic growth, the challenges the country faces, and the actions currently being undertaken to address them.[16] The neopolitical turn—changing rhetoric, centralization, anti-corruption, public repression, and more—is a two-pronged response to these challenges. The neopolitical turn is both an attempt to fix that old system and a hedge against the chance that the old system is unfixable. The fix addresses the prior system's accumulated costs by increasing control over local officials, while the hedge provides new political tentpoles supporting regime continuance should economic performance deteriorate further.

The chapter continues as follows. After emphasizing the conventional view of the significance of the transition between Mao and post-Mao China, I examine the reform era through the lens of information. This lens exposes the center's increasing problems of local officials hiding facts—about pollution, corruption, and debts, among others. Next, I argue that the new normal is a neopolitical turn in Chinese politics, highlighting institutional and rhetorical facets. I contrast my argument with alternative conceptions of the new normal. Finally, I conclude with a brief comparison with the Russian case and call for more research on the subtleties of authoritarian rule using this framework.

Transformation and Information

While continuities certainly exist between CCP rule under Mao and after his death, Chinese politics was fundamentally altered. Scholars and students of contemporary China, as well as the regime itself, have taken to dividing CCP rule of China into two distinct periods, the Mao era and the reform era.[17] On the other hand, cross-national analyses of non-democratic polities tend to treat the reign in an uninterrupted fashion.[18]

The half decade of 1976 to 1981 saw the who, what, where, when, how, and why of Chinese politics transformed with profound consequences for citizens living under this regime and its agents at local levels. Technocrats replaced revolutionaries (who), to pursue economic development rather than communist utopia (what), retreating from the front lines of economic production (where), while learning from the disasters of the Great Leap Forward and Cultural Revolution (when), using market mechanisms (how), to maintain the institutional power of the Chinese Communist Party (why).[19]

It is well understood that central political control of the day-to-day lives of Chinese declined after Mao.[20] However, information's critical role in reform era politics tends to be overlooked in favor of depersonalization of elite power, experimentation, adaptation, and pragmatism when considering policy, rhetoric, and state-society relations. While each of these lenses sheds some light on different aspects of the three and a half decades that have followed in Mao's wake, in the early reform era decisions about central monitoring of local governments—that is, information—can clarify the problems that the regime faced at the time, how its choices resolved these issues in the short term, and how those choices came to induce new problems over the long term.[21]

The transformation of Chinese politics following Mao was not simply replacing one paramount leader with another ruler possessing different policy priorities. Rather, the entire machinery of the Chinese Communist Party and the government of the People's Republic of China was reinstitutionalized.

Most Party members and state officials were distant from the machinations of the super-elite. However, they keenly experienced the policy and rhetorical shifts, moving away from Maoist economic and ideological dogmatism. Leaders at all levels felt cognitive dissonance with the regime's changing justification strategy. Crucially, central elites emphasized bottom-up experimentation with minimal oversight for two reasons. First, they believed that such local initiatives were more likely to produce solid economic outcomes. Second, they gave local officials opportunities to move beyond the past at their own pace.

Reform entails many costs and risks for an authoritarian regime. As Tocqueville put it, "The most critical moment for bad governments is the one which witnesses their first steps towards reform."[22] An existing government initiating a reform signals a belief that the status quo can be improved. As a regime was the status quo until altering it, reforms signal that the regime had erred. Such signals can split regime elites as well as create resistance and cognitive dissonance among the regime's agents and the population, especially one emerging out of a totalitarian regime that demanded ideological conformity.

Jettisoning Mao-era politics created significant obstacles, as can be seen in the difficulties facing rural reforms. Introduction of the profit motive as a regime-approved technique of generating development represented a radical shock to the intellectual frameworks, self-conceptions, and policy environments of cadres and Chinese citizens. Some cadres feared that the rural reforms, by distancing policy from Maoist ideals, would increase inequality as well as possibly lead to the return of landlords.[23] These officials had been indoctrinated; they had come to accept the values that the regime had been using to justify itself and were not willing to hastily shift away from them. Relatedly, those who believed in the prior ideological vision might have concerns not only about the values inherent in the reform but also because of their beliefs about what kinds of policies would produce strong outcomes.[24] Others resisted out of fear, because they were unwilling or too cautious to move so far down what looked like a capitalist road.[25] Under Mao, sudden policy reversals away from profit-minded activities—perhaps most clearly with the post–Great Leap Forward policies and campaigns, such as the Socialist Education Movement and the Four Cleanups—scared many away from such actions. Others resisted or dragged their feet since the household responsibility system and marketization more generally shifted the power structure in the countryside.

Decollectivization of agriculture also cut off revenue streams to local leaders, who—particularly at the village level—went from ordering all economic and political efforts of the collective to a more hands-off role overseeing a community.[26] While their control over the agricultural work of the village was declining, local officials latched onto a new opportunity and fostered an explosion of rural industry.[27] Some officials took advantage of their positions and extracted value from these enterprises for personal gain, while others facilitated the development of these enterprises in a less corrupt manner. The lack of monitoring from higher levels gave local governments significant room to maneuver in ways that greased the wheels of marketization, as officials accepted the trade-off of less influence over a larger set of resources.[28]

Party-state elites were aware that relaxing central controls would entail an increased risk of profiteering and corruption, as demonstrated when they simultaneously recreated monitoring institutions while constraining their ability to monitor. The Party reconstituted the CCDI in 1979 as an investigatory and monitoring agency looking at the political performance of cadres.[29] Multiple economic agencies were also tasked with overseeing the activities of the party-state's local agents: the State Planning Commission, the State Statistical Bureau, and the General Accounting Administration (GAA).[30] At the founding of the GAA in 1983, Tian Jiyun, then vice premier, explicitly acknowledged that the increased economic freedom of localities would generate divergences between national and local interests.[31] The center acted to encourage growth and accepted that its plans to do so would create divides between the desires of central and local officials, yet limited its ability to monitor and punish local actions that moved away from central aims.

These monitoring institutions failed to serve as strong checks on local behavior because of their bureaucratic weakness and lack of capacity. One crucial factor was their subordinate relationship with local Party committees. That is, these agencies were tasked to monitor and report to higher authorities about the actions of their immediate political superiors, who often controlled their budgets. Second, they were given staffs inadequate to closely observe local actions. In 1988, Qiao Shi, a Politburo Standing Committee member and leader of the CCDI at the time, told auditors that since they were responsible for overseeing 800,000 organizations, even a staff of 500,000 would be inadequate; yet rather than suggesting funding a staff of sufficient scale to tackle the task, he emphasized the importance of aiding "internal auditing bureaus" inside these organizations.[32] State leaders acknowledged this problem yet fashioned these institutions in this shorthanded manner, pointing toward a deliberate decision to create a monitoring apparatus with limited vision. To be sure, other institutional channels, such as petitions, existed in China during this period, but the emphasis here is that these information-gathering institutions were limited in their funding and empowerment.[33]

The limited vision into localities meant that local officials were judged primarily by their performance on a few critical quantitative indicators. The Cadre Evaluation System (干部考核制度) is a system of quantitative metrics or targets by which higher-ups can measure local economic and political performance, and reward (or punish) officials based upon such figures.[34] Different targets are seen as more or less critical, hard and soft targets respectively, and there are also particular items of singular import—one-item vetoes—which historically have included population growth (via birth rate rather than in-migration, a one-child policy issue) and social stability (with eruptions of instability torpedoing promotions).[35] GDP and its growth became the most visible and significant of these statistics, with fiscal revenues and investment also weighted heavily.

Under technocratic rule, local government or party-state officials were embedded in a competition over figures in spreadsheets. Simplifying the complexities of local performance made localities legible to the center but came with numerous consequences, some of which were quite perverse.[36] This system in some ways insulated the center from the raw heat of the aggrieved, channeling discontent into "rightful resistance," which blamed local officials for problems and called on higher levels to ride to the rescue.[37]

Scholars debate about the extent to which numbers cause promotions (and which numbers matter),[38] or to put it differently, the extent to which the figures that fed into the cadre evaluation system dominated the patterns of promotions inside the party-state hierarchy.[39] However, even those who see non-numerical components of a given politician's profile (i.e., factions or networks) as critical to promotions concede that these numbers do aid in accounting for who moves up the chain of command, especially at the lower levels.[40]

Hiding Facts

The significance of a few particular indicators and the general lack of monitoring created incentives for lower-level officials to hide the truth from their superiors.[41] Facts that could have exposed problems of environmental pollution, wasted investments, corruption, and manipulated statistics were instead concealed. Rather than provide accurate records of reality, the numbers at the heart of the machine increasingly failed to count what mattered, and what was counted failed to measure up.

Local governments and firms measured on outputs such as GDP and profits ignored pollution produced by their activities. The system did not count or weight the costs imposed on others by the burning, spilling, and dumping of these toxins, befitting a classic negative externality. Fossil fuels powered China's run of remarkable economic growth, leading to China becoming the world's number one contributor to global greenhouse emissions in 2006,[42] but they also contributed to lower air quality to such an extent that estimates of annual excess deaths due to air pollution vary from tens of thousands to hundreds of thousands.[43] "Airpocaplyses"—air so thick with particulate matter that day becomes night—displaced gleaming skyscrapers as the images dominating international coverage of China's cities.[44] Beginning in 2008, the U.S. embassy in Beijing released hourly fine-particulate-matter measures on Twitter that showed much higher numbers than the government's official statistics but which better accorded with the experience of those trying to breathe while getting around in Beijing.[45] Air pollution is the most visible and discussed, but water pollution and soil pollution also cause serious harm to the health of people and the agricultural productivity of Chinese land.[46]

Government use of land to support local efforts in contravention to central priorities has become another reason local officials hide facts from Beijing. The most spectacular example here is the phenomena of "ghost cities"—as one piece describes them, "monumentally scaled urban developments, even entire new cities featuring skyscrapers and enormous public spaces, all built at breakneck pace but with scant population."[47] Chinese property market dynamics, including local government capture of urban land revenues and real estate speculation, have led to significant building ahead of demand for housing in many cities, with ghost cities only the most extreme examples of a widespread phenomenon. From the central government's perspective, the concern is massive overinvestment that turns out to be uneconomical. Local government plans for the real estate sector certainly indicate that this concern is real, as reports in 2016 suggested that China's cities had proposed projects with enough housing units for 3.4 billion people—more than twice China's likely maximum total population in 2050.[48]

Hard data on the extent of corruption is difficult to observe in China, as elsewhere. Corruption preceded China's economic reforms, but its scale grew with the rise of markets and especially in the wake of the revival of market reform generated by Deng's Southern Tour.[49] However, putting numbers to these claims is complex, as different metrics proliferate, none of them particularly satisfying.[50] Regardless of the impossibility of knowing the size of corruption perfectly, some cases show its massive scale in mid-2010s China. For example, during an anti-corruption action, it took twenty police officers two nights to empty Lt. General Gu Junshan's mansion in Puyang, Henan, and they filled four trucks with gold, high-end liquors, and other valuables.[51] In a separate real estate deal in Shanghai, Gu reportedly took a 6 percent cut of a 2 billion yuan land sale.[52]

The center's limited vision allowed for graft but also gave incentives for locals to adjust the statistics that ostensibly measure their performance. Trusting numbers comes with difficulty for Chinese leaders concerned about the possibility of data manipulation. As Zhu Rongji stated about grain production estimates:

> I don't entirely believe that figure for grain production, the people at the State Statistical Bureau say they calculated it using the most advanced techniques in the world. I said I recognized that and can't deny the achievements of the statistical departments. I fully stand by their work, but this sort of thing is hard to verify.[53]

The quality of the quantitative data of things less tangible than grain are even more concerning. In a report released by WikiLeaks, Executive Vice Premier

Li Keqiang noted his skepticism of official GDP figures from lower-level governments as "man-made," "unreliable," and "for reference only."[54] Systematic evaluation of GDP growth measures at the provincial level also points toward officials "juking the stats," as growth in GDP exceeds growth rates in other close correlates at moments of political significance such as turnovers.[55] Air quality statistics have also come under scrutiny as discrepancies between official and unofficial measurements come to light and photographs reveal that "blue sky days" fail to require a sky resembling the color blue.[56] In light of these and other problems such as slowing of economic growth, the regime has taken a neopolitical turn, especially since 2012.

From Technocratic to Neopolitical

The regime has shifted its mix of political strategies and itself has joined commentators in declaring a "new normal" (新常态), yet in some ways the new system may not look so different at first glance. What are we to make of these changes? Obviously views differ on this point, from those emphasizing continuity (e.g., Lardy 2014; Shen 2014) to those emphasizing differences (e.g., Minzner 2014, 2015a). I take a middle position that acknowledges the real changes that have taken place but situates them within the broader stream of the reform era's emphasis on performance. The core changes are an institutionalized centralization of political authority and changes in how the regime justifies itself to various audiences.

The first change has been a substantial centralization of power.[57] Beyond Xi's personalization of power, perhaps the centralization's most important component is the increased activity and prominence of the Party's CCDI.[58] While the CCDI operated prior to this period, its efforts were not as pervasive, feared, or commented upon as under Wang Qishan during the anti-corruption "campaign," which has also targeted more and higher-level officials than previous efforts in the reform era.[59] These anti-corruption activities represent a centralization of power because they expand the auditing of local governments, officials, bureaucrats, and firms by central authorities to a greater extent and with more independence than previously. The CCDI has opened new offices at local levels and its place in the political hierarchy in localities has expanded, as evidenced by its leaders being responsible to central authorities vertically instead of only horizontally to the local Party committee.[60] The Party's principal actors in Beijing are increasing their monitoring activities over their agents in the provinces, cities, and counties of China.

The centralization of authority can even be seen in policy dimensions that at first appear relatively distant from organizational issues of the party-state, such as urbanization policy. The CCP-led regime has managed urbanization throughout its reign, promoting urban stability and attempting to restrict migration to and the size of the country's largest cities.[61] However, in recent years there has been a push in the opposite direction, toward building true megacities in and around Beijing, Shanghai, and Guangzhou. At the same time, Beijing demolished the residences of tens of thousands of migrants, referring to them as the "low-end population," and both Beijing and Shanghai have put into place ceilings on their population.[62] Yet this push appears to be more related to the desire for increased central control—assaulting the "fortress economies" of the different regions—than purely about urban planning.[63] As Zhang Gui, a researcher at Hebei Technology University, put it, "Right now, every official will think of his own region first—from the construction of projects to investment," since heretofore officials had been judged primarily on such metrics.[64]

A second change associated with the new normal can be seen in the increased importance of party over state organs, exemplifying the rise of the political over the technocratic. The CCDI's increased role as the principal actor of centralization makes the prospect of a rule of law that constrains the CCP even more unlikely in the near term. The Fourth Plenum of the Eighteenth Party Congress in October 2014 pointed toward the heightened position of the Party and the center's efforts to monitor and control local officials through the legal system. The official communiqué from the plenum called for concrete steps that should allow judges to hold local officials more accountable for their actions.[65] In particular, the creation of circuit courts and regional courts with jurisdictions across extant subnational borders should give judges room to rule against local leaders without putting the court's resources and their own salaries at risk. That is, while the reform of the legal system and other state institutions fits with the centralizing thread of the politicized new normal, the CCDI and the reinvigoration of Party institutions reflect a break from the practices of the past thirty years of reform.

The post-2012 neopolitical turn also differs from before in the regime's new public and explicit efforts to use traditional morality to justify its rule.[66] Earlier in the reform era, such an emphasis was placed on technical expertise that the Politburo Standing Committee formed in 1997 was completely made up of individuals who held degrees in science or engineering.[67] These years of peak technocracy clearly marked the successful rise of China's "Red Engineers."[68] During this period, the political base of the regime shifted from urban industrial workers to include capitalists and intellectuals.[69] These two populations, which had been targets of political campaigns under Mao, became crucial to the Party, which now represented them, co-opting these potentially threatening groups before any trouble arose.[70] The idea that politics could be reduced to a series of engineering problems has been upended in the new normal.

The Mass Line (群众路线) campaign is another piece of the shifting-justification strategy of this neopolitical turn. The goal of Xi's campaign—his personal image has been closely tied to it[71]—is to rectify "four undesirable work styles" of Chinese local officials: "formalism, bureaucracy, hedonism and extravagance."[72] High provincial officials, as well as those of lower ranks, have eaten and lived in the homes of local residents to increase their connections with the people in their jurisdictions.[73] They also have engaged in self-criticisms that were broadcast on national television, such as Zhou Benshun's statement about the weakness of quantitative metrics of development mentioned in the introduction.[74] Public discussion of the political failings of leaders who remain in office was much less common during the reform era's first three decades.

Fighting hedonism and extravagance has become a major point in these changes; the imposed austerity of governmental officials is referred to by the expression "four dishes, one soup" after a simple meal that Xi ate in Hebei's Fuping county.[75] This simple meal differs greatly from the elaborate banquets for officials of local governments, paid for either out of public coffers or by local business leaders and developers to influence policy decisions.

Emphasizing the need to judge local officials by their morality fits into the centralization efforts, as it can inculcate obedience to central dictates and perhaps reduce monitoring costs. It also represents a partial move away from technocratic or scientific measures of performance as a technology of legitimation and toward traditionalism, as can be seen in Xi Jinping's invocation of Chinese classics in defining virtue.[76] The change in the regime's public-facing justification is significant: it reframes the discourse, emphasizing virtue and process over an output-centric rhetoric (via performance legitimacy arising from litanies repeating the rapid growth of GDP and other statistics associated with scientific development).

Interestingly, in the campaign explicit references are made to the idea that such changes are not singular or temporary. Xi himself is quoted as telling officials that they "should not have the wrong idea that they have passed the test just because the sessions are over."[77] Indeed, in August 2014, fourteen months after the launch of the campaign, the regime promulgated further details about reinvigorating the implementation of anti-corruption measures.[78] Years later, new cases of corrupt officials—high and low—continue to dominate the headlines.[79]

While much of the transformation in the new normal exists inside the party-state hierarchy, the neopolitical turn can also be seen in acts of repression against those taken to be opponents of the regime. Rights lawyers, feminist activists, and Hong Kong booksellers exemplify this return to more aggressive treatment for those outsiders trying to push agendas. More than 140 rights lawyers were detained in a sweep in July 2015.[80] Five leading feminist activists were detained earlier in 2015—on the night of March 6, before International Women's Day (March 8)—and were brutally interrogated while in captivity despite their cause going viral on international social media.[81]

Another sensational example of China's neopolitical repression has been its use of televised confessions.[82] In 2013, highly successful corporate executives and public intellectuals began appearing on CCTV to confess their crimes, something that had been nearly absent from Chinese politics during the prior decades of the reform era. These humiliation rituals then expanded to include a number of booksellers from Hong Kong, including one who vanished while traveling in Thailand.[83] Rather than silently imposing costs on activists or opponents, or generating self-censoring actions through perceptions of fear, these displays blast messages of state power, authority, and willingness to attack those deemed critical.

The ultimate expression of the CCP's reassertion of its authority over the lives of Chinese citizens comes from Xinjiang, which in 2017 was described as a "21st-century police state," with checkpoints along highways, iris-scanning machines, facial recognition technology at gas stations, police searching phones for banned applications, and omnipresent security forces; the situation has become only grimmer in 2018 (Rajagopalan 2017). A vast system of detention facilities, officially deemed "reeducation centers," has been created, and here hundreds of thousands of Uyghurs (almost all men) have been confined without formal criminal proceedings, cut off from those outside the centers, detained in prison-like facilities with barbed-wire fences and gun towers, and forced to endure and regurgitate propaganda.[84] After months of denying the existence of such facilities despite considerable evidence from satellite imagery, former inmate testimony, government contracts and budgets, and street photography all demonstrating their presence, state media did an about-face in mid-October 2018 when "the CCTV prime-time program 'Focus Talk' (焦点访谈) dedicated a 15-minute episode to the topic of Xinjiang's 'vocational skills educational training centers' (职业技能教育培训中心)" (Koetse 2018; Zhang 2018; Zenz 2019). Some estimates of the numbers detained exceed one million, nearly 10 percent of the Uyghur population (Zenz 2019).

The differences in China before and after the neopolitical turn are numerous and significant. Institutionalized authority has been centralized through the expansion and increased prominence of the CCDI. With Xi's growing personal influence diminishing perceptions of collective leadership, the elite bargain that seemed to protect officials of high rank from investigation has been shaken up. Decision-making power increasingly rests in an expanded set of Xi Jinping–dominated "leading small groups" (领导小组).[85] The system of assessments for local officials has been changed. Political discussions, including self-criticisms, have been broadcast on various Chinese media. Maoism and classical Chinese political rhetoric and ideology have returned, with both portrayed positively as a way of judging officials and the regime as a whole.[86] The Party's use of bald repression is broadcast to demonstrate its power and the dangers of questioning its domination.

Alternative Conceptions of the Neopolitical Turn

The argument proposed here separates the reform era into a period of previous technocratic politics and the current neopolitical turn, providing context for understanding the variety of changes in internal power dynamics and state rhetoric in China over the past few years. Other interpretations and alternatives have been offered. I briefly discuss some of these as well as evidence that could aid in distinguishing opposing observable implications.

A first alternative to my argument discounts the changes and puts forward simply that there has not been a political transition. This line of argument, more common in the early days after Xi's ascension, claims that the anti-corruption crusade is of a piece with prior purges, part of the regular politics of new leaders being installed in China's increasingly institutionalized reform era. Indeed, both Jiang Zemin and Hu Jintao initiated similar attacks on corruption after coming to power and called for probity with efforts that conveniently sidelined potential elite rivals.[87] However, Xi's various campaigns have led to more investigations and the removal of more and higher-level officials than did previous iterations. Politburo and former Politburo Standing Committee members Bo Xilai and Zhou Yongkang have been pushed out of the Party, as has a leading military figure, Xu Caihou.[88] Xi's anti-corruption campaign is distinct from those of his reform era predecessors because of its duration, intensity, and willingness to pursue higher-level officials. All of these indicate a new political direction, confrontational rather than bloodless.

A related account acknowledges changes but argues that the reform era is best understood as a series of centralizing and decentralizing cycles, with the current moment an example of the former. For example, in *Factions and Finance*, Shih argues that decentralization and centralization of banking and financial operations moved in cycles.[89] A generalist faction, led by Deng, Hu, and Zhao, pushed to devolve investment decisions to localities where their allies/experience lay, while what Shih terms a technocratic faction, led by Chen Yun, attempted to walk back these changes and have central authorities control the financial levers. In the recent period, however, the centralizing changes under Xi are principally political rather than economic and appear less likely to be reversed. That is, while these changes undoubtedly have economic consequences and perhaps even economic causes, the mechanisms of centralization are primarily political and institutional. The CCDI's expansion and its ascent up the local Party hierarchy increase the power of the center's monitors in the localities. The reform era has seen episodes of significant economic centralization, such as the 1994 fiscal reforms, but political centralization has been significantly rarer. The long duration of the anti-corruption crusade also distinguishes this effort from those in prior cycles.

As Xi's anti-corruption crusade persists, claims that today's politics are the same as yesterday's are increasingly being replaced by arguments that we have entered a third era of Chinese politics. The most direct and persuasive case is made by Minzner.[90] He credits "institutionalization" with keeping China stable during the reform era and focuses on a number of norms that had been solidifying but now appear to be eroding away. Succession politics bounded by age limits forcing turnover, the rise of a meritocratic bureaucracy, the decline of purges based on factional connections, and an increased willingness to engage with the outside world and foreign ideas provided the core content of the reform era's institutionalization.[91] Since the start of the new millennium and especially after Xi came to power, these policies, beliefs, and patterns of behavior are shifting.

Distinguishing between this "new era" perspective and the "neopolitical turn" formulation presented here is subtle but important. A chasm divides Chinese politics in 2017 from those in 1967. The engagement of the military in politics, the acceptability of wealth accumulation, and the use of markets and prices to allocate goods rather than centralized economic plans are all radically different across that fifty-year span. On the other hand, today's situation remains similar to that of China two or three decades ago. The changes taking place are not as dramatic as those separating the Mao and reform eras. Beijing is not throwing out the rule book; it is simply changing some of the rules, with critical shifts on centralization emphasized here as well as personalization.

The ending of term limits for the office of president allows Xi Jinping to extend his rule beyond 2023 and represents an acquiescence by other top Party leaders to the diminishment of collective and collaborative rule.[92] The orderly succession of leaders has been a hallmark of the Chinese reform era. In 1998, five years before he took over as general secretary and president, Hu Jintao was widely acknowledged to be the heir apparent, as Xi Jinping was when he was appointed to the Politburo Standing Committee in 2007. Yet Xi did not follow suit, appointing no leaders of the next generation to that top political body in 2017. In the end, China both today and two decades ago appears to be ruled by similar groups of elites through similar mechanisms pursuing similar, although modified, ends. Clarification about what is happening can arise from attempting to ascertain the reasons for these changes.

Why has this neopolitical turn emerged in the PRC under Xi Jinping? I argue that the new normal represents both an attempt to fix technocratic pathologies as well as an effort to hedge against the possibility of an end to strong economic performance through the construction of an alternative narrative to justify the regime based on Chinese tradition, clean governance, and strength.[93] The center is increasing its monitoring to better understand the situation in the provinces and control the behavior of local government officials. The utility of the prior technocratic, decentralized, and low-information politics has become overwhelmed by its accumulated costs, particularly economic and political risks.[94] For instance, the incentives led to overproduction of particular goods and underproduction of others as local officials gamed the system; as other examples, during different periods local governments had tariff fights that fell into violence, and environmental protection was undersupplied throughout.[95]

As China moved from severely undercapitalized to possessing greater stocks of extant investment, the most valuable projects tended to be completed first. The set of potential projects remaining after years of heavy investment tended to have weak underlying economics.[96] Even economists sanguine about China's growth prospects acknowledge overinvestment.[97] Doomsayers, on the other hand, point to the rise of ghost cities and airports built years ahead of anticipated demand as uneconomical.[98]

China's reliance on investment and exports for growth has long been noted, and calls for it to rebalance to a more consumption-based model of economic development have been heard for years.[99] Cross-national evidence points to economic growth's significance for explaining authoritarian regime survival. Far from destabilizing authoritarian regimes, periods of economic growth tend to foster political stability.[100] Yet the repeated interventions of the Chinese regime in its economy to mitigate potential hard times point to the regime's concerns about the politics of an economic downturn.

The new reality facing local officials appears more complicated. Now that scientific measurement of performance has been accepted into the system's DNA, it is hard to remove, even given the various pathologies already discussed. Rather than ceasing to use quantitative measures, the system is moving in multiple directions. First is a move to diversify the number of different measures used to evaluate officials.[101] In 2014, the National Bureau of Statistics released a list of forty indicators that would help to end the reign of "GDP supremacy."[102] Second is the rhetorical and real emphasis on central dominance, clean governance, and the increased presence of monitoring. Anti-corruption teams going into top organizations, corporations, and local governments and prosecuting individuals for failing to uphold high standards have become routine. Some officials have postponed decisions in the hopes that this unwanted attention is simply a phase that they can wait out, but the institutionalization of this monitoring makes waiting unlikely to be successful. Depictions of dominance and strength over international disputes and domestic adversaries join continued crowing about statistical achievements as major elements of the regime's presentation and self-understanding.

Conclusion

The principal claim of this chapter is that China's reform era is undergoing an important neopolitical turn. The changes centralize political authority, raise standards of behavior for local officials, extend the institutional capacities of extant inspection units, and promulgate new norms of behavior. These changes are not so extensive as to declare the beginning of a new era in Chinese politics, nor do they undermine the significance of the post-Mao transformation into China's reform era.

More broadly, the discussion of China's neopolitical turn can help illuminate areas of non-democratic politics that the existing literature has overlooked. Political science has made substantial progress differentiating the end of authoritarianism in a country and the end of a given authoritarian regime's rule in a country. This distinction captures the reality that most authoritarian regimes are replaced not by democracies but by other dictators, giving us insights into the political risks that these regimes face and concerns that they have. Indeed, these survival patterns have directed researchers to focus on elite politics, since coups predominate as the ultimate mechanism ending one regime and beginning another.[103]

For as much as they can account for the deaths of regimes, elite-focused approaches have difficulty saying much about what life is like under them, beyond broad assessments of growth rates, levels of violence, and foreign policies.[104] Yet regimes vary, and the politics that they inculcate and the policies that they pursue matter for their populations. This is not the whole of their import, however. Mass politics is rarely just up to the whims of the dictator or epiphenomenal to elite politics; instead, mass politics shapes elite politics. In *Cities and Stability*, I show that populations matter in authoritarian regime survival. Even basic differences across countries and regimes such as the size of capital cities and the concentration of urbanization shape survival patterns.[105] And not simply those regime changes caused by urban rebellions but also intra-elite coups. Mass politics (or state-society relations, as it is often referred to in the literature on Chinese politics) is a crucial factor in authoritarian regimes, both for the possibility of revolution and also, critically, in determining the character of intra-elite politics. In other words, while coups are proximate causes of regime deaths, mass politics is the underlying condition that makes a regime susceptible, makes an ambitious colonel consider such a move, and makes an elite willing to side with the new leader over the old one.

China's centralization and broader neopolitical turn respond to the political failures of the prior system but come with their own downsides. As recent research on Russia demonstrates, political insulation has benefits for dictators. Taking advantage of differences in the ways in which mayors come to office—either appointed from above by regional leaders or elected by the population—Beazer and Reuter (2019) show that the higher-level leadership takes more blame when the economic tides turn in communities governed by appointed leaders. This analysis shows how preempting threats can also generate them. Centralizing authority may increase control and allow the center to eliminate some problems at the local level, but it also increases central ownership of any subsequent issues that might arise. That ownership could be harmful should those issues threaten the arguments that the regime uses to justify its continued rule. Free lunches, as ever, remain hard to find. Further,

Beazer and Reuter show that the blaming effect is targeted to the level that conducts the appointments (regions) rather than generically affecting the central government in Moscow. This may suggest that Xi's efforts at centralization and personalization could place blame on his shoulders personally should crises come to pass.

China's neopolitical turn highlights the types of transitions that non-democratic regimes experience and initiate but which remain underexamined in the literature. Rhetorical changes put politics front and center instead of shunting it off to the side. Institutional changes give the center more ability to oversee the activities of lower-level officials but also reduce its ability to slough off responsibility to local bad actors for problems or malfeasance. Non-democratic politics is not transparent, which has pushed scholarly inquiry to focus on easily measurable quantities, such as the personal history of the leader and the presence of legislatures, elections, and parties, to differentiate regimes. However, non-democratic politics is not as opaque as work has suggested, because rhetoric and policy detail exude from even the most closed-off regimes and give access to some of their political machinations.

Notes

An earlier version of this chapter was presented at the conference Citizens and the State: Comparing Mass Politics and Policy in China and Russia, University of Notre Dame, March 10–11, 2017. Thanks to workshop participants at Yale University and the University of Chicago, as well as Andrew Mertha, Sara Newland, Lisa Wedeen, Dan Slater, Mike Albertus, Jessica Weiss, Mike Neblo, Ben Lessing, Dali Yang, Tom Pepinsky, Kristen Looney, Kate Baldwin, Peter Lorentzen, and Gautam Nair for comments and suggestions. All errors remain my own.

1. "大胆使用批评和自我批评有力武器," 2013; 央视网, 2013. See also "Critical Masses," 2013; Huang 2013b; Zhang 2013.

2. "Critical Masses," 2013; 央视网, 2013.

3. The Chinese phrase 新常态 (xinchangtai, "new normal") has been invoked recently to describe the apparent slowdown of China's breakneck economic growth; see, e.g., Spence 2015. I use the term more broadly to reflect the changes in both the economic and political systems of China.

4. Claims have been made about his building a personality cult like Chairman Mao, and questions have been raised about his willingness to leave office in 2022 when his second term as president concludes. For examples of Xi's influence and personality cult, see Jacobs and Buckley 2015; Lam 2015; Phillips 2014. Martin and Cohen (2014) point in this direction but note limits in the comparison between Mao and Xi.

5. On official statements about the anti-corruption and morals campaigns, see Xinhua 2013a, 2013b. On self-criticisms being aired on Chinese TV, see Demick 2013. The centralization appears to be located in Beijing rather than being a boon for provincial governments, as was a previous moment's "soft centralization" (Mertha 2005). "Traditional" here refers to a blend of Maoist and imperial political thought. The Central Commission on Discipline Inspection has both CCDI and CDIC as common English acronyms.

6. E.g., Browne 2016; Goldkorn, Bandurski, Rosenzweig, and Cheung 2016; Zeng 2015.

7. Zhang 2018; Zenz 2019.

8. Cheibub, Gandhi, and Vreeland 2010; Geddes, Wright, and Frantz 2014; Wahman, Teorell, and Hadenius 2013.

9. Stromseth, Malesky, and Gueorguiev 2017

10. Marquez 2016; Svolik 2012.

11. Another formulation focuses on the questions: who rules, why, and how.

12. E.g., Minzner 2015a.

13. Although the populace-facing local governments are bound to fail to remain unseen, and, of course, do not help themselves on this score by building grandiose monuments to their own power and for their own comfort. For examples of such grandiose buildings, see Kuo and Watts 2013; the overawing nature of such facilities also should not be overlooked (e.g., Scott 1998).

14. See Minzner 2014, 2015a.

15. For the latter, see Minzner 2015a.

16. See Huang 2015.

17. See Heilmann and Perry 2011.

18. As noted earlier, analyses that rely solely on typologies of authoritarian regimes have trouble distinguishing between these periods, See, e.g., Cheibub, Gandhi, and Vreeland 2010; Geddes, Wright, and Frantz 2014; Wahman, Teorell, and Hadenius 2013.

19. See Wallace n.d., ch. 3, for more detail on these changes.

20. See, e.g., Fewsmith 1994; Lieberthal 2004; Naughton 2007.

21. Another interpretation, following Bunce 1999, could treat the limited vision as a "subversive institution" rather than a known trade-off between short-run gains and long-term costs. One could argue that it is the success of the ideological transformation itself that undermines the regime that put it in place. Evidence that at least some of the individuals making and implementing these choices raised the specter of troubles down the line point against a view that such potential consequences were unforeseen as well as unintended.

22. Tocqueville 1856, 214. This book was mentioned by top leaders (Li Keqiang and Wang Qishan) in 2012 with the Eighteenth Party Congress (Huang 2013a).

23. Zweig 1983.

24. That is, ideological beliefs could create resistance through values or efficacy concerns.

25. See, for instance, Zweig 1983, 1986. Central elites also waffled on these and other successive moments, with periods of openness almost inevitably paired with closed periods (alternating between放 [fang] and收 [shou]).

26. Nee 1989. Nee argued that the power of local officials would ebb as market incentives shifted power to producers but was sanguine on officials' acquiescence to this eventuality.

27. A serious debate has emerged on the nature of the township and village enterprises (TVEs) that were critical to rural industrial growth in China during the 1980s, with Oi and Naughton presenting the standard view—particularly Oi's "local state corporatism"—contrasting with Huang's view of TVEs as overwhelmingly private rather than owned and operated by local states. See Huang 2008; Naughton 2007; Oi 1999. While Huang is correct in noting that private TVEs account for most of the increase in their number, the change in TVE employment comes from both private and local state-owned firms.

28. It is obviously not simply exploitive corruption but real development (often with officials taking the lead and personally profiting while benefitting their localities) that took place (Oi 1999).

29. Guo 2014; Huang 1996. The CCDI (aka CDIC) state-side institution is the Ministry of Supervision (监察部), formed in 1987 (Huang 1996).

30. Huang 1996. These organizations are now the National Development and Reform Commission (NDRC, 中央法改委), the National Bureau of Statistics (NBS), and the National Audit Office (NAO).

31. Tian, cited in Cui and Shao 1990.

32. Qiao Shi, cited in Cui and Shao 1990.

33. See Dimitrov 2014 on petitions. While political authority in China may have been fragmented throughout CCP rule, it certainly became more fragmented following Mao's death (Lieberthal and Oksenberg 1990).

34. See, e.g., Birney 2014; Edin 2003;. Minzner 2009; Wang 2013; Whiting 2000.

35. See, e.g., Ong 2012.

36. On legibility, see Scott 1998. For examples of local machinations in China, see Smith 2009.

37. Li and O'Brien 1996; O'Brien and Li 2006.

38. Lü and Landry 2014.

39. See, e.g., Edin 2003; Landry 2008; Lü and Landry 2014; Shih, Adolph, and Liu 2012; Whiting 2000.

40. One prominent example is Shih et al. 2012.

41. Along typical principal-agent problem lines. See, for instance, Miller 1992.

42. "China Overtakes U.S. In Greenhouse Gas Emissions," 2007; US EPA n.d.

43. World Bank 2007; Wong 2013. The Chinese government has on occasion pressured international organizations to refrain from releasing quantitative estimates of deaths from air pollution as well (Wong 2013).

44. See, e.g., Hauser 2015; Li 2013; Wong 2014.

45. Andrews 2013; Demick 2011. @BeijingAir is the Twitter handle. Historical data available from US Dept. of State ("U.S. Department of State Air Quality Monitoring Program" n.d.).

46. Hornby 2014; Larson 2014; Zuo 2014.

47. Woodworth and Wallace 2017. See also Shepard 2015; Sorace and Hurst 2015.

48. "Chinese Cities' Expansion Plans Could House 3.4 Billion People" 2016; Zhuang 2016.

49. Wedeman 2012.

50. Wedeman 2012 alone presents the following: revealed rate of corruption, actual rate of corruption, cumulative level of corruption, emerging rate of corruption, perceived level of corruption, incidence vs. intensity of corruption. With observed quantities giving information that helps point toward the hidden reality. Others have looked at different kinds of business expenses from annual reports to extract estimates of corruption and variation over space (e.g., Wang 2014).

51. Wang 2014; Zhou and Wang 2015.

52. Meng 2014.

53. Zhu 2013, 348.

54. WikiLeaks, Cable 07BEIJING1760, 15 March 2007.

55. Wallace 2016. For evidence of village-level officials manipulating statistics, see Tsai 2008.

56. See, for example, Andrews 2013; Demick 2011. For academic work, see Oliver 2011.

57. Whether there has been centralization within the Politburo Standing Committee, as some argue and others question, remains to be seen, although the extent to which outsiders

will ever know the "truth" of such dynamics is limited at best. On difficulties of assessing elite politics in China, see Teiwes 2015.

58. Xi's personalization is discussed later but is difficult to fully assess outside the regime's "inner sanctum."

59. "Campaign" is placed in quotes, as it seems to be something of more permanence—something institutionalized—rather than a temporary campaign; the term "crusade" is also used. Higher-level targets include Zhou Yongkang, former Politburo Standing Committee member, and Xu Caihou, former Politburo member and vice chairman of the central military commission (Barreda and Yan 2014; Caixin 2014; "Zhou Yongkang's Downfall," 2014).

60. Zhou 2014.

61. For more on China's management of urbanization, see Wallace 2014.

62. On Beijing's 2017 demolitions, see Friedman 2017. On population caps, see Roxburgh 2018.

63. Reuters 2014.

64. Reuters 2014. The piece goes on to argue: "They [experts] say China's 'every region for itself' approach to economic growth is a cause of a wide variety of problems, including overinvestment, pollution and corruption." Others have also noted that urbanization and metropolitan planning has become a battlefield for inter-level conflict in some provinces, as each attempts to claim turf (Jaros 2015).

65. "Official Central Committee Communiqué on 4th Plenum," 2014. Members of the CCDI standing committee attended the Fourth Plenum as non-voting delegates.

66. Mixing Maoist and imperial (principally Confucian but also legalist) ideals of behavior is fascinating since so much of Mao's thought went into criticizing the problems associated with the old society's Confucianism and the inequality that it perpetuated and justified. Their fusion appears on its way to becoming an "invented tradition" (Ranger and Hobsbawm 1983).

67. "The clout of technocrats reached a pinnacle in 1997, when all seven members of the Politburo Standing Committee formed that year had degrees in the sciences or engineering" (Li 2012).

68. Andreas 2009.

69. Solinger 2003; Yang 2006.

70. Dickson 2003; Teiwes 1997. "Incorporating" here is used instead of the more common "co-opting" because the latter implies a level of opprobrium and perhaps permanent neutralization.

71. See, for instance, Xinhua 2014a. Interestingly, some argue that the style and operations of Xi's Mass Line campaign are actually following Bo Xilai's Mass Line program in Chongqing before he was toppled (Downie 2014).

72. Xinhua 2014b.

73. Xinhua Insight 2013.

74. "Critical Masses," 2013.

75. "Four Dishes and One Soup," 2013; "Xi Eats Plainly Amid Focus on Official Waistlines," 2012.

76. See, e.g., Tatlow 2014.

77. Xinhua Insight 2013.

78. Xinhua 2014b.

79. TJ interim party secretary, September 2016.

80. Amnesty International 2015; Buckley 2015; "China's 'Rule by Law' Takes an Ugly Turn" 2015. See also "China Apprehends Suspected Paid Protest Organizers" 2015, "Detention of 'Trouble-Making' Lawyers in Accordance with Law: Legal Experts" 2015.

81. Fincher 2016; Tatlow 2016; Zeng 2015.

82. Goldkorn et al. 2016; Yoon 2015.

83. Forsythe and Jacobs 2016; "Hong Kong Bookseller Who Vanished in Thailand Held in China" 2016.

84. Literally "transformation through education work" (*jiaoyu zhuanhua gongzuo*) (Zenz 2018, 4). Other language includes "de-extremification" (*qu jiduanhua*) campaign (Zenz 2018, 12).

85. See Johnson et al. 2017.

86. Minzner 2014 also references the closing off of foreign influences or connections.

87. Wedeman 2005, 2012.

88. Barreda and Yan 2014; Caixin 2014; "Zhou Yongkang's Downfall," 2014.

89. Shih 2009.

90. Minzner 2015a, 2015b.

91. Minzner 2015a, 2015b.

92. Buckley and Bradsher 2018.

93. Thanks to Ben Lessing for pushing me to clarify on this point. For similar arguments related to the economic costs of China's existing bureaucratic system, see Huang 2015, 267.

94. To clarify, the center operated with limited information about localities during technocratic dominance; that is, the center judged local performance on a few key metrics rather than with more sustained attention or multidimensional assessments.

95. See, for example, Wedeman 2003 on various commodity fights and local protectionism during price reform from the 1980s through mid-1990s. See, for example, Wang 2006, 2013 on environmental degradation as a result of the incentives emerging from the CES.

96. Similarly with state planning, expectations of the economic viability of different concerns decreases over time as China's labor costs increase.

97. Lardy 2014.

98. E.g., Pettis 2012; Shih 2010. For example, the heavily covered disaster of Ordos (Sanderson 2013; Woodworth 2012, 2015; Zhou 2013). On the phenomenon of ghost cities more generally, see ("China's Ghost Cities Are About to Get Spookier" 2014; Sorace and Hurst 2015; Woodworth and Ulfstjerne 2016). Symbolically, ghost cities are the polar opposites of slums. They demonstrate a capacity and willingness to invest in infrastructure rather than allow individuals to exist without state penetration. However, the emptiness shows waste and problems of decision-making akin to that of slums.

99. E.g., Eurasia Group 2011. In 2007, Wen Jiabao made similar comments (IMF Survey 2007; Wen 2007).

100. Cheibub et al. 2010; Gandhi 2008; Geddes 1999; Wallace 2013, 2016; Wright 2008.

101. Wildau 2014.

102. Xinhua 2014c. That being said, the regime has referred to moving away from GDP on a number of previous occasions. In 2015, Shanghai became the first provincial unit to not release a GDP growth target in decades ("GDP Apostasy" 2015; Huang 2015).

103. Geddes 1999; Geddes et al. 2014; Svolik 2012; Wahman, Teorell, and Hadenius 2013.

104. Blaydes 2010; Debs and Goemans 2010; Greitens 2016; Svolik 2012; Weeks 2008; Weiss 2014; Wright 2008.

105. Wallace 2013, 2014.

References

Amnesty International. 2015. *China: Lawyers and Activists Detained or Questioned by Police Since 9 July 2015.* https://www.amnesty.org/en/documents/document/?indexNumber=asa17%2f2094%2f2015&language=en.

Andreas, Joel. 2009. *Rise of the Red Engineers: The Cultural Revolution and the Origins of China's New Class.* Stanford: Stanford University Press.

Andrews, Steven Q. 2013. "How Beijing Hid the Smog." *Wall Street Journal,* February 5.

Barreda, David, and Cong Yan. 2014. "Spoils of the 'Tiger' Hunt." *China File,* July 3.

Beazer, Quintin H., and Ora John Reuter. 2019. "Who Is to Blame? Political Centralization and Electoral Punishment under Authoritarianism." *The Journal of Politics* 81, no. 2 (April 1, 2019): 648–62.

Birney, Mayling. 2014. "Decentralization and Veiled Corruption Under China's 'Rule of Mandates.'" *World Development* 53: 55–67.

Blaydes, Lisa. 2010. *Elections and Distributive Politics in Mubarak's Egypt.* Cambridge: Cambridge University Press.

Browne, Andrew. 2016. "Self-Criticism Makes a Comeback in Xi Jinping's China." *Wall Street Journal,* February 2.

Buckley, Chris. 2015. "People's Daily Details Allegations Against Lawyers Detained in China." *New York Times,* July 13.

Buckley, Chris, and Keith Bradsher. 2018. "China Moves to Let Xi Stay in Power by Abolishing Term Limit." *New York Times,* February 25.

Bunce, Valerie. 1999. *Subversive Institutions: The Design and the Destruction of Socialism and the State.* Cambridge: Cambridge University Press.

Cheibub, José A., Jennifer Gandhi, and James R. Vreeland. 2010. "Democracy and Dictatorship Revisited." *Public Choice* 143, no. 1: 67–101.

"China Apprehends Suspected Paid Protest Organizers." 2015. Xinhua, July 12

"Detention of 'Trouble-Making' Lawyers in Accordance with Law: Legal Experts." 2015. *People's Daily Online,* July 15.

"China Overtakes U.S. in Greenhouse Gas Emissions." 2007. *New York Times,* June 20. Retrieved from

"China's 'Rule by Law' Takes an Ugly Turn." 2015. *China File,* July 14.

"Chinese Cities' Expansion Plans Could House 3.4 Billion People." 2016. Bloomberg News, July 15.

"Critical Masses." 2013. *The Economist,* October 5.

Cui, Jianmin, and Boqi Shao. 1990. 党政领导谈审计. 北京: 中国审计出版社.

Debs, Alexandre, and H. E. Goemans. 2010. "Regime Type, the Fate of Leaders, and War." *American Political Science Review* 104, no. 3: 430–445.

Demick, Barbara. 2011. "U.S. Embassy Air Quality Data Undercut China's Own Assessments." *Los Angeles Times,* October 29.

Demick, Barbara. 2013. "Mao-Era Style of Self-Criticism Reappears on Chinese TV." *Los Angeles Times,* September 26.

Dickson, Bruce J. 2003. *Red Capitalists in China: The Party, Private Entrepreneurs, and Prospects for Political Change.* Cambridge: Cambridge University Press.

Dimitrov, Martin K. 2014. "Internal Government Assessments of the Quality of Governance in China." *Studies in Comparative International Development* 50, no. 1: 50–72.

Downie, Edmund. 2014. "One City, Many Models: The Chinese Left's Debates over Chongqing." Academia.edu, April 14. https://www.academia.edu/8919324/One_City_Many_Models_The_Chinese_Left_s_Debates_over_Chongqing.

Edin, Maria. 2003. "State Capacity and Local Agent Control in China: CCP Cadre Management from a Township Perspective." *China Quarterly* 173: 35–52.

Eurasia Group. 2011. "China's Great Rebalancing Act." http://eurasiagroup.net/item-files/China's%20Great%20Rebalancing%20Act/China%20Rebalancing.pdf.

Fewsmith, Joseph. 1994. *Dilemmas of Reform in China: Political Conflict and Economic Debate*. Armonk, NY : M. E. Sharpe.

Fincher, Leta Hong. 2016. "China's Feminist Five." *Dissent*, Fall.

Friedman, Eli. 2017. "Evicting the Underclass." *Jacobin*, December 6, 2017. http://jacobinmag.com/2017/12/beijing-fire-migrant-labor-urbanization.

"Four Dishes and One Soup." 2013. *China Economic Review*, January 22.

Gandhi, Jennifer. 2008. *Political Institutions Under Dictatorship*. Cambridge: Cambridge University Press.

"GDP Apostasy." 2015. *The Economist*, January 31.

Geddes, Barbara. 1999. "Authoritarian Breakdown: Empirical Test of a Game Theoretic Argument." Paper presented at the Annual Meeting of the American Political Science Association, Atlanta, GA.

Geddes, Barbara, Joseph Wright, and Erica Frantz. 2014. "Autocratic Breakdown and Regime Transitions: A New Data Set." *Perspectives on Politics* 12, no. 2: 313–331.

Goldkorn, Jeremy, David Bandurski, Joshua Rosenzweig, and Alvin Y. H. Cheung. 2016. "Beijing's Televised Confessions." *China File*, January 20.

Greitens, Sheena C. 2016. *Dictators and Their Secret Police: Coercive Institutions and State Violence*. Cambridge: Cambridge University Press.

Guo, Xuezhi. 2014. "Controlling Corruption in the Party: China's Central Discipline Inspection Commission." *China Quarterly* 219: 597–624.

Hauser, Christine. 2015. "'Airpocalypse': Beijing Smog Red Alert on Social Media." *New York Times*, December 8.

Heilmann, Sebastian, and Elizabeth J. Perry, eds. 2011. *Mao's Invisible Hand: The Political Foundations of Adaptive Governance in China*. Cambridge, MA: Asia Center, Harvard University.

Hobsbawm, Eric J., and Terence Ranger. 1983. *The Invention of Tradition*. Cambridge: Cambridge University Press, Cambridge.

"Hong Kong Bookseller Who Vanished in Thailand Held in China." 2016. Bloomberg News, January 17.

Hornby, Lucy. 2014. "China Admits Widespread Soil Pollution in 'State Secret' Report." *Financial Times*, April 18.

Huang, Cary. 2013a. "Tocqueville's Advice on French Revolution Captures Chinese Leaders' Attention." *South China Morning Post*, February 22.

Huang, Cary. 2013b. "Xi Jinping Oversees Self-Criticism Sessions in Hebei." *South China Morning Post*, September 26.

Huang, Cary. 2015. "Shanghai's Shunning of GDP Obsession Seen as Welcome Move Towards Quality Growth." *South China Morning Post*, February 1.

Huang, Philip C. C. 2015. "How Has the Chinese Economy Developed So Rapidly? The Concurrence of Five Paradoxical Coincidences." *Modern China* 41, no. 3: 239–277.

Huang, Yasheng. 1996. *Inflation and Investment Controls in China: The Political Economy of Central-Local Relations During the Reform Era*. Cambridge: Cambridge University Press.

Huang, Yasheng. 2008. *Capitalism with Chinese Characteristics: Entrepreneurship and the State*. Cambridge: Cambridge University Press.

IMF Survey. 2007. "China's Difficult Rebalancing Act," September 12. http://www.imf.org/external/pubs/ft/survey/so/2007/car0912a.htm.

Jacobs, Andrew, and Chris Buckley. 2015. "Move over Mao: Beloved 'Papa Xi' Awes China." *New York Times*, March 7.

Jaros, Kyle A. 2015. "Forging Greater Xi'an The Political Logic of Metropolitanization." *Modern China*, 42, no. 6 (November 16): 638–673.

Johnson, Christopher, Scott Kennedy, and Mingda Qiu. 2017. "Xi's Signature Governance Innovation: The Rise of Leading Small Groups." Center for Strategic and International Studies, October 17. https://www.csis.org/analysis/xis-signature-governance-innovation-rise-leading-small-groups.

Koetse, Manya. 2018. "CCTV Airs Program on Xinjiang's 'Vocational Training Centers': Criticism & Weibo Responses." November 12. https://www.whatsonweibo.com/cctv-airs-program-on-xinjiangs-vocational-training-centers-criticism-weibo-responses/.

Kuo, Lily, and Jake M. Watts. 2013. "These Gilded Government Buildings Explain Exactly Why Beijing Is Banning New Ones." *Quartz*, July 24.

Lam, Willy. 2015. "A Modern Cult of Personality? Xi Jinping Aspires to Be the Equal of Mao and Deng." Jamestown Foundation, Washington, DC, March 6.

Landry, Pierre F. 2008. *Decentralized Authoritarianism in China: The Communist Party's Control of Local Elites in the Post-Mao Era*. Cambridge: Cambridge University Press.

Lardy, Nicholas R. 2014. *Markets over Mao: The Rise of Private Business in China*. Washington, DC: Institute for International Economics.

Larson, Christina. 2014. "China Gets Serious About Its Pollutant-Laden Soil." *Science 343*, no. 6178: 1415–1416.

Li, Lianjiang, and Kevin O'Brien. 1996. "Villagers and Popular Protest in Contemporary China." *Modern China* 22, no. 1: 28–61.

Li, Mia. 2013. "'Airpocalypse' Hits Harbin, Closing Schools." *New York Times*, October 21.

Li, Raymond. 2012. "Six Politburo Standing Committee Members Are Not Technocrats." *South China Morning Post*, November 20.

Lieberthal, Kenneth. 2004. *Governing China: From Revolution Through Reform*. 2nd ed. New York: W. W. Norton.

Lieberthal, Kenneth, and Michel Oksenberg. 1990. *Policy Making in China: Leaders, Structures, and Processes*. Princeton: Princeton University Press.

Lü, Xiaobo, and Pierre F. Landry. 2014. "Show Me the Money: Inter-Jurisdiction Political Competition and Fiscal Extraction in China." *American Political Science Review* 108, no. 3: 706–722.

Mai, Jun. 2016. "Acting Communist Party Chief of Tianjin Placed under Investigation for Suspected Graft." *South China Morning Post*, September 11. https://www.scmp.com/news/china/policies-politics/article/2018315/tianjin-mayor-huang-xingguo-placed-under-investigation.

Marquez, Xavier. 2016. *Non-Democratic Politics: Authoritarianism, Dictatorship and Democratization*. London: Palgrave.

Martin, Peter, and David Cohen. 2014. "Mao and Forever." *Foreign Affairs*, June 3.

Meng, Angela. 2014. "Gold, Liquor, and Houses: New Details Emerge of Disgraced General Gu Junshan's Graft Loot." *South China Morning Post*, January 15.

Mertha, Andrew C. 2005. "China's Soft Centralization: Shifting Tiao/Kuai Authority Relations." *China Quarterly* 184: 791–810.

Miller, Gary J. 1992. *Managerial Dilemmas: The Political Economy of Hierarchy.* Cambridge: Cambridge University Press.

Minzner, Carl. 2009. "Riots and Cover-Ups: Counterproductive Control of Local Agents in China." *University of Pennsylvania Journal of International Law* 31, no. 1: 53–123.

Minzner, Carl. 2014. "China Is Again Slowly Turning In on Itself." *Los Angeles Times*, October 18.

Minzner, Carl. 2015a. "China After the Reform Era." *Journal of Democracy* 26, no. 3: 129–143.

Minzner, Carl. 2015b. "Is China's Reform Era Over and, If So, What's Next?" *China File*, July 21.

Naughton, Barry. 2007. *The Chinese Economy.* Cambridge, MA: MIT Press.

Nee, Victor. 1989. "A Theory of Market Transition: From Redistribution to Markets in State Socialism." *American Sociological Review* 54, no. 5: 663–681.

O'Brien, Kevin J., and Lianjiang Li. 2006. *Rightful Resistance in Rural China.* Cambridge: Cambridge University Press.

"Official Central Committee Communiqué on 4th Plenum." 2014. *China Copyright and Media* (blog), October 23. http://chinacopyrightandmedia.wordpress.com/2014/10/23/official-central-committee-communique-on-4th-plenum.

Oi, Jean C. 1999. *Rural China Takes Off: Institutional Foundations of Economic Reform.* Berkeley: University of California Press.

Oliver, Steven. 2011. "Smoke and Mirrors? Systematic Manipulation of Air Quality Data by Chinese Municipalities." October 13. Available at SSRN: http://papers.ssrn.com/abstract=1943782.

Ong, Lynette H. 2012. *Prosper or Perish: Credit and Fiscal Systems in Rural China.* Ithaca, NY: Cornell University Press.

Pettis, Michael. 2012. "People Are Finally Waking Up To China's Massive Over-Investment Problem." *Business Insider*, December 28. http://www.businessinsider.com/the-imf-on-overinvestment-2012-12.

Phillips, Tom. 2014. "Xi Jinping: The Growing Cult of China's 'Big Daddy Xi.'" *Telegraph*, December 8.

Rajagopalan, Megha. 2017. "This Is What A 21st-Century Police State Really Looks Like." *BuzzFeed.* October 19. https://www.buzzfeed.com/meghara/the-police-state-of- the-future-is- already-here.

Reuters. 2014. "Beijing-Hebei-Tianjin Integration to Challenge Local Leaders' Power." *South China Morning Post*, July 23.

Roxburgh, Helen. 2018. "China's Radical Plan to Limit the Populations of Beijing and Shanghai." *The Guardian*, March 19. https://www.theguardian.com/cities/2018/mar/19/plan-big-city-disease-populations-fall-beijing-shanghai.

Sanderson, Henry. 2013. "China Slowdown Brings Ordos Bust as Li Grapples with Credit." Bloomberg News, July 16.

Scott, James C. 1998. *Seeing Like a State: How Certain Schemes to Improve the Human Condition Have Failed.* New Haven: Yale University Press.

Shen, Dingli. 2014. "With Xi's New Power Is Collective Leadership Over?" East Asia Forum, October 19. https://www.eastasiaforum.org/2014/10/19/with-xis-new-power-is-collective-leadership-over.

Shepard, Wade. 2015. *Ghost Cities of China: The Story of Cities Without People in the World's Most Populated Country*. London: Zed Books.

Shih, Victor, Christopher Adolph, and Mingxing Liu. 2012. "Getting Ahead in the Communist Party: Explaining the Advancement of Central Committee Members in China." *American Political Science Review* 106, no. 1: 166–187.

Shih, Victor. 2009. *Factions and Finance in China: Elite Conflict and Inflation*. Cambridge: Cambridge University Press.

Shih, Victor. 2010. "Local Government Debt, Big Rock-Candy Mountain." *China Economic Quarterly* 14, no. 2: 26–32.

Smith, Graeme. 2009. "Political Machinations in a Rural County." *China Journal* 62: 29–59.

Solinger, Dorothy J. 2003. "State and Society in Urban China in the Wake of the 16th Party Congress." *China Quarterly* 176: 943–959.

Sorace, Christian, and William Hurst. 2015. "China's Phantom Urbanisation and the Pathology of Ghost Cities." *Journal of Contemporary Asia* 46, no. 2: 1–19. https://doi.org/10.1080/00472336.2015.1115532.

Spegele, Brian. 2012. "Xi Eats Plainly Amid Focus on Official Waistlines." *WSJ Blogs - China Real Time Report* (blog), December 31. http://blogs.wsj.com/chinarealtime/2012/12/31/xi-eats-plainly-amid-focus-on-official-waistlines/.

Spence, Michael. 2015. "China's Slowing New Normal." Project Syndicate, April 28. http://www.project-syndicate.org/commentary/china-new-normal-investment-by-michael-spence-2015-04.

Stromseth, Jonathan R., Edmund J. Malesky, and Dimitar D. Gueorguiev. 2017. *China's Governance Puzzle: Enabling Transparency and Participation in a Single-Party State*. Cambridge: Cambridge University Press.

Svolik, Milan W. 2012. *The Politics of Authoritarian Rule*. Cambridge: Cambridge University Press.

Tatlow, Didi. 2014. "Xi Jinping on Exceptionalism with Chinese Characteristics." *New York Times*, October 14.

Tatlow, Didi. 2016. "Police Remove Bail Conditions on 5 Chinese Feminists Detained Last Year." *New York Times*, April 13.

Teiwes, Frederick C. 1997. "The Establishment and Consolidation of the New Regime, 1949–1957." In *The Politics of China: The Eras of Mao and Deng*, 2nd ed., ed. R. MacFarquhar. Cambridge: Cambridge University Press.

Teiwes, Frederick C. 2015. "Politics Inside the Black Box: The Study of Elite Political Conflict in the PRC." In *Handbook of the Politics of China*, ed. D. S. G. Goodman, 21–41. Cheltenham: Edward Elgar.

Tocqueville, Alexis de. 1856. *The Old Regime and the Revolution*. New York: Harper and Brothers.

Tsai, Lily L. 2008. "Understanding the Falsification of Village Income Statistics." *China Quarterly* 196: 805–826.

"U.S. Department of State Air Quality Monitoring Program." n.d. Retrieved March 2, 2017, from http://www.stateair.net/web/historical/1/1.html.

U.S. EPA. n.d.. "Global Greenhouse Gas Emissions Data." U.S. Environmental Protection Agency. Retrieved March 2, 2017, from https://www.epa.gov/ghgemissions/global-greenhouse-gas-emissions-data%20.

Wahman, Michael, Jan Teorell, and Axel Hadenius. 2013. "Authoritarian Regime Types Revisited: Updated Data in Comparative Perspective." *Contemporary Politics* 19, no. 1: 19–34.

Wallace, Jeremy. 2013. "Cities, Redistribution, and Authoritarian Regime Survival." *Journal of Politics* 75, no. 3: 632–645.

Wallace, Jeremy. 2014. *Cities and Stability: Urbanization, Redistribution, and Regime Survival in China.* New York: Oxford University Press.

Wallace, Jeremy. 2016. "Juking the Stats? Authoritarian Information Problems in China." *British Journal of Political Science* 46, no. 1: 11–29. https://doi.org/10.1017/S0007123414000106

Wallace, Jeremy. n.d. "Seeking Truth and Hiding Facts: China's Evolving State Capitalism." *Manuscript.*

Wang, Alex. 2006. "The Role of Law in Environmental Protection in China: Recent Developments." *Vermont Journal of Environmental Law* 8: 195.

Wang, Alex. 2013. "The Search for Sustainable Legitimacy: Environmental Law and Bureaucracy in China." *Harvard Environmental Law Review* 37, no. 2: 365–440.

Wang, Heyan. 2014. "How a PLA General Built a Web of Corruption to Amass a Fortune." *Caixin,* January 16.

Wang, Yuhua. 2014. *Tying the Autocrat's Hands: The Rise of the Rule of Law in China.* New York: Cambridge University Press.

Wedeman, Andrew. 2003. *From Mao to Market: Rent Seeking, Local Protectionism, and Marketization in China.* Cambridge: Cambridge University Press.

Wedeman, Andrew. 2005. "Anticorruption Campaigns and the Intensification of Corruption in China." *Journal of Contemporary China* 14, no. 42: 93–116.

Wedeman, Andrew. 2012. *Double Paradox: Rapid Growth and Rising Corruption in China.* Ithaca, NY: Cornell University Press.

Weeks, Jessica L. 2008. "Autocratic Audience Costs: Regime Type and Signaling Resolve." *International Organization* 62, no. 1: 35–64.

Weiss, Jessica Chen. 2014. *Powerful Patriots: Nationalist Protest in China's Foreign Relations.* New York: Oxford University Press.

Wen, Jiabao. 2007. *Government Work Report (Zhengfu Gongzuo Baogao).* FBIS CPP20070317066003. Wen Jiabao.

Whiting, Susan H. 2000. *Power and Wealth in Rural China: The Political Economy of Institutional Change.* Cambridge: Cambridge University Press.

Wildau, Gabriel. 2014. "Small Chinese Cities Steer Away from GDP as Measure of Success." *Financial Times,* August 13. https://www.ft.com/content/a0288bd4-22b0-11e4-8dae-00144feabdc0.

Wong, Alan, Michael Forsythe, and Andrew Jacobs. 2016. "Defying China, Hong Kong Bookseller Describes Detention." *New York Times,* June 16.

Wong, Edward. 2013. "Air Pollution Linked to 1.2 Million Deaths in China." *New York Times,* April 1.

Wong, Edward. 2014. "'Airpocalypse': Smog Hits Beijing at Dangerous Levels." *New York Times,* January 16.

Woodworth, Max D. 2012. "Frontier Boomtown Urbanism in Ordos, Inner Mongolia Autonomous Region." *Cross-Currents: East Asian History and Culture Review* 1, no. 1: 74–101.

Woodworth, Max D. 2015. "Ordos Municipality: A Market-Era Resource Boomtown." *Cities* 43: 115–132.

Woodworth, Max D., and Michael Ulfstjerne. 2016. "Taking Part: The Social Experience of Informal Finance in Ordos, Inner Mongolia." *Journal of Asian Studies* 75, no. 3: 649–672.

Woodworth, Max D., and Jeremy Wallace. 2017. "Seeing Ghosts: Parsing China's 'Ghost City' Controversy." *Urban Geography* 38, no. 8: 1–12.

WorldBank. 2007. "Cost of Pollution in China: Economic Estimates of Physical Damages." No. 39236. The World Bank. http://documents.worldbank.org/curated/en/782171468027560055/Cost-of-pollution-in-China-economic-estimates-of-physical-damages.

Wright, Joseph. 2008. "Do Authoritarian Institutions Constrain? How Legislatures Impact Economic Growth and Foreign Aid Effectiveness." *American Journal of Political Science* 52, no. 2: 322–343.

Xinhua. 2013a. 习近平主持中共中央政治局会议 部署开展党的群众路线教育实践活动工作. 人民日报海外版. April 20. http://paper.people.com.cn/rmrbhwb/html/2013-04/20/content_1228272.htm.

Xinhua. 2013b. 党的群众路线教育实践活动工作会议召开习近平发表重要讲话—群众路线网—人民网. June 18. http://qzlx.people.com.cn/n/2013/0618/c364565-21884589.html.

Xinhua. 2014a. "Xi Urges Further 'Mass Line' Efforts." January 20.

Xinhua. 2014b. "China Central Authority Calls for Implementation of 'Mass Line.'" August 5.

Xinhua. 2014c. "New Accounting Regime Ends 'GDP Supremacy.'" *China Daily*, September 22.

Xinhua Insight. 2013. "Yearender: CPC Gets Closer to Masses to Ensure a 'Red China.'" December 21. http://news.xinhuanet.com/english/china/2013-12/21/c_132986046.htm.

Yang, Dali. 2006. "Economic Transformation and Its Political Discontents in China: Authoritarianism, Unequal Growth, and the Dilemmas of Political Development." *Annual Review of Political Science* 9, no. 1: 143–164.

Yoon, Joana. 2015. "Orange as the New Black." In *Shared Destiny: China Story Yearbook 2015*, ed. G. Barmé, J. Goldkorn, and L. Jaivin. Canberra: ANU Press.

Yung, Chester. 2014. "China's Ghost Cities Are About to Get Spookier." *Wall Street Journal*, May 16.

Zeng, Jinyan. 2015. "China's Feminist Five: 'This Is the Worst Crackdown on Lawyers, Activists and Scholars in Decades.'" *The Guardian*, April 17.

Zenz, Adrian. 2019. "'Thoroughly Reforming Them Towards a Healthy Heart Attitude': China's Political Re-Education Campaign in Xinjiang." *Central Asian Survey* 38, no. 1: 102–28.

Zhang, Hong. 2013. "Sweating and on the Verge of Tears: Chinese Officials Carry Out Self-Criticism on TV." *South China Morning Post*, September 28.

Zhang, Shawn. 2018. "List of Re-Education Camps in Xinjiang 新疆再教育集中营列表." *Shawn Zhang on Medium* (blog), May 20. https://bit.ly/35XWqwA.

"Zhou Yongkang." 2014. *Caixin*. August 10

Zhou, Dongxu. 2014. "Market Reforms, Fight Against Corruption Go Hand in Hand, Expert Says." *Caixin*, July 22.

Zhou, Wei, and Heyan Wang. 2015. "How Disgraced Military Official Led Murky Property Development." *Caixin*, August 12.

Zhou, Xin. 2013. "China's Ordos Struggles to Repay Debt: Xinhua Magazine." Bloomberg News, July 8.

"Zhou Yongkang's Downfall." 2014. *China File*, July 31.

Zhu, Rongji. 2013. *Zhu Rongji on the Record: The Road to Reform 1991–1997*. Washington, DC: Brookings Institution Press.

Zhuang, Pinghui. 2016. "How High Can China's Population Possibly Go? Ambitious Urban Plan to House 3.4 Billion People Sparks Concern." *South China Morning Post*, July 15.

Zuo, Mandy. 2014. "Initial Results of 8-Year Soil Pollution Study Not Accurate Enough, Experts Say." *South China Morning Post*, April 20.

Zweig, David. 1983. "Opposition to Change in Rural China: The System of Responsibility and People's Communes." *Asian Survey* 23, no. 7: 879–900. https://doi.org/10.2307/2644294

Zweig, David. 1986. "Prosperity and Conflict in Post-Mao Rural China." *China Quarterly* 105: 1–18.

大胆使用批评和自我批评有力武器. 2013. *Renmin Ribao*, September 27.

央视网. 2013. 批评和自我批评是一剂良药_新闻频道. 《焦点访谈》. September 25. Retrieved from http://news.cntv.cn/2013/09/26/VIDE1380140758843768.shtml.

Political Opportunities for Participation and China's Leadership Transition

Diana Fu and Greg Distelhorst

Since Xi Jinping took office in China, state power has become increasingly personalized. Xi became the "core leader" (*hexin lingdao*) and assumed the title of military commander in chief in 2016.[1] Headlines have declared a sweeping transformation in politics under Xi, from the broad-reaching anti-corruption drive to a strong-arm campaign against grassroots civil society. The state has aggressively policed boundary-pushers, from the disappearance of Hong Kong publishers of politically sensitive books to a crackdown on mainland labor activists, lawyers, feminists, and Protestant churches. By most accounts, the present administration has departed from previous trajectories by closing political opportunity structures for participation and backtracking on incremental liberalization.

This chapter interrogates the prevailing narrative that pathways to grassroots political participation have narrowed in the transition from Hu Jintao (2002–2012) to Xi Jinping (2013–present). It argues that there are both continuities and discontinuities in political participation during the transition. Opportunities for contentious participation—defined as disruptive behavior ranging from grassroots advocacy to outright protests—have been severely restricted, but on the other hand, formal institutions for participation that expanded under Hu Jintao continue to provide channels for dialogue between local officials and citizens across China. We find little evidence of institutional decay when examining several of China's quasi-democratic institutions. On the contrary, evidence suggests that these institutions are becoming more widely used under Xi (Fu and Distelhorst 2017).

This case offers insights into political opportunity structures in authoritarian settings. Whereas political opportunities are normally thought of as either opening or closing, political participation in contemporary China shows that these two dynamics can occur simultaneously. Although one channel of participation closes, another may remain open and even expand. The manipulation of the political opportunity structure may be strategic for authoritarian rulers, as it provides a managed outlet for grievances during a period of intense repression of civil society.

Contentious and Institutional Political Participation

Shi Tianjin defined political participation in China as "activities by private citizens aimed at influencing the actual results of government policy" (Shi 1997, 21). Although Chinese citizens have only limited opportunities to select government officials and directly shape policy, they have other pathways to political influence. China scholars have studied citizen participation through appeals to officials (Cai 2004; Chen 2012), civil society advocacy (Yang 2005), lawsuits against government agencies (Pei 1997; O'Brien and Li 2004), and more recently submitting suggestions and complaints over the internet (Meng, Pan, and Yang 2017).

We divide grassroots participation into two modes: contentious and institutionalized. Contentious participation entails using disruptive methods—protests, petitioning, strikes, and forming illegal associations—to influence officials or to make a symbolic statement. In contrast, institutionalized participation uses state-sanctioned channels such as local elections, government hotlines and mailboxes, and courts to influence policy, to handle and resolve complaints, or to adjudicate disputes that arise between the public and government entities. Institutionalized participation is not a recent innovation. Such participation dates to imperial China, when ordinary people presented petitions to officials (Chen 2012, 44–53), yet new institutions of participation have emerged in the early twenty-first century.

Contentious participation occurs outside of official institutions (Ong and Göbel 2014). Rather than relying on formal processes to shape the actions of government, contention drives change through the disruption of ordinary activities and by creating a public spectacle. A large body of literature examines contentious actions taken by Chinese villagers (O'Brien and Li 2006), workers (Chan 2001; Chen 2003; Lee 2007; Friedman 2014; Gallagher 2014), pensioners (Hurst and O'Brien 2002), lawyers (Fu and Cullen 2008; Stern and O'Brien 2012; Pils 2014; Liu 2016), religious groups (Vala 2012; Koesel 2014), and journalists (Hassid 2008). In addition, studies have examined NGOs' contentious participation in environmental activism (Yang 2005; Mertha 2008; Steinhardt and Wu 2016) and in labor mobilization (Lee and Shen 2011).

Although we analyze contentious and institutionalized participation separately in this study, it is important to recognize that they are not strictly exclusive. Contentious activities often make use of participatory institutions to achieve their ends (O'Brien and Li 2006). In some cases, public mobilization shapes the actions of nominally impartial public institutions. For instance, activists can place pressure on judges by staging flash protests outside courtrooms (Fu 2018, ch. 5). The news media can mobilize public opinion, leading to more draconian criminal sentences (Liebman 2005). Activists can also exploit the unresponsiveness of participatory institutions to publicize government failings (Distelhorst 2017). The two modes of participation sometimes occur in tandem, but they still differ in whether they primarily seek to achieve their goals through formal, state-sanctioned processes or through disruption and confrontation with authority.

We first theorize how this case can contribute to disaggregating political opportunity in an authoritarian state. We then examine a major discontinuity in governing contentious participation under the two administrations. In tracing state repression under Hu of illegal labor organizations, human rights lawyers, and heterodox religious practitioners, we show that although grassroots activists were harassed, they were nevertheless able to mobilize contentious participation without sacrificing organizational survival. Repression was relatively decentralized and ad hoc, leaving room for civil society activists to maneuver. In contrast, the Xi administration has ushered in a campaign of repression against civil society characterized by national security rhetoric, the criminalization of threatening activism, and proactive repression. The result was not only an increased *degree* of repression but also a shift in its *form*, which contracted opportunities for contentious participation.

The second part of the chapter turns to everyday participation that takes place within institutions established by the state. We examine how people use three quasi-democratic institutions: constituency service institutions that enable citizens to appeal for help from local authorities; China's Regulations on Open Government Information, which permit citizens to apply for disclosure of government-held data; and China's courts, which allow citizens to file administrative lawsuits against government agencies. Public use of these participatory institutions has persisted across the leadership transition and even expanded in some cases, producing continuity in institutionalized participation.

Disaggregating Political Opportunity

These empirical shifts have theoretical implications for understanding political opportunity structures in authoritarian settings. Political opportunities include a host of structural openings for contention, including the opening of political access, unstable alignments, influential allies, and dividing elites (Tarrow 1996, 55–56). Political opportunities can change over time and are thus more "conjunctural" than static openings in any given political system (Tarrow 1996, 58). In other words, changing institutional arrangements may affect protest differently over time. In this view, institutional changes are viewed as structures that condition the type and timing of mobilization.

Adapting this concept to authoritarian or hybrid regimes requires certain modifications to this framework. Existing literature on Russia suggests that elite cleavages within state institutions may be an even more salient factor in hybrid regimes than in democratic ones. The sharpening of such elite cleavages can create heightened contention, whereas the resolution of them tended to end popular contention (Robertson 2010, 209). Stability may also reflect ad hoc bargains struck with various potential sources of contention, rather than durable institutional arrangements (Greene 2017). In the former Soviet Union, common institutional characteristics such as ideologies, modes of domination, and cultural affinities between different states created opportunities for "tidal influences of one nationalism on another" (Beissinger 2002, 32–37). Moreover, the presence of competitive elections in which there is a chance for an oppositional leader to win can provide a channel for anti-regime mobilization (Koesel and Bunce 2012).

Whereas scholarship on Russia and post-Soviet states emphasizes changes in elite cleavages and other institutional arrangements at the top echelons of the state, China scholars have argued that political opportunities need to be disaggregated by the level of government, the issue, the identity of participants, and the region (O'Brien and Stern 2009, 13–17). At the central state level, political opportunities have been characterized as vacillating from periods of contraction (*shou*) and liberalization (*fang*) (Gold 1990). By all accounts, the current period under Xi Jinping is characterized by increasing constraints, as the tightening on civil society and the consolidation of central state power have closed prior political openings. In addition to opportunities created by the differences between the central state and local states (Cai 2010, 31–32; O'Brien and Li 2006), opportunities must also be disaggregated horizontally. Different party-state agencies at the same administrative level can offer different opportunities for contention, with one agency facilitating protest while another represses (Chen 2012, 15–16; Fu 2017b).

We take an alternative approach by highlighting how the authoritarian state at the central level can *simultaneously* open institutional channels of participation while closing other, more contentious avenues of participation. The changes in political opportunity under the Xi administration illustrate this pattern. While much scholarly literature and reportage have highlighted decreasing resistance opportunities, we show that institutional opportunities for participation remain open and in some cases have even expanded.

Theoretically, this shows that the opportunity structure can simultaneously expand and contract, even during a period of high repression. Contracting opportunities for contentious participation do not necessarily mean the disappearance of institutionalized participation. In some ways, keeping institutionalized channels open benefits the regime during a period of increased repression because it allows the leadership to maintain a veneer of openness while curbing disruptive contention. The case of China under Xi thus shows the interplay between opening and closings of opportunities for participation, which can be an effective governing tactic.

This is not the first study to suggest that repression and facilitation can go hand in hand. Charles Tilly argued that rulers can choose a mixture of repression and facilitation: "Various combinations of facilitation and repression (whether anticipatory or responsive) mark the boundaries among prescribed, tolerated, and forbidden" (Tilly 2006, 75). However, what distinguishes this case is that it shows how the regime applies this mixture of tactics to different spheres of participation rather than to the same group of contenders. In other words, instead of holding out both carrots and sticks to protesters, it holds out carrots to those who pursue institutional forms of redress while using sticks to beat protesters who choose disruption.

Discontinuities in Contentious Participation

SOCIAL MANAGEMENT UNDER HU JINTAO

The Hu administration (2002–2012) took a fragmented approach toward governing contention on an everyday basis (Fu 2018). To be sure, the administration did not hesitate to round up dissidents seeking to promote democracy and human rights, as evidenced by the detention of Charter 08 signatories in 2008 and harsh measures against ethnic minorities in the aftermath of the Tibetan and Xinjiang riots in 2008 and 2009, respectively.[2] These commands came from the national leadership. In governing civil society, the Hu administration also continued to develop and reform the state corporatism model that regulated the number of organizations that could be formally registered with the state and limited their activities (Unger and Chan 1995; Hildebrandt 2013; Teets 2014).

Despite such centralized regulatory controls and coercion, everyday governance of contention—spontaneous protests, petitioning, and organizing—allowed local governments considerable discretion to deploy whatever control tactics they saw fit. This fragmented repression was part of a broader agenda of social management that promoted Hu's hallmark idea of establishing a "harmonious society."[3] The goal of this agenda was to secure social stability, a cornerstone of the party-state's legitimacy in the Hu era (Shue 2004), by targeting societal elements that threatened disorder. To this end, the central state issued a mandate to local authorities to maintain social stability at all costs and incentivized them to do so with a so-called one-veto system (*yipiao foujue*) (Edin 2003), which stipulated that outbreaks of mass incidents would negatively affect local officials' careers.

As a result, the local authorities commonly used extralegal means to intimidate persistent petitioners, including detaining them in informal jails and forcing them to return to their hometowns (Cai 2010). Some local authorities hired thugs to threaten dissenters in what has become an increasingly commercial practice of outsourcing coercion to third parties (Wang and Minzner 2015; Chen 2017).[4] In labor disputes, some localities bought off individuals or groups who staged collective action with a stability maintenance fund (Lee and Zhang 2013; Su and He 2010). In fact, paying for stability was an informal institution under Hu, which allowed the state and protesters to negotiate over the price of rights (Chen 2012, 44–53; Lee and Zhang 2013). In housing demolition disputes, municipal authorities have also used "relational repression" (Deng and O'Brien 2013), which taps into a protester's network of friends and relatives to demobilize them. By shifting responsibility for maintaining social stability downward (Lee and Zhang 2013), the central leadership under Hu delegated the dirty work of repression to local authorities, thereby implicitly channeling repression into more informal and extralegal means.

The discretion afforded to local authorities in governing civil society resulted in fragmentation: conflicting strategies of control across bureaucracies at the local levels (Howell 2015; Fu 2017b). While state security apparatuses sought to repress labor organizations, the official labor union attempted to co-opt these groups. This fragmented approach created opportunities for collaboration between local states and civil society groups such as environmental NGOs and service provision NGOs (Mertha 2008; Teets 2014). Driven by the need to minimize political uncertainty and secure their own political power, local authorities often collaborated with civil society groups, offering protection in exchange for support (Spires 2011), even as other branches of the local state engaged in repression.

Fragmented repression under Hu also gave rise to forms of mobilization in which grassroots actors continuously tested the ambiguous political boundaries of activism (Stern and O'Brien 2012). This operating environment permitted activists to experiment with a range of "boundary-spanning contention" that straddled the line between permissible and transgressive (O'Brien and Stern 2009), including "rightful resistance" (O'Brien and Li 2006), "cellular activism" (Lee 2007, 10–11), spontaneous protests (Chen 2012, 44–53; Cai 2010, 149), and "disguised collective action" (Fu 2017a).

While these diverse forms of contentious participation have persisted under Xi, three qualitative shifts in repression have significantly changed the political opportunity structure for contentious participation.

PARTY MANAGEMENT UNDER XI JINPING

When Xi took the reins in 2013, repressing boundary-pushers in civil society was a cornerstone of his political campaign to consolidate power. He departed from social management to establish what we term "party management" over civil society. This entailed bringing existing civil society groups under the direct leadership of party organs and closing the space for unwanted organizations. Embarking upon the largest ideological campaign since Mao Zedong (Zhao 2016), Xi viewed civil society as a conduit through which dangerous Western ideas flowed into China. A 2013 internal directive known as Document No. 9 listed an independent civil society among the seven perils to the Chinese state.[5] Placing it in the company of other Western perils such as media freedom and universal human rights, Xi's document saw civil society as both a practical threat to everyday social stability and an ideological threat, which called for a qualitatively different, stronger approach to repression. Referring to people who hold "ulterior motives" in fostering civil society, Document No. 9 stated:

> Promoting civil society and Western-style theories of governance, they [advocates of civil society] claim that building a civil society in China is a precondition for the protection of individual rights and forms the basis for the realization of constitutional democracy. *Viewing civil society as a magic bullet for advancing social management at the local level* [emphasis added], they have launched all kinds of so-called citizen's movements.[6]

Although the language did not directly attribute the term "social management" to Hu, it clearly signaled that the party-state should not view civil society as an instrument to manage society. Instead, the Xi administration saw it as a dangerous political force that was in direct opposition to the Chinese Communist Party:

> Advocates of civil society want to squeeze the Party out of leadership of the masses at the local level, even setting the Party against the masses, to the point that their advocacy is becoming a serious form of *political opposition* [emphasis added].[7]

Characterizing civil society as a form of political opposition means that social organizations cannot be used to govern society and must instead be treated as a threat to national security.

Party management extended into three major spheres of civil society. In governing the press, Xi declared that the media must be the voice of the Party. In a much-quoted speech to state-run media during an inspection tour in 2016, Xi declared: "They [the Party's media] must love the party, protect the party, and closely align themselves with party leadership in thought, politics, and action."[8] An editorial in the *China Daily* followed by arguing that trust in the state media must be restored during a period where social media has proliferated:

> The Party has always held "the mass line," maintaining an open attitude toward people's opinions, as an essential principle of governance. That applies to its journalistic work, too. If the current split [that between traditional and social media] continues, the legitimacy of the Party might decline. It is necessary for the media to restore people's trust in the Party, especially as the economy has entered a new normal.[9]

Likewise, in legal reform, the administration has affirmed the Party (not the government) as the author and interpreter of the law:

> Letting Party leadership penetrate into the entire process and all aspects of ruling the country to the law is a basic experience of the construction of our country's Socialist rule of law. Our country's Constitution has established the leading position of the Chinese Communist Party.[10]

In governing non-state organizations, the Party has called on the Organization Department to increase party membership in non-state organizations. According to a statement by the department and reported by Xinhua News agency, the goal of increasing party membership is to "mobilize and educate ordinary people to stand against negative influence and illegal activities."[11] By boosting membership in social organizations, the Xi administration seeks to establish party dominance in the non-state sphere. Consolidating the Party's leadership in media, law, and social organizations is at the core of Xi's party management.

Equating civil society with anti-Party forces calls for extreme measures against dissident activists and groups. While much press coverage has focused on the intensified *degree* of repression, there have also been three important shifts in the *nature* of repression under Xi: from sporadic harassment to criminalization, from post facto to preemptive, and from social stability to national security framing. All three tactical shifts have resulted in a more consolidated form of repression, a departure from the fragmented repression under Hu.

FROM SOCIAL STABILITY TO NATIONAL SECURITY FRAMING

Hu's administration upheld social stability as one of the guiding principles of governance.[12] Accordingly, the portion of its budget allocated to maintaining domestic security surpassed the national defense budget for three consecutive years from 2011 to 2013.[13]

Maintaining social stability remains an important priority under Xi. However, the lack of full disclosure on the domestic security budget makes it difficult to judge the extent to which social stability maintenance is prioritized by the current administration. Recent data released by the Ministry of Finance suggests that 2016 spending on public security was earmarked at 166.8 billion yuan ($25.6 billion), which represented a 5.3 percent increase from the previous year. In contrast, defense spending for 2016 reached as high as 950 billion yuan ($146 billion), 783.2 billion yuan more than domestic security.[14] Although the budget for domestic security is likely an underestimate, these allocations suggest a reversal in priority from the Hu era.

Accompanying this reversal in budgetary allocation is a shift in the rhetorical framing of repression that underscores national security in addition to the maintenance of social stability. The Xi administration is much more likely than its predecessor to frame crackdowns of NGOs and detention of activists as part of safeguarding national security. This rhetorical change is also reflected in the bureaucratic restructuring of the security apparatus. Xi demoted the once-powerful Politics and Law Committee in charge of maintaining domestic security and purged its retired head, Zhou Yongkang, who had been considered "China's security czar."[15] In its place, Xi established the National Security Commission and installed himself as the head of this coordinating body (Wang and Minzner 2015).

This pivot toward national security affected the government's management of civil society in two respects. First, the emphasis on national security is reflected in recent laws and regulations governing civil society. In addition to the National Security Law passed in 2015, which outlaws a number of potential threats to the economy, society, and cyberspace, the Xi administration also passed the Overseas Non-Governmental Organization (NGO) Law, which came into effect January in 2017.[16] This law effectively isolates Chinese NGOs from outside funding bodies and influences, using the language of national security, and gives the Ministry of Public Security the power to regulate foreign organizations operating in China.[17] Article 5 stipulates that NGOs "must not endanger China's national unity, security, or ethnic unity; must not harm China's national interests, societal public interest and the lawful rights and interests of citizens, legal persons, and other organizations; . . . must not engage in or fund for-profit activities or political activities, and must not illegally engage in or fund religious activities."[18] Local governments have responded accordingly, with Jilin province's state security bureau setting up a hotline for its citizens to report on those suspected of breaching national security.[19] Effectively, the new law's political goal is to ensure that foreign interests do not infiltrate China through linking up with domestic civil society. Whereas foreign groups used to operate in a legal gray zone, any that seek to set up a representative office in China are now required to register with the Ministry of Public Security. To do so, foreign entities such as foundations, NGOs, think tanks, and trade associations must first obtain formal approval from a supervisory government-related unit.

The national security frame goes beyond written laws. Foreign activists operating in China have also been accused of threatening China's national security. For instance, the detainment and deportation of Swedish activist Peter Dahlin in 2016 were framed in the official media as a national security case:

> In recent days, national security and relevant agencies coordinated to break a case of national security, successfully cracking down on a group that called itself "China Rights Emergency Aid." This group has accepted foreign funding and has trained and supported a number of "legal representatives" who have engaged in illegal activities harming national security.[20]

According to his own testimony, Dahlin was investigated for violating Article 107 of the criminal law for using foreign funding for illegal and subversive activities. However, he was never formally charged in court for violating national security and was later deported under the Espionage Law without a hearing.[21] In 2017, Taiwanese NGO worker Li Ming-che was detained and prosecuted on suspicion of "threatening national security."[22] These cases highlight the links drawn by the Xi administration between civil society activities and threats to national security.

The passage of a series of national security laws combined with a concerted propaganda effort further justifies extending the security apparatus's reach into civil society. Activists can now be targeted as internal enemies who threaten national security. Moreover, the new law regulating foreign NGOs is a form of soft repression of civil society, as it effectively restricts foreign funding from flowing to domestic organizations that the government does not favor. In addition, the fewer the number of foreign NGO workers in China, the harder it is for knowledge transfer to take place.[23]

Xi's personification of power, as exemplified in his self-installation as the head of the National Security Commission in 2014, directly impacts the political opportunity structure for contention. Although the commission has not thus far executed any of its stated plans to crack down on domestic unrest and foreign infiltration, it nevertheless has served a symbolic purpose.[24] It made an unequivocal statement that coercion is directed by the supreme leader, not by an institution such as the Central Political and Legal Affairs Commission. This personification of power sends an immediate and powerful signal. With Xi denouncing civil society as among the seven Western perils most deadly to state power, local officials are less willing to risk even tacitly tolerating contention by civic organizations, regardless of the issue, participants, or region.

FROM SPORADIC HARASSMENT TO CRIMINALIZATION

The second shift under Xi is from sporadic harassment to the criminalization of contentious participation. Ever on guard against the ideological perils of a growing civil society, Xi's government has a propensity for criminalizing contention, which includes mass arrests of activists and staging of public confessions. As a result, a number of individuals and organizations across different sectors that had been tacitly tolerated by local states became targets.

Under Hu's leadership, the party-state also charged boundary-pushers with disruption of social order and subversion of the state. However, according to data analysis by the Duihua Foundation, the number of people indicted with endangering state security (ESS crimes) under Xi has significantly increased. The number of trials in the category that includes ESS increased by 20 percent in 2013, the year during which the leadership transition took place.[25] In 2014, this figure reached the highest level recorded by the *China Law Yearbook* since

1999. Overall, the number of ESS charges in 2013 and 2014 under Xi's reign was close to the highest figure recorded under Hu, which was in 2008, when the Beijing Olympics were held. According to official statistics, the number of ESS indictments dropped by 50 percent in 2015, but analysts believe this may be due to an increased number of charges against activists in non-ESS categories, including "picking quarrels and provoking trouble."[26]

Qualitative research also suggests that the Xi administration has criminalized a wider range of activism. A case in point is the 2015 mass arrest of labor activists who had been previously tolerated under Hu. Between 2009 and 2011, local authorities in Guangdong province had periodically harassed labor activists and shuttered organizations from time to time, but the fragmented nature of local state control had allowed activists to resurrect their organizations in other localities and to "mobilize without the masses"— coordinate contention without rallying large-scale collective action.[27]

This limited space for activism all but collapsed under Xi. In December 2015, the party-state launched an unprecedented crackdown on labor organizations in Guangdong province, arresting at least twenty-five staff members and activists from five different organizations. At least three activists, including the director of the province's largest labor NGO, were charged: one for alleged embezzlement and two others for "organizing a crowd to disrupt social order."[28] The coordinated raids and criminal detentions of leaders represent a departure from the period 2009–2011, in which arrests and organizational closures were reserved for mass disturbances.

In addition to the crackdown on labor activists, in July 2015 nearly 250 rights lawyers were rounded up in the largest mass detainment of lawyers since the 1990s.[29] Several lawyers were formally charged with subversion and inciting subversion of state power, both serious charges normally reserved for challenges to the party-state's rule.[30] The authorities have also effectively legalized forced disappearances of activists by using the amended Article 73 of China's Criminal Procedure Law, which permits incommunicado residential surveillance of up to six months for individuals suspected of crimes against national security.[31] A lawyer belonging to the New Citizens' Movement was also charged with inciting to subvert state power in June 2016.[32]

In what has become a routine feature under Xi's reign, the party-state created a public spectacle of these arrests by compelling some detained lawyers to make confessions on television.[33] Similarly, the regime forced Hong Kong book publishers who were detained in October 2015 to confess their crimes on television, as it did with the Swedish activist Peter Dahlin, who confessed to providing funding to human rights lawyers.[34] These public confessions are part and parcel of the criminalization of activism. They have Maoist characteristics, as they are reminiscent of the parading and public shaming of counterrevolutionaries during the Cultural Revolution. This public form of repression also constitutes part of a larger agenda under Xi to create a "new normal" (*xin changtai*), in which challengers are targeted and destroyed for all to see (Wallace 2017).

FROM REACTIVE TO PROACTIVE REPRESSION

Reactive repression seeks to contain social unrest by demobilizing protesters *after* the outbreak of mass incidents, while preemptive repression seeks to contain contention from the outset. There has been no shortage of reactive repression under Xi's administration, as evidenced by the examples given earlier. However, a more insidious form of repression is proactive, with the goal of cutting emergent threads between networks of activists and civil society organizations. If reactive repression is akin to putting out small fires of dissent, then proactive repression is akin to ensuring that the disaffected do not possess the wood chips needed to kindle a fire.

In the realm of civil society, proactive repression involves a combination of meticulous oversight of existing organizational networks and cutting links between civil society groups and protesters. One of the most threatening elements of civil society is its ability to mobilize citizens. The Chinese government is keenly aware of civil society organizations' role abroad as facilitators of mobilization in the color revolutions and Arab Spring, and it keeps a hawkish watch on budding activism that has an organizational backbone. While neo-Tocquevillians may applaud the formation of such social capital (Putnam 1995), the larger networks that can be created on the backs of civil society associations seem far more ominous to the Chinese party-state than small-scale collective action. Thus, proactive repression that aims to preempt organized contention is deemed critical to sustaining state power.

The recent squelching of China's burgeoning feminist movement is a prime example of proactive repression that targets activism supported by an organizational backbone. The "Feminist Five," who had planned to hand out anti-sexual-harassment pamphlets on public buses, were preemptively detained even before they could distribute their literature (Zheng 2015). They were initially informally charged with "picking quarrels," later changed to a charge of illegal assembly.[35] Their planned actions were considered threatening because they were coordinated across several different cities, including Beijing, Guangzhou, and Hangzhou (Fincher 2016). The government proactively rounded up these women even though they appeared to be lobbying for a goal the Chinese Communist Party propagated—against sexual harassment and on behalf of "women holding up half the sky." By proactively policing the younger generation of feminists, Xi's government is sending a signal to other potential rabble-rousers—especially if their actions are done in multiple localities and in conjunction with social organizations and networks outside of the Party.

The feminists were also considered a serious threat because of their alliances with other civic organizations. The Feminist Five did not carry out their actions in isolation. They were embedded in a broader network of NGOs and informal groups at universities that regularly exchanged information, discussed tactics, and provided mutual support. Staff members from the anti-discrimination organization Yirenping sent regular email updates to international supporters and circulated public statements calling for the release of the Feminist Five.[36]

In February 2016, just one month prior to the arrest of the Feminist Five, China's most influential women's rights organization, Beijing Zhongze Women's Legal Counseling Service Center, was forced to close.[37] In the Hu era, the center had taken on a number of politically sensitive cases that attracted national media coverage and was a key proponent of China's first domestic violence law, passed in 2015.[38] Repression had begun under the Hu administration, as Beijing University (which used to be the center's supervisory unit) ended its affiliation with the center in 2009, though it allowed the center to continue operating under a different name.[39] Under Xi, the organization was shuttered completely. Some have speculated that the center's closure was triggered in part by its leader's growing international reputation and the center's close ties to foreign politicians such as Hillary Clinton. Although the center was not directly involved in the new feminist movement, it was part of a broader network of women's advocacy organizations that the Xi administration found deeply threatening because of its ties to the international community. Proactive repression under Xi seeks to completely dismantle advocacy organizations and clip their ties to activist networks before the outbreak of organized mass incidents.

Institutionalized Participation Under Hu Jintao and Xi Jinping

The shift in governing contentious participation was stark, but contention is not the only avenue to political participation. Although few would characterize China's political trajectory under Hu as "democratizing," the first decade of the twenty-first century witnessed the introduction or expansion of quasi-democratic institutions that enable grassroots political participation.[40] First, government agencies, Party organizations, and legislative bodies used information technology to make it easier for citizens to make direct appeals to political authorities, establishing channels like the Mayor's Mailbox (Hartford 2005). Second, government transparency regulations were introduced locally and later formalized nationally by the 2008 Regulation on Open Government Information (Distelhorst 2017; Chen 2016). This statute obligated government agencies to respond to freedom-of-information requests from ordinary citizens. Third, throughout this period, citizens took government agencies to court by filing administrative lawsuits in the Chinese justice system. Although this kind of participation is less confrontational than the activism discussed earlier, it nonetheless constitutes attempts to change "the actual results of government policy" (Shi 1997, 21). In fact, both writing letters to officials and taking officials to court are participatory acts observed by Shi in the late 1980s. Opportunities to submit Open Government Information requests and to make electronic appeals to officials only emerged later.

In light of the change in approach to contentious participation, did the state also reduce access to participatory *institutions* under Xi Jinping? Did the government take actions either to reduce the quality of participatory institutions (e.g., make them less responsive) or to increase barriers to accessing these institutions? We look for empirical evidence of these trends in three participatory institutions: online appeals to officials, Open Government Information requests, and lawsuits against government agencies.

WRITTEN APPEALS TO OFFICIALS

Contacting public officials through letters and visits has a long history in China (Chen 2012, 44–53). In its modern form, petitions (*xinfang*) to political authorities are managed through the National Administration of Letters and Visits, as well as similarly named departments within administrative, Communist Party, legislative, and justice organs (Dimitrov 2015). The purpose of these institutions is to resolve conflicts, improve policy, and collect information about the complaints and dissatisfaction of the public. In Beijing in the 1980s, filing complaints with work units and through the bureaucratic hierarchy was among the most common forms of political participation (Shi 1997, 94). Archival evidence suggests that Chinese officials believe that responsiveness to inquiries and letters of complaint is important. If citizens' appeals fall on deaf ears—or worse, induce retribution from authorities—the public may cease contacting officials altogether and thereby deprive the government of useful information (Dimitrov 2015).

Due to the decentralized nature of the various channels to make appeals, both written and in person, estimates of the number made are hard to find. One widely cited figure put the national total at 12.7 million personal visits in 2003, and estimates based on provincial reporting show petitions peaking in 2004 before falling to roughly 10 million in 2009 (Dimitrov 2015).[41] By these figures, one petition was filed for every 133 people in 2009. Using an alternative methodology, the 2010 China General Social Survey asked respondents how they dealt with "unjust" treatment by political authorities, and directly appealing to officials or agencies was the most frequent action. Estimates based on this survey put the overall prevalence of direct appeals to upper-level authorities through any channel—not just formal petitions—at roughly one for every 60 people.[42]

One reform during the Hu Jintao administration added a new channel to submit written appeals to officials. Local governments throughout China established mechanisms to receive citizen letters over the internet. The city of

Nanjing allowed citizens to contact government departments online starting in 2001, and Hangzhou established a web-based 12345 Mayor's Mailbox in 2003 (Hartford 2005). Since then, online mechanisms have spread across China. Although observers are understandably skeptical about their efficacy, evidence suggests that the mere presence of these online opportunities has a positive impact on public opinion about government (Truex 2017). We obtained and analyzed publicly posted letters from 293 local governments. We found that people use these mailboxes to seek official intervention in property disputes, make queries about household registration (*hukou*) and childbearing regulations, complain about garbage and noise pollution, air grievances about local schools and hospitals, and bring up disputes with employers.

Do we observe any change in the quality of online appeals institutions across the two administrations? Although researchers can observe publicly posted letters and official responses (Su and Meng 2016), it is difficult to assess what proportion of citizens' appeals led to helpful actions by authorities. Officials may omit some letters from public records. Instead, researchers have studied the quality of online appeals institutions through field audits that submit information requests to local agencies. These studies cannot tell us about any concrete actions that officials take in response to citizens' grievances, but they do offer evidence of changes in staffing or funding over time. If local Mayor's Mailboxes lost funding or staff in the Xi era, we would expect local responsiveness to citizens' queries to decline.

A series of field studies of such online institutions conveniently spans the Hu-Xi leadership transition (Distelhorst and Hou 2017). In July 2012, prior to the leadership transition, an initial study found that 43 percent (111 of 258) of contacted prefectural governments offered helpful replies to requests for information. Subsequent surveys were undertaken between May and August 2013, after the leadership transition. The average rate of helpful replies across the later studies was precisely identical to the prior year's: 43 percent (417 of 967).[43] There is little evidence that local Mayor's Mailboxes suddenly lost funding or personnel in the first year of Xi's leadership.

FREEDOM-OF-INFORMATION REQUESTS

Under Hu's leadership, the party-state embarked on a government transparency reform. The reform not only involved top-down mandates for agencies to disclose more information but also sought to stimulate government transparency through public participation. When the Regulations on Open Government Information took effect in May 2008, ordinary citizens were permitted to request information from tens of thousands of government agencies across the country. The reform thus created a new channel of citizen participation in China, broadening the freedom to request information.

It may seem puzzling that a regime widely known for censoring and manipulating information (King, Pan, and Roberts 2013) would also pursue reforms to increase government transparency. However, two imperatives in the early 2000s motivated transparency reforms, as reflected in the writings of reform architect Zhou Hanhua. The first was a long-standing concern among the leadership in Beijing about monitoring local governments to reduce local corruption, ineptitude, and deviations from laws. The second was China's entry to the World Trade Organization in 2001. China's accession agreement included a commitment to make local policies more transparent, a pledge that Zhou cited when arguing for the reform (Zhou 2002, 81–83).

Opening freedom-of-information requests to ordinary citizens was proposed in the earliest drafts of the new Open Government Information regulation. Zhou viewed public participation in improving transparency as integral to aligning public administration with legal statutes:

> Other than strictly following the law, administration by law emphasizes the openness and participatory nature of government activities, so as to allow the public to truly participate in the policymaking process. It may be said that openness and participation are the most concentrated embodiment of contemporary administration by law. (Zhou 2002, 83)

These transparency reforms began at local levels. Fujian province and the municipality of Guangzhou adopted China's earliest local transparency regulations. Throughout the decade similar regulations diffused across China's municipal and provincial governments. When the national Regulations on Open Government Information took effect in May 2008, more than 50 percent of China's local governments had already enacted local government transparency regulations.

How well did these participatory transparency institutions function in practice under Hu? Several field studies of the new Regulations on Open Government Information showed that the response and disclosure rates were discouragingly low. On environmental transparency, a 2009 study found that fewer than half of 113 city governments responded to requests for information

TABLE 3.1 } Key Local Government Transparency Reforms

Year	Prefectures	Provinces
2001	—	Fujian
2002	Guangzhou	—
2003	Harbin, Shantou, Taiyuan	—
2004	Anshan, Changchun, Chengdu, Datong, Hangzhou, Jinan, Kunming, Ningbo, Wuhan	Chongqing, Hubei, Jilin, Shanghai
2005	Guiyang, Haikou, Suzhou, Urumqi, Zhengzhou	Beijing, Guangdong, Hainan, Hebei
2006	Benxi, Shenzhen	Heilongjiang, Jiangsu, Liaoning, Shaanxi, Sichuan

Notes: Years of enactment listed. The national Open Government Information reform was enacted in 2007, effective May 1, 2008.

about enterprises violating pollution regulations (IPE & NDRC 2010). On financial transparency, one audit rated the majority of provinces as responding to less than 30 percent of requests (SUFE 2010). The response rate was even poorer at lower levels of government. A 2010 audit submitted requests for basic information about local public services to a random sample of county-level governments and found that county agencies fulfilled just 14 percent of these basic requests (Distelhorst 2017). Inquiries about the educational qualifications of local teachers received the highest disclosure rate (22 percent); disclosure of registered businesses in the public transport sector was second most likely (17 percent); and disclosure of enterprises penalized for regulatory violations was provided by only a small handful of counties (5 percent).

Given the Xi administration's embrace of censorship, we might expect public participation through transparency institutions to contract or even collapse under his leadership. Yet the available data suggest that public enthusiasm for freedom-of-information requests has not changed across the two administrations. Recent data examining trends in participation across twenty provinces in China show that total requests slightly declined between 2012 and 2013, recovered in 2014 during the second year of Xi's administration, and exceeded previous years in 2015.

Assessing changes in the *quality* of the information that was accessed is more challenging. However, the available evidence again suggests more continuity than change from Hu to Xi. On financial transparency, the Shanghai University of Finance and Economics has maintained a largely consistent transparency evaluation methodology through the leadership transition. Its mean provincial financial transparency score nearly doubled between 2011 and 2016, from 23 points to 42 points, suggesting that financial transparency actually improved under Xi.[44]

On environmental transparency, the Pollution Information Transparency Index provides data, but its scoring system changed across time periods,

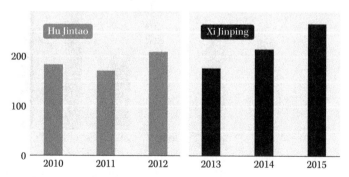

FIGURE 3.1 Public Participation in Freedom-of-Information Requests (thousands)

Notes: Total requests under the Open Government Information regulations from twenty provinces collected from annual provincial reports by Yongxi Chen, University of Hong Kong. Only twenty provinces reported annual totals for each of the six years under study.

making it difficult to directly compare results across the two administrations. The new scoring system adopted in 2014 for freedom-of-information requests added "completeness" of government responses to the scoring criteria, which previously focused on whether a government agency provided a channel and offered timely responses to inquiries. The share of prefectures achieving a perfect score declined from 56 percent under the old scoring system to just 23 percent in the new system. However, the researchers reported similar three-year trends in the performance of information disclosure in both the Hu and Xi administrations by local Environmental Protection Bureaus. When the local environmental bureaus in both administrations were exposed to information showing their shortcomings, they responded by improving the quality of those channels. If the Xi administration took a fundamentally different approach, we might have expected these local bureaus to ignore poor marks rather than invest in improvements in informational disclosures.

Comparing two studies that filed information requests with provincial governments under Hu and Xi, we again find no evidence of discontinuity across the two administrations. The Center for Public Participation and Support at Peking University reported that at least fifteen of thirty provinces (Tibet was excluded) responded to their applications for government information in 2010 (CPPSS 2011). When the Chinese Academy of Social Sciences conducted a similar study in 2015, it received on-time replies from twenty-three provinces (77 percent) via postal mail (CASS 2016). In requests sent via email, 12 of 17 provincial authorities (71 percent) replied on time. Although these two evaluations sought different information and did not make detailed results publicly available to researchers, they offer little suggestion that provincial governments have become more closed to information requests under Xi.

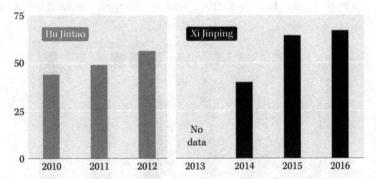

FIGURE 3.2 Local Environmental Protection Bureau "Disclosure by Application" Scores

Notes: Average percentage scores of city-level Environmental Protection Bureaus for "Disclosure by Application" in the Pollution Information Transparency Index reports, 2010–2016. The scoring system became more stringent in 2014 by incorporating completeness of government responses. One hundred thirteen cities are analyzed in 2010–2012, and 120 are analyzed in 2014–2016. Examining only cities available in all six years does not change the results. Original reports available from http://wwwen.ipe.org.cn/reports/Reports.aspx?cid=18336.

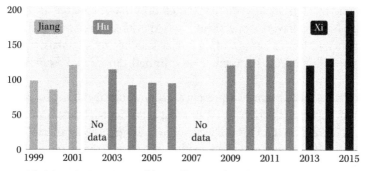

FIGURE 3.3 Administrative Lawsuits Tried (per million population)

Notes: Administrative lawsuits tried in courts reported in the annual Work Report of the Supreme People's Congress under Jiang Zemin, Hu Jintao, and Xi Jinping, normalized by national population. No data were reported in the reports for 2002, 2007, and 2008.

ADMINISTRATIVE LAWSUITS

Finally, we briefly examine a third institutionalized channel of political participation: administrative lawsuits, colloquially known as "folks suing officials" (民告官案件) (Pei 1997; O'Brien and Li 2004). Although the courts tend to defer to core regime interests (Chen 2016), every year judges rule on many thousands of claims against government authorities. This reflects a combination of the willingness of citizens to invest their time and money and the capacity of courts to process and rule on their claims.

If Xi's clampdown on participation extended to administrative lawsuits, we might expect such lawsuits to decline under his leadership, through increased barriers to entry or reduced judicial resources. Instead, we observe broad continuity in the popularity of administrative lawsuits across the two administrations. Total administrative lawsuits heard by Chinese courts declined slightly in the first year of Xi's administration, followed by a rebound in 2014. Administrative lawsuits increased dramatically in 2015, reaching a per capita level almost 50 percent higher than in any of the previous fifteen years. The increased volume of cases heard suggests the institution is attracting increased public interest, is the recipient of additional resources, or both.

Conclusion

By distinguishing between two pathways for political participation—contentious and formal—we showed that there are both continuities and discontinuities in the political opportunity structure for participation under Hu Jintao and Xi Jinping. On the one hand, Xi's accession to power has had dire consequences for civil society and contentious participation more broadly.

Repression of civil society under Xi not only has increased in *degree* but also has changed in *form*. Specifically, we identified three major shifts: from framing repression as safeguarding social stability to safeguarding national security; from sporadic harassment to criminalization; and from reactive to proactive repression.

Taken together, these shifts represent a discontinuity in political opportunities for contentious participation. Xi is pursuing a more consolidated, top-down approach to repression than his predecessor, which signals a significant change in opportunities for contentious participation. Whereas activists and organizations were able to exploit both vertical and horizontal divisions within the state to carve out spaces for maneuvering in the Hu era, they are less able to do so under Xi. Few state actors are willing to aid activists and organizations in a political system that celebrates repressive acts by extracting public confessions from boundary-pushers. The act of making repression a public spectacle evidences the party-state's desire to buttress its legitimacy not only by maintaining stability but also through ostentatious displays of state power.

This consolidation of coercive power should not be conflated with the formalization of coercion. While the number of activists formally charged for criminal activities has increased, the state has also continued to use informal coercion.[45] This entails the extensive use of third-party agents such as thugs and private security companies (Chen 2017) as well as state-organized disappearances. These informal coercive tactics occur simultaneously with the increasing criminalization of activism, thus leading to an overall shrinking opportunity structure for contentious participation.

This does not mean, however, that Xi has restricted access to institutionalized participation. As the second part of this chapter has shown, several formal institutions for public participation under Hu Jintao have persisted under Xi's reign. These institutions facilitate relations between local governments and the public and provide channels to address complaints. We find little evidence of institutional decline; in fact, the evidence suggests that these institutions are becoming more rather than less effective. Local responsiveness to online appeals remained steady or increased across the two administrations. Both freedom-of-information requests and lawsuits against government agencies have recently hit new highs. Admittedly, these are only a subset of China's participatory institutions. Others, including local elections and deliberative meetings, are omitted from our analysis and may be experiencing different trends under Xi (Unger, Chan, and Chung 2014).

Although a shift to institutionalized participation may appear to be in the interest of the state, there are potential shortcomings to repressing contentious participation. Both institutionalized and contentious participation help the party-state to collect information about society (Lorentzen 2013), but it is not clear that both reveal the same kind of information. From the state's perspective, institutionalized participation may offer only a suboptimal substitute for the information that disruptive contention brings to the fore. The high costs of participating in collective action demonstrate the intensity of public feeling. In comparison, clicking "send" on an email to the mayor's office costs citizens relatively little. That kind of participation may provide information about low-stakes quibbles rather than major grievances.

This case can be used to further theorize political opportunity structures under authoritarianism. It evidences that at the central level, the authoritarian state can simultaneously open and close political opportunities for partici-pation. This dual strategy was used by the former Chinese leader Hu Jintao, who adopted a type of "flexible repression" to govern civil society (Fu 2018, ch. 3) by facilitating obedient civil society organizations (Koesel 2014; Teets 2014; Hildebrandt 2013) while repressing contentious groups. This chapter has shown that the same strategy has been taken to a new level and modified under Xi's leadership. The latter administration has little tolerance for civil society of any kind but has left certain institutionalized channels of participa-tion virtually untouched. The Chinese state's strategy of balancing repression with institution building may prove to be an effective governance maneuver. Previous scholarship notes how participatory institutions incorporate and ap-pease social actors who might otherwise pose threats to the regime (Gandhi and Prezeworski 2007). This use of participatory institutions stands in contrast to striking individual bargains with potential threats to stability, as observed in contemporary Russia (Greene 2017).

It remains to be seen whether simply preserving institutions of public partic-ipation from the Hu administration will be sufficient to meet public demands for input into policymaking and responsive governance. If not, the decision to repress more contentious activity may have the undesirable effect of political dis-engagement, pushing discontent out of the view of public officials. Losing sight of the concerns of the public is a dangerous situation for any political regime.

Notes

The authors thank Mark Beissinger, Valerie Bunce, Titus Chen, Manfred Elfstrom, Karrie Koesel, Sida Liu, Maria Repnikova, Margaret E. Roberts, Graeme Robertson, Rory Truex, Jeremy Wallace, Jessica Weiss and workshop participants at the University of Notre Dame and National Sun Yat-Sen University for thoughtful feedback on this research. They also gratefully acknowledge Yongxi Chen for sharing his data on provincial information requests. This chapter was adapted from Fu and Distelhorst (2017)

1. "Xi Jinping Xinren Junweilianzhi Zongzhihui [Xi Jinping assumes commander in chief of the Central Military Commission]," Renmin Wang [People Net], April 21, 2016, http://cpc.people.com.cn/xuexi/n1/2016/0421/c385474-28293613.html; "Zhonggong Shouci Xingrong Xi Jinping Lingdao Wei Hexin [Politburo describes Xi as a core leader for first time]," BBC, October 27, 2016, http://www.bbc.com/zhongwen/simp/china/2016/10/161027_china_xi_core.

80 { Citizens and the State in Authoritarian Regimes

2. Human Rights Watch, "China: Retaliation for Signatories of Rights Charter," December 10, 2008, https://www.hrw.org/news/2008/12/10/china-retaliation-signatories-rights-charter; Yonghong Han, "7-5 Shijian Hou Shouci Dao Xinjiang Kaocha Hu Jintao: Xinjiang 'Wending Yadao Yiqie'" [Hu Jintao's first visit to Xinjiang since 7-5 incident: In Xinjiang 'stability takes precedence over all'"], August 25, 2009, http://prd.zaobao.com/special/report/politic/xinjiang/story20090826-111931; "Marking Time at the Fringes," Economist, July 8, 2010.

3. "Chinese President Urges Improved Social Management for Greater Harmony, Stability," *Xinhua*, February 19, 2011, http://news.xinhuanet.com/english2010/china/2011-02/19/c_13739874.htm.

4. Louisa Lim, "The Thugs of Mainland China," *New Yorker*, October, 8, 2014.

5. Shi Shui Sheng, "Wangchuan 9 Hao Wenjian Yuanwen" [Original text of Document No. 9], August 21, 2013.

6. "Communiqué on the Current State of the Ideological Sphere: A Notice from the Central Committee of the Communist Party of China's General Office," April 22, 2013, trans. China File, http://www.chinafile.com/document-9-chinafile-translation.

7. "Communiqué on the Current State of the Ideological Sphere."

8. "Xi Jinping Asks for 'Absolute Loyalty' from Chinese State Media," *Guardian*, February 19, 2016.

9. "State Media Should Play Due Role in Properly Guiding Public Opinion," *China Daily*, February 22, 2016.

10. "Zhongguo Zhongyang guanyu quanmian tuijing yifazhiguo ruogan zhongda wenti de jiejue" [CCP Central Committee decision concerning some major questions in comprehensively moving governing the country according to the law forward], *Zhongguo Gongchandang Xinwenwang*, http://cpc.people.com.cn/n/2014/1029/c64387-25927606.html.

11. "CPC to Increase Presence in NGOs, Trade Unions," Xinhua, September 28, 2015.

12. Willy Lam, "Beijing's Blueprint for Tackling Mass Incidents and Social Management," *China Brief*, March 25, 2011.

13. "China Withholds Full Domestic Security Spending Figure," Reuters, March 4, 2014.

14. "China to Spend 'At Least' U.S. $25 Billion on 'Maintaining Stability," Radio Free Asia, March 8, 2016.

15. "Zhongong Zhongyang Jueding Geiyu Zhou Yongkang Kaichu Dangji Chufen" [Central Committee of Party decides to revoke Zhou Yongkang's Party membership]," Xinhua, December 6, 2014, http://news.china.com/focus/zhouyongkang/11163098/20141206/19063885.html.

16. A similar law was passed in Russia in 2012 requiring that all organizations receiving foreign funding be registered as foreign agents. See Chapter 7 in this volume.

17. "The People's Republic of China's Law on the Management of the Activities of Overseas NGOs Within Mainland China," *China Development Brief*, May 3, 2016.

18. "Foreign NGO Law Emphasizes National Security," *China Digital Times*, April 30, 2016.

19. Austin Ramzy, "Seen a Spy? With New Hotline, China Invites You to Call It In," *New York Times*, November 2, 2015.

20. "Woguo Zhifabumen Pohuo Yiqi Weihai Guojiaanquan Anjian: Bide Deng Fanzui Xianyiren Bei Yifa Caiqu Xingshiquangzhi Cuoshi" [Law enforcement agencies break

national security case; Peter Dahlin and other suspects subject to criminal procedures according to law], Xinhua, January 19, 2016, http://news.xinhuanet.com/legal/2016-01/19/c_ 1117827737.htm.

21. "Q & A with Peter Dahlin, the Swedish NGO Worker Who 'Endangered the National Security' of China," *China Change*, January 3, 2017.

22. "Yin Shexian Weihai Guojia Anquan Li Mingzhe Bei Youguan Bumen Diaocha" [Li Mingche investigated by relevant agencies on suspicion of threatening national security], Xinhua, March 30, 2017, http://news.sina.com.cn/w/2017-03-30/doc-ifycwunr8112530. shtml.

23. "How Foreign Non-profit Organizations Should Respond to China's New Overseas NGO Management Law," *China Development Brief*, March 5, 2016.

24. "China's Much Heralded NSC Has Disappeared," *Foreign Policy*, June 30, 2016.

25. "China State Security Indictment Hits Record High in 2014," *Duihua Human Rights Journal*, November 25, 2015.

26. "China State Security Trials Fell 50 Percent in 2015, Official Data Suggest," *Duihua Human Rights Journal*, April 6, 2016.

27. Fu 2018, ch. 1.

28. Yaxue Cao, "Chinese Authorities Orchestrate Surprise Raid of Labor NGOs in Guangdong," *China Change*, December 10, 2015. This raid may have been instigated by the labor organization's involvement in two incidents of collective action—the Lide Shoe Factory strike and the Shatou sanitation workers' strike. In both cases, the organizations coached workers in collective bargaining.

29. Eva Pils, " 'If Anything Happens . . .': Meeting the Now-Detained Human Rights Lawyers," *China Change*, July 8, 2016.

30. "Zhou Shifeng An Yishen Dangting Xuanpan Dianfu Guojia Zhengquan Zuiming Chengli Panchu Youqi Tuxing Qi Nian" [First trial finds Zhou Shifeng guilty of attempting to overthrow the regime, sentenced to seven years], Xinhua, August 4, 2016, http://news. xinhuanet.com/legal/2016-08/04/c_1119336487.htm; Chris Buckley, "China Arrests Rights Lawyer and Her Husband on Subversion Charges," *New York Times*, January 13, 2016.

31. Eva Pils, "The '709 Incident': Some Testimony from the Human Rights Lawyer Community," *China Change*, July 8, 2016.

32. "China Tries Civil Rights Activist for Subversion, Detains Supporters," Radio Free Asia, June 24, 2016.

33. Xiong, Zhi, "Dianshi Renzui Gai Chengwei Lishi Le" [Put televised confessions in the past], *Fenghuang Wang*, March 2, 2016, http://news.ifeng.com/a/20160302/47658390_ 0.shtml; Emily Rauhala, "Jailed Chinese Lawyer Reappears to Deliver a 'Confession,' but the Script Seems Familiar," *Washington Post*, August 1, 2016.

34. "Hong Kong Booksellers Reappear, Offer 'Confession' on Chinese TV," CBC News, February 29, 2016; "Ruidian Renquan Gongzuozhe Yangshi Renzui Yin Yulunchang Reyi" [CCTV confession of Swiss human rights worker leads to fierce debate], *Duowei Xinwen*, January 20, 2016, http://china.dwnews.com/news/2016-01-20/59712248.html.

35. Yaxue Cao, "A Café Chat with Li Tingting," *China Change*, July 26, 2016.

36. "Beijing Yirenping Zhongxin: Zhengzai Huyu Shifang Wuwei Nvquan Renshi De Fanqishi Gongyi Jigou Beijing Yirenping Zhongxin Bei Duoming 'Jingcha' Chachao" [Beijing Yirenping Center: Beijing Anti-Discrimination Organization Calling for Release of Feminist Five Searched by Multiple "Police"], Human Rights in China,

March 25, 2015, http://www.hrichina.org/chs/zhong-guo-ren-quan-shuang-zhou-kan/
bei-jing-yi-ren-ping-zhong-xin-zheng-zai-hu-xu-shi-fang-wu-wei-nu.

37. Yaxue Cao, "Guo Jianmei, Zhongze, and the Empowerment of Women in China,"
China Change, February 14, 2016.

38. Didi Kirsten Tatlow, "China Is Said to Force Closing of Women's Legal Aid Center,"
New York Times, January 29, 2016.

39. The center was previously called the Beijing University Legal Aid and Research
Center.

40. "Grassroots" participation refers to acts to that are open to individuals without
special political designations. Excluded in this definition is participation through serving as
a political official, such as a People's Congress deputy or Village Committee head. However,
voting in these elections qualifies.

41. Yu Jianrong, "Zhongguo Xinfang Zhidu De Kunjing He Chulu" [The predica-
ment and way out for China's petitioning system], *Zhanlue Yu Guanli* [Strategy and
management], 2009.

42. Zhongguo Zonghe Shehui Diaocha [China General Social Survey], Renmin
University of China, http://www.cnsda.org/index.php?r=projects/view&id=15553986.

43. This "helpful response" rate of 43 percent is in the middle of the distribution of previous studies of similar contacting channels in the United States, Italy, Brazil, and South
Africa. Unsurprisingly, the quality of online contacting channels in China declines at lower
levels of government. In a study of county governments, only 32 percent of requests for information were answered (Chen et al. 2015, table 2).

44. "Caizheng Touming, Jin Liang Shengfen Jige" [In financial transparency only two
provinces pass], *Bandao Dushibao* [Peninsula metropolis daily], November 28, 2016.

45. "China State Security Indictment Hits Record High in 2014," *Duihua Human Rights
Journal*, November 25, 2015.

References

Beissinger, M. R. 2002. *Nationalist Mobilization and the Collapse of the Soviet State.*
Cambridge: Cambridge University Press.

Cai, Y. 2004. "Managed Participation in China." *Political Science Quarterly* 119, no. 3: 425–451.

Cai, Y. 2010. *Collective Resistance in China: Why Popular Protests Succeed or Fail.* Stanford,
CA: Stanford University Press.

CASS (Chinese Academy of Social Sciences). 2016. 中国政府信息公开第三方评估报告
[Third-party evaluation report of Open Government Information in China (2015)].
Beijing: CASS.

Chan, Anita. 2001. *China's Workers Under Assault: The Exploitation of Labor in a Globalizing
Economy.* Armonk, NY: M. E. Sharpe.

Chen, F. 2003. "Between the State and Labour: The Conflict of Chinese Trade Unions'
Double Identity in Market Reform." *China Quarterly* 176: 1006–1028.

Chen, J., J. Pan, and Y. Xu. 2016. "Sources of Authoritarian Responsiveness: A Field
Experiment in China." *American Journal of Political Science* 60, no. 2: 383–400.

Chen, X. 2012. *Social Protest and Contentious Authoritarianism in China.*
New York: Cambridge University Press.

Chen, X. 2017. "Origins of Informal Coercion in China." *Politics and Society* 45, no. 1: 67–89.

Chen, Y. 2016. "Transparency Versus Stability: The New Role of Chinese Courts in Upholding Freedom of Information." *Tsinghua China Law Review* 9: 79–138.

CPPSS (Center for Public Participation Studies and Support, Peking University). 2011. 中国行政透明度观察报告 [China administrative transparency observations report]. Beijing: CPPSS.

Deng, Y., and K. J. O'Brien. 2013. "Relational Repression in China: Using Social Ties to Demobilize Protesters." *China Quarterly* 215: 533–552.

Dimitrov, M. K. 2015. "Internal Government Assessments of the Quality of Governance in China." *Studies in Comparative International Development* 50, no. 1: 50–72.

Ding, X. L. 1994. "Institutional Amphibiousness and the Transition from Communism: The Case of China." *British Journal of Political Science* 24, no. 3: 293–318.

Distelhorst, G. 2017. "The Power of Empty Promises: Quasi-Democratic Institutions and Activism in China." *Comparative Political Studies* 50, no. 4: 464–498.

Distelhorst, G., and Y. Hou. 2016. "Constituency Service Under Nondemocratic Rule: Evidence from China." *Journal of Politics* 79, no. 3: 1024–1040.

Edin, M. 2003. "State Capacity and Local Agent Control in China: CCP Cadre Management from a Township Perspective." *China Quarterly* 173: 35–52.

Fincher, L. H. 2016. "China's Feminist Five." *Dissent* 63, no. 4: 84–90.

Friedman, E. 2014. *Insurgency Trap: Labor Politics in Postsocialist China*. Ithaca, NY: Cornell University Press.

Fu, D. 2017a. "Disguised Collective Action in China." *Comparative Political Studies* 50, no. 4: 499–527.

Fu, D. 2017b. "Fragmented Control: Governing Contentious Labor Organizations in China." *Governance* 30, no. 3: 445–462.

Fu, D. 2018. *Mobilizing Without the Masses: Control and Contention in China*. Cambridge: Cambridge University Press.

Fu, D., and G. Distelhorst. 2017. "Grassroots Participation and Repression Under Hu Jintao and Xi Jinping." *China Journal* 79: 100–122.

Fu, H., and R. Cullen. 2008. "Weiquan (Rights Protection) Lawyering in an Authoritarian State: Building a Culture of Public-Interest Lawyering." *China Journal* 59: 111–127.

Gallagher, Mary. 2014. "China's Workers Movement and the End of the Rapid-Growth Era." *Daedalus* 143, no. 2: 81–95.

Gandhi, J., and A. Przeworski. 2007. "Authoritarian Institutions and the Survival of Autocrats." *Comparative Political Studies* 40, no. 11: 1279–1301.

Gold, T. B. 1990. "The Resurgence of Civil Society in China." *Journal of Democracy* 1, no. 1: 18–31.

Greene, S. 2017. "From Boom to Bust: Hardship, Mobilization and Russia's Social Contract." *Daedalus* 146, no. 2: 113–127.

Hartford, K. 2005. "Dear Mayor: Online Communications with Local Governments in Hangzhou and Nanjing." *China Information* 19, no. 2: 217–260.

Hassid, J. 2008. "China's Contentious Journalists: Re-conceptualizing the Media." *Problems of Post-communism* 55, no. 4: 52–61.

Hildebrandt, T. 2013. *Social Organizations and the Authoritarian State in China*. New York: Cambridge University Press.

Howell, Jude. 2015. "Shall We Dance? Welfarist Incorporation and the Politics of State-Labour NGO Relations." *China Quarterly* 223: 702–723.

Hurst, W., and K. J. O'Brien. 2002. "China's Contentious Pensioners." *China Quarterly* 170: 345–360.

IPE & NDRC (Institute of Public and Environmental Affairs & Natural Resources Defense Council). 2010. *Environmental Open Information: Between Advance and Retreat: The 2009–2010 Pollution Information Transparency Index (PITI) Second Annual Assessment of Environmental Transparency in 113 Chinese Cities.* Beijing: IPE/NRDC.

King, G., J. Pan, and M. E. Roberts. 2013. "How Censorship in China Allows Government Criticism but Silences Collective Expression." *American Political Science Review* 107, no. 2: 326–343.

Koesel, K. J. 2014. *Religion and Authoritarianism: Cooperation, Conflict, and the Consequences.* New York: Cambridge University Press.

Koesel, K. J., and V. J. Bunce. 2012. "Putin, Popular Protests, and Political Trajectories in Russia: A Comparative Perspective." *Post-Soviet Affairs* 28, no. 4: 403–423.

Lee, C. K. 2007. *Against the Law: Labor Protests in China's Rustbelt and Sunbelt.* Berkeley: University of California Press.

Lee, C. K., and Y. Shen. 2011. "The Anti-Solidarity Machine? Labor Nongovernmental Organizations in China." In *From Iron Rice-Bowls to Informalization: Markets, State, and Workers in a Changing China,* ed. S. Kuruvilla, C. K. Lee and Mary Gallagher. Ithaca, NY: Cornell University Press.

Lee, C. K., and Y. Zhang. 2013. "The Power of Instability: Unraveling the Microfoundations of Bargained Authoritarianism in China 1." *American Journal of Sociology* 118, no. 6: 1475–1508.

Liebman, B. L. 2005. "Watchdog or Demagogue? The Media in the Chinese Legal System." *Columbia Law Review* 105, no. 1: 1–157.

Liu, S. 2016. "The Changing Roles of Lawyers in China: State Bureaucrats, Market Brokers, and Political Activists." In *The New Legal Realism: Studying Law Globally,* ed. H. Klug and S. E. Merry, 2:180–197. Cambridge: Cambridge University Press.

Lorentzen, P. 2013. "Regularizing Rioting: Permitting Public Protest in an Authoritarian Regime." *Quarterly Journal of Political Science* 8, no. 2: 127–158.

Meng, T., J. Pan, and P. Yang. 2017. "Conditional Receptivity to Citizen Participation: Evidence from a Survey Experiment in China." *Comparative Political Studies* 50, no. 4: 399–433.

Mertha, A. 2008. *China's Water Warriors: Citizen Action and Policy Change.* Ithaca, NY: Cornell University Press.

O'Brien, K. 2002. "Neither Transgressive nor Contained: Boundary-Spanning Contention in China." *Mobilization: An International Quarterly* 8, no. 1: 51–64.

O'Brien, K. J., and L. Li. 2004. "Suing the Local State: Administrative Litigation in Rural China." *China Journal* 51: 75–96.

O'Brien, K. J., and L. Li. 2006. *Rightful Resistance in Rural China.* Cambridge: Cambridge University Press.

O'Brien, K. J., and R. E. Stern. 2009. "Studying Contention in Contemporary China." In *Popular Protest in China,* vol. 15, ed. K. J. O'Brien. Cambridge, MA: Harvard University Press.

Ong, L., and C. Göbel. 2014. "Social Unrest in China." In *China and the EU in Context: Insights for Business and Investors,* ed. Kerry Brown, 178–213. Basingstoke: Palgrave Macmillan.

Pei, M. 1997. "Citizens v. Mandarins: Administrative Litigation in China." *China Quarterly* 152: 832–862.

Pils, E. 2014. *China's Human Rights Lawyers: Advocacy and Resistance*. Milton Park, UK: Routledge.

Putnam, Robert. 1995. "Bowling Alone: America's Declining Social Capital." *Journal of Democracy* 6, no. 1: 65–78.

Robertson, G. B. 2010. *The Politics of Protest in Hybrid Regimes: Managing Dissent in Post-communist Russia*. New York: Cambridge University Press.

Shi, T. 1997. *Political Participation in Beijing*. Cambridge, MA: Harvard University Press.

Shue, V. 2004. "Legitimacy Crisis in China?" In *State and Society in 21st Century China: Crisis, Contention, and Legitimation*, ed. P. H. Gries and S. Rosen, 59–89. New York: Routledge Curzon.

Spires, A. 2011. "Contingent Symbiosis and Civil Society in an Authoritarian State: Understanding the Survival of China's Grassroots NGOs." *American Journal of Sociology* 117, no. 1: 1–45.

SUFE (Shanghai University of Finance and Economics). 2010. *Zhongguo caizheng toumingdu baogao—shengji caizheng xinxi yu bumen xingzheng shouzhi gongkai zhuangkuang pinggu* [2010 China financial transparency report—An evaluation of provincial finance information and departmental administrative expenditures disclosure]. Shanghai: Shanghai University of Finance and Economics Press.

Steinhardt, H. C., and F. Wu. 2016. "In the Name of the Public: Environmental Protest and the Changing Landscape of Popular Contention in China." *China Journal* 75, no. 1: 61–82.

Stern, R. E., and K. J. O'Brien. 2012. "Politics at the Boundary: Mixed Signals and the Chinese State." *Modern China* 38, no. 2: 174–198.

Su, Y., and X. He. 2010. "Street as Courtroom: State Accommodation of Labor Protest in South China." *Law and Society Review* 44, no. 1: 157–184.

Su, Z., and T. Meng. 2016. "Selective Responsiveness: Online Public Demands and Government Responsiveness in Authoritarian China." *Social Science Research* 59: 52–67.

Tarrow, S. 1996. "States and Opportunities: The Political Structuring of Social Movements." In *Comparative Perspectives on Social Movements*, ed. D. McAdam, J. D. McCarthy, and M. Zald, 41–61. Cambridge: Cambridge University Press.

Teets, J. 2014. *Civil Society Under Authoritarianism: The China Model*. New York: Cambridge University Press.

Tilly, C. 2006. *Regimes and Repertoires*. Chicago: University of Chicago Press.

Truex, R. 2017. "Consultative Authoritarianism and Its Limits." *Comparative Political Studies* 50, no. 3: 329–361.

Unger, J., and A. Chan. 1995. "China, Corporatism and the East Asian Model." *Australian Journal of Chinese Affairs* 33: 29–53.

Unger, J., A. Chan, and H. Chung. 2014. "Deliberative Democracy at China's Grassroots: Case Studies of a Hidden Phenomenon." *Politics and Society* 42, no. 4: 513–535.

Vala, C. T. 2012. "Protestant Christianity and Civil Society in Authoritarian China: The Impact of Official Churches and Unregistered 'Urban Churches' on Civil Society Development in the 2000s." *China Perspectives* 3: 43.

Wallace, J. 2017. "The New Normal: A Neo-Political Turn in China's Reform Era." Paper presented at the conference "Citizens and the State: Comparing Mass Politics and Policy in China and Russia," University of Notre Dame, March 10–11, 2017.

Wang, Y., and C. Minzner. 2015. "The Rise of the Chinese Security State." *China Quarterly* 222: 339–359.

Yang, G. 2005. "Environmental NGOs and Institutional Dynamics in China." *China Quarterly* 181: 46–66.

Zhao, S. 2016. "Xi Jinping's Maoist Revival." *Journal of Democracy* 27, no. 3: 83–97.

Zheng, W. 2015. "Detention of the Feminist Five in China." *Feminist Studies* 41, no. 2: 476–482.

Zhou, H. 2002. "起草《政府信息公开条例》(专家建议稿) 的基本考虑" [Basic considerations on drafting the Regulations on Open Government Information (expert recommendation draft)], *Faxue Yanjiu* [Legal research] 6: 75–97.

4 }

Diffusion-Proofing

RUSSIAN AND CHINESE RESPONSES TO
WAVES OF POPULAR MOBILIZATION AGAINST
AUTHORITARIAN RULERS

Karrie J. Koesel and Valerie J. Bunce

"Diffusion is the process whereby past events make future events more likely."[1]

"If you open the window for fresh air, you have to expect some flies to blow in."[2]

Do authoritarian leaders take measures to insulate their regimes from the possibility of the contagion effects associated with the cross-national diffusion of popular challenges to authoritarian rulers? This important question helps us rethink our understanding of both international diffusion and the strategic foundations of authoritarian politics—two issues that are rarely joined but that have invited considerable scholarly attention in recent years. (On diffusion, see, for example, Jacoby 2006; Weyland 2009; Simmons, Dobbin, and Garrett 2008; Givan, Soule, and Roberts 2010; Bunce and Wolchik 2011. On authoritarian strategies, see Wintrobe 2001; Gandhi and Przeworski 2006; Gandhi 2007; Bueno de Mesquita and Downs 2005; Bueno de Mesquita and Smith 2011; Dobson 2012; Svolik 2012.) In particular, many studies of cross-national diffusion—that is, the transfer among countries of an innovative idea, product, policy, institution, or repertoire of behavior—take as their central mission the identification of structural factors that drive the spread of change. (On definitions of diffusion, see Rogers 2005; Bunce and Wolchik 2011. On structural factors, see Brinks and Coppedge 2006; Simmons, Dobbin, and Garrett 2008.) What is often missing in these studies, however, is not just an identification of the innovation that is producing change but also such equally important issues as the role of agency in these processes and factors that deter diffusion, including the strategies deployed by defenders of the status quo. (But see Bunce and Wolchik 2011; Finkel and Brudny 2012a, 2012b; Radnitz 2012.)

At the same time, virtually all studies of authoritarian resilience focus on the strategies authoritarian rulers use to contain domestic threats. (But see Ambrosio 2009, 2007; Silitski 2010.) Here we encounter two problems. One is the failure to examine the management of international challenges. This is surprising, because most contemporary authoritarian regimes (unlike their predecessors during the Cold War) are deeply integrated into the international system, and international influences figure prominently in the cross-national spread of democratic change—a dynamic that obviously constitutes one of the biggest threats to the tenure of authoritarian rulers (Bueno de Mesquita and Downs 2005; Simmons, Dobbin, and Garrett 2008; Brinks and Coppedge 2006).

The other problem is that analyses of the strategic calculations of authoritarian leaders often emphasize the benefits associated with their actions but fail to take into account their costs (see especially Bueno de Mesquita and Smith 2011). On the one hand, there is little doubt that the threats posed by such waves are real. Over the past twenty-five years, there have been three such cross-national waves; the popular challenges to Communist Party rule in the Soviet Union, Eastern Europe, and China from 1989 to 1991, the color revolutions (1998–2005), and the Arab uprisings (2010–2012). These waves, moreover, have managed to remove twenty-one authoritarian leaders from office, despite in many cases their long tenure, their considerable coercive powers, and their alliances with powerful international actors (Bunce 1999; Bunce and Wolchik 2011; Brownlee 2012; Patel, Bunce, and Wolchik 2014; Lynch 2012, 2014). Thus, if authoritarian rulers are vigilant stewards of their powers, they can be expected to deploy strategies that seek to discourage their citizens from modeling their behavior on the rebellious precedents set by their counterparts elsewhere.

On the other hand, measures to contain diffusion entail some risks. Repression can lead to the growth of popular resentments and, in the case of the regime's governing coalition, transform "obedient agents into political rivals" (Svolik 2012, 159). Moreover, one of the foundations of authoritarian resilience is the ability of the leader to make a credible claim that she is invincible (Maglaoni 2006; Svolik 2012). Just as such an image deters ordinary citizens and opposition groups from taking the risks associated with mounting challenges to the leader, so it reduces the likelihood that allies of the regime will choose to defect and thereby risk at the least their rents and at the most their lives. However, by their very nature, measures that seek to contain the contagion effects associated with waves of popular uprisings in other authoritarian regimes send a clear signal to ordinary citizens, opposition groups, and regime allies that authoritarian leaders are worried about their hold on power. In contrast to those that respond to challenges arising solely in the domestic arena, such actions are closely tied in terms of timing and content to the proven ability of popular uprisings against authoritarian rulers to occur, succeed in their mission, and spread rapidly among states.

Our purpose is to use a controlled comparison in order to assess whether and under what conditions authoritarian leaders take preemptive action to deter their citizens from joining cross-national waves of popular mobilizations against authoritarian rulers (Quinlivan 1999; also Silitski 2010; Finkel and Brudny 2012a, 2012b). In particular, we compare the responses of the Russian and Chinese leadership to two recent waves: the color revolutions in post-communist Europe and Eurasia from 1998 to 2005 and the 2010 to 2012 Arab uprisings. Russia and China were selected for this study because of their similarities, yet their differences make for an illuminating comparison. On the one hand, both regimes are authoritarian; they have long histories of Communist Party rule and even longer experiences with authoritarian politics; and they have transitioned over the past several decades from international isolation and political-military competition with the West to greater integration with the global security order and especially with the global economic order. On the other hand, because these two regimes represent different types of authoritarian rule, their reactions to these waves should be different. While the Russian regime holds competitive national elections, albeit ones that favor the incumbent or his anointed successor, the Chinese regime does not. Russia, in short, represents a competitive variant on authoritarian politics and China a non-competitive variant (Levitsky and Way 2010). This distinction suggests that Chinese leaders have more weapons at their disposal to contain diffusion than their Russian counterparts, and that while leaders of both countries are vulnerable to popular uprisings for the simple reason that they are authoritarian, Russian leaders face an additional threat: the possibility of electoral challenges to their power (Robertson 2011; Acemoglu and Robinson 2006).

A comparison of the color revolutions and the Arab uprisings helps us leverage these and other distinctions. While both waves focused on the removal of authoritarian rulers from power, they diverged in several important respects. Most obviously, they took place in different parts of the world. Less obviously, while the color revolutions involved innovative approaches to challenging authoritarian rulers at the polls, the second wave involved a different repertoire: large-scale mobilizations in the streets. While the former approach was tailored to exploit the political opportunities provided by competitive authoritarianism, the second one reflected the fact that such opportunities were unavailable in the Middle East and North Africa (MENA)—either because the regime did not hold such elections (Libya) or because the outcome of national elections, despite ostensible competition, had become a foregone conclusion (Egypt). This left the opposition with only one option, especially after the 2010 Egyptian elections: large-scale popular protests, albeit in new forms that enabled the Egyptian model to succeed and to travel (Patel 2012; Patel, Bunce and Wolchik 2014). In this sense, while the color revolutions "specialized" in competitive authoritarian regimes, the MENA uprisings targeted non-competitive systems.

Diffusion-Proofing

We address two questions in our analysis. First, is there evidence that the leaders of Russia and China have taken preemptive measures to reduce the likelihood that these waves will engulf their countries as well? At issue, therefore, is whether authoritarian leaders perceive such external developments as threatening and whether the leaders decide to contain them by taking countermeasures, as they have been shown to do in response to domestic threats. Here we can introduce a useful concept that borrows from James Quinlivan's study of the actions that authoritarian leaders have taken (and, given recent trends, with evident success) to reduce the likelihood of one common, domestic threat to their power—that is, decisions by leaders of the military and security forces to launch coups d'état (Quinlivan 1999). Can we argue, therefore, that authoritarian leaders do not just engage in "coup-proofing" but also engage in "diffusion-proofing"?

The second question builds on the costs noted earlier regarding decisions to contain diffusion. Are Russian and Chinese leaders more likely to launch diffusion-proofing measures when the cross-national spread of popular uprisings poses, at least in theory, more contagious precedents?[3] Here, combining our earlier observations about limitations on authoritarian rulers with the literature on diffusion, we can argue that leaders of authoritarian regimes are more likely to introduce measures to preempt diffusion when sites are close to one another, such as when neighboring countries have joined the wave, or when there are similarities among sites, such as when their regime type matches those in countries that have participated in the wave (Rogers 2005; Brinks and Coppedge 2006; Bunce and Wolchik 2011).

This line of argument suggests that if geography is a critical consideration, then both the Russian and the Chinese leaderships would be more threatened by the color revolutions than by the MENA uprisings. Second, if regime "fit" matters, then the Russian leadership should be more threatened by the color revolutions than their Chinese counterparts. The Arab uprisings, however, present a less clear-cut expectation. Because they took place in non-competitive systems, they should be more threatening to the Chinese than the Russian leadership. However, because popular uprisings are the Achilles heel of all authoritarian regimes, the MENA protests should represent a dangerous precedent to the leaders of both of these countries (Acemoglu and Robinson 2006).

How can we determine whether these regimes have engaged in diffusion-proofing? There is no simple answer to this question, because authoritarian leaders keep their motivations hidden, and at least some elements of a diffusion-proofing strategy are likely to overlap with the strategies leaders use to manage threats that arise solely from the domestic arena (see especially Radnitz 2012). For example, whether we focus on diffusion-proofing or its domestic equivalent, "protest-proofing," we would expect authoritarian leaders to deprive citizens and opposition groups of "coordinative resources" and to maintain control over the "organizational space" (see, in particular, Bueno de Mesquita and Downs 2005; Robertson 2011).

These considerations lead us to use three measures in this study to evaluate whether diffusion-proofing is taking place. One is to focus on changes in rhetoric, not just changes in policies. By tracking both, we emerge with a more well-rounded reading of the ensemble of strategies authoritarian leaders deploy while putting the concept of diffusion-proofing to a more stringent test. In addition, we will pay particular attention to timing and whether changes in rhetoric and actions occur in conjunction with waves of popular mobilizations against authoritarian rulers. Finally, we take a cue from the literature on diffusion, which argues in effect that the spread of change depends upon whether local actors, monitoring these events from the outside, have the incentives and the resources to emulate the precedents set by their counterparts who have joined the wave (Rogers 2005). The job of authoritarian leaders, therefore, is to reduce, where possible, these incentives to emulate and the coordinative resources available to their citizens. This leads us to Table 4.1, where we compare the factors that drive diffusion with those that deter it.

As the table indicates, protests are more likely to spread across state boundaries when citizens have an incentive to engage in similar behaviors (because they know about these events, see them as having positive effects, and see similarities between their situation and the situation in regimes that have

TABLE 4.1 } Drivers and Deterrents of Diffusion

Drivers of Diffusion	Diffusion-Proofing Strategies
Incentives to emulate • Access to information about uprisings • Similarities in grievances, region, and regimes • Favorable views of uprisings and outcomes	Deterrents • Control information about uprisings • Frame uprisings and outcomes negatively • Draw sharp contrasts between domestic conditions and regimes, rulers, and socioeconomic conditions where uprisings occur • Introduce democratic "decorations" or promises of reform
Coordinative resources • Opportunities to organize opposition and civil society groups • Opportunities to protest • Access to external support (financial, informational, and strategic networks)	Constraints • Demobilization of civil society and control of the organizational space • Coercion and co-optation of key constituencies (opposition parties, youth, etc.) • Punitive policies on protest, dissent, and associational groups

hosted the waves) and when they have the resources to do so (because there are opportunities to organize and to protest, given a relatively open organizational space and external support for such activities). In contrast, protests are less likely to spread when regimes adopt diffusion-proofing strategies that deprive citizens of these incentives and resources—for example, by limiting information about the waves, portraying their effects in negative ways, drawing sharp contrasts between their regime and those that have hosted these waves, cracking down on external support of civil society, and using a mixture of coercion and co-optation in order to demobilize opposition groups, civil society organizations, and students.

In the analysis that follows, we use this table to compare the reactions of the Russian and Chinese leaderships to the color revolutions and then to the Arab uprisings. Contrary to our expectations, we find strong evidence that the rulers of both regimes were threatened by both of these waves. Moreover, they responded by taking relatively similar and equally ambitious countermeasures to contain their local impact. Thus, irrespective of the wave's geography and the type of regime it targeted, it prompted the rulers of Russia and China to use rhetoric and policies to diffusion-proof their rule and their regimes.

The Color Revolutions

There is strong evidence that the success of the color revolutions in using elections to oust dictators across Eastern Europe and Eurasia prompted Russian and Chinese leaders to code these events as existential threats that required many of the countermeasures listed in Table 4.1. Thus we can conclude that authoritarian leaders—or at least the leaders of these two countries and in this particular wave—went to considerable lengths to deny their citizens the incentives and the coordinative resources they needed to carry out their own color revolutions. While the similar responses of the two regimes introduce the possibility that the geography of the wave played an important role, since these electoral mobilizations took place on the borders of both of these states (though in many more cases for Russia), they call into question the impact of regime type and its associated repertoires of protest. Because it lacks the competitive national elections of Russia, China is not a logical candidate for a color revolution. We can now elaborate on this conclusion by turning first to the issue of reducing the incentives to emulate popular uprisings.

Deterrents

While neither the Russian nor the Chinese leadership went to unusual lengths to censor information about the color revolutions, they did make extensive use of negative framing (Chong and Druckman 2012). Just as this helped them distance their regimes from these events, so it allowed them to bolster the very arguments that these two regimes have repeatedly used to legitimate their rule—that is, their proven ability to protect the nation from foreign (especially Western) interference and to promote economic growth and political stability (Ambrosio 2009; Shambaugh 2008; Kots 2007; Li 2006). For example, in a September 2005 meeting with Western academics and journalists, Vladimir Putin was asked about the wave of electoral turnovers that had taken place from 2003 to 2005 in Georgia, Ukraine, and Kyrgyzstan. Putin responded by, first, locating these three countries in the "former Soviet Union," thereby reminding his audience of Russia's role as the regional hegemon, and, second, by characterizing these three neighbors of Russia as "banana republics." This is an efficient term for his purposes, because in drawing parallels with Central America during the Cold War, it highlights the small size of these countries and their vulnerability to Western domination (both in contrast to Russia), while linking these features in turn to political disorder and economic crises in the wake of these electoral transitions (*RFE/RL* 2005; Kniazov 2005).[4] Not surprisingly, the Russian media subsequently picked up these themes by reporting, for example, that the color revolutions were not "real revolutions" but rather power struggles orchestrated and financed by the West to weaken Russia and promote Western hegemony in Eastern Europe and Eurasia (Nikonov 2007; *Moscow News* 2005; *Kommersant* 2005; also Neverov 2012).

The Russian campaign against the color revolutions succeeded, at least until the outbreak of protests following the December 2011 parliamentary elections, largely because the themes that were developed resonated so well with popular memories of the 1990s when, not coincidentally in the minds of many Russians, the Yeltsin regime forged a close alliance with the West, and the Russian experiment with democracy and capitalism led to economic and political implosion. It is telling that a nationwide survey found that only 3 percent of Russians think that life in Georgia and Kyrgyzstan has improved following the color revolutions, and only 6 percent report that they believe that life has improved in Ukraine following its Orange Revolution (*Public Opinion Foundation* 2005). It is noteworthy, given the role of youth movements in toppling authoritarian rulers in Ukraine, but also in Serbia and Georgia, that the negative portrayals of the color revolutions have been particularly successful in influencing Russian youth. For example, a poll of sixteen- to twenty-nine-year-olds found that 72 percent opposed an Orange Revolution taking place in Russia (Mendelson and Gerber 2005, n. 1).

China's state-run media and academic circles have also painted a dismal portrait of this wave of electoral turnovers. Similar to the Russian framing, the color revolutions have been largely reduced to events that were orchestrated by the United States, though there was some recognition, which also served the interests of the regime, of the role of high levels of poverty and economic crises in providing fertile ground for these uprisings. Like their Russian counterparts, moreover, the Chinese media have reported that the so-called revolutionaries have not delivered on their election promises—an argument that also serves the purpose of disparaging the value, more generally, of Western-style electoral competition. Rather than portraying the color revolutions as improving people's lives, the Chinese media report them as instead ushering in an era of inflation, rampant corruption, and a dramatic decline in the quality of life (Kuang and Liu 2006; Ning 2006; Zhang 2005; Li 2006).

In the Chinese media (and to a lesser extent the Russian media), a great deal of the blame for this sorry state of affairs has been placed on the international community of non-governmental organizations (NGOs), such as the U.S.-based National Endowment for Democracy, the National Democratic Institute, the International Republican Institute, and the Open Society (Tang, Chang, and Wang 2005; Wang 2005; Zyatkov 2007; Nikonov 2007). These organizations are characterized as claiming to be in the business of supporting human rights but in reality dedicating themselves to the instigation of public protest or, to use a phrase favored by the Chinese, "street politics" (*jietou zhengzhi*) (Liu 2006; Wang 2005). For instance, one editorial suggested that foreign NGOs are staffed by "regime change professionals" who "flaunt democracy and freedom and under the banner of humanitarianism, hold signs of assistance and poverty reduction, while their real intention is to export their ideology and values, to set off a 'democratic wave'" (Wang 2005, 12). Academic sources tell a similar story, insisting that international NGOs are Trojan horses in the West's multistep plan of using elections to promote regime change and encourage street politics (Pan and Dai 2005; Tian 2006).

Constraints

The campaign by Chinese and Russian officials to reduce the incentives of their citizens to launch their own color revolutions has been joined with measures that also limit their ability to engage in such actions. Here, the primary emphasis has been on demobilizing key constituencies—that is, opposition groups, civil society associations, and youth, all of whom played a prominent role in mounting both the electoral challenges to authoritarian leaders in Europe and Eurasia and the protests that often followed these electoral confrontations. For both China and Russia, the weapon of choice used to reduce the influence of the first two actors has been repression, while in the case of youth it has been co-optation and at times outright courtship.

Since Vladimir Putin's rise to power in Russia in 2000, there have been concerted efforts to weaken opposition parties by harassing them, raiding their offices, disbanding their organizations, and impairing their ability to participate in elections and, if participating, to conduct credible campaigns. These kinds of actions seemed to have escalated in the aftermath of the color revolutions. For example, during the 2006–2007 campaign season opposition parties, ranging from Yabloko (Apple) to the Communists (KPRF), logged complaints against law enforcement agencies for obstructing their activities (Kostenko 2007). The Respublikanskaja Partija (Republican Party), one of the oldest opposition parties in the country, was denied registration before the elections took place.[5] Maksim Reznik, the head of Yabloko in St. Petersburg, was detained for two months after collecting information on voter fraud in connection with the 2007 parliamentary elections. Garry Kasparov, the leader of the opposition party Drugaja Rossija (Other Russia), was temporarily jailed for trying to organize a protest in Moscow. Thereafter, he was forced to drop his bid for the Russian presidency, because Russian law required candidates to rent a hall for a nominating convention, but Kasparov was prevented from doing so (Kramer 2007). In the process of limiting threatening opposition groups, Kremlin elites have also promoted "virtual" opposition parties to create the image of a pluralist political landscape (Wilson 2005). It is also a telling comment about the lack of a level playing field in elections that the national convention of the party in power, Edinaja Rossija (United Russia), that took place in October 2007 (in anticipation of the 2007 parliamentary elections, the first national elections to take place after the Orange Revolution), was dispro-portionately covered in the Russian media.[6]

While the Chinese Communist Party (CCP) does not have to contend with an organized opposition, it has taken strong measures to repress even modest forms of opposition to the regime. Thus even small groups, such as the co-signers of the pro-democracy Charter 08, have become targets of state aggression in the wake of the color revolutions (Potter and Woodman 2012, 107).

Constraining the drivers of diffusion has also meant the close management of popular protests by both the Russian and Chinese leadership. However, their approach to this issue has been somewhat different—though in ways that are often surprising, given the differences, as discussed earlier, between competitive and non-competitive authoritarian regimes. During the early years under Putin, a priority was placed on preventing protests from taking place or limiting them to very small-scale actions that have been characterized by the Kremlin as "pocket protests" (Lyall 2006). When demonstrations have managed to take place, moreover, the police have been given the go-ahead to carry out militant attacks on protesters (Robertson 2011).

In China, violent repression of protests certainly falls within the strategic arsenal of the regime. However, recent scholarship demonstrates that protests have been tolerated and even used to prolong authoritarian rule. As has been hypothesized, protests help particularly to identify local "troublemakers" (who can later be punished), provide some quality control with respect to service delivery by making local cadres more accountable, and deflect popular criticism away from the center (Chen 2012; Wu 2009; O'Brien 2008; Lorentzen 2008). Whether these functions are actually served, however, depends upon two factors: whether the CCP will be able to control their dynamics such that demonstrators continue to hold local government and Party officials—and not Beijing—responsible for their problems, and whether protests remain contained within jurisdictional boundaries rather than spilling across them and laying the groundwork for more ambitious political challenges.

The color revolutions were also followed by the introduction in both countries of new laws and institutions that serve the purpose of managing and monitoring associational life Robertson 2011; Wilson 2010; Nygren 2008; Ambrosio 2007). In a 2004 presidential address to the Federal Assembly, for example, Putin followed up the concerns expressed about Western involvement in the color revolutions by criticizing civil society groups for being financed from abroad and serving "dubious groups and commercial interests" (Putin 2004). Soon thereafter, these warnings were codified into law restricting civil society associations. Following the Orange Revolution, the Russian parliament passed legislation increasing the restrictions on NGOs, including mandatory reregistration with special emphasis on those receiving Western funding. If NGOs successfully reregister with authorities, they are required to operate under much more stringent conditions, such as the newly granted rights of government officials to sit in on internal meetings, request audits, monitor activities, and deport foreign staff (Finkel and Brudny 2012b). This law or some version of it seems to have served as a model for leaders in other authoritarian states, including not just China but also Venezuela, Kazakhstan, Uzbekistan, Tajikistan, Belarus, Egypt, and Zimbabwe (Committee on Foreign Relations, 2006; see also Kamhi 2006, Chivers 2006).

Finally, both regimes have made the courtship of youth a high priority. This strategy is driven in part by recognition of the prominent role of youth movements during the color revolutions, such as Otpor (Resistance) in Serbia, Kmara (Enough) in Georgia, and Pora (It's Time) in Ukraine.[7] Building on the ideas behind the Young Pioneers during Soviet times, the Russian government has developed a large pro-Kremlin youth movement committed to promoting patriotism and defending the Russian nation, its core values, and policies. The youth movement is well financed—sponsoring summer camps, providing members with mobile phones, and promising career advancement—and reaches out to all ages. For instance, pro-Kremlin groups at the core of the movement, including Nashi (Ours), Otechestvo (Fatherland) and Molodaya Gvardiya (Young Guards), target secondary-school and college students; others, such as Mishki (Teddy Bears), organize patriotic activities for children seven to fifteen years olds (Stanovaya 2005; Kosobokov 2008).[8] Pro-Kremlin youth often have an expansive interpretation of what falls within their patriotic purview. They have served as moles in opposition parties and harassed journalists critical of Putin. The Chelyabinsk headquarters of Molodaya Gvardiya even organized a series of training drills to thwart a potential color revolution from occurring. Under the code name Poligon (Firing Range), members rehearsed military drills, orchestrated a pro-government rally, repelled an attack by potential opposition activists, and then staged an impromptu takeover of a local TV station in order to prevent an "illegitimate seizure of power" by color revolutionaries (Arapova and Savino 2007). The goal seemingly shared among all youth associations is to defend the Kremlin from threats, especially those posed by the color revolutions (Odynova 2009; Krainova 2009).

Like Russia, the Chinese state has also courted younger generations, but in somewhat different ways. In the mid-1980s, university students represented less than 1 percent of all Party members. This problem, especially when joined with the central role of youth in the demonstrations in China in 1989 and in the color revolutions, led the CCP to particularly focus on expanding youth membership.[9] Over the course of the 1990s, for example, students came to represent roughly 10 percent of the Party. However, from 2002 to 2007 (years that spanned the color revolutions), college recruits increased by over 250 percent. Since that time, student membership in the Party has consistently outpaced other loyal constituencies, including workers, farmers, and army officers (Guo 2002, 98–105; Xinhua 2009).

The Chinese regime has also used the National Postgraduate Entrance Examination (Boshi Yanjiusheng Renxue Kaoshi), the equivalent of the U.S.-based Graduate Record Examinations (GRE), to socialize students about the proper reading of the color revolutions. In 2005, the examination included a question on the 2004 election crisis that led to the Orange Revolution. Test-takers were asked to analyze the strategic position of Ukraine and evaluate how the election standoff would affect relations among Russia, the United States, and Europe.

While the inclusion of the question reveals the Chinese leadership's concern over the Orange Revolution, it also performs another function: sending a clear signal, reinforced by a compendium of model essays, of how students should interpret the protests. For example, one such "model essay" explains the events in the following way:

> The essence of the Ukrainian election crisis is a conflict of interest between the U.S. and Russia. After the U.S. brought down the Soviet Union, on the surface the U.S. has had decent relations with Russia, but the U.S. has never put down its guard against Russia. The U.S. endeavored to win over other CIS countries and bring them into its own sphere of influence. . . . In this strategic context, Ukraine became the latest target of U.S. efforts of expansion. (Zhang 2007, 174–175)

The model essay concludes by suggesting that the United States is "immorally" intervening, in the name of democracy, with the underlying goal of using elections to promote disorder, marginalize Russia, and unleash a "domino effect" across the region (Zhang 2007, 175). Once again, the Chinese have crafted a self-serving message that performs two functions: warning students about the dangers posed by the color revolutions and drawing a linkage between electoral competition, on the one hand, and political disorder and Western interference, on the other.

Explaining the Chinese Reaction

There seems to be strong evidence, therefore, that *both* the Russian and Chinese regimes saw the color revolutions as threatening developments that required elaborate preemptive measures. The question then becomes why the Chinese, given the absence of a national electoral venue, worried so much about the possibility of contagion. One could account for the Chinese reaction by arguing, in line with some recent studies, that the durability of the dictatorship rests upon two pillars: a proactive leadership and the incentives that some ambitious members of the Party and some leaders of the security agencies have to exaggerate the potential for contagion and thereby improve their opportunities for upward mobility in the first case and expand their political influence and access to resources in the second (Wright 2010; Chen 2010).[10] While this is plausible, there are some other explanations we can offer that are more rooted in the issue of diffusion. One is that the information deficits of authoritarian leaders make it rational for them to assume the worst and to act accordingly (see especially Schedler 2015). Because the color revolutions did produce in fact the "worst" outcome, which is the removal of authoritarian leaders from office, it made sense for authoritarian leaders to take preemptive measures (see Silitski 2010).[11]

In addition, when color revolutions took place in more repressive political contexts, the electoral mobilizations were followed by street-based protest. In this way, the color revolutions became relevant to all authoritarian leaders, whether they headed competitive or non-competitive systems. Moreover, the experiences of the 2005 Kyrgyz revolution might have been particularly instructive for China, not just because the two countries share a border and their leaders knew each other through their participation in the Shanghai Cooperation Council but also because Kyrgyzstan borders Xinjiang, a deeply divided province that has experienced violent Uyghur-Han riots over the past decade and has an active, if now repressed, separatist movement (Brinks and Coppedge 2006; Bovingdon 2010). The uprisings in Kyrgyzstan also followed a pattern that would seem to have been particularly disturbing to the Chinese in view of their situation at home—that is, unrest began outside of the capital in an area heavily populated by disgruntled minority communities and then spread quickly to the rest of the country, resulting in the president's decision to vacate office (Bunce and Wolchik 2011).

Finally, it is important to recognize the involvement of the West in general and the United States in particular in the diffusion of these electoral challenges to authoritarian rulers throughout post-communist Europe and Eurasia. Western participation was no doubt very threatening to the Chinese (and to the Russians) because of what these interventions suggested about Western willingness to promote democratic change in authoritarian regimes. Just as disturbing was the fact that protests against authoritarian rulers managed to spread even to places such as Georgia and Kyrgyzstan, where the West did not have a strong commitment to leadership change—at least not in the elections held in 2003 and 2005, respectively. Thus, for the Chinese as for the Russians, the color revolutions carried two equally disturbing messages: they could be attributed to the power of the United States or to the power of the diffusion dynamic itself.

The MENA Uprisings: Incentives to Emulate

The MENA uprisings also prompted the Chinese and the Russian leadership to take ambitious countermeasures to curtail the spread of change. Two key planks in this newer version of "containment policy" have been to expand state control over the information their citizens have been able to get about the MENA wave and to introduce more punitive laws governing the actions of the broadcast and print media (Stockman and Gallagher 2011; Whitmore 2012; Tsvetkova and Bryanski 2011; Barry 2012; Arutunyan 2012).[12] Beginning with the color revolutions, the Chinese and the Russians began to share technologies with each other and with other authoritarian states such as Kazakhstan, Belarus, and Venezuela that block the free flow of information and enhance the ability of the regime to monitor the exchange of information. As one might expect, especially given the role of social media in the Arab uprisings, the second wave of anti-authoritarian protests has led to a further tightening of electronic information sources. China's extensive influence over the internet—including the army of state-sponsored bloggers and online police, monitoring mechanisms and technical filters, requirements for private companies to self-censor and filter search results, and bans on Facebook, YouTube and Twitter—translated into the blocking of the terms "Egypt," "jasmine," and "freedom" from Google searches and popular microblogging sites (*weibo*) once protesters began to fill Egypt's Tahrir Square, as well as crippling several popular virtual private network services (VPNs) used to bypass what was known as the "Great Firewall" (Page 2011; LaFrainere and Barboza 2011).[13] The state-run media justified these restrictions by warning that "some people with sinister ulterior motives both inside and outside China attempt to divert troubled water to China and 'fan flames' via the internet in a hope also to . . . make China chaotic" (Jiang 2011). In the process, the government has stirred up nationalistic sentiments by calling on grassroots bloggers to defend China against hostile external forces (People's Daily 2011).

Russian authorities have taken a more subtle approach to controlling information. Just as they have consolidated ownership and influence over mainstream broadcast and print media, with respect to the regulation of the internet they have targeted sites, blogs, and even specific time periods such as electoral campaigns that are considered to represent significant threats. The fact that the internet remains the least regulated source of information in Russia, at least until the protests that broke out in December 2011, seems to reflect three factors (Finkel and Brudny 2012a).[14] Because Russia is a competitive, not fully authoritarian regime, there are pockets of liberalization; a majority of Russians already rely on government-controlled or -influenced news sources, so there is no pressing need to overtly manipulate cyberspace; and there seems to be no consensus among the ruling elite on how best to control the internet (Finkel and Brudny 2012a, 18). For instance, while still president, Medvedev argued that the state would not impose any top-down restrictions. By contrast, the Federal Security Service (FSB) has advocated a Chinese model of banning independent internet, telephone, and email services because of their potential to encourage large-scale mobilizations (*RIA Novosti-Moscow* 2012; Lebedev 2011). There has also been some discussion of creating an army of patriotic, pro-Kremlin commentators modeled after China's "Fifty Cent Party" (*wumao dang*)—the term used for anonymous online commentators who were allegedly paid 50 cents by the government for each pro-regime posting (Allnutt 2011; Soldatov 2011).[15]

Deterrents

Similar to their handling of the color revolutions, the Chinese and the Russian regimes have characterized the Arab uprisings in very negative ways. It has been argued that the protests in the Middle East and North Africa were financed by Western countries interested in oil and NATO expansion; the demonstrations were orchestrated and manipulated by Western regime-change professionals; and the outcome of these events have not been democracy but rather social and economic instability throughout the region and in global markets (Huang 2011; Shi 2011; Li 2011; Shishkin 2011; Razimov 2011). Indeed, in reporting on the MENA wave, the *Beijing Daily* reminded citizens that "stability is a blessing and chaos a calamity," while other newspapers ran photographs of Jon Huntsman, the U.S. ambassador, at one of the few Jasmine demonstrations in Beijing and suggested that the United States was coordinating the protests (Ren 2011; Global Times 2011). In Russia, leaders of Edinaja Rossija have also claimed that Russians are "too smart" to allow the West to engineer an Arab Spring there, because it would negatively "affect common folk . . . trigger higher interest rates on loans, industrial deterioration, desta-bilization of the ruble exchange rate [and] curtailment of social programs" (Neverov 2012).

This recycling of their negative depictions of the color revolutions was also joined with two new narratives that are intended to evoke sympathetic reactions from their citizenry. One was that the implosion of long-ruling au-thoritarian regimes will likely empower Islamic extremists. Here, Moscow (and to a lesser degree Beijing) was particularly keen on emphasizing that the second wave will favor Islamic fanatics, destabilize Central Asia (and more importantly the North Caucasus), and generate tensions among Muslim populations (Dannreuther 2011; Williams 2011; Niu 2011).[16] It is interesting to note, however, that this anti-Islamic framing did not seem to resonate strongly with their publics. For example, a 2011 poll revealed that only 10 percent of Russians believe the MENA uprisings are "Islamic revolutions" that will bring fanatics to power, while 27 percent viewed the events as popular revolutions against corrupt, despotic regimes (Levada Center 2011b; Kipp 2011). More striking was that nearly 40 percent of Russians expect that positive changes will follow the MENA wave and consider "an Egypt Scenario" (as it was de-fined in February 2011) to be a possibility for Russia—an interpretation that contrasts sharply with popular sentiments about the color revolutions (Levada Center 2011a; Coalson and Sokolov 2011).

The other innovative framing introduced by the Arab Spring is the type of contrast that has been drawn between the Russian and Chinese regimes versus the toppled MENA governments. In China, regime elites downplayed the idea of revolutionary contagion by emphasizing their ability to ensure sta-bility and improve the quality of life for ordinary citizens. At a 2012 conference in Munich, China's vice foreign minister remarked: "Some people suggested the Arab Spring will come to China, but that is [no] more than a fantasy be-cause the policies and governance of the country have the overwhelming support of the people" (McDonald 2012; also People's Daily 2012). While ad-miration of the Party's many contributions is hardly a new observation in the Chinese press or among senior Party leaders, the comparison drawn between China and the failures of autocracy in the Middle East and North Africa is. To channel this narrative effectively, the state-run media was quick to remind cit-izens that China is not run by a family or a single dictator and has "abolished the life-long tenure of leading officials . . . and [made] the change of leader-ship . . . a conventional practice" (Jiang 2011). Therefore, unlike the deeply entrenched and corrupt autocrats of the Arab world, Chinese leaders change regularly and "have always complied with public will and are bent on tackling social problems . . . including unemployment, high housing prices, a rise in food and other commodities prices and a gap between the rich and the poor" (Jiang 2011; also Zhang 2011). Thus their depiction of the MENA uprisings carried the underlying message that "China is definitely not the Middle East, and any vain scheme to deliver Middle East turmoil to China is doomed to fail" (Jiang 2011).

Constraints

These self-serving framings have occured in conjunction with heightened sensitivity to popular protests, whether they are large or small or have real or imagined ties to the MENA uprisings. In late February 2011, for instance, after anonymous web postings called for Chinese citizens to "stroll" (*sanbu*) through central squares in thirteen cities and participate in a domestic "Jasmine Revolution," the authorities responded with an unusual show of force (Chang 2011).[17] Although turnout for these protests was low (totaling less than one hundred, including the U.S. ambassador), uniformed and plainclothes police officers constructed barriers around the protest sites, filmed and detained demonstrators and journalists, temporarily shut down public transportation to city centers, and placed well-known pro-democracy activists under house arrest (Wright 2011; Swartz 2011; Demick 2011; Link 2011). Such a harsh response may be in part because protestors were openly critical of the central party-state; however, even when local government officials have been the targets, the Chinese authorities have responded swiftly and severely. For example, in June 2011 a security guard in Guangdong allegedly assaulted a pregnant street vendor while attempting to move her unlicensed cart. As rumor spread of the incident, migrant workers rioted for three days, burning police cars and ransacking local government offices. Anxious that the anti-government riots might spread, and perhaps that the incident would be associated with the Tunisian street vendor who inspired the Arab Spring, authorities declared martial law, called in the riot police, jailed demonstrators, and launched a top-down campaign to quiet anti-regime sentiments (Zheng 2011).

In the case of Russia, riot police continue to disband small "anti-authoritarian" protests and harass opposition organizers (*Moskovskiy Komsomolets* 2011; Cullison 2011). For example, with respect to the large-scale protests that broke out following the 2011 parliamentary elections, the Russian regime demonstrated, at least initially, remarkable tolerance, in contrast to its counterpart in Bahrain. Moreover, the Kremlin decided to restore popular elections of Russian governors and to minimize the hurdles involved in registering a political party—though the latter action is less indicative of its support of competition than a calculation that easier registration encourages further fragmentation of an already divided opposition. These democratic "decorations," however, have been followed by other actions that suggest that Russian leaders are concerned about popular protests at home and in the MENA. Once Putin was reelected in March 2012, the Kremlin took unprecedented steps to restore the image of his invincibility and to undermine the opposition. Thus, the Russian leadership immediately blamed the West for inciting unrest in their country and organized pro-regime demonstrations across the country as a counterbalance (Herszenhorn and Barry 2012; Lipman and Petrov 2012; Neverov 2012). Here is it striking to observe a return to Soviet-era tricks, such as orchestrating public demonstrations of popular support by requiring (and paying) state employees to rally around the Kremlin (*RIA Novosti* 2012; Dzhanpoladova 2012). At the same time, the regime has passed a number of laws to minimize the possibility of future dissent. For example, fines increased 1,500 percent on protesters (up to 1.5 million rubles, or $46,000); NGOs receiving funds from abroad must reregister as "foreign agents" or face penalties of up to 1 million rubles and four years in prison; democracy-promoting organizations that are funded by the U.S. Agency for International Development (USAID) have been forced to shut down or leave the country; the definition of both slander and libel has been broadened and the fines leveled for these transgressions have increased dramatically; and, in November 2012 the government's supervisory agency for communications, Roskomnadzor, was given the legal right to blacklist websites and require internet providers to censor "harmful" content (*RFE/RL* 2012a, 2012b; Tsvetkova and Bryanski 2011). For these and other reasons, a report by Human Rights Watch concluded that repression in Russia during 2012 reached a level not seen since the communist era (Human Rights Watch 2013).

Perhaps even more than was the case for the color revolutions, the MENA uprisings have led the Russian and Chinese leaderships to launch elaborate campaigns to diffusion-proof their rule and their regimes. While such reactions were expected in the sense that the Chinese and Russian leaders, like all authoritarian rulers, fear popular unrest, especially when (as in the Arab cases) it is so unexpected and able to spread so quickly, it is nonetheless somewhat surprising that events so far away generated such strong responses. One reason for this might be the timing of the MENA wave; the Arab publics rose up on the eve of scheduled successions in both Russia and China. It is instructive to note here that succession is a nagging problem for virtually all authoritarian regimes, in part because it is strongly associated with divisions within the ruling circle and upsurges in popular unrest (Svolik 2012; Bunce 1981; Trejo 2012).

At the same time, we suggest that the color revolutions had primed the Russian and the Chinese leadership to react forcefully and quickly to the Arab uprisings, especially since the latter erupted in a region that had been long seen as the last bastion of authoritarian politics. Indeed, at least in the case of Russia, there was some concrete evidence that the leadership had good reason to fear the precedents set by this wave. In a poll taken shortly after the departure of Ben Ali in Tunisia and Mubarak in Egypt, there was a substantial increase in comparison with polls taken during the previous eight months in the percentage of respondents expressing a willingness, despite Putin's popularity, to participate in protests (Davidoff 2011; Ponomareva 2012). Of course, this is exactly what happened in December 2011 (Koesel and Bunce 2012; Robertson 2013).

Conclusions

Our purpose has been to assess whether and under what conditions authoritarian leaders take preemptive actions to insulate their regimes from the cross-national diffusion of popular mobilizations against other authoritarian rulers. We addressed this issue by comparing how the leaders of two variants of authoritarian politics—the competitive form in Russia and the non-competitive version in China—have responded to two waves: the color revolutions, which targeted competitive authoritarian regimes, and the Arab uprisings, which took place in non-competitive authoritarian systems. As we discovered, the Russian and the Chinese leaderships seemed to code the precedents set by each of these waves as very dangerous to their future and the future of their regimes. As a result, they deployed an array of ambitious—and relatively similar—strategies at both the rhetorical and policy levels to contain the reach of these waves. Irrespective of the wave's regional or regime theater of operation, diffusion-proofing has been the norm for the leaders of both countries and with respect to both waves.

These findings have implications for our understanding of the strategic foundations of authoritarian rule. While we concur with the claim that authoritarian leaders are vigilant and therefore deploy strategies that preempt and manage threats to their power, we introduce additional points to this discussion. One is that there are good reasons to bring comparative evidence to bear on this issue, especially when that evidence allows us to introduce variation in leaders, regimes, and likely perceptions of threat. The other is that the tool kit authoritarian leaders use to maintain their powers needs to be expanded to include measures, such as those we have detailed, that serve the purpose of containing international as well as domestic threats.

Our study also contributes to the understanding of diffusion in important ways. This body of work has tended to focus on a single wave, the participants seeking change, and the sources and impact of mobilization. By contrast, our study compares multiple waves, the defenders of the status quo, the containment of diffusion, and the origins and consequences of demobilization. Our analysis, therefore, counsels students of diffusion to pay more attention to those who resist, as well as to those who adopt change, and to the role of agency as well as structural factors in influencing the course of diffusion (Simmons, Dobbin, and Garrett 2008; Brinks and Coppedge 2006. But see Ambrosio 2009 on resistance).

These observations suggest in turn two additional points. One is that those who map diffusion dynamics have often been geographically too conservative, failing to take into consideration the measures that actors—even those located very far from the epicenter of the process—take to contain the reach of change (Beissinger 2007). Broadening the spatial arena of diffusion would seem to be particularly warranted when the guardians of the authoritarian status quo are very resourceful and the external threat involves a fundamental challenge to their political survival.

The other implication is confirmation from some unexpected sources—that is, the leaders of Russia and China—of how the scholarly community has understood diffusion processes. Authoritarian leaders seem to understand that "diffusion is no illusion," and that it is a dynamic that requires both a supply side (for example, Western support for civil society and the establishment elsewhere of appealing and transferrable precedents) and a demand side (for instance, similarities between those countries that hosted the wave and other countries that could join it, along with the opportunities and incentives available to local actors to embrace those precedents) (Brinks and Coppedge 2006). Thus the Chinese and Russian responses were precisely what students of diffusion would predict (were they to take a more agency-oriented approach): block external supply and suppress local demand.

Indeed, we can go one step further. Russian and Chinese leaders carried out these tasks by neutralizing the impact of precisely the two drivers of diffusion that have received the most attention in the literature. One is demonstration effects. The argument here is that innovations in one site are more likely to sponsor emulation elsewhere when three conditions are met: they have been introduced in contexts that appear to be similar to other settings, they are perceived to have been successful, and they rest on a repertoire that seems to be relatively easy to transfer. As a result, individuals watching these developments from the outside engage in a recalculation of their behavior such that the benefits of emulation rise, while the perceived costs of doing so decline. They have become, in short, more optimistic about change. The other and less often recognized driver of diffusion is a more deliberate and orchestrated dynamic. Here we refer to the role of transnational networks, or the formation of coalitions among domestic and international actors that play the role of designing and applying an innovation in one setting and then carrying it to others.

While analysts of diffusion disagree about which driver is more important, the Chinese and the Russian leaderships appear to be agnostic. Rather than choosing between them, their rhetoric and their policies—as we saw in Table 4.1 and its application to our two waves—rested on the shared premise that both could play a role. In this sense, the Chinese and Russian leaders hedged their bets.

Notes

This chapter was previously published in *Perspectives on Politics* 11, no. 3 (September 2013): 753–768.

1. Oliver and Meyers 2003, 174.

2. Quoted in MacKinnon 2008, 32.

3. On this question, also see Finkel and Brudny 2012a, 2012b.

4. Similar themes emerged following the 2011 parliamentary protests; see Koesel and Bunce 2012 and Barry 2011.

5. In 2007 the Russian Supreme Court ruled that the Republican Party should be denied registration for failing to meet the minimum legal requirements. In May 2012 this decision was reversed.

6. Freedom House reports opposition parties have been denied equal coverage in the media since 2004. These efforts intensified in 2007, when "Putin and his allies used state resources, particularly state-controlled television, to support the pro-Kremlin parties and crush any conceivable opposition." See *Nations in Transit—Russia 2008 Report* and "Freedom of the Press Reports," http://www.freedomhouse.org/country/russia.

7. On the pro-Kremlin youth movement, see Finkel and Brudny 2012b, 18–26.

8. For a very different approach to youth campaigns and authoritarian rule, see McGlinchey 2009.

9. In the aftermath of the 1989 student uprisings, the CCP organized a national conference targeting the development of youth; see "Quanguo gaoxiao danjian huiyi," http://210.34.4.20/news/detail.asp?serial=57953&key.

10. Our appreciation to Bruce Dickson for suggesting this second point. Indeed, in 2011–2012 the Chinese budget for domestic security (including police, jails, and surveillance) was larger than that of the PLA.

11. Similarly, Sarotte 2012 finds that the Chinese use of preemptive force in 1989 was driven in part by Communist Party losses in Eastern Europe and fears of contagion.

12. Freedom House evaluates the freedom of the press in Russia in 2002 as "partially free" and from 2003–2012 as "not free." China is consistently rated "not free." See http://www.freedomhouse.org/report/freedom-press/freedom-press-2012.

13. But see King, Pan, and Roberts 2012 for a discussion of censorship and collective action online in China.

14. For a discussion of selective and event-based internet controls, see Deibert and Rohozinski 2010, 20–29. See also Novikova 2011; Kimmage 2009, 56. Freedom House rates the Russian internet as "partially free" and the Chinese internet as "not free" (2009, 2011–2012), http://www.freedomhouse.org/report/freedom-net/freedom-net-2012. For attacks on opposition websites and bloggers following the 2011 elections, see *Freedom of the Net–Russia, 2012*, http://www.freedomhouse.org/report/freedom-net/2012/russia.

15. The total membership of the Fifty Cent Party is unknown, but some estimate that there are over 280,000 active participants who police and post in Chinese and foreign chat rooms; see Bandurski 2008.

16. Also see Ortmann 2008, 371, who notes that the Islamic terrorist narrative was introduced during the Tulip Revolution.

17. In China, "to stroll" has become a euphemism for protest.

References

Acemoglu, Daron, and James A. Robinson. 2006. *Economic Origins of Dictatorship and Democracy.* New York: Cambridge University Press.

Allnutt, Luke. 2011. "Russia's Thirty Ruble Army Emerges Again." *RFE/RL*, March 23. http://www.rferl.org/content/russia_30_ruble_army_emerges_again/24477703.html.

Ambrosio, Thomas. 2007. "Insulating Russia from a Colour Revolution: How the Kremlin Resists Regional Democratic Trends." *Democratization* 14, no. 2: 232–52.

Ambrosio, Thomas. 2009. *Authoritarian Backlash.* Burlington, VT: Ashgate.

Arapova, Natalia, and Ekaterina Savino. 2007. "Ne revoljuciju, a protivodejstvie ej!" [No revolution, an opposition to it!]. *Peredovaja gazeta*, April 25.

Arutunyan, Anna. 2012. "Media Bill Controversy." *Moscow News*, July 23. http://russialist.org/russia-kremlin-reprimand-duma-media-foreign-agent-bill-590.php.

Bandurski, David. 2008. "China's Guerrilla War for the Web." *Far Eastern Economic Review*, July 19.

Barry, Ellen. 2011. "On TV, Putin Is Dismissive of Critics Far and Near." *New York Times*, December 16.

Barry, Ellen. 2012. "Russian Legislators Approve Greater Government Control over the Internet and Non-Profits." *New York Times*, July 19.

Beissinger, Mark. 2007. "Structure and Example in Modular Political Phenomena: The Diffusion of Bulldozer, Rose, Orange and Tulip Revolutions." *Perspectives on Politics* 5, no. 2: 259–276.

Bovingdon, Gardner. 2010. *The Uyghurs: Strangers in Their Own Land.* New York: Columbia University Press.

Brinks, Daniel, and Michael Coppedge. 2006. "Diffusion Is No Illusion: Neighbor Emulation in the Third Wave of Democracy." *Comparative Political Studies* 39, no. 4: 463–489.

Brownlee, Jason. 2012. *Democracy Prevention: The Politics of the U.S.–Egyptian Alliance.* New York: Cambridge University Press.

Bueno de Mesquita, Bruce, and George W. Downs. 2005. "Development and Democracy." *Foreign Affairs* 84, no. 5: 77–86.

Bueno de Mesquita, Bruce, and Alastair Smith. 2011. *The Dictator's Handbook: Why Bad Behavior Is Almost Always Good Politics.* New York: Public Affairs.

Bunce, Valerie. 1981. *Do New Leaders Make a Difference? Executive Succession and Public Policy under Capitalism and Socialism.* Princeton: Princeton University Press.

Bunce, Valerie. 1999. *Subversive Institutions: The Design and the Destruction of Socialism and the State.* New York: Cambridge University Press.

Bunce, Valerie, and Sharon Wolchik. 2011. *Defeating Authoritarian Leaders in Postcommunist Countries.* New York: Cambridge University Press.

Chang, Anita. 2011. "'Jasmine Revolution' Causes China to Flex Its Force." Associated Press, February 21.

Chen, Titus C. 2010. "China's Reaction to the Color Revolution: Adaptive Authoritarianism in Full Swing." *Asian Perspective* 34, no. 2: 5–51.

Chen, Xi. 2012. *Social Protest and Contentious Authoritarianism in China.* New York: Cambridge University Press.

Chivers, C. J. 2006. "Kremlin Puts Foreign Private Organizations on Notice." *New York Times*, October 20.

Chong, Dennis, and James N. Druckman. 2013. "Counter-Framing." *Journal of Politics* 75: 1–16.

Coalson, Robert, and Mikhail Sokolov. 2011. "Authoritarian Russia Watches as Middle East Unravels." *RFE/RL*, March 3. http://www.rferl.org/content/authoritarian_russia_watches_as_mideast_unravels/2327204.html.

Committee on Foreign Relations, U.S. Senate. 2006. "The Role of Non-Governmental Organizations in the Development of Democracy." Hearings before the Committee on Foreign Relations, U.S. Senate, 109th Congress, Second Session. June 8.

Cullison, Alan. 2011. "Anti-Authoritarian Protest in Moscow Meet Stern Response." *Wall Street Journal*, June 1.

Dannreuther, Roland. 2011. "Russia and the Arab Revolutions." *Russian Analytical Digest* 98, no. 6: 4–6.

Davidoff, Victor. 2011. "Missiles Can Help Stop Riots." *Moscow Times*, February 28.

Deibert, Ronald, and Rafal Rohozinski. 2010. "Control and Subversion in Russian Cyberspace." In *Access Controlled*, ed. Ronald Dibert, John Palfrey, Rafal Rozhozinski, and Jonathan Zittrain, 15–34. Cambridge, MA: MIT Press.

Demick, Barbara. 2011. "China Police Show Up in Masse at Hint of Protest." *Los Angeles Times*, February 21.

Dobson, William J. 2012. *The Dictator's Learning Curve: Inside the Global Battle for Democracy*. New York: Doubleday.

Dzhanpoladova, Natalya. 2012. "Workers of the World, Rally!" *RFE/RL*, February 8. http://www.rferl.org/content/rent_a_crowd_pro-putin_protests_in_moscow/24478076.html.

Finkel, Evgeny, and Yitzhak M. Brudny. 2012a. "No More Colour! Authoritarian Regimes and Colour Revolutions in Eurasia." *Democratization* 19, no. 1: 1–14.

Finkel, Evgeny, and Yitzhak M. Brudny. 2012b. "Russia and the Colour Revolutions." *Democratization* 19, no. 1: 15–36.

Gandhi, Jennifer. 2007. "Authoritarian Institutions and the Survival of Autocrats." *Comparative Political Studies* 40, no. 11: 1279–1301.

Gandhi, Jennifer, and Adam Przeworski. 2006. "Cooperation, Cooptation, and Rebellion under Dictatorships." *Economics and Politics* 18, no. 1: 1–26.

Givan, Rebecca Kotlins, Sarah A. Soule, and Kenneth Roberts, eds. 2010. *The Diffusion of Social Movements*. New York: Cambridge University Press.

Global Times. 2011. "Mei shiguan: Hong Bopei zai molihua shiwei didian shu qiaohe" [US ambassador: Jon Huntsman at the Jasmine demonstrations is a coincidence]. *Global Times*, February 25. http://www.gcpnews.com/articles/2011-02-25/C1046_62196.html.

Guo, Ruiting. 2002. *Zhongguo Gongchandang dang nei tongji ziliao huibian, 1921–2000* [Collection of CCP inner statistics, 1921–2000]. Beijing: Danjian du wu chubanshe.

Herszenhorn, David M., and Ellen Barry. 2012. "Putin Contends Clinton Incited Unrest over Vote." *New York Times*, December 8.

Huang, Peizhao. 2011. "Jizhe qinli Aiji zhengzhi weiji: Meiguo taidu zhide wanwei" [Reporters witnessed Egyptian political crisis: think over the United States's attitude]. *Global People*, February 21. http://news.sina.com.cn/w/sd/2011-02-21/145721988856.shtml.Human Rights Watch. 2013. "Russia's Worst Crackdown Since Soviet Era: Government Should

Stop Pressure, Reprisals on Civil Society." January 31. http://www.hrw.org/news/2013/01/31/russia-worst-crackdown-soviet-era.Jacoby, Wade. 2006. "Inspiration, Coalition and Substitution." *World Politics* 58, no. 4: 623–651.

Jiang, Shangyu. 2011. "Zhongguo bushi zhongdong" [China is definitely not the Middle East]. *People's Daily*, March 10. http://paper.people.com.cn/rmrbhwb/html/2011-03/10/content_765003.htm?div=-1.

Kamhi, Alison. 2006. "The Russian NGO Law: Potential Conflicts with International, National and Foreign Legislation." *International Journal for Not-for-Profit Law* 9, no. 1: 1–16.

Kimmage, Daniel. 2009. "Russia: Selective Capitalism and Kleptocracy." In *Undermining Democracy: 21st Century Authoritarians, Freedom House, RFE/RL and Radio Free Asia.* http://www.underminingdemocracy.org.

King, Gary, Jennifer Pan, and Margaret Roberts. 2012. "How Censorship in China Allows Government Criticism but Silences Collective Expression." Unpublished manuscript. October 2. http://gking.harvard.edu/publications/how-censorship-china-allows-government-criticism-silences-collective-expression.

Kipp, Jacob W. 2011. "Moscow Responds to the Arab Revolutions: Focus on Libya (Part One)." *Eurasia Daily Monitor* 8, no. 79.

Kniazov, Alexander. 2005. *Gosudarstvennyi perevorot 24 Marta 2005g v Kirgizii* [Coup d'état in Kyrgyzstan, March 24, 2005]. Moscow: Europa.

Koesel, Karrie, and Valerie Bunce. 2012. "Putin, Popular Protests and Political Trajectories in Russia: A Comparative Perspective." *Post-Soviet Affairs* 28, no. 4: 403–423.

Kommersant. 2005. "Putin Appoints Velvet-Counter-Revolutionary." March 23.Kosobokova, Tatiana. 2008. "Nashi' menjajut amplua" [Nashi movement changes role]. *RBC Daily*, July 21. http://www.rbcdaily.ru/politics/562949979036590.

Kostenko, Natalia. 2007. "Demokratizatory—2007" [The democratizers of 2007]. *Nezavisimaya Gazeta*, November 15. http://www.ng.ru/politics/2007-11-15/1_democratizator.html.

Kots, Aleksandr. 2007. "Politics: A KP Investigation, Interview with Sergei Markov." *Komsomolskaja Pravda*, February 27.

Krainova, Natalya. 2009. "Nashi Activist Tells of Snooping for Kremlin." *Moscow Times*, February 6.

Kramer, Andrew. 2007. "Kasparov Says He Was Forced to End Bid for Presidency." *New York Times*, December 13.

Kuang, Xiaoyang, and Yu Liu. 2006. "Yanse geming: meiguo de minzhu zhanlue duice" [The color revolutions: America's "exporting democracy" strategy and our countermeasures]. *Yangzhou daxue xuebao (Renwenshe hui kexue ban)* 2: 22–27.

LaFrainere, Sharon, and David Barboza. 2011. "China Tightens Censorship of Electronic Communication." *New York Times*, March 22.

Lebedev, Pavel. 2011. "Plany FSB zakryt' Skype dlja rossijan v Belom dome schitajut 'vpolne argumentirovannymi'" [FSB plan to close Skype for Russians in the White House considered "completely reasonable"]. April 8. http://www.gzt.ru/topnews/hitech/-plany-fsb-zakrytj-skype-dlya-rossiyan-v-belom-/356071.html.

Levada Center. 2011a. "Russians on the Revolution in Egypt." Representative Opinion poll, February 11–14. http://levada.ru/press/2011022101.html.

Levada Center. 2011b. "47% Respondents Object to the Situation in Libya." Representative Opinion poll, March 18–21. http://levada.ru/press/2011032509.html.

Levitsky, Steven, and Lucan A. Way. 2010. *Competitive Authoritarianism: Hybrid Regimes After the Cold War*. New York: Cambridge University Press.

Li, Hongmei. 2011. "Play the Middle East Card Subtly and Deftly." *People's Daily*, April 13.

Li, Peng. 2006. "Tuise de 'yansegeming' " [The fading "color revolutions"]. *Xuexi shibao* 3, April 2. http://www.china.com.cn/chinese/zhuanti/xxsb/1173040.htm.

Link, Perry. 2011. "The Secret Politburo Meeting Behind China's New Democracy Crackdown." *New York Review of Books*, February 20.

Lipman, Maria, and Nikolay Petrov. 2012. "What the Russian Protests Can—and Can't—Do." *Foreign Affairs*, February 9.

Liu, Ming. 2006. *Jietouzhengzhi yu "yansegeming"* [Street politics and color revolutions]. Beijing: Communication University of China Press.

Lorentzen, Peter. 2008. "Regularized Rioting: The Strategic Toleration of Public Protest in China." Unpublished manuscript, June 2. University of California, Berkeley.

Lyall, Jason. 2006. "Pocket Protests: Rhetorical Coercion and the Micropolitics of Collective Action in Semiauthoritarian Regimes." *World Politics* 58, no. 3: 378–412.

Lynch, Marc, ed. 2012. *The Arab Uprising: The Unfinished Revolutions of the New Middle East*. New York: Public Affairs/Perseus.

Lynch, Marc. 2014. *The Arab Uprisings Explained*. New York: Columbia University Press.

MacKinnon, Rebecca. 2008. "Flatter World and Thicker Walls? Blogs, Censorship and Civic Discourse in China." *Public Choice* 134, nos. 1–2: 31–46.

Magaloni, Beatriz. 2006. *Voting for Autocracy: Hegemonic Party Survival and Its Demise in Mexico*. New York: Cambridge University Press.

McDonald, Mark. 2012. "The Arab Spring Is Coming to China." *New York Times*, February 5.

McGlinchey, Eric. 2009. "Searching for Kamalot: Political Patronage and Youth Politics in Uzbekistan." *Europe-Asia Studies* 61, no. 7: 1137–1150.

Mendelson, Sarah, and T. Gerber. 2005. "Local Activist Culture and Transnational Diffusion: An Experiment in Social Marketing Among Human Rights Groups in Russia." Unpublished manuscript.

Moscow News. 2005. "Putin Names Spin Doctor to Counter CIS Revolutions." March 23.

Moskovskiy Komsomolets, 2011."Gnevu mesta ne nashlos' " [Wrath didn't occur]. June 12. http://www.mk.ru/politics/article/2011/06/12/596873-gnevu-mesta-ne-nashlos.html.

Neverov, Sergei. 2012. "Pochemu v Rossiju ne pridet arabskaja vesna" [Why there will be no Arab Spring in Russia]. *Nezavisimaya Gazeta*, February 10. http://www.ng.ru/politics/2012-02-10/1_arab_vesna.html.

Ning, Jinhe. 2006. "Yansegeming yu Meiguo" [Color revolution and America]. *Chengdu xingzheng xueyuan xuebao* 1: 53–55.

Nikonov, Vjacheslav. 2007. "Chernaja magija" [Black magic]. *Izvestia*, May 30. http://izvestia.ru/news/325150.

Niu, Xinchun. 2011. "Zhongdong beifei dongdang dailai de yinyou" [The potential problems coming from the chaos in the Middle East and North Africa]. *Guangming Daily*, March 15. http://theory.gmw.cn/2011-03/15/content_1720069.htm.

Novikova, Irina. 2011. "V zone chastichnoj svobody: Rossija uhudshila svoi pozicii v rejtinge nezavisimosti v Internete" [In a zone of partial freedom: Russia has slipped down the internet independence rating]. *Novye Izvestija*, April 20. http://www.newizv.ru/society/2011-04-20/143878-v-zone-chastichnoj-svobody.html.

Nygren, Bertil. 2008. "Putin's Use of Natural Gas to Reintegrate the CIS Region." *Problems of Postcommunism* 56, no. 4: 3–15.

O'Brien, Kevin ed. 2008. *Popular Protest in China*. Cambridge, MA: Harvard University Press.

Odynova, Alexandra. 2009. "Kremlin Advisers Warn Nashi Youth." *Moscow Times*, October 6.

Oliver, Pamela E., and Daniel J. Myers. 2003. "Networks, Diffusion, and Cycles of Collective Action." In *Social Movement Analysis*, ed. Mario Diani and Doug McAdam, 173–203. Oxford: Oxford University Press.

Ortmann, Stefanie. 2008. "Diffusion as Discourse of Danger: Russian Self-Representations and the Framing of the Tulip Revolution." *Central Asian Survey* 27, nos. 3–4: 363–378.

Page, Jeremy. 2011. "Beijing Restricts Internet over Egypt." *Wall Street Journal*, January 31.

Pan, Rulong, and Zhengqin Dai. 2005. "Yansegeming yu guoji feizhengfuzuzhi" [Color revolutions and international NGOs]. *Dianzi keji daxue xuebao (she ke ban)* 7, no. 4: 77–79.

Patel, David. 2012. "Preference Falsification, Diffusion, and the Centrality of Squares in the Arab Revolutions." Paper presented at the American Political Science Association annual meeting, New Orleans, August 30–September 2.Patel, David, Valerie Bunce, and Sharon Wolchik. 2014. "Diffusion and Demonstration." In *The Arab Uprisings Explained: New Contentious Politics in the Middle East*, ed. Marc Lynch, 57–74. New York: Columbia University Press.

People's Daily. 2012. "Zhongguo zai Munihei chongshen heping fazhan de juexin" [China in Munich reiterates determination for a peaceful development]. February 4. http://world. people.com.cn/GB/17021620.html.

Ponomareva, Yulia. 2012. "A Summer of Discontent?" *Moscow Times*, February 9.

Potter, Pitman B., and Sophia Woodman. 2012. "Boundaries of Tolerance: Charter 08 and Debates Over Political Reform." In *Liu Xiaobo, Charter 08, and the Challenges of Political Reform in China*, ed. Jean-Philippe Beja, Huanling Fu, and Eva Pils, 56–81. Hong Kong: Hong Kong University Press.

Public Opinion Foundation. 2005. "'Cvetnye revoljucii' v stranah SNG" ['Color revolutions' in the CIS]. July. http://bd.fom.ru/report/cat/polit/col_rev/dd052824.

Putin, Vladimir V. 2004. "Annual Address to the Federal Assembly of the Russian Federation." Moscow, May 26. http://archive.kremlin.ru/eng/speeches/2004/05/26/ 1309_type70029type82912_71650.shtml.

Quinlivan, James T. 1999. "Coup-Proofing: Its Practice and Consequences in the Middle East." *International Security* 24, no. 2: 131–165.

Radnitz, Scott. 2012. "Oil in the Family: Managing Presidential Succession in Azerbaijan." *Democratization* 19, no. 1: 60–77.

Razimov, Yaroslav. 2011. "Arabskie 'revoljucii' jeto rezul'tat sochetanija i vnutrennih problem i 'proektov' zapadnyh stran" [The Arab revolutions are the result of combining domestic problems and Western "projects"]. Russian Institute for Strategic Research, April 4. http://www.riss.ru/vystuplenija_v_smi/?newsId=340.

RIA Novosti-Moscow. 2012. "Mass Protests Force Kremlin to Take Heed of Opposition Demands." February 5.

Ren, Siwen. 2011. "Zijue weihu shehui hexie wending" [Safeguard social harmony and stability]. *Beijing Daily*, March 5. http://news.xinhuanet.com/politics/2011lh/2011-03/05/c_ 121151263.htm.

RFE/RL. 2005. "Newsline." September 6. http://www.rferl.org/content/article/1143474.htm.

RFE/RL. 2012a. "Russian State Duma Passes Bill to Increase the Fines on Protesters." August 1. http://www.rferl.org/content/russia-fines-protesters/24589103.html.

RFE/RL. 2012b. "Russian Duma Gives Initial Backing to 'Foreign Agents' Bill." July 6. http://www.rferl.org/content/russia-duma-backing-ngo-bill-foreign-agent-first-reading/24637487.html.Robertson, Graeme. 2011. *The Politics of Protest in Hybrid Regimes: Managing Dissent in Post-Communist Russia*. New York: Cambridge University Press.

Robertson, Graeme. 2013. "Protesting Putinism: The Election Protests of 2011–2012 in Broader Perspective." *Problems of Postcommunism* 60, no. 2: 11–23.Rogers, Everett. 2005. *Diffusion of Innovations*. New York: Free Press.

Sarotte, M. E. 2012. "China's Fear of Contagion: Tiananmen Square and the Power of the European Example." *International Security* 37, no. 2: 156–182.

Schedler, Andreas. 2015. "The Politics of Uncertainty: Sustaining and Subverting Electoral Authoritarianism." Oxford University Press.

Shambaugh, David. 2008. *China's Communist Party: Atrophy and Adaptation*. Berkeley: University of California Press.

Shi, Jianxun. 2011. "Middle East Turbulence Scares People Worldwide." *People's Daily*, March 1. http://english.people.com.cn/90001/90780/91343/7304617.html.

Shishkin, Igor. 2011. "Zachem Amerika vzorvala Bol'shoj Blizhnij Vostok?" [Why did America explode the Middle East?]. *Regnum*, April 17. http://www.regnum.ru/news/polit/1395636.html.

Silitski, Vitali. 2010. "Contagion Deterred: Preemptive Authoritarianism in the Former Soviet Union (the Case of Belarus)." In *Democracy and Authoritarianism in the Postcommunist World*, ed. Valerie Bunce, Michael McFaul and Kathryn Stoner-Weiss, 274–299. New York: Cambridge University Press.

Simmons, Beth A., Frank Dobbin, and Geoffrey Garrett, eds. 2008. *The Global Diffusion of Markets and Democracy*. New York: Cambridge University Press.

Soldatov, Andrei. 2011. "Kremlin's Plan to Prevent a Facebook Revolution." *Moscow Times*, February 28.

Stanovaya, Tatyana. 2005. "Molodezhnye organizacii v sovremennoj Rossii" [Youth organizations in contemporary Russia]. Politikum.ru. http://www.compromat.ru/page_11491.htm.

Stockman, Daniel, and Mary Gallagher. 2011. "Remote Control: How the Media Sustain Authoritarian Rule in China." *Comparative Political Studies* 44, no. 4: 436–467.

Svolik, Milan W. 2012. *The Politics of Authoritarian Rule*. New York: Cambridge University Press.

Swartz, Dale. 2011. "Jasmine in the Middle Kingdom: Autopsy of China's (Failed) Revolution." *American Enterprise Institute for Public Policy Research* 1: 1–5.

Tang, Yong, Zhe Chang, and Honggang Wang. 2005. "Suoluosi jijinhui shentou quanqiu" [The Soros Foundation infiltrates all over the world]. *Huanqiu shibao*, April 18, 7.

Tian, Fang. 2006. "Lun quanqiuhua beijingxia feizhengfuzuzhi dui guoji shehui de zhengzhi zuoyong" [The political influence of NGOs in the international society under globalization]. *Lilun yuekan* 2: 146–147.

Trejo, Guillermo. 2012. *Popular Movements in Autocracies: Religion, Repression, and Indigenous Collective Action in Mexico*. Cambridge: Cambridge University Press.

Tsvetkova, Maria, and Gleb Bryanski. 2011. "Russia Looks About for Law to Regulate Internet." Reuters, April 16.

Wang, Jiabo. 2005. "Shui zai dulianti caozong jietou zhengzhi" [Who is manipulating "street politics" in the CIS?]. *Guangming Daily*, March 18.

Weyland, Kurt. 2009. "The Diffusion of Revolution: '1848' in Europe and Latin America." *International Organization* 63, no. 3: 391–423.

Whitmore, Brian. 2012. "The Empire Strikes Back—At Independent Media." *RFE/RL*, February 16. http://www.rferl.org/content/the_empire_strikes_back_-_at_independent_media/24486805.html.

Williams, Stuart. 2011. "Medvedev Warns Arab Unrest May Empower Fanatics." Agence France-Presse, February 22.

Wilson, Andrew. 2005. *Virtual Parties: Faking Democracy in the Post-Soviet World*. New Haven: Yale University Press.

Wilson, Jeanne L. 2010. "The Legacy of the Color Revolutions for Russian Politics and Foreign Policy." *Problems of Postcommunism* 57, no. 3: 31–36.

Wintrobe, Ronald. 2001. "How to Understand and Deal with Dictatorship: An Economists' View." *Economics of Governance* 2: 35–58.

Wright, Teresa. 2010. *Accepting Authoritarianism: State-Society Relations in China's Reform Era*. Stanford: Stanford University Press.

Wright, Teresa. 2011. "Perpetuating Communist Party Rule in China." *Journal of International Affairs* 65, no. 1: 31–45.

Wu, Zhang. 2009. "Public Woes in Agrarian China: Local Government and Peasant Protest in Hunan." Ph.D. diss., Cornell University.

Xinhua. 2009. "Communist Party Retains Vigor, Charisma Among Chinese Youth 88 Years After Its Founding." July 2. http://english.people.com.cn/90001/90776/90785/6691284.html.

Zhang, Jianfeng. 2007. *2008 Nian, zhengzhi lilun linnian zhenti biaozhun daan yu kaoshi fenxi* [2008 year, political theory examinations 1997–2007]. Beijing: Xinhua chubanshe.

Zhang, Weiwei. 2011. "China Should Follow Own Course in Political Reform." *People's Daily*, April 2.

Zhang, Zhongyun. 2005. "Yao zhongshi jietou zhengzhi de xiaoying" [Pay attention to the impact of street politics]. *Gaoxiao lilun zhanxian* 5: 62–63.

Zheng, Caixiong. 2011. "Unfounded Rumor Sends Local Crowd into Frenzy." *China Daily*, June 13, 4.

Zyatkov, Nikolai. 2007. "Kontrrazvedka: shpionov segodnja lovjat tak" [Counter-intelligence: how spies are caught these days]. *Argumenty i Fakty* 41, October 10. http://gazeta.aif.ru/online/aif/1406/09_01.

Media Politics

Critical Journalists in China and Russia

ENCOUNTERS WITH AMBIGUITY

Maria Repnikova

China and Russia are known as coercive authoritarian regimes with low press freedoms, suppressed activism, and little to no political competition.[1] In recent years, moreover, there appears to be some convergence between the two in the realm of political control, with both states expanding internet censorship, rewriting punitive laws and regulations, and showing no mercy for their critics.[2] Putin's main remaining adversary, Alexey Navalny, was predictably jailed in June 2017 (Walker 2017), while China's most famous dissident, Nobel Peace Prize winner Liu Xiaobo, died in prison in July of that year (Buckley 2017).

At the same time, control in both China and Russia continues to be implemented selectively, leaving some (albeit shrinking) spaces for critical expression and mobilization from below. This selective or partial nature of control is especially apparent in the media sphere, where some news outlets, online platforms, and individual voices persist on the margins and disseminate alternative, and at times critical, perspectives on politics and society.

While critical media and journalists are often linked to democratization prospects (Curry 2010; McNair 1991), we still know surprisingly little about how these semi-controlled spaces work under resilient authoritarian regimes, especially in comparative perspective. How does the gray zone of critical reporting differ between China and Russia? How do journalists experience and navigate political uncertainty, and what does that tell us not just about the varieties of authoritarianism when it comes to media politics but also about the manifestations of ambiguity as a strategic tool in the authoritarian arsenal of political legitimation?

This chapter explores these questions through the perspectives of critical journalists in China and Russia, media practitioners who routinely push the boundaries of permissible reporting. It examines how they understand the parameters of critical journalism, how they experience signals from the state, and how they navigate or negotiate them. By grappling with the complexity of media management from below, this chapter attempts to capture the dynamism of media politics in the two countries.

MEDIA POLITICS UNDER AUTHORITARIANISM: BETWEEN DEMOCRACY AND A HARD PLACE

The analysis of media-state relations in authoritarian regimes is largely captured by the dichotomy between democratization and resilience. Media is analyzed either as a force (direct or indirect) for political liberalization or as a tool of a resilient authoritarian state. As for the former, since the 1960s political scientists and communication scholars have argued that media can play a critical role in destabilizing authoritarianism. Earlier scholarship, drawing on modernization theory, associated access to mass media with more dynamic public participation in politics, and thereby a higher probability for a democratic transition (Lerner and Riesman 1965).

In the 1990s, in the wake of the collapse of the Soviet Union, an expansion of more critical or independent news sources has been linked to the empowerment of democratic movements (Huntington 1996; McNair 1991). Gorbachev's glasnost or media liberalization policy, some argue, mobilized public support for systemic political change, unanticipated by regime reformers (McNair 1991). Studies on political change in other transitional contexts, such as Taiwan, also found that independent media has played a role in eroding regime legitimacy (Rawnsley and Rawnsley 1998). In the past decade, Information and Communication Technologies have been linked to the Arab Spring (Howard and Hussain 2011), as well as to the emergence of the public sphere and gradual liberalization in authoritarian regimes such as China (Yang 2009).

At the same time, extensive studies on media control emphasize the capacity of authoritarian states to deploy the media and digital technologies to remain in power. Recent scholarship has delved into the many dimensions of censorship (Greitens 2013; King, Pan, and Roberts 2013), media regulation (Creemers 2017), surveillance (Deibert and Rohozinski 2010), and co-optation (Gunitsky 2015) that authoritarian regimes use to suppress and manipulate public opinion. The "failed" revolutions in the Middle East and North Africa, combined with unbending authoritarianism in China, Russia, Iran, and much of Central Asia, have further obscured the linkages between media and democratization, pointing to the adaptive nature of authoritarian leaders when it comes to navigating communication channels to their advantage (Oates 2013; MacKinnon 2011; Gunitsky 2015).

Between the binaries of democratization and resilience, however, some critical voices continue to reside in the gray zone or on the margins of authoritarian systems. They don't immediately provoke a democratic change, but they take advantage of limited freedoms to challenge state discourses and advocate for official accountability. Grasping how these voices and spaces for alternative media interact with the state can illuminate the parameters of political sensitivity and state tolerance toward criticism, as well as the opportunities for routine or everyday bottom-up resistance. Most importantly, analyzing these gray spaces informs us about the dynamics of authoritarian adaptation through the lens of state-media interaction.

This chapter does that by comparing how critical journalists in China and Russia experience control and resistance. It demonstrates that while both groups navigate significant political uncertainty, Chinese journalists receive more intensive signals from the state than their Russian counterparts, who exist in a relatively freer but more arbitrary political environment. As a result, Chinese journalists more routinely negotiate with the state as part of their survival strategy, whereas Russian journalists engage in more preemptive risk-taking and subtle self-censorship.

CHINA AND RUSSIA: PARALLELS AND DISTINCTIONS IN MEDIA GOVERNANCE

Chinese and Russian media systems are known for being heavily state-controlled, featuring a mix of censorship and propaganda. In Russia, after a decade of democracy, Putin's trajectory of authoritarianism has brought the media back into the state's orbit (Lipman and McFaul 2001). Most major news outlets in today's Russia now either directly or indirectly belong to the state, which dictates the messages to be transmitted to the public. Chinese media has officially been part of the Chinese Communist Party since the founding of the People's Republic and has been heavily managed by the party-state's institutions (Brady 2008), including the Central Propaganda Department (CPD) and its local branches, the General Administration for Publication and Press (GAPP), and now also the Cyberspace Administration. Despite the transformative commercialization of the media in the 1980s and 1990s, the party-state continues to hold a 51 percent stake in all the news outlets, and to regularly censor and shape media content (Stockmann 2012). Both regimes are also renowned for their sophisticated propaganda, ranging from official state media to armies of trolls that spread pro-regime messages and strike down critics online (Han 2015; Walker 2015).

In recent years, there are also emerging signs of possible cross learning in media management between China and Russia, including in the realm of censorship, propaganda, and global internet governance. The Russian regime intensified internet censorship after the 2011 protests, borrowing some techniques from China when it comes to content blocking (Parker 2017). The Chinese state, in turn, has been incorporating a more Putin-like personalistic governance mode, reflected in unusually intensive media focus on the leader, President Xi, in contrast to the previous decades (Shi 2017). The two states have broadcast joint declarations on global media governance, namely their support for internet sovereignty, in opposition to the internet freedom discourse channeled by the West (Roth 2015).

The less apparent similarity between the two media systems, however, is the continued ambivalent tolerance of critical voices in the media sphere. In Russia, scholars refer to the "islands of press freedom" that continue to exist in isolation of mainstream politics (Lipman 2010), whereas in China, scholars have documented the practice of media oversight or supervision, in part endorsed by the state (Repnikova 2017; Zhao 2000). How this so-called partial tolerance works in practice is the subject of the analysis that follows. Specifically, considering the other overlaps in media governance, should we expect to see these gray zones of critical journalism working in similar ways in China and Russia? How does political ambivalence play out in the realm of critical reporting?

This chapter presents the first account of these dynamics. It argues that despite the apparent overlaps in media governance, when it comes to the gray zone of critical reporting there are important distinctions in media-state interactions in these two cases. While both groups of journalists experience uncertainty when it comes to state control, Chinese journalists exist within a more structured ambiguity than their Russian counterparts. Whereas the former navigate routine signals from the state, the latter face the risk of arbitrary coercion.

SOURCES

In unpacking state-journalist interactions in the gray zone of critical media, this chapter primarily draws on in-depth interviews with media practitioners, as well as participant observation of journalistic practices online and offline. Eighty interviews were conducted with journalists and editors between 2009 and 2014, with some follow-up interviews done in 2016 and 2017.

Interviewees were selected from outlets that have a national reputation for quality investigative journalism and in-depth coverage of contentious societal issues.[3] In China, these include the Guangzhou-based *Nanfang Zhoumo*, *Nanfang Dushibao*, and *Nanfang Renwu Zhoukan*, as well as the Beijing-based *Caijing* and *Caixin* magazines, *Bingdian* (a supplement to *Zhongguo Qingnian Bao*), and the CCTV program *Jiaodian Fangtan*. In Russia, these outlets include the Moscow-based newspapers *Novaya Gazeta* and *Vedomosti* (especially the op-ed page), the magazines *Vlast'* and the *New Times*, and the liberal investigative digital news outlets Agentura.ru and Grani.ru. Interviews were also carried out with some retired investigative journalists and freelance commentators in both countries.

It's important to note a geographic distinction between China and Russia in the selection of interviewees. Whereas all Russia interviewees are based in Moscow, Chinese interviewees work for news outlets based out of Beijing and Guangzhou. This distinction is rooted in different degrees of political and economic centralization in the two cases. Whereas in Russia the epicenter for intellectual and critical thinking has consistently remained in Moscow, in China, up until recently, the southern province of Guangzhou was one of the key centers for liberal thinking due to its economic vibrancy, distance from Beijing, and progressive provincial authorities.[4]

The author carried out the interviews without a translator and ensured the interviewees' anonymity unless otherwise agreed upon with an interviewee. The selection of interviewees was done through the snowball strategy, whereby a core group of contacts would make further introductions.

Other than the in-depth interviews, the analysis also draws on observations of media workshops on investigative journalism and media ethics in Beijing, as well as seminars on media politics in Moscow. In China the author participated in discussions on media oversight role and journalists' strategies for managing political ambiguity. In Russia, the author gave a presentation to Moscow's prominent liberal journalists about the state of Chinese media, which sparked intriguing debates on the differences between Moscow and Beijing when it comes to holding government accountable.

Part I: The Encounters with Ambiguity

CHINA: FACING STRUCTURED AMBIGUITY

Interviews with Chinese media professionals over the past decade illuminate the consistent distinctions between the so-called red zone of untouchable topics and the gray zone of semi-sensitive issues that can be probed with caution. The red line is surprisingly consistent and includes stories on secessionist movements (i.e., Taiwan, Xinjiang, Tibet, Hong Kong), questioning of the Party's legitimacy, and any writings promoting democratization or systemic change. "If you were to start working at our magazine today, very quickly you would grasp which topics are not to be touched at all. The list of the completely inaccessible topics is pretty clear and stable, and it is not difficult to get used to," noted an experienced editor in Beijing (CJ10 2009).

The gray zone, in contrast, is constantly fluctuating and tends to include hot societal issues such as corruption, social inequality, local protests, environmental degradation, rural-urban migration, and crisis management, among others. Topics in the gray zone are not banned at the outset but are viewed as potentially politically sensitive by the state. Journalists tackling these topics operate in the atmosphere of what I call "structured ambiguity." They receive constant signals from the state, many of which are preemptive directives; the instigators of these signals are relatively transparent or traceable; and political pressures tend to follow certain repetitive patterns familiar to experienced reporters. In working to manage the contours of the gray zone by actively engaging with media professionals and social media content, the state also creates some order in the overarching climate of "political ambivalence" (Stern 2014).

Frequent interaction between officials and media professionals is at the core of media management in China. The instructions or directives are constantly trickling down from different Party and state agencies to media gatekeepers and then to practicing journalists. Editors shared that they receive official requests and criticisms via phone calls, text messages, and now also the WeChat platform.[5] During the most recent fieldwork in Beijing and Shanghai (summer 2016 and 2017), the author observed editors getting messages from the Cyberspace Administration via a WeChat circle that included other media professionals, creating group pressure when it comes to following the rules. Journalists and editors are so conditioned to the frequency of official notifications that they tend to respond indifferently, exhibiting little surprise at these interruptions.

Many of these instructions, moreover, are sent preemptively, before an article is published. Journalists and editors from China's critical news outlets have consistently shared that about 50 percent of their stories don't make it into print, and their pursuits are often cut short while they are in the field investigating a sensitive issue. "The most challenging part of my work is that I am often forced to give up on a story I would spend a long time working on because of an abrupt directive from the Central Propaganda Department," commented a longtime investigative journalist from *Caixin* magazine (CJ34 2012). Similar revelations were made during most recent trips to Beijing. According to the journalists, preemptive directives can range from a complete publication ban to a ban on original reporting (but not the discussion of an issue) to a request for positive reporting or hopeful narratives. The fact that journalists are preemptively notified about the shifting sensitivity of certain issues limits how far they can go, but also creates a cushion of stability when it comes to anticipating state responses to their reports and figuring out negotiation strategies.

On top of these preemptive signals, of course, editors often receive more directives after a story is published, including instructions on specific line-by-line adjustments as well as orders to delete content. These adjustments are enabled by media's transformation from print to online editions, giving way to endless possibilities for changing content. Some editors share that their workflow has significantly increased as a result, as they are now responsible not only for producing appropriate content but also for adjusting it in real time. If preemptive and post-factum signals don't work, harsher post-factum pressures can be leveled against the journalists, including official warnings and criticisms, professional demotion, and in rare cases detention.[6] The signaling, therefore, is somewhat gradual and multilayered, with most pressure happening preemptively and then expanding further if necessary.

Other than the frequency of signals, the origins and patterns of these signals are somewhat traceable for experienced professionals. When it comes to traditional media, editors receive warnings directly from officials at the propaganda department (typically the regional one) as well as the GAPP and, now, from the Cyber Administration, which is in charge of all internet content (Cairns 2016). While pressures from other entities and actors, such as advertisers and investors, are noteworthy and can affect investigations of certain issues, the daily contact with restrictions seems to have more of a political nature (even if it originates elsewhere) due to the intensive oversight from the party-state, and thereby remains relatively transparent to journalists.

Moreover, interviews reveal that journalists can often trace the patterns in what may initially appear as arbitrary censorship directives. For example, they can link censorship to popularity of a topic on social media, or to pressures from local officials and other actors negatively implicated in a report. When a topic becomes popular on social media, it quickly appears on the radar of media-regulating officials, according to journalist interviewees. The capacity of social media, like Weibo, to transform isolated incidents into national scandals and events raises the censorship bar when it comes to investigative and in-depth reporting. Many journalists observe that authorities often first try to gauge public interest in an online discussion and then instruct journalists how to shape public opinion, leaving less space for independent investigations. The 2012 large-scale pollution protest in Shifang, Sichuan province (Branigan 2012), for instance, was openly discussed on Weibo but restricted in traditional media. Similar dynamics have been notable in recent years, with major incidents such as the 2015 Shenzhen landslide and the 2015 Kunming terrorist attack widely discussed online but censored in traditional media.[7]

Other than online popularity, Chinese interviewees connect censorship to local-level intrusions from officials who fear negative professional repercussions from media investigations. Journalists share that local officials try to inhibit their reporting by lobbying higher-level authorities to issue a censorship ban, as well as by bribing journalists, threatening them, and limiting their access in the field. An excerpt from an interview below details the dynamics of interactions with local-level officials:

> There have been times I would approach local officials and instead of accepting or declining my interview, they would report about my presence to local propaganda authorities, who in turn would complain to central authorities. A number of times my report was cut off as a result. (CJ52 2012)

While local propaganda authorities can't directly control the media outside their jurisdiction, they can complain to higher authorities, using the risk of social instability as an excuse to argue in favor of censorship. In addition, journalists report being offered bribes in the field and at times being physically harassed, detained, or even followed on the train to Beijing. While obviously unsetting and detrimental to their work, these negative encounters with local-level officials also expose journalists to the webs of political pressure that may stand behind an unexpected censorship ban.

The experience of Chinese journalists with arbitrary control suggests that the high level of destabilizing uncertainty also paradoxically comes with a degree of predictability or order. Chinese journalists experience routine signals that are fairly transparent (they all stem from Party and state agencies), and they are capable of finding patterns in state censorship fluctuations that can help explain or a shift or allow them to anticipate one. Of course, these signals can also be conflicting, with local officials often being more sensitive to media investigations than central authorities—but these conflicts are apparent to media professionals, and they take advantage of them to push boundaries, which will be explained in the second part of the chapter.

RUSSIA: OPERATING IN THE SHADOW OF ARBITRARY COERCION

In contrast to China, the distinctions between the red zone and the gray zone are less apparent for Russia's critical journalists. When asked about topics that are consistently off-limits, most struggle to immediately identify them. "We don't have topics we can't cover. We never censor ourselves, we pretty much say what we want," shared a senior journalist at *Novaya Gazeta* (RJ05 2010). Russian critical media probe into issues unimaginable for their Chinese counterparts, including investigations into Putin's wealth, critical discussions about Russia's authoritarianism, and coverage of opposition movements, among others. Most sensitive issues appear to fit into the gray zone, which occasionally gets readjusted by the state.

While generally less controlled than China's critical journalists, Russian journalists live in the shadow of a more arbitrary state. They receive few signals from the state, and what signals they do get come mostly in the aftermath of their reporting. Specifically, they find out about official dissatisfaction through reprimands from their owners, legal warnings and restrictions, and encounters with unexpected violence. These signals are indirect, are not easily traceable to a specific agency or individual, and appear to serve the purpose of scaring journalists and demonstrating to other, more mainstream media the risks of becoming too critical.

Interviewees stressed that post-factum political signals are often fused with economic ones, as media owners are often the ones restraining editors and journalists. With the exception of a very few outlets, such as *Novaya Gazeta* and the *New Times*, most liberal media are owned by oligarchs with direct linkages to the Kremlin. While generally adhering to a non-interference strategy, these owners occasionally reshuffle editorial positions or intimidate editors into leaving. After openly supporting the 2011 anti-Putin protests, for instance, a prominent editor at *Kommersant Vlast'* was forced to resign by the billionaire owner of the publication, Alisher Usmanov (Mauldin and Kolyandr 2011). In May 2016, Mikhail Prokhorov, another billionaire and a former presidential candidate, pressured the RBC Media Group editorial team into resigning, again as a way of pleasing the Kremlin (Greenslade 2016). Other than direct intimidations via owners, political retributions in economic form also manifest themselves via landlords and advertisers. For instance, Russia's only independent TV channel, TVRain, was forced to leave its production studio and move its operations into a private apartment after a landlord unexpectedly broke the lease (Dougherty 2015).

Post-factum legal pressure presents another form of political signaling. Specifically, journalists note anti-extremism legislation and corruption charges as instruments of media control. The anti-extremism laws, first enacted in 2012 and significantly expanded since then, are described by some interviewees as the new form of censorship, as explained by a long-time investigative reporter in Moscow:

> In the past, there was a real system of censorship, and now we have a legal framework, which allows to censor. Based on extremism, someone can be blamed for false accusations of political leaders and officials, and even for coverage of social protests. In reality, the anti-extremism legal framework works like censorship regime . . . not in terms of permitting but in terms of punishment [post-facto]. During Soviet times, your article would be scrutinized before the article comes out. . . . But now you write it first, and then you get pressured for it. (RJ11 2010)

A senior editor at the magazine *Kommersant Vlast'* further presents some specific examples of how these warnings are implemented, some seemingly predictable while others keep the editors guessing:

> One warning was for publishing an interview with a famous Ingush writer, who is very much respected there, one of his sons was murdered by Russians, and the other one is in jail . . . The magazine got a warning for spreading extremist statements. The second was about rocket troops [*roketnie voiska*], a typical report for us, based on open sources. This time the Ministry of Defense wrote to Rosnadzor that this is state secret, and Rosnadzor, without checking whether it's state secret, just sent us a warning automatically.[8] It's fairly serious to have two warnings because if the authorities believe it's important or necessary to shut us down, they

can take us to court. . . . It is entirely up to them. We didn't expect these warnings. When we had interview with Saakashvili we expected some reaction . . . but they had nothing to hold on to . . . so it's possible that these warnings were a response to the interview with Saakashvili. (RJ31 2000)

As explained by this interviewee, editors are informed that an anti-extremism law has been broken via warnings, two of which can result in closure of a news outlet. Though this rarely happens, the warnings create an atmosphere of uncertainty, whereby editors try to get to the roots of the warning or to calculate potential reactions to future sensitive reports, as will be explained later.

In 2016, anti-extremism legislation was expanded to include social media, which previously had been unaffected by these regulations (Freedom House 2016). In 2014, Grani.ru, a well-known liberal media site, was blocked after accusations of spreading extremism (Benyumov 2016). Later that year, a chief editor at Lenta.ru, another popular news site, was fired by the managing shareholder after receiving an extremism warning (Benyumov 2016). This legislation, therefore, has turned into a flexible tool for punishing individual journalists and entire media groups.

Other than anti-extremism legislation, Russian interviewees note arbitrary criminal charges as another legal punishment mechanism. Individual journalists and media activists have occasionally been singled out on fraudulent corruption charges. In 2007, for instance, Natalia Morar, a Bulgarian national working for the magazine *New Times*, was accused of posing a national security threat and refused entry into Russia, allegedly in retaliation for her investigation of Russian security services (Reporters Without Borders 2007). Manana Aslamazian, the head of Russia's branch of Internews, a leading media development organization, was accused of smuggling cash into Russia (Baldwin 2008). Most recently, corruption charges were also leveled against Russia's leading anti-corruption blogger and activist, Alexey Navalny, who was accused of stealing lumber (Ioffe 2017). These cases of trumped-up corruption charges are rarer than legal pressures but serve to demonstrate the infinite power of the state and the relative weakness of critical voices.

Finally, journalists working for the most risk-taking media outlets, such as *Novaya Gazeta* and the *New Times*, invoke the implicit physical threat as part of their professional reality:

> What was difficult to come to terms with is that every two to three years someone from our team is murdered. Of course, we try not to think of who is next. . . . You see photos of those murdered hanging in our office. When I get interns in the summer, I first show them these pictures and explain how and why they were murdered. Some get a bit frozen, but mostly they're quite OK. It's important for interns to understand this, because then I will be sure that they know the risks they're getting into. (RJ05 2010)

Novaya Gazeta has lost four journalists since 2001. Anna Politkovskaya, a fierce reporter who relentlessly investigated war crimes in Chechnya, is the most famous victim (Finn 2006). The Committee to Protect Journalists estimates a total of fifty-eight journalist murders since 1992, the majority of them reporters covering politics and corruption.[9] It is nearly impossible to directly trace or prove the state's involvement in these murders, but the climate of impunity exacerbates journalists' fears and suspicions.

In contrast to Chinese journalists, who receive routine and relatively transparent signals from different arms of the party-state, Russian journalists are largely left alone to navigate the risks of sensitive reporting. Signals are delivered post-factum and it is challenging to trace them to a particular source. In the minds of the journalists, they seem to be vaguely linked to official dissatisfaction at the highest echelons of power, but precisely where the signal originates from is hard to decipher. Moreover, unlike Chinese journalists who can discern some patterns in the maze of state censorship, Russian journalists are left guessing as to why a certain case was deemed as sensitive and why the punishment came when it did. While clearly enjoying a broader gray zone of semi-sensitive issues, Russian journalists are also operating in a more arbitrary environment, which leaves them with fewer negotiation strategies, as will be discussed in the following section. But first we return to China and the journalists' strategies of routine survival.

Part II: Reactions to Uncertainty: Negotiating the Gray Zone

CHINA: THE GAME OF ROUTINE SURVIVAL

The frequency and intensity of state signals bind China's media professionals in a game of routine negotiation with political pressures. Every story involves some degree of creative maneuvering, and Chinese journalists use a variety of strategies to stretch the boundaries of the gray zone.

Journalists navigate preemptive censorship by using social media to try to get to stories early, and by pursuing stories in other jurisdictions and undertaking cross-media collaborations to stave off pressures from local officials. Media professionals monitor social media and pay close attention to emerging hot topics and incidents, rushing to the scene before a censorship order is issued by media-regulating officials, who also closely monitor social media. This risk-taking was observed by the author throughout the 2000s as well as in the subsequent Xi era, which is known for its harsher media climate. Following the 2015 deadly Tianjin explosion, for instance, some investigative journalists reacted by instantly going for the story and worrying about the repercussions later. "The restrictions will come sooner or later, so we have to get a move on! Let the bans race against truth!" said one such journalist (Xiao 2015). The fact that nearly half the stories do make it into print suggests that journalists' opportunistic approach often pays off, allowing them to outpace the censors, at least temporarily.

Other than trying to win with speed, Chinese media professionals also play with different layers of restrictions by focusing on stories outside their jurisdiction. Since Chinese media is first and foremost overseen by local (or provincial) authorities, reporting is most sensitive within their respective regions. This sensitivity subsides as they move further from these political borders. This practice, known as *yidi jiandu*, has long characterized China's investigative reporting, and is fueled by cross-media collaborations. Journalists from local outlets, unable to report a story, would spill it to their colleagues at larger, more daring news outlets, such as *Caixin* magazine or *Nanfang Zhoumo*, which would then consider sending its reporters to investigate. "When conducting reporting, I established connections with journalists across China. Sometimes when a story breaks that they are banned from covering, they would get in touch and ask if I would be interested in it," shared a journalist from *Nanfang Zhoumo* (CJ46 2012). At times it is victims that get in touch with journalists and try to persuade them to write about them, and here too there is a cross-territorial dimension, whereby victims contact news outlets outside their own jurisdiction.

When asked whether *yidi jiandu* is still feasible in China amid a media crackdown, one interviewee responded, "If not that, then what would be left for us to investigate in China?" (CJ70 2017). This suggests that "going outward" is one of the remaining strategies that allow journalists to dance around censorship. A prominent example of a news outlet that has successfully been carrying out cross-territorial investigations under Xi is *Pengpai*, a Shanghai-based, state-funded digital media outlet that emerged in 2014. With news bureaus around China, *Pengpai* tackles issues from corruption to judicial governance in many locales, but Shanghai itself is mainly covered through a positive lens (Repnikova and Fang 2017).

When it comes to navigating post-factum censorship, journalists may attempt to soften official reactions by veiling negative stories in a constructive or hopeful tone. Interviewees reveal that they try to be constructive in their criticisms by drawing on official and expert voices, advocating solutions, and fusing a sense of hope into otherwise devastating stories. The following excerpt from an interview with a *Caixin* editor unravels the journalists' understanding of constructive critique:

> When we provide opinions and suggestions, we do so in an objective manner, including perspectives of scholars and officials. . . . If you criticize for the sake of criticizing, then of course, they will get very angry, and there is a higher risk of getting into trouble. (CJ25 2012)

Other studies that analyze the content of investigative reports demonstrate how the critical articles often express critique between the lines, carefully letting official voices channel the more controversial statements, and often concluding with solutions or steps taken to resolve a crisis and move forward (Repnikova 2017).

Journalists may also try to disseminate censored stories through social media platforms. At times the unpublished stories they share may even include editorial markings and comments. Following the 2012 fatal floods in Beijing, for instance, a *Nanfang Zhoumo* journalist used Weibo to leak an unpublished investigation into the number of victims (*China Digital Times* 2012). The posting was widely circulated online. More recently, journalists tend to share censored materials in WeChat circles, which are more private than the Weibo platform. Leaking is also often done via the help of netizens or social media users outside of the journalistic community. While censors can ban a news article, it often keeps circulating in other platforms until vanishing entirely.

Finally, in some cases a waiting strategy can work, whereby journalists wait for the sensitivity of a certain topic to subside before trying again to publish an in-depth story. "Censorship bans do not have official expiration dates; they are meant to be effective for extended periods of time . . . but their control capacity can slowly diminish, as time passes and the incident becomes less relevant," shared a journalist from *Nandu Zhoukan*, a Guangzhou-based magazine (CJ50 2012). What waiting it out means in practice is leaving the story aside until another opportunity presents itself. Considering that many breaking stories in China, such as those on protests, environmental and man-made disasters, and corruption, are on topics that will come up again in the future, journalists can at times use materials gathered earlier to present a more in-depth or systemic account of an issue at a later time. Such practices were observed by the author in the analysis of media investigations of mining disasters. *Caixin* magazine, for instance, made mining safety the topic of the year in 2004 and 2005 and published in-depth investigations drawing on many similar incidents (Repnikova 2017).

While this section presented a selective analysis of the core strategies journalists use to negotiate routine censorship, the actual tools can change depending on the context; the constant factor is the improvisation critical journalists use in their interactions with the state. The state's routine signaling leaves them with little choice but to trace the webs of these signals and try to buy a little time and space in the system. As can be seen in the analysis of these strategies, this negotiation takes place within the wide shadow of self-censorship. Self-censorship is an almost accepted practice, something inevitable if one wants to survive in the system. Journalists don't probe the red zone of forbidden topics and experiment mainly in the safer, gray zone of subjects not outlawed by the state. Much of their negotiation also takes the form of appeasement, whereby they try to protect the interests of their jurisdiction and largely align with central-level objectives of constructive critique and solutions-driven governance.

RUSSIA: A MIX OF FATALISM AND RESIGNED
SELF-CENSORSHIP

The post-factum nature of state signaling to critical journalists in Russia leaves them with little room for an instant creative response. When it comes to owners dismissing or reshuffling editorial teams, journalists can quit voluntarily or be forced to leave. In some cases, as with the RBC News (Vasilyeva 2017), editors resign collectively as a sign of protest, but even such symbolic gestures don't necessarily buy more space in the system or create new opportunities for re-sistance. Few Russian citizens come out in support of these strikes, and the incidents get quickly buried amid other news stories.

When journalists and media activists are falsely charged with corruption, there is little they can do, as the legal system is skewed in favor of the state, es-pecially when it comes to high-level targets. Neither Morar nor Aslamazyan, nor Navalny for that matter, has been able to brush off the unfair verdicts. The state may use anti-extremism legislation to issue warnings or close media outlets, and journalists are unable to get these decisions overturned; often they struggle to unravel the logic behind these unexpected punishments. In an echo of the post-factum pressures in the Chinese context, once a warning is issued, it mostly facilitates compliance, not pushback.

Finally, the physical violence is nearly impossible to negotiate. Beyond the mere physical harm, in some cases resulting in death, getting justice for the victims of such crimes is a challenge. Unpunished crimes against journalists are prevalent at all levels of the system. As the director of the Glasnost Fund, in charge of protecting freedom of speech in Russia, noted: "One of the key problems that our journalists face is the lack of punishment for abuse of their rights. . . . A journalist going from town A to town B is killed by a truck, seems like a normal crime, but it turns out he was carrying the latest circulation of an opposition newspaper to another region" (RSE03 2010). The chances of proving the real motive behind such crimes targeted at journalists remain very slim. Societal apathy further weakens any possibility for wider pressure on the state to address these crimes. As a former editor of *Itogi* magazine noted, "When repression happens against journalists, the question is not only why and how it happened, but that the public didn't side with journalists" (RJo9 2010). Similar to journalists' public resignations, their murders and physical assaults in Russia don't spur wide public outrage and are ignored or quickly forgotten.

Unable to routinely push back and actively engage with state authorities, Russian media professionals navigate the arbitrary state signals with a mix of determined fatalism and subtle self-censorship. On the one hand, Russian media practitioners engage in constant and perhaps even subconscious risk-taking as they face an unknown state reaction. Russian journalists express an almost fatalistic outlook when it comes to living in the shadow of an arbitrary state. As noted an editor at *Kommersant Vlast'*: "Our position is that while we can work, we will. . . . Do what you can, and what will be, will be" (RJ13 2010). Others similarly brush off future scenarios by enacting entrenched resistance or even political opposition. Some interviewees note that they are "forced to be doing that because of the changing circumstances" (RJ06 2010), referring to the political tightening under President Putin. Unlike Chinese journalists who consciously try to align with the state in order to reap some benefits, Russia's critical journalists survive the political uncertainty by adopting a mission of fighting the political status quo.

At the same time, while Russian media practitioners exhibit a certain discomfort at admitting that they might occasionally restrain themselves and are quick to denounce censorship, many express and practice caution indirectly. In interviews with Russian media professionals, self-censorship is veiled in discussions of stylistic limitations, journalistic indifference, security concerns, legal considerations, and preoccupations with maintaining relationships with sources. "There are some particular limits, accepted limits, not to be too aggressive, rude, etc. But we all understand that. It's more of a stylistic issue," noted a senior investigative journalist at *Novaya Gazeta* (RJ05 2010). In referring to limits as merely "stylistic," this interviewee distances himself from the practice of self-censorship, which he clearly opposes.

Another interviewee differentiates between self-censorship and conformism when it comes to the weakening of investigative journalism in Russia: "It's conformism because no one needs it, and you can come across real problems in doing so—it's the entrance into a zone that is very unpleasant and problematic" (RJ10 2010). When asked whether this constitutes a form of self-censorship, he continued to stress the distinction: "I would really say it's conformism—it's not self-censorship in a sense that people don't allow themselves to engage in it . . . they don't want to bother" (RJ10 2010). The concept of the problematic zone invoked in this interview echoes that of the gray zone in the Chinese context. In the Russian case, this interviewee suggests, journalists are not so much afraid to probe into sensitive issues as unwilling to take the risk. The line between the fear of repercussions and general apathy, however, is a slippery one, something that this interviewee leaves ambivalent.

The other way that self-regulation peeks through in Russian interviews is in discussions of security risks. "In the past few years, we don't write about Chechnya—the reason is our human losses, we lost six people. Not all six died because of their professional interests toward Chechnya, but four out of six did. This happened from 2000, in the past nine years," explained *Novaya Gazeta* editor (RJ02 2010). In referring to safety issues, this editor doesn't link the journalists' deaths with potential state involvement or even with the state's condoning of the growing climate of insecurity when it comes to investigating the Chechnya war. After all, Politkovskaya, a vocal critic of Putin's war in Chechnya, was gunned down outside the elevator in her apartment building in Moscow. While the editor primarily explains his decision in terms of journalists' safety, it could also be interpreted as soft self-censorship in reporting the Chechnya conflict.

Discussion of legal repercussions or considerations also alludes to editorial restraint. "Every time the topic is somewhat problematic, we have to think one thousand times and speak to lawyers about it. Once a week we discuss the possibility of libels," shared a former editor of *Russian Newsweek* (RJ12 2010). An editor at *Kommersant* specifically referred to cautiousness concerning articles about the former mayor, Yury Luzhkov: "You always have to keep in mind that Luzhkov would win any court decisions in Moscow and that he can criticize your every word. I read every story connected to Luzhkov much more carefully than others" (RJ01 2010). When asked whether this constitutes self-censorship, he agreed, but indirectly: "It's like in a city, some streets you can walk on anytime day and night . . . some streets you can walk around at night but have to be careful . . . and some streets you can't walk around at night at all. Luzhkov fits into the third category" (RJ01 2010).

Finally, self-censorship can be justified in terms of maintaining relationships with important sources. "The president's administration is very sensitive [*obitchivaia*]. Communists are fairly sensitive. . . . The key thing is about not ruining your sources . . . to maintain a balance between the ability to write something this time, and also to be able to return to this same source for more information at a later point. It's very easy to refuse a journalist's question in Russia," shared a *Kommersant* editor (RJ01 2010). The notion of building relationships came up in a number of interviews as something integral to conducting investigative journalism. This very objective is also implicitly tied to self-censorship when it comes to the scope of investigations.

To conclude, unlike China's media professionals, who use a palette of creative strategies to improvise on the spot when dealing with political pressure, Russian journalists are left with a limited arsenal in dealing with arbitrary postfactum signals from the state. For the most part, the punishments are nonnegotiable. In navigating this complex political climate, Russian journalists fuse fatalistic resistance with subtle self-censorship that is often masked in practical concerns and dismissed as voluntary forgoing of editorial freedom.

Discussion and Conclusions

This chapter presented a rare comparison of media-state relations under authoritarian rule through the prism of critical journalists in China and Russia. It demonstrated journalists' distinct experiences within the gray zone of political sensitivity, on the boundary of permissible reporting. It showed that whereas Chinese journalists experience more frequent preemptive signals from the state, Russian journalists must deal within a more arbitrary state that sends few but harsh post-factum signals. As a result, journalists' pushback or creative resistance also differs between the two cases. Chinese journalists embark on a routine game of cautious improvisation with the state, whereas Russian journalists are largely unable to negotiate political pressures, and in turn adopt a mixed strategy of defiant opposition and resigned self-censorship.

These findings hold implications for our thinking about China-Russia comparisons and about the manifestations of political ambivalence under authoritarianism. First, this analysis suggests that despite the overarching similarities in media politics between China and Russia and the growing overlaps in terms of media control, when it comes to managing the gray zone of critical voices, the two states adopt different approaches: the Chinese state takes a more proactive strategy, in contrast to the more reactive attitude of the Russian authorities. The Chinese state is more vigilant about and responsive to public opinion trends, and more active in engaging critical journalists in its effort at persuasion. Chinese regulators regularly issue directions to journalists about the latest fluctuations in the gray zone of semi-sensitive issues, censoring and guiding a lot of the content. The Russian state, in contrast, manages critical reporting by sending occasional, reactive signals in the aftermath of contentious reports, aimed more at instilling fear than at persuasion.

These different approaches might suggest that the Chinese state is more preoccupied with legitimizing its rule through engagement with public opinion, as it tries to co-opt critical voices into this mission. The Russian state, by contrast, sees critical voices not as allies but rather as insignificant players that can be kept in check with occasional interference. The apparent alignment of Chinese journalists with the party-state and the radicalizing opposition of Russian journalists vis-à-vis the system, however, suggests that while the Chinese approach is more resource-intensive, it might be more effective in the long run when it comes to stability maintenance.

Beyond China and Russia, the analysis in this chapter reveals different manifestations of political ambivalence as a governance tool in authoritarian contexts. Whereas uncertainty has long been considered a feature of authoritarian regimes, associated with fear and self-censorship, few studies have attempted to examine how political unpredictability plays out for actors testing the boundaries of the permissible. This chapter demonstrates that political ambivalence can take both a more structured form, as is the case in China, and a more amorphous form, as it does in Russia. The more structured ambiguity is more limiting when it comes to testing the boundaries, as journalists are capable of improvising only along the routes indirectly sanctioned by the state. The amorphous form of political ambiguity comes with fewer initial restrictions, allowing journalists to go as far as criticizing the entire system until they are abruptly stopped by unexpected, coercive measures from the top. More research is needed into the implications of these distinctions when it comes to the possibilities for larger political mobilization. The China-Russia comparison suggests that structured ambiguity breeds resistance from within, whereas arbitrary coercion incites more isolated but also more radically disposed political contestation. More comparative studies in authoritarian politics would help distill how these initial hypotheses apply to other contexts.

Notes

1. On restrictions on the independent press, see Jennifer Dunham, "Press Freedom's Dark Horizon," Freedom House 2017 Report, https://freedomhouse.org/report/freedom-press/freedom-press-2017. And political activism has seen renewed crackdowns in recent years under Xi and Putin. In particular, both regimes have restricted foreign funding for civil society organizations. On Russia, see Fred Weir, "Russia's Growing NGO Crackdown Turns to Environmental, Cultural Groups," *Christian Science Monitor,* June 10, 2013. On China, see Edward Wong, "Clampdown in China Restricts 7,000 Foreign Organizations," *New York Times,* April 28, 2016. In both cases, control rather than political liberalization has been the key feature of state governance in recent years.

2. The latest sign of convergence in online censorship is Russia following China in cracking down on virtual private networks (VPNs), which allow social media users to bypass domestic internet regulations and access the World Wide Web. See Lily Hay Newman, "The Attack on Global Privacy Leaves Few Places to Turn," *Wired,* August 4, 2017. Both countries also have tighter controls on foreign NGO funding and foreign NGO operations.

3. The selection of news outlets was done through preliminary fieldwork interviews with Chinese and Russia media experts, as well as readings of original materials, to determine which outlets have the best reputations for in-depth and investigative coverage at the national level. There are many local-level outlets, especially in Russia, that carry out some investigative reporting. In this comparison, however, the key focus was on the gray zone, or the very boundaries of what is permissible, at the national level.

4. This trend started to shift in 2013 with the decline of *Southern Weekend.* See Maria Repnikova and Kecheng Fang, "Behind the Fall of China's Greatest Newspaper," *Foreign Policy,* January 29, 2015. Shanghai has now started to emerge as the newest center for more critical media, as exemplified by *Pengpai.*

5. The WeChat platform is a social media application developed by Tencent. It allows for communication via circles of friends and colleagues, and it has become increasingly popular amid the recent crackdown on the Twitter-like Weibo platform. It has also been used as a tool for censorship and surveillance, however.

6. Few journalists expressed fear of imprisonment or even physical harassment as a possible outcome of their reporting. Most worried about losing the story, as well as potentially being forced out of their jobs if they are labeled as troublemakers. For more on the harsher measures, see Repnikova 2017.

7. These recent examples were shared via online correspondence with journalists at *Caixin* magazine, who have remained actively involved in investigative reporting in the Xi era.

8. Roskomnadzor, the Federal Service for Supervision of Communications, Information Technology and Mass Media, was reestablished in 2008, and it is responsible for passing down warnings to the media, as well as for creating lists of blocked sites based on their extremist content.

9. The Committee to Protect Journalists has a database of attacks on the press at https://cpj.org/data. See: https://cpj.org/europe/russia/

References

Baldwin, Chris. 2008. "Russian Court Throws Out NGO Smuggling Charges." Reuters, May 27.

Benyumov, Konstantin. 2016. "How Russia's Independent Media Was Dismantled Piece by Piece." *The Guardian*, May 25.

Brady, Anne-Marie. 2008. *Marketing Dictatorship: Propaganda and Thought Work in Contemporary China*. Lanham, MD: Rowman & Littlefield.

Branigan, Tania. 2012. "Anti-Pollution Protesters Halt Construction of Copper Plant in China." *The Guardian*, July 3.

Buckley, Chris. 2017. "Liu Xiaobo, Chinese Dissident Who Won Nobel While Jailed, Dies at 61." *New York Times*, July 13. https://www.nytimes.com/2017/07/13/world/asia/liu-xiaobo-dead.html?mcubz=3

Cairns, Christopher. 2016. "Prerequisites for Selective Censorship: Leaders' Evolving Beliefs and Bureaucratic Re-Centralization." PhD diss., Cornell University.

China Digital Times. 2012. "Beijing Flood Stories Cut from *Southern Weekend*." *China Digital Times*, July 26.

Creemers, Rogier. 2017. "Cyber China: Upgrading Propaganda, Public Opinion Work and Social Management for the Twenty First Century." *Journal of Contemporary China* 26, no. 103: 85–100.

Curry, Jane. 2010. "Revolutionary Reporting: The Media, Democratization, and Eastern Europe." *Harvard International Review* 32, no. 3: 53.

Deibert, Ronald, and Rafal Rohozinski. "Liberation vs. Control: The Future of Cyberspace." *Journal of Democracy* 21, no. 4: 43–57.

Dougherty, Jill. 2015. "How the Media Became One of Putin's Most Powerful Weapons." *The Atlantic*, April 21. http://www.theatlantic.com/international/archive/2015/04/how-the-media-became-putns-most-powerful-weapon/391062.

Finn, Peter. 2006. "Outspoken Putin Critic Shot Dead in Moscow." *Washington Post*, October 8.

Freedom House. 2016. "Freedom on the Net 2015: Russia Country Profile." https://freedomhouse.org/report/freedom-net/2016/russia.

Greenslade, Roy. 2016. "Three Russian Editors Resign amid Threats to Press Freedom." *The Guardian*, May 17.

Greitens, Sheena. 2013. "Authoritarianism Online: What Can We Learn from Internet Data in Nondemocracies?" *P.S. Political Science and Politics* 46, no. 2: 262–270.

Gunitsky, Seva. 2015. "Corrupting the Cyber-Commons: Social Media as a Tool of Autocratic Stability." *Perspectives on Politics* 13, no. 1: 42–54. doi:10.1017/S1537592714003120.

Han, Rongbin. 2015. "Manufacturing Consent in Cyberspace: China's 'Fifty-Cent Army.'" *Journal of Current Chinese Affairs* 44, no. 2: 105–134.

Howard, Philip N., Sheetal D. Agarwal, and Muzammil M. Hussain. 2011. "The Dictators' Digital Dilemma: When Do States Disconnect Their Digital Networks?" *Issues in Technology Innovation* no. 13, Brookings Institution, October.

Huntington, Samuel P. 1989. *The Clash of Civilizations and the Remaking of World Order*. New York: Simon & Schuster.

Ioffe, Julia. 2017. "Another Day in Court for Alexey Navalny." *The Atlantic*, February 8.

King, Gary, Jennifer Pan, and Margaret Roberts. 2013. "How Censorship in China Allows Government Criticism but Silences Collective Expression." *American Political Science Review* 107, no. 2: 1–18.

Lerner, Daniel, and David Riesman. 1965. *The Passing of Traditional Society: Modernizing the Middle East.* New York: Free Press.

Lipman, Maria. 2010. "Freedom of Expression Without Freedom of the Press." *Journal of International Affairs* 64, no. 2: 153–169.

Lipman, Masha, and Michael McFaul. 2001. "'Managed Democracy' in Russia: Putin and the Press." *Harvard International Journal of Press/Politics* 6, no. 3: 116–127.

MacKinnon, Rebecca. 2011. "China's 'Networked Authoritarianism.'" *Journal of Democracy* 22, no. 2: 32–46.

Mauldin, William, and Alexander Kolyandr. 2011. "Moscow Editor Fired over Coverage of Putin." *Wall Street Journal*, December 14.

McNair, Brian. 1991. *Glasnost, Perestroika and the Soviet Media.* London: Routledge.

Oates, Sarah. 2013. *Revolution Stalled: The Political Limits of the Internet in the Post-Soviet Sphere.* New York: Oxford University Press.

Parker, Emily, and April Glaser. 2017. "Russia Is Trying to Copy China's Approach to Internet Censorship." *Slate*, April 4. http://www.slate.com/articles/technology/future_tense/2017/04/russia_is_trying_to_copy_china_s_internet_censorship.html.

Rawnsley, Gary D., and Ming-Yeh T. Rawnsley. 1998. "Regime Transition and the Media in Taiwan." *Democratization* 5, no. 2: 106–124.

Repnikova, Maria. 2017. *Media Politics in China: Improvising Power Under Authoritarianism.* Cambridge: Cambridge University Press.

Repnikova, Maria, and Kecheng Fang. 2017. "From Economic to Social Media Experiments: The Tensions of Fragmented Authoritarianism." Paper presented at the Annual Meeting of the Association for Asian Studies, March 17.

Reporters Without Borders. 2007. "Reporter Who Wrote About Kremlin Slush Fund Banned from Reentering Russia." December 18. http://archives.rsf.org/article.php3?id_article=24793.

Roth, Andrew. 2015. "Russia and China Sign Cooperation Pacts." *New York Times*, May 8.

Shi, Ting. 2017. "Here's a Window into How Xi Has Reshaped China." *Bloomberg*, June 18.

Stern, Rachel E. 2014. *Environmental Litigation in China: A Study in Political Ambivalence.* Cambridge: Cambridge University Press.

Stockmann, Daniela. 2012. *Media Commercialization and Authoritarian Rule in China.* New York: Cambridge University Press.

Vasilyeva, Nataliya. 2016. "3 Top Editors Resign from Top Russian Media Firm RBC." *Business Insider*, May 13.

Walker, Shaun. 2015. "Salutin' Putin: Inside a Russian Troll House." *The Guardian*, April 2.

Walker, Shaun. 2017. "Putin Critic Alexei Navalny Jailed After Calling for Moscow Protests." *The Guardian*, June 12.

Xiao, Han. 2015. "Chinese Media and the Tianjin Disaster." China Media Project, August 20. http://cmp.hku.hk/2015/08/20/39159.

Yang, Guobin. 2009. *The Power of the Internet in China: Citizen Activism Online.* New York: Columbia University Press.

Zhao, Yuezhi. 2000. "Watchdogs on Party Leashes? Contexts and Implications of Investigative Journalism in Post-Deng China." *Journalism Studies* 1, no. 4: 577–597.

6 }

How Russian Media Control, Manipulate, and Leverage Public Discontent

FRAMING PROTEST IN AUTOCRACIES

Tomila Lankina, Kohei Watanabe, and Yulia Netesova

The capacity of present-day authoritarian rulers to weather social discontent and to enjoy phenomenally high levels of citizen adulation has often baffled scholars.[1] Increasingly, scholars are recognizing that autocrats are not im- mune to accountability mechanisms, as is evident in such leaders' concerns about generating economic growth, securing order and stability and other legitimacy-enhancing measures (see Chapters 1, 8, 9, and 11 in this volume, and Tertytchnaya and Lankina 2019). To explain the dynamics of popular endorsement for authoritarian leaders—or, conversely, citizens' willingness to press for alternatives through protest—social scientists are increasingly turning to an analysis of how non-democratic rulers manipulate modern forms of communication (Enikolopov, Petrova, and Zhuravskaya 2011; White, Oates, and McAllister 2005; Oates 2006; Mickiewicz 2008; Toepfl 2013; Rød and Weidmann 2015; Treisman and Guriev 2015). Yet despite the growing awareness of the media's significance in authoritarian rulers' survival tool kit, there is little scholarly agreement on the exact strategies that rulers will em- ploy in manipulating information on mass discontent. Two sets of interrelated questions in particular have been subjects of debate in emerging theorizing on the role of state media in manipulating protest in autocracies. The first set of questions relates to state control of information on rallies. Will rulers seek to uniformly suppress any information that signals the willingness of citizens to organize (King, Pan, and Roberts 2013)? Or will they selectively allow in- formation on some popular protests to enter into the public domain, while suppressing news on other protests (Dimitrov 2008; Hutchings and Tolz 2015;

Treisman and Guriev 2015)? The second set of questions relates to the nature of manipulation of information on protests. Will authoritarian regimes stigmatize all protests because they are perceived to be inherently threatening and destabilizing? Or will state media strategically tailor their framing depending on the protesters' targets and grievances? Arguably, anti-regime protests would be one straightforward type of protest warranting negative media coverage. Conversely, following Jessica Chen Weiss (2013, 2), we also conjecture that some mass organized or spontaneous street acts—for instance, nationalist rallies or riots—may well have some perceived utility to the regime and therefore may be presented in a relatively positive light.

To address these theoretically important and policy-relevant questions, we borrow insights on issue framing from the rich literature on Western social movements (Snow and Benford 1992; Snow et al. 1986) to analyze media manipulation of news on protest in Russia. Specifically, we analyze coverage of protest during the 2011–2013 protest cycle, during which occurred protests that were unprecedented in scale, only to be followed by state repression, political demobilization, and a significant reduction in political anti-regime protest activity.

We rely on a content analysis method called Latent Semantic Scaling (LSS) developed by Watanabe (Lankina and Watanabe 2017). Applying the LSS technique, we constructed a Russian-language dictionary of words frequently appearing in stories about protests. The dictionary construction process involved assigning scores along a *disorder–freedom to protest* scale to lines of text in randomly selected batches of news stories on protest. Because this process involved both human coding and electronic analysis, it is known as "supervised machine learning." The dictionary could be applied to perform electronic content analysis of large volumes of news stories so as to explore shifts over time in the media's framing of protest.

For our analysis, we gathered time series data for six leading state-controlled television channels and newspapers spanning the years 2011–2013. We also harvested stories from sources that fall outside of state control. The stories are sourced from the Russian media database Integrum. We find that around December 2011–February 2012, corresponding to the relatively liberal political environment associated with the presidency of Dmitriy Medvedev, the state-controlled media produced large volumes of news stories on anti-regime protest. Although when protests first erupted in December 2011 media coverage tended to adopt a critical frame toward protesters, the state-controlled outlets quickly switched gears, employing a *freedom to protest* frame, covering protests in a relatively sympathetic way. In the weeks following the reelection of Vladimir Putin to his third presidential term on March 4, 2012—during which time the protests showed no sign of abating—we observe a drop in the volume of coverage of anti-regime contention and a significant shift toward the *disorder* framing of street activism. We also find a news burst that essentially consists of manufactured stories of protests that portray anti-regime protesters in a negative light. This trend contrasts sharply with coverage of the October 2013 Russian nationalist rallies in a Moscow suburb. These events also received a significant amount of attention in state media. Although they degenerated into right-wing extremist-fueled violence, vandalism of public property, and arrests of hundreds of rioters, we do not observe a significant tendency of the most widely watched state TV channels to resort to the *disorder* framing of those events.

This chapter is structured as follows. In the first section, we discuss the literature on media control and framing of protest in authoritarian states and generate hypotheses for our study. In the second section, we discuss our data and methodological tool kit. In the third section, we perform quantitative analysis of our data and supplement it with qualitative analysis of news stories. The final section concludes with a summary of findings and a discussion of the wider comparative implications of our work.

Analytical Framework

Scholars are increasingly recognizing that state-controlled media represent an important weapon in the "resilience-building" strategies of authoritarian rulers (Dimitrov 2008; Gehlbach and Sonin 2014). Protests—defined here as gatherings of citizens in public spaces with the aim of articulating particular demands—are beginning to feature prominently in this literature (Lorentzen 2013; King, Pan, and Roberts 2013; Weiss 2013).

Precisely how, then, do autocracies use the media to pursue those objectives? Two interrelated sets of tactics that apply to the media generally and protest coverage in particular could be discerned in the literature. For the sake of analytical clarity, we label these tactics *control* and *manipulation*. The tactics of control would encompass straightforward old-fashioned censorship; self-censorship, in which coercion is unnecessary because journalists are aware of the bounds of what is permissible; co-optation; repression; and harassment of journalists, all with the aim of controlling the flow of information on anti-regime protests. Evidence of such tactics would be lack of media coverage or limited diversity of media content.

At the same time, empirical scholarship from autocracies with political institutional, regime, and media contexts as varied as those of China, Egypt, and Russia has highlighted that such straightforward techniques of blocking coverage of particular events could be counterproductive—and the rulers recognize this. It is true that even in a controlled media environment, citizens often regard state media as trustworthy (Truex 2014), even when they find themselves selectively filtering out information perceived to be biased (Mickiewicz 2006). Surveys have revealed that in present-day Russia state-run television remains "one of the most trusted and authoritative institutions in the country" (Smyth and Oates 2015, 289). Yet the media landscapes in present-day autocracies are also considerably more complex than they were several decades ago, before the advent of the internet and social media (Smyth and Oates 2015; Hassid 2008; Egorov, Guriev, and Sonin 2009; Hamdy and Gomaa 2012; Gehlbach and Sonin 2014). Globalization has increased the porousness of domestic information spaces. As Mark Beissinger comments in Chapter 12 in this volume, "In both countries [Russia and China] citizens are potentially exposed to foreign information in ways that were absolutely unthinkable in earlier Russian and Chinese regimes." In what Maria Repnikova (Chapter 7) aptly terms the phenomenon of "semi-controlled spaces," authoritarian rulers recognize that to keep viewers' and readers' attention and to discourage citizens from turning to independent media, the information projected on state television screens or in newspapers has to reflect political reality at least to some extent—including when it comes to covering social discontent (Jones-Rooy 2012; Klein 2012; Stockmann and Gallagher 2011; Gehlbach and Sonin 2014). Autocrats also do not see contentious news as something that is inherently to be subjected to stringent controls, for it could provide a source of useful resilience-building material. As Bunce, Koesel, and Weiss write in Chapter 1, "autocrats depend on the public . . . for good information," and information on public discontent specifically may reveal underlying sources of grievances, which autocrats could seek to address to hold on to power. "Bad information," they write, "means bad decisions, which contribute to a decline over time in the regime's performance." News coverage of contentious issues may also reflect the peculiarities of bureaucratic decision-making by news agencies. As Hutchings and Tolz (2015) argue in their analysis of news coverage by Russia's leading TV anchors, these individuals are not puppets slavishly carrying out precise regime instructions about how to cover political events. Significant agency is present in their day-to-day decisions. The regime may be also caught unawares by particular events, and journalists may enjoy a significant degree of freedom in fashioning narratives describing these events. That said, when it comes to events of key national significance—as would be the case, for instance, with Russia's annexation of Crimea—the analysis performed by Lankina and Watanabe (2017) indicates that we would expect the regime to tighten the screws regarding the scope and framing of news coverage. Although, as Maria Repnikova points out in Chapter 5, significant differences are observed between Russia and China in that China's journalists receive far clearer instructions about red lines than do their Russian counterparts, we would expect Russian state-controlled media's news coverage of pivotal and highly politically sensitive events to exhibit greater similarity to the Chinese model in terms of greater levels of control over the media in their coverage of these events. Whatever the nuances of the environments in which the media operate, Russia-China comparisons and analyses of other autocracies reveal that present-day non-democratic regimes have tended to combine media control with news coverage somewhat more characteristic of democratic settings, where the media are often biased but in more subtle ways than would be the case with the projection of crude ideology-driven propaganda or outright blockage of undesirable information (Iyengar and Kinder 1987; Jones-Rooy 2012). We refer to these tactics as *manipulation*.

A useful concept for capturing the subtleties of manipulation of information on protest is issue framing. Frame analysis was originally popularized in sociology by Erving Goffman (Goffman 1975; Noakes and Johnston 2005), and it has been widely employed in social movement scholarship in western settings. Nelson, Clawson, and Oxley (1997, 567) define framing as a "process by which a communication source such as a news organization, defines and constructs a political issue or public controversy." According to one classic formulation, the objective of framing is "selecting and highlighting some faces of events or issues, and making connections among them so as to promote a particular interpretation, evaluation and/or solution" (Entman 2004, 5). Implicit in the concept is the instrumental nature of the mechanism of framing by both movement leaders and the state (Snow and Benford 1992; Snow et al. 1986; Gamson and Meyer 1996; Zald 1992; Peng 2008; Cottle 2008).

Even in Western contexts, where data are far easier to come by, frame analysis is plagued by issues of causal inference, considering the difficulties of ascertaining the effects of framing—as opposed to a variety of other variables that may be at play—on public opinion formation. Nevertheless, a small number of studies have demonstrated the utility of empirical applications of framing to study manipulation of news on protests in autocracies (Hamdy and Gomaa 2012; Lankina and Watanabe 2017).

Following Nelson, Clawson, and Oxley (1997), we distinguish between two broad shades of media framing of protest: protest as public disorder (the *disorder* frame) and protest as representing citizens' democratic right (the *freedom to protest* frame). These frames could be regarded as representing extremes on a scale of framing that at one end stigmatizes protest and, at the other, endorses it as something legitimate and even desirable in an open society. In what has been described as the "protest paradigm," even in democracies the media often tend to employ a "status quo" perspective (McLeod and Detenber 1999), subtly delegitimizing protest (Smith et al. 2001; Deluca, Lawson, and Sun 2012). At the same time, politicians and the media often have an incentive to portray particular rallies in a more positive light because of the ideological convictions or political orientations of a particular media outlet; due to the nature of the causes pursued in protests; or for other reasons specific to the political context in which the event occurs (Nelson, Clawson, and Oxley 1997). Where coverage is located on the scale could also convey information about attempts to ascribe legitimacy, whether to protesters' demands, to the authorities being targeted, or to the protesters themselves. The semantics of coverage could convey regime responsiveness to public demands, as when these demands are presented in a positive light. Finally, there may be a time lag in the reaction and learning effect of specific events. State leaders may be caught unawares by the magnitude of some protests; internal divisions may emerge among the inner circle of rulers as to how to respond. The hesitation and wavering in responses could provide journalists with greater freedom in pursuing particular narratives or, alternatively, with greater room for inferring how the regime would like the journalists to respond (Hutchings and Tolz 2015).

Yet we still know little about the conditions under which state media are more or less likely to apply a particular frame. Protests are in fact a routine occurrence in non-democratic countries (Lankina and Voznaya 2015; Robertson 2013). Logically, we would expect the nature of the events themselves and protesters' demands to influence ruler propensity to deploy a particular frame, not least because they shape the perception of threats to the regime. We label this aspect of protest framing the *issue* dimension of protest coverage.

Although we are seeing outlines of comparative theorizing on how protest issues might influence state media strategies in autocracies, scholars have come up with widely diverging assumptions and expectations. King, Pan, and Roberts (2013) distinguish between the "state critique" and the "mobilization potential" theories of autocratic responses to protest. While the state critique theory predicts that autocrats are wary of citizen criticisms of the state, the mobilization potential theory predicts that autocrats are far more fearful of signals that citizens are capable of organizing to protest—even if protests feature such "diffuse" targets as local authorities, ethnic minority communities, or private businesses. An objection to these assumptions is that state critique—including that articulated in citizen protests—can provide the regime with important information; it is thus not a given that all forms of citizen discontent will be controlled or manipulated in media coverage (Egorov, Guriev, and Sonin 2009; Chen 2012; Jones-Rooy 2012; Stockmann and Gallagher 2011; Lorentzen 2013; Nathan 2003; Dimitrov 2008). Autocrats may also find utility in some types of protests that show evidence of citizen anger being channeled toward non-regime targets. Nationalist protests in particular have featured prominently in these debates (Dimitrov 2008; Morozov 2012; King, Pan, and Roberts 2013; Hutchings and Tolz 2015). In this volume, Diana Fu and Greg Distelhorst (Chapter 3) provide a useful distinction between contentious and institutionalized routes of articulation of grievances. Their analysis of China's treatment of citizen participation reveals that various types of activism produce distinct state responses, with the regime in particular showing greater tolerance for institutionalized forms of participation (see also Chapter 8, by Manfred Elfstrom).

Finally, we expect that media control and manipulation of protest would reflect an element of learning on the part of rulers. Fearful of a rising tide of political protests, the government may tacitly endorse, or fail to explicitly condemn, other events with a very different set of targets, in order to show that it is being responsive to the public mood. Or previous citizen mobilization—whatever the goals—may instill in autocrats fear of wider implications for citizen capacity to organize and mount collective action of a political kind in the future. Indeed, "diffusion-proofing" transcends responses to national discontent. As Karrie Koesel and Valerie Bunce point out in Chapter 4, the tactical domestic adaptations of Putin in Russia and Xi in China in the aftermath of external color revolutions and the Arab Spring protests illustrate that autocracies are sensitive to, and seek to preempt the repetition in their own countries of, the scenarios of uprisings in contexts that may be geographically far removed. Elizabeth Plantan (Chapter 7) discusses how the manipulation of legal and institutional landscapes in which NGOs operate in both China and Russia—and that includes foreign-funded media agencies or news outlets—represents one such mechanism designed to preemptively deter citizen activism. Ultimately, it is the capacity for tactical shifts in media responses given the information about past, ongoing, and new popular challenges to the regime at home and to fellow autocrats abroad that may well contribute to "authoritarian resilience." Alternatively, the peculiarities of protest framing could reveal important regime vulnerabilities that may be obscured by apparent invincibility to discontent.

HYPOTHESES

We now formulate general hypotheses that will be tested in our media analysis: (H1) Large-scale anti-regime political protests will lead the media to frame them in terms of *disorder* (media manipulation). (H2) The imposition of media control of coverage of protests will occur with a time lag after the eruption of a large-scale protest event (*learning effect*).

Because of disagreements among scholars about precisely how autocrats will respond to protests that do not have the regime as its key target, we formulate our third and fourth hypotheses as follows: (H3) Large-scale protests with non-regime key targets are more likely to be framed in the media in terms of *disorder*. Alternatively: (H4) Large-scale protests with non-regime key targets are less likely to be framed in the media in terms of *disorder*.

Empirical Analysis

MEDIA SOURCES

Our sample is drawn from newspapers and television channels, traditional media that are widely consumed in Russia despite the growth of online media platforms. Although analyzing regime narratives on protest in social media and discussion forums—for instance, relying on trolls and fake news—would provide valuable supplementary information about media manipulation techniques, it is beyond the scope of our study.

The newspapers included in our analysis are *Rossiyskaya Gazeta, Izvestiya,* and *Komsomolskaya Pravda. Rossiyskaya Gazeta* is a daily fully owned by the Russian government.[2] It adheres to a formal writing style and features state laws, directives and official announcements in addition to political commentary and news. Russia's state agencies tend to have a subscription to *Rossiyskaya Gazeta.* Our second newspaper, *Izvestiya,* is also a daily newspaper, with a large readership. First printed in 1917 as one of the main official Soviet newspapers, it was privatized in the early 1990s (Jones 2002). It is now owned by the National Media Group Company, which also has a 25 percent stake in Channel 1.[3] *Izvestiya* became known for aggressive pro-Kremlin news coverage in particular after the winter 2011–2012 anti-government protests in Russia. The daily *Komsomolskaya Pravda* is a tabloid-style source owned by the ESN Group, which belongs to Grigory Berezkin, who is a board member of a number of state corporations, notably Russian railroads.[4] All of the newspapers have online versions.

Television has been a key source of information for many Russians, particularly as print newspaper circulation dwindled in the 1990s (Nelson, Orttung, and Livshen 2015; Cottiero et al. 2015; Smaele 2010; Akhterov 2011; McNair 2000; Mickiewicz 2008; Smyth and Oates 2015; Oates 2006; Enikolopov, Petrova, and Zhuravskaya 2011). For our analysis, we selected three leading state TV channels: Russia 1, Channel 1, and NTV. Russia 1 is fully state owned and forms part of the All-Russian State Television and Broadcasting Company (VGTRK) group.[5] Channel 1 is regarded as Russia's leading TV channel. The Russian state owns a majority 51 percent stake in the company, while the closed joint stock company National Media Group owns 25 percent and the Kremlin-friendly oligarch Roman Abramovich owns a 24 percent stake.[6] NTV is owned by Gazprom Media and is widely regarded as a Kremlin-controlled outlet.[7]

We also selected three sources that fall outside of Kremlin control in the period under investigation in this chapter: Rosbalt, Interfax, *Novaya Gazeta,* and Namarsh.ru.[8] Coverage of protest by the news agencies Rosbalt and Interfax is included to control for the nature of the event in our framing and keyword analyses. Because these sources often reproduce material broadcast in state-controlled sources, we cannot treat them as fully reliable benchmarks against which to compare media control and manipulation in the Kremlin-controlled sources. For those latter purposes, we employ *Novaya Gazeta* and Namarsh.ru. Rosbalt is generally known to provide relatively impartial political news coverage, though it is also not known to be associated with Russia's political opposition. Nevertheless, similar to other media sources that fall outside of Kremlin control, Rosbalt was subjected to state-sponsored harassment.[9] Interfax is a non-governmental media agency that is likewise considered to be a source of comparatively balanced media coverage (Boyd-Barrett 2014). Like Rosbalt, it is not a source associated with Russia's political opposition or one preoccupied with exposing corruption in the echelons of power. By contrast, *Novaya Gazeta* is an online newspaper that not only is widely regarded as a source of independent news but also is known for investigative reporting on Russian politics and for staunch criticism of the regime. Our third source of independent coverage of protest, Namarsh.ru, is a web platform exclusively dedicated to reporting protests occurring across Russia, set up by the political opposition activist and chess champion Garry Kasparov. Although it is known to be of liberal-leaning orientation and so may underreport forms of labor activism such as strikes (Robertson 2011), Namarsh.ru is regarded as one of the most systematic sources of data on Russia's protest activism. Because Namarsh.ru is almost exclusively dedicated to the coverage of protest, in contrast to the other, mainstream sources employed in our analysis, it provides us with additional baseline data against which to compare coverage of protests by other sources, both state and non-state.

DATA COLLECTION

For our electronic content analysis of news stories, we harvested TV transcripts and newspaper articles from the Integrum Russian news database by employing the search term "protest*" (протест*). Where online editions of the news sources were available in the database, they were also downloaded but stored separately from the print or broadcast editions. The total number of news stories downloaded for the period January 1, 2011, to December 31, 2013, is 31,068. We present a breakdown of the figure in Table 6.1. The number of TV transcripts for Channel 1 is small because its broadcast edition is available only from July 31, 2012. We are, however, able to use online news as a proxy for news coverage for the earlier months considering that there is little difference

TABLE 6.1 } Number of media news stories downloaded

	Newspaper	TV	Online	Newswire
Izvestiya	1,315	-	3,650	-
Komsomolskaya pravda	1,605	-	5,496	-
Rossiyskaya gazeta	1,682	-	0	-
Channel 1	-	840	2,342	-
NTV	-	3,180	4,035	-
Russia 1	-	4,386	0	-
Rosbalt	-	-	-	6,097
Interfax	-	-	-	9,460
Novaya gazeta	-	-	1,584	-
Namarsh.ru	-	-	953	-
Total	4,602	8,406	18,060	15,557

between online and offline editions in that period. (We discuss the similarities between online and broadcast content in Supplementary Appendix 1 [SA 1]). We excluded stories about protests in other countries by employing a geographic classifier developed by Watanabe (2018). The classifier ensures that at least 90 percent of protest material analyzed covers Russian protests. (Details are contained in SA 2).

Since our corpus of 7,689 full-text news stories is still too large for in-depth text analysis by humans, and considering that human coders are less capable of coding documents spanning three years highly consistently, we performed dictionary-based content analysis by constructing a *disorder-freedom to protest* framing dictionary from scratch. The dictionary construction technique that we use, which was developed by Kohei Watanabe and which is based on work by Peter Turney and Michael Littman (Turney and Littman 2003), is called Latent Semantic Scaling (LSS). LSS enables the construction of domain-specific dictionaries for content analysis from corpora with either manually chosen exemplary words (seed words) or human-coded documents that are then used in machine content analysis (Lankina and Watanabe 2017). In the machine content analysis, the computer program "learns" what news stories should be given low or high scores on a particular topic of interest (in our case, protest) based on scores assigned to randomly selected batches of news stories by human coders. This process is known as supervised machine learning. We adopted the supervised approach in dictionary making because of the challenges of identifying seed words representing the social disorder and freedom dimensions of framing. Further details on the dictionary construction process are provided in SA 3 and SA 4.

STATISTICAL ANALYSIS

MEDIA CONTROL

We begin by obtaining numbers of news stories published within seven-day periods by the state-controlled news sources in order to identify key episodes of popular protest in Russia in the period 2011–2013. Analyzing what protests received substantial coverage and how the coverage of similar events varied over time would in turn help us ascertain whether state-controlled media restrict—that is, control—the coverage of particular events depending on the issue dimension of street contention. Figure 6.1 allows us to see distinctive spikes of news coverage during that period, from which we selected the four largest bursts of news about popular protests for our analysis.

The first news burst falls on December 8, 2011 (S1), the period immediately following the December 5, 2011, parliamentary elections that were widely

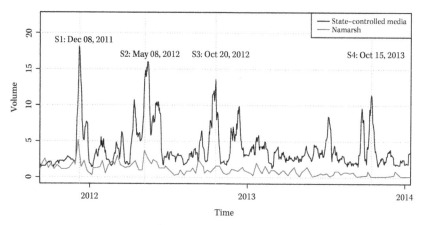

FIGURE 6.1 7-Day Moving Average, Volume of News on Protests

condemned as fraudulent. Fueling protests was also the announcement by President Dmitry Medvedev in October 2011 that Vladimir Putin would contest the March 2012 presidential elections. The announcement angered many Russians in that it signaled a potential end to Medvedev's political reforms. Although analysts doubted the depth of Medvedev's commitment to liberal democracy, he pursued a range of popular initiatives, including allowing for a relatively permissive environment for street activism (Gel'man 2013).

The second period (S2), around May 8, 2012, centers on mass protests that followed the reelection of Vladimir Putin. The protest, which the opposition termed "March of the Millions" and which took place in Moscow on the eve of the presidential inauguration, featured skirmishes between some protesters and the police. These events came to be known as the "Bolotnaya disturbances," named after the square toward which the protesters were heading. Both the opposition activists and police accused the other party of instigating clashes. Some four hundred activists were arrested following the Bolotnaya protests and several have been given prison sentences.

The third news burst (S3) corresponds to October 20, 2012, following the state media's allegations that the opposition was conspiring to overthrow the regime. The allegations were initially aired on October 5, 2012, in the *Anatomiya protesta—2* (The anatomy of protest—2) television documentary on NTV.[10] The documentary "exposed" the reportedly externally funded plot of the leader of the opposition Left Front movement, Sergey Udal'tsov, to provoke disorder in the country. The claims were based on supposed eavesdropping on Udal'tsov's conversation with an "emissary" of Mikhail Saakashvili, who, as the leader of Georgia's color evolution, was now allegedly supporting a plot to unseat Putin. The claims were then widely reproduced across Russia's state-controlled media outlets and served as a basis for arrests and persecution of anti-regime activists.

The fourth news burst (S4) falls on October 15, 2013, and coincides with media coverage of nationalist rallies and riots following the murder on October 10 of a young Russian man, Yegor Shcherbakov. Shcherbakov had been knifed to death allegedly by a trader from Azerbaijan when he was walking with his girlfriend past a vegetable market and trade warehouse in Biryulyovo, a suburb of Moscow known for its large concentration of migrant workers. Following the murder, what began as a peaceful protest gathering of a handful of distressed neighborhood residents degenerated into violence and vandalism involving hundreds of soccer hooligans, Russia's neo-Nazi groups, and ordinary citizens. Many of the rioters—over 450 were arrested on October 14 (Fitzpatrick 2013)—were promptly released.

We found the highest number of news stories in S1: 207 stories on protest appeared in our state-controlled sources during a period of two weeks before and after the date when the large spike in coverage was observed. The second-largest volume of news coverage is in the S2 cluster, with 210 news stories. The S3 and S4 news clusters feature fewer stories; there are 167 and 129 stories in the S3 and S4 clusters, respectively. Overall, we do not find evidence that state-controlled media refrained from covering the large-scale anti-regime protests that occurred in the winter and spring of 2011–2012; or, as the coverage of the Biryulyovo events (S4) indicates, that it shied away from covering other protests and disturbances—what we refer to as the control of the media's response to public discontent.

Nonetheless, there is a possibility that important anti-regime protest events are not covered in our dataset of regime-controlled media stories. To evaluate this possibility, we collected all the articles that mention protests and that are harvested by Namarsh.ru (red line, Figure 6.1) during the period of investigation. We assume that Namarsh.ru is unlikely to refrain from covering anti-regime or other large-scale protest events. We can confirm based on these alternative data that there is no surge in the number of stories on protest other than in the periods covered by clusters obtained by analyzing state media coverage of protest.

TABLE 6.2 } Characteristics of clusters

	Date of news spike	Issues	Regime as key target	Size of cluster
S1	8 December 2011	Duma election	Yes	568
S2	8 May 2012	Presidential election	Yes	595
S3	20 October 2012	Allegations of planned mass protests and disturbances aimed at dislodging the regime; trials of activists engaged in past protests and "plotters" of future rallies	Allegations of planned protests targeting the regime	408
S4	15 October 2013	Migration/immigration/non-Russian minorities	No	295

MEDIA MANIPULATION

We now turn to analyzing variations in the semantic nuances of the coverage of protest in state-controlled media sources, which would also help us ascertain whether the regime's manipulation strategies vary depending on the issues of protest. In our computerized content analysis, we coded all news stories on protests on a scale of *disorder* versus *freedom to protest* employing our author-constructed dictionary. Higher values on the score indicate a greater tendency to employ a *freedom to protest* frame, while lower values on the score indicate a tendency toward employing a *disorder* frame. Figure 6.2 provides a visual illustration of the observed variations in framing scores in all the articles in our corpus of state-controlled news in 2011–2013; each circle in the figure indicates framing scores of individual articles. The local regression line is clearly showing a shift toward the *freedom to protest* frame between S1 and S2, and a sharp drop in the direction of the *disorder* frame between S2 and S3; following S3, there is a gradual upward shift in the direction of the *freedom to protest* frame until S4; after S4, we do not observe a dip in the direction of the *disorder* frame. Furthermore, we observe significant variation in news coverage in S3 and S4. Specifically, S4 (the period corresponding to the Biryulyovo riots) is significantly less likely to feature a *disorder* frame compared to S3 (the spike in news corresponding to "exposure" of alleged plots to stage anti-regime protests and disturbances).

A more direct comparison of the S1, S2, S3, and S4 clusters is presented as a box plot in Figure 6.3. The ANOAVA test that we performed on the data reveals that the differences of cluster means are very strongly significant ($p < 0.001$); pairwise comparison of cluster means employing Tukey's test also shows that differences are highly significant ($p < 0.001$) with the exception of the means scores between the S1 and S4 clusters ($p = 0.015$); the largest differences are

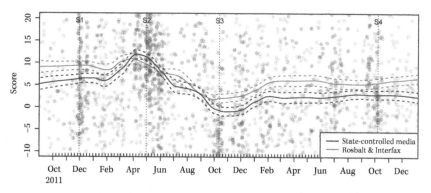

FIGURE 6.2 Framing of Protests by State-Controlled Media and News Agencies, October 2011–December 2013

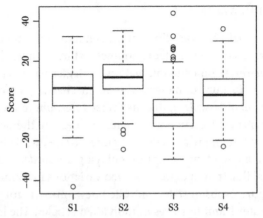

FIGURE 6.3 Quantile Ranges of Framing Scores of News Stories Published by the
State-Controlled Media

found between the S2 and S3 cluster (-17.8 points; p < 0.001) and between the S1
and S3 clusters (1.17 points; p < 0.001). Thus, we observe a significant trend of
the media framing of protest as *disorder* in the period following the reelection
of Putin as president in 2012; this trend starkly contrasts with coverage of nationalist protests and riots in October 2013 (S4), which were significantly more
likely to be covered as *freedom to protest* in state media.

These results indicate that when the magnitude of anti-regime anger became evident after the December 2011 rallies, state media began to project a
relatively positive narrative about protests—the *freedom to protest* frame—
only to switch gears after the spring 2012 Bolotnaya rallies and, by autumn
2012, to employ frames stigmatizing protests. In performing this set of robustness checks, we also observe that when it comes to coverage of the S4
protests, the general trend is for state-controlled newspapers to employ
framing similar to that used in the coverage of the S1 protests—that is, there
is little evidence to suggest that the Biryulyovo protests, despite being significantly more violent, were more likely to be presented in the state media in
terms of *disorder*. Moreover, we observe that the two most widely watched
TV outlets, Russia 1 and Channel 1, were significantly more likely to trend in
the direction of *freedom to protest* framing in the coverage of the S4 protests
as compared to the framing of protests by these sources in S1. This paradoxical result indicates that these media channels were in essence siding with
the nationalist protesters and rioters, who were in turn venting their anger
against migrants, foreigners, and other "outsiders." This result echoes the
findings of other scholars, who have argued that at the beginning of 2012 the
state-controlled TV channels in particular began to engage in systematic nationalist and anti-migrant rhetoric as one way of boosting the failing support
for the Putin regime (Hutchings and Tolz 2015).

In our final set of tests, we employ a simple keyword search technique to ascertain what issues advanced by protesters were highlighted in particular by the state-controlled sources. The keywords for this analysis were chosen based on recent studies of protest activity in Russia, which have distinguished between protest issues, agendas with wage- and housing-related concerns, political agendas (as would be the case with electoral rallies challenging electoral misconduct), and urban/post-material rallies (prominent among which are protests against illegal construction, ecological harm, and corruption of street-level bureaucrats dealing with housing and construction permits and cultural preservation) (Robertson 2011; Lankina 2015). We searched our dataset for keywords related to construction (строительств*, застройк*, or "дольщик*"), wages (заработн* or плат*), immigration (приезж* or мигрант*), ecology (экологическ*), election (выбор*), and corruption (коррупц*). Combining keyword counts with framing scores would potentially allow us to perform a more in-depth analysis of news content, but this strategy presents endogeneity issues because some of these words are loaded with positive or negative scores in our framing dictionary. Therefore, we limit our analysis to exploring variations in the volume of news articles that contain these keywords.

Figure 6.4 shows normalized frequencies of our keywords in news stories published by the state-controlled media in S1–S4. As expected, a large proportion (84 percent) of the S1–S2 news stories in the state-controlled media featured frequent mentions of elections; this is consistent with the fact that state-controlled media did not refrain from covering the anti-regime street protests in which citizens rallied around the issue of electoral fraud. Although the share of stories in our protest news sample featuring the keywords related to wage (14 percent) and corruption (21 percent) was quite high in the S4 time period (corresponding to the Biryulyovo riots), we also found a surge in frequency of mentions of migration/immigration. While less than 2 percent of protest stories contained these terms in the earlier time periods, for S4 the figure is 22 percent. Again, this finding would appear unremarkable considering that protesters and rioters in Biryulyovo rallied against non-ethnic-Russian migrants and immigrants.

When we compare and contrast the frequencies of words related to specific protest issues in the state-controlled sources and news agencies, interesting contrasts emerge. In the non-state-controlled media (Figure 6.5), we do find variations in the frequency of keywords, which suggests that different media sources chose to highlight particular aspects of the causes advanced in rallies over others. We find that the frequency of the migration/immigration keywords also increased in the S4 cluster in the news agencies. Nevertheless, only 10 percent of stories featured in the non-state-controlled media in the S4 period contained the migration/immigration-related keywords, half the number of those in the state-controlled media; instead, mentions of wages in

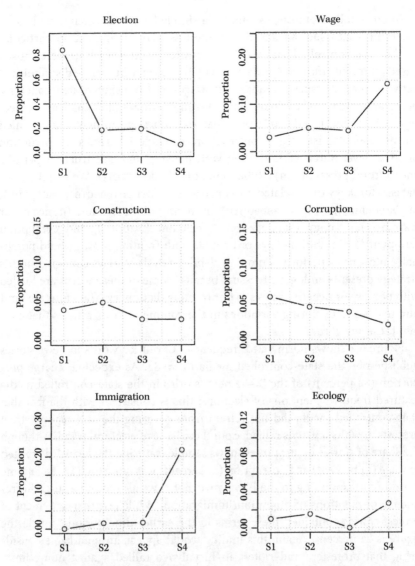

FIGURE 6.4 Frequency of Keywords Related to Protest Agendas in State-Controlled Media

the non-state-controlled media sharply increase to 19 percent in this period. In Namarsh.ru and *Novaya Gazeta* (Figure 6.6), we do not find stories with mentions of migration/immigration in S4, and references to wages remained approximately at the same level as in S3 (11 percent). Thus the state-controlled media clearly, more than the non-state-controlled sources, sought to emphasize the nationalist rather than socioeconomic aspect of the protesters' grievances in the Biryulyovo events.

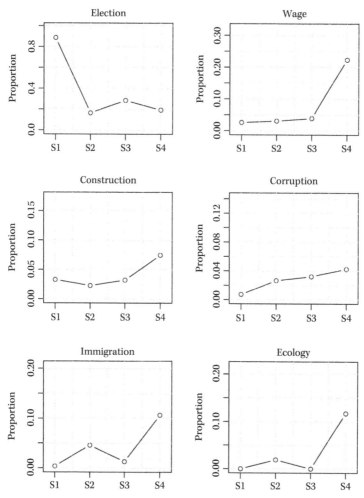

FIGURE 6.5 Frequency of Keywords Related to Protest Agendas in News Agencies

QUALITATIVE ANALYSIS OF NEWS STORIES

We now provide illustrative examples of coverage of the relevant stories by the tabloid newspaper *Komsomolskaya Pravda*. We chose this paper because it is Russia's most popular daily newspaper. As noted earlier, we do not observe significant deviation among the six outlets in trends in protest framing in the various time periods covered in our study. The one exception to this finding is the Russia 1 TV channel, which had a higher tendency to employ a *disorder* frame in S1 and S2, while showing convergence with the frames dominant in the other outlets in S3 and S4. How *Komsomolskaya Pravda* covers a particular story is therefore likely to provide us with a fair assessment of the slant in coverage by most of the state-controlled outlets analyzed in our study.

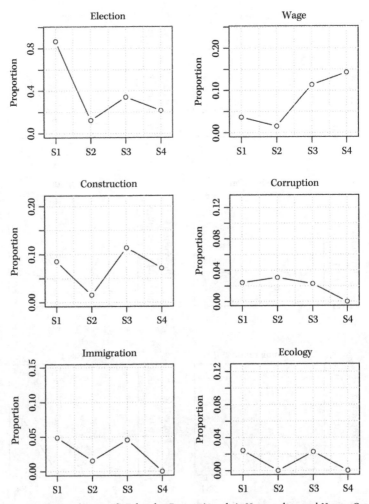

FIGURE 6.6 Frequency of Keywords Related to Protest Agenda in Namarash.ru and *Novaya Gazeta*

S1: The December 2011 Protests

The story that appeared on December 10, 2011, was titled "Tsoi pel, OMON ulybalsya, a Bolotnaya likovala" (Tsoi was singing, the special police forces were smiling, while Bolotnaya was jubilant). Among the first images in this story was a glamorous, beaming media star, Tina Kandelaki, taking a selfie of herself with the protesters in the background.[11] Both the title of the feature and the image clearly prime the reader to sympathize with participants in the event. The title of the piece contains a reference to Viktor Tsoi, a pop singer who became an icon of the perestroika era with his cult song "We Want Change!" It also characterizes the special police forces as having a positive attitude toward the event—they were "smiling." Not only does the title characterize the protesters with reference to the large square in which the event is taking place—Bolotnaya Square, thereby impressing upon the reader the full magnitude of the assembly—but it also subtly frames this assembly as one of happy, jubilant people. The fact that the image is of a famous TV star who is clearly supportive of the protesters' agenda—rather than, for instance, of police in riot gear—likewise primes readers to sympathize with the event.

The feature went on to highlight the mass nature of the rally ("The rally had been already on for two hours . . . but the people kept streaming in"; "There were no less than 50,000 people, that's for sure"). It also alluded to the peaceful conduct of the protesters, either in the journalist's direct references to the participants or in quotes from opposition activists interviewed on the spot: "Those who turned up are people who have self-respect and respect for their country, and the law in principle; the people . . . had been swearing that they are vigilant and will not succumb to any provocations." The overall positive atmosphere reigning during the rally was also conveyed ("'We want change!' blasted the loudspeakers. . . . Yes! agreed the jubilant crowd").

S2–S3: Bolotnaya and Aftermath

The piece that illustrates coverage in the period that corresponds to the significant shift toward a disorder frame appeared in *Komsomolskaya Pravda* on October 2, 2012. It was titled "Politbyuro Bolotnoy: Nezavisimyy ekspertnyy doklad" (The Politburo of Bolotnaya: independent expert report).[12] The feature was dedicated to members of the political opposition who staged the anti-regime rallies in December 2011 and May–June 2012. The image that accompanied the feature was of something resembling an organizational flowchart of the opposition's "Politburo." The chart listed such departments as the "Department for Ideology and Propaganda" and the "Department for External Liaisons," among others. It also featured photos of ostensible members of the "Politburo," including the performance art group Pussy Riot star Nadezhda Tolokonnikova as "Secretary in Charge of Ideology" and the anti-corruption blogger and political activist Alexey Navalny as "General Secretary." The reference to the Soviet-era Politburo—the Communist Party body that made key domestic and foreign policy decisions in the USSR—was a clear attempt to stigmatize the activists, as was the suggestion that they were part of a highly organized group, equipped with their own propaganda and foreign policy divisions.

The story sought to delegitimize the most prominent figures of the rallies as individuals with whom Russians—including those who attended the rallies—do not identify and whom they do not consider as speaking on their behalf. The news piece clearly resorted to a *disorder* frame when describing speeches by activists in those rallies:

> The crowd booed [*osvistany*] nearly all of the leaders who took to the podium during the protest. . . . The people were not receptive to calls

emanating from the podium, while they were particularly negative toward provocative calls to stage a Maidan and revolution.

The feature referred to the opposition's attempt to unite under a loose Coordination Council body, branding it as a Western- and oligarch-funded grouping composed of "marginals," "opportunists," individuals of "nontraditional sexual orientation," "intermediaries between Bolotnaya and Gosdep [U.S. State Department]," "radical nationalists," "playboys," and washed-up "has-beens" (*ustarevshye politiki*).[13]

S4: The Biryulyovo Protests and Riots

A *Komsomolskaya Pravda* article that provides a flavor of the tabloid's coverage of the Biryulyovo events appeared on October 14, 2013.[14] It was titled "Zhiteli Biryulyova: draki, iznasilovaniya i strel'ba pod oknami dlya nas—budni" (Birulyovo residents: fights, rapes and shootouts under our windows for us is the day-to-day reality). The first image in the story was of people carrying flags and marching on a wide street. There is nothing in the image that would indicate disorder; men and women of different ages are seen on the image. The journalist commented: "No one wants to live in a district where after 11 [p.m.] it is hard to encounter a Russian person. It is truly scary." The news piece cited residents commenting on the events: "We, residents of Biryulyovo-West, want order. Nothing more"; "All these endless migrants, I think there are no less than 15,000 of them, have flooded the district, they live here, go around, rest, and here too they kill Russians."

Neither *Komsomolskaya Pravda* nor the other state-controlled outlets shied away from reporting on the violence and rioting in those events and the vandalism (smashing of shop windows, damage to property, and crushing of cars) perpetrated by some of the right-wing extremists and bystanders. Nevertheless, in this particular piece, like in the other Kremlin-friendly sources, *Komsomolskaya's* editorial line appeared to be sympathetic to their wider anti-immigrant and anti-migrant agenda (protesters were chanting "Vyselyat'!" [Move out!]).[15]

Discussion

Dovetailing with earlier research about regime responses to complex media landscapes in modern-day autocracies, our analysis suggests that state-controlled media provide substantial coverage of mass protests even when they openly target the regime. In the case of the mass protests of 2011–2012, their unprecedented size, especially that of the "March of the Millions," made it impossible for the regime to hide the event from public eyes. Simply pretending that these events did not happen would discredit state-controlled media, compromising the effectiveness of future media manipulation strategies. Yet we also find that Russian state-controlled media do resort to both media control and manipulation tactics in coverage of large-scale protest events, and this is done in ways that may not be always straightforwardly apparent absent systematic media analysis over time and across news outlets. The choice of tactics is in turn contingent upon the issues around which protesters rally and the targets of their grievances. Furthermore, the regime tailors its responses to the evolving processes of citizen mobilization in a dynamic fashion.

We find support for hypothesis H1, in that large-scale anti-regime political protests will lead the media to frame them in terms of *disorder* (media manipulation), but, in what supports H2, the shift toward negative framing will occur with some time lag, reflecting a learning effect, because such large-scale mobilizations may catch the regime unprepared or unaware. Indeed, as our analysis also shows, early on in the protest cycle, the regime sought to systematically project a positive spin on protests, framing them in terms of *freedom to protest*, only to switch gears later on when this tactic failed to pacify the public and protests continued. In what fails to support H3 but supports our final hypothesis (H4), our analysis of coverage of the Biryulyovo events indicates that such protests are also less likely to be framed in leading state media in terms of *disorder* as compared to anti-regime protests. Taken together, our study highlights the interconnected nature of responses to the different protest events: not only do rulers learn from past events in fashioning their responses to protests, but they also strategically leverage protests with particular agendas for regime-reinforcing purposes.

Our analysis has important implications for wider comparative theorizing on authoritarian vulnerabilities and resilience. Much of our awareness about responses to protest in authoritarian states comes from studies of China. Yet not only is there considerable disagreement among China scholars themselves about the regime's strategies for dealing with discontent, but we have yet to systematically ascertain the extent to which the particular strategies are mirrored in other autocracies (Dimitrov 2008; Chen 2012; King, Pan, and Roberts 2013; Lorentzen 2013). The chapters in this volume illuminate both the similarities when it comes to specific strategies of containing, manipulating, or leveraging discontent—for information generation and other purposes—and the differences in regime responses to discontent in China and Russia.

When it comes to theorizing on media coverage of nationalist protest in particular, our findings differ from those of King, Pan, and Roberts (2013), who have studied responses to nationalist mobilization (among other protest causes) in China. They find that ethnonationalist mobilizations are perceived to be dangerous and are to be nipped in the bud even if in those mobilizations the regime is glorified but the minorities or external groups are stigmatized. We owe an intellectual debt to King, Pan, and Roberts's study because it provides perhaps the most sophisticated analytical lens for scholars to begin to make sense comparatively about how authoritarian state leaders deal with different kinds of protests beyond the high-profile color-revolution-type scenarios. Yet the patterns uncovered in our own study of Russia are more in tune with arguments that other scholars have made about Chinese leaders' responses to ethnonationalist protest, variously characterizing these responses in terms of ambivalence, tacit endorsement, manipulation, or even active encouragement (Morozov 2012; Jones-Rooy 2012; Dimitrov 2008; Pei 2012; Weiss 2013). In fact, these assumptions would be consistent with a long-standing line of social science inquiry into the political uses and abuses of ethnic and nationalist sentiment (Wilkinson 2004; Beissinger 2002).

Our analysis supports the argument that protests with a nationalist agenda (broadly defined) may not necessarily elicit a *disorder* frame even if anti-regime protests occurring around the same time may well elicit such a frame. This is not only because nationalist protests often target a specific ethnic or religious group, local authorities, or external powers, rather than state leaders, but also because the regime would be tempted to strategically leverage these protests. Furthermore, even when the sentiment expressed in ethnic protests and riots may be at odds with the preferred (more tolerant and more inclusive) national idea, authoritarian power-holders may show adaptability to the domestic "public mood" (Hutchings and Tolz 2015, 101), tailoring the media narratives accordingly. Although ethnically exclusive rhetoric would have clashed with some Kremlin-supported thinkers' Eurasianist ideas, which fused nostalgia for empire and Soviet patriotism to offer a more tolerant and inclusive version of Russian nationalism, the regime ideologues also apparently took note of the unlikely alliance between liberal forces in the political opposition and Russian nationalists in the December 2011 protests (Umland 2012; Popescu 2012; Laruelle 2014).

One further area of research that would represent an extension of our work would be to analyze in greater depth the inner mechanisms of control and the construction of media frames (manipulation). This would in turn further illuminate the intentionality of shifts in control and manipulation—that is, the specific audiences who are targeted. State-controlled media may represent as much a signaling mechanism vis-à-vis the broader publics (as would be the case with signals that street protests would not be tolerated) as a device for coordinating the behavior of state agents (such as local authorities consuming state-controlled media for clues about appropriate actions when street protests occur). The extent of media agencies' bureaucratic autonomy and the extent of freedom of bureaucratic maneuver may vary from issue to issue and should be considered as well. Another possible angle would be to regard news media as a source of moral authority. Considering the known influence of leading state media on public opinion formation, the narratives of popular news anchors such as *Russia Today*'s Dmitry Kiselyov may not just reinforce popular prejudices but sway public opinion. The state may well promote such charismatic TV presenters as facilitators for the interpretation of nationally significant events. Messages would be simplified to offer cognitive shortcuts for populations that may otherwise lack an opinion on important public events or are struggling to make sense of such events. For instance, Kiselyov and other leading anchors may well have helped steer public opinion toward ready-made patriotic interpretations of complex events such as the annexation of Crimea or the Donbas violence.[16]

Because our dictionary and method are replicable, we suggest a number of further empirical extensions to our analysis that could enrich scholarship on protest dynamics in authoritarian contexts. Given what we know about the use of state resources to manipulate public information in Russia and other authoritarian states, it has become common in survey research to ask respondents to identify sources from which they derive news. While some surveys provide a list of newspapers and TV channels in the questionnaire, others limit the media questions to ascertaining whether television or the internet is the main source. Neither of these strategies, in our view, adequately captures how state media outlets can mold public opinion. Considering the overwhelming cross-national evidence about the persuasive power of specific media messages (Iyengar and Kinder 1987; Enikolopov, Petrova, and Zhuravskaya 2011), it is imperative for scholars of public opinion in autocracies to employ more nuanced measures of media influence than simple measures of exposure. Fortunately, our framing measures could be easily incorporated into multiple regression analysis—for instance, as additional right-hand variables in cross-sectional time series models gauging the determinants of public support for leaders and how support levels shift over time, or public support for a "tough line" on protesters. This would be a valuable extension of our research, which stops short of ascertaining the impact of media control and manipulation on public opinion and behavior. Conversely, our media measures could be used as a dependent variable, for instance in a study that would explore the effect of changing protest dynamics or changing support for rulers on media responses. They could be also leveraged in protest event count studies analyzing how media stigmatization of protest could undermine attempts by movement leaders to rally bystanders behind the protesters' cause. Our framing analysis thus represents an important contribution to scholars' theoretical and methodological tool kit for systematic analysis of media strategies to cope with public discontent in authoritarian settings.

Notes

1. Following Svolik (2012), we use the terms "dictatorship," "autocracy," and "authoritarian regime" interchangeably.

2. "O gazete," *Rossiiskaya Gazeta*, https://rg.ru/about, accessed July 8, 2016.

3. "Sostav holding," NMG, http://nm-g.ru/#sostav-holdinga, accessed July 8, 2016; "Osnovnyye etapy razvitiya gazety Izvestiya," *RIA Novosti*, February 13, 2012, http://ria.ru/spravka/20120313/592628788.html.

4. "Grigory Berezkin," *Forbes*, March 21, 2013, http://www.forbes.ru/profile/grigorii-berezkin; "Sovet direktorov," *Rossiiskie Zheleznye Dorogi*, http://rzd.ru/ent/public/ru?STRUCTURE_ID=5185&layer_id=5554&id=1209, accessed July 8, 2016.

5. "O kompanii," VGTRK, http://vgtrk.com/#page/221, accessed July 8, 2016.

6. "Sostav holding," NMG, http://nm-g.ru/#sostav-holdinga, accessed July 8, 2016; "Kto vladeyet SMI v Rossii: Vedushchiye holdingi," BBC Russian Service, July 11, 2014, http://www.bbc.com/russian/russia/2014/07/140711_russia_media_holdings.

7. "O kompanii," Gazprom Media, http://www.gpm.ru/ru/about/index, accessed July 8, 2016.

8. We prefer not to use the term "independent sources" because the ownership structure of many news outlets is likely to influence their editorial line.

9. The editor of Rosbalt, Natalya Cherkasova, is married to Viktor Cherkasov, who occupied senior positions in the government and security services. This, however, has been regarded as providing the outlet with a certain degree of protection from harassment suffered by other media sources. Interview with a Rosbalt correspondent, December 2015.

10. The documentary *Anatomiya protesta-1*, aired on March 15, 2012, alleged that protesters were paid to attend the anti-regime rallies and that the protests were stage-managed by the United States. See Daria Ivashkina, "'Anatomiyu protesta—2' posvyatili Udal'tsovu," *Komsomolskaya Pravda*, October 5, 2012, http://www.kp.ru/daily/25961/2901269. See also Roman Vorobyov, "Anatomy of Protest Stirs Trouble," *Russia Beyond*, October 12, 2012, http://rbth.co.uk/articles/2012/10/12/documentary_stirs_trouble_for_opposition_19039.html.

11. Aleksey Ovchinnikov, "Tsoy pel, OMON ulybalsya, a Bolotnaya likovala," *Komsomolskaya Pravda*, December 10, 2011, https://www.kp.kg/daily/25802/2783071.

12. "Politbyuro Bolotnoy: Nezavisimyy ekspertnyy doklad," *Komsomolskaya Pravda*, October 2, 2012, https://www.kp.ru/daily/25959/2899348.

13. "Intermediar[y]" was intended to be a reference to the human rights activist Lyudmila Alekseeva; "has-been" was intended to be a reference to Boris Nemtsov, prominent in the democratic movement. "Politbyuro Bolotnoy: Nezavisimyy ekspertnyy doklad," *Komsomolskaya Pravda*, October 2, 2012, http://www.kp.ru/daily/25959/2899348. For coverage of the May 6 Bolotnaya protests, see Alexander Grishin, "'Marsh millionov' zakonchilsya massovymi besporyadkami," *Komsomolskaya Pravda*, May 6, 2012,http://www.kp.ru/daily/25879/2842584.

14. Artur Galeev, "Zhiteli Biryuleva: Draki, iznasilovaniya i strel'ba pod oknami dlya nas—budni," *Komsomolskaya Pravda*, October 14, 2013, http://www.kp.ru/daily/26145.5/3034689.

15. See, for instance, "Biryulyovskiy bunt, osmyslennyy i besposhchadnyy," *Moskovskiy Komsomolets*, October 13, 2013, http://www.mk.ru/incident/article/2013/10/13/929758-biryulevskiy-bunt-osmyislennyiy-i-besposchadnyiy.html. For another article that showed police in riot gear and reported on the disturbances in ways that was sympathetic to the protesters' demands, see Dmitry Steshin, "Biryulevo-pogromnoye," *Komsomolskaya Pravda*, October 13, 2013, http://www.kp.ru/daily/26145.7/3034513.

16. We are grateful to Greg Distelhorst for making these valuable comments about the intentionality of framing and censorship during the Notre Dame workshop.

References

Akhterov, Victor. 2011. "Voiceless Glasnost: Responding to Government Pressures and Lack of a Free Press Tradition in Russia." In *The Handbook of Global Communication and Media Ethics*, ed. Robert S. Fortner and Mark P. Fackler, 677–699. Hoboken: Wiley-Blackwell.
Beissinger, Mark R. 2002. *Nationalist Mobilization and the Collapse of the Soviet State.* Cambridge: Cambridge University Press.
Boyd-Barrett, O. 2014. *Interfax: Breaking into Global News.* Scotforth Books.
Chen, Xi. 2012. *Social Protest and Contentious Authoritarianism in China.* New York: Cambridge University Press.
Cottiero, Christina, Katherine Kucharski, Evgenia Olimpieva, and Robert W. Orttung. 2015. "War of Words: The Impact of Russian State Television on the Russian Internet." *Nationalities Papers* 43, no. 4: 533–555.
Cottle, Simon. 2008. "Reporting Demonstrations: The Changing Media Politics of Dissent." *Media, Culture and Society* 30, no. 6: 853–872.
Deluca, Kevin M., Sean Lawson, and Ye Sun. 2012. "Occupy Wall Street on the Public Screens of Social Media: The Many Framings of the Birth of a Protest Movement." *Communication, Culture and Critique* 5, no. 4: 483–509. doi: 10.1111/j.1753-9137.2012.01141.x.
Dimitrov, Martin. 2008. "The Resilient Authoritarians." *Current History* 107, no. 705: 24–29.
Egorov, Georgy, Sergei Guriev, and Konstantin Sonin. 2009. "Why Resource-Poor Dictators Allow Freer Media: A Theory and Evidence from Panel Data." *American Political Science Review* 103, no. 4: 645–668.
Enikolopov, Ruben, Maria Petrova, and Ekaterina Zhuravskaya. 2011. "Media and Political Persuasion: Evidence from Russia." *American Economic Review* 101, no. 7: 3253–3285. doi: 10.1257/aer.101.7.3253.
Entman, R. M. (2004). *Projections of Power: Framing News, Public Opinion, and U.S. Foreign Policy.* University of Chicago Press.
Fitzpatrick, Catherine A. 2013. "Their Brains are Like a Wrecking Ball." *The Interpreter*, October 14.
Gamson, William A., and David S. Meyer. 1996. "Framing Political Opportunity." In *Comparative Perspectives on Social Movements*, ed. Doug McAdam, John D. McCarthy, and Mayer N. Zald, 275–290. Cambridge: Cambridge University Press.
Gehlbach, Scott, and Konstantin Sonin. 2014. "Government Control of the Media." *Journal of Public Economics* 118: 163–171.
Gel'man, Vladimir. 2013. *Iz ognya da v polymya: Rossiyskaya politika posle SSSR* [From fire to flame: Russian politics after the USSR]. St. Petersburg: BHV-Petersburg.
Goffman, Erving. 1975. *Frame Analysis: An Essay on the Organisation of Experience.* Harmondsworth: Penguin Books.
Hamdy, Naila, and Ehab H. Gomaa. 2012. "Framing the Egyptian Uprising in Arabic Language Newspapers and Social Media." *Journal of Communication* 62, no. 2: 195–211. doi: 10.1111/j.1460-2466.2012.01637.x.
Hassid, Jonathan. 2008. "Controlling the Chinese Media: An Uncertain Business." *Asian Survey* 48, no. 3: 414–430.
Hutchings, Stephen, and Vera Tolz. 2015. *Nation, Ethnicity and Race on Russian Television.* Abingdon: Routledge.
Iyengar, Shanto, and Donald Kinder. 1987. *News That Matters.* Chicago: University of Chicago Press.

Jones-Rooy, Andrea E. 2012. "Communication and Commitment: The Strategic Use of the Media in Autocracies." Ph.D. diss., University of Michagan.

King, Gary, Jennifer Pan, and Margaret E. Roberts. 2013. "How Censorship in China Allows Government Criticism but Silences Collective Expression." *American Political Science Review* 107, no. 2: 326–343.

Klein, Adam. 2012. "Measuring Media Compliance and Divergence in the Nondemocratic Press System." *Communication Monographs* 79, no. 1: 115–136. doi: 10.1080/03637751.2011.646488.

Lankina, Tomila. 2015. "The Dynamics of Regional and National Contentious Politics in Russia: Evidence from a New Dataset." *Problems of Post-Communism* 62, no. 1: 26–44.

Lankina, Tomila, and Alisa Voznaya. 2015. "New Data on Protest Trends in Russia's Regions." *Europe-Asia Studies* 67, no. 2: 327–342.

Lankina, Tomila, and Kohei Watanabe. 2017. "'Russian Spring' or 'Spring Betrayal'? The Media as a Mirror of Putin's Evolving Strategy in Ukraine." *Europe-Asia Studies* 69, no. 10: 1526–1556.

Laruelle, Marlene. 2014. "Alexei Navalny and Challenges in Reconciling 'Nationalism' and 'Liberalism.'" *Post-Soviet Affairs* 30, no. 4: 276–297. doi: 10.1080/1060586x.2013.872453.

Lorentzen, Peter. 2013. "Regularizing Rioting: Permitting Protest in an Authoritarian Regime." *Quarterly Journal of Political Science* 8: 127–158.

McLeod, Douglas M., and Benjamin H. Detenber. 1999. "Framing Effects of Television News Coverage of Social Protest." *Journal of Communication* 49, no. 3: 3–23. doi: 10.1111/j.1460-2466.1999.tb02802.x.

McNair, Brian. 2000. "Power, Profit, Corruption, and Lies: The Russian Media in the 1990s." In *De-Westernizing Media Studies*, ed. Myung-Jin Park and James Curran, 79–94. London: Routledge.

Mickiewicz, Ellen. 2006. "The Election News Story on Russian Television: A World Apart from Viewers." *Slavic Review* 65, no. 1: 1–23. doi: 10.2307/4148520.

Mickiewicz, Ellen T. 2008. *Television, Power, and the Public in Russia*. Cambridge: Cambridge University Press.

Morozov, Evgeny. 2012. *The Net Delusion: The Dark Side of Internet Freedom*. Philadelphia: PublicAffairs.

Nathan, Andrew J. 2003. "Authoritarian Resilience." *Journal of Democracy* 14, no. 1: 6–17.

Nelson, Elizabeth, Robert Orttung, and Anthony Livshen. 2015. "Measuring RT's Impact on YouTube." *Russian Analytical Digest* 177: 2–9.

Nelson, Thomas E., Rosalee A. Clawson, and Zoe M. Oxley. 1997. "Media Framing of a Civil Liberties Conflict and Its Effect on Tolerance." *American Political Science Review* 91, no. 3: 567–583.

Noakes, John A., and Hank Johnston. 2005. "Frames of Protest: A Road Map to a Perspective." In *Frames of Protest: Social Movements and the Framing Perspective*, ed. John A. Noakes and Hank Johnston, 1–29. Oxford: Rowman and Littlefield.

Oates, Sarah. 2006. *Television, Democracy and Elections in Russia*. New York: Routledge.

Pei, Minxin. 2012. "Is CCP Rule Fragile or Resilient?" *Journal of Democracy* 23, no. 1: 27–41.

Peng, Zengjun. 2008. "Framing the Anti-War Protests in the Global Village: A Comparative Study of Newspaper Coverage in Three Countries." *International Communication Gazette* 70, no. 5: 361–377.

Popescu, Nicu. 2012. "The Strange Alliance of Democrats and Nationalists." *Journal of Democracy* 23, no. 3: 46–54.

Robertson, Graeme. 2011. *The Politics of Protest in Hybrid Regimes: Managing Dissent in Post-communist Russia.* Cambridge: Cambridge University Press.

Robertson, Graeme. 2013. "Protesting Putinism." *Problems of Post-Communism* 60, no. 2: 11–23.

Rød, Espen Geelmuyden, and Nils B. Weidmann. 2015. "Empowering Activists or Autocrats? The Internet in Authoritarian Regimes." *Journal of Peace Research* 52, no. 3: 338–351. doi: 10.1177/0022343314555782.

Smaele, Hedwig de. 2010. "In Search of a Label for the Russian Media System." In *Comparative Media Systems: European and Global Perspectives*, ed. Bogusława Dobek-Ostrowska, Bogusława Dobek-Ostrowska, Michał Głowacki, Karol Jakubowicz and Miklós Sükösd, 41–62. Budapest: Central European University Press.

Smith, Jackie, John D. McCarthy, Clark McPhail, and Boguslaw Augustyn. 2001. "From Protest to Agenda Building: Description Bias in Media Coverage of Protest Events in Washington, D.C." *Social Forces* 79, no. 4: 1397–1423.

Smyth, Regina, and Sarah Oates. 2015. "Mind the Gaps: Media Use and Mass Action in Russia." *Europe-Asia Studies* 67, no. 2: 285–305. doi: 10.1080/09668136.2014.1002682.

Snow, David A., and Robert D. Benford. 1992. "Master Frames and Cycles of Protest." In *Frontiers in Social Movement Theory*, ed. Aldon D. Morris and Carol M. Mueller, 133–155. New Haven: Yale University Press.

Snow, David A., E. Burke Rochford, Steven K. Worden, and Robert D. Benford. 1986. "Frame Alignment Processes, Micromobilisation, and Movement Participation." *American Sociological Review* 51 (August): 464–481.

Stockmann, Daniela, and Mary E. Gallagher. 2011. "Remote Control: How the Media Sustain Authoritarian Rule in China." *Comparative Political Studies* 44, no. 4: 436–467. doi: 10.1177/0010414010394773.

Svolik, Milan. 2012. *The Politics of Authoritarian Rule.* New York: Cambridge University Press.

Tertytchnaya, Katerina, and Tomila V. Lankina. 2019. "Electoral Protests and Political Attitudes under Electoral Authoritarianism." *Journal of Politics* 82, no. 1: 285–299.

Toepfl, Florian. 2013. "Making Sense of the News in a Hybrid Regime: How Young Russians Decode State TV and an Oppositional Blog." *Journal of Communication* 63, no. 2: 244–265. doi: 10.1111/jcom.12018.

Treisman, Daniel, and Sergei Guriev. 2015. "How Modern Dictators Survive: Cooptation, Censorship, Propaganda, and Repression." Discussion Paper Series: Development Economics and Public Economics, London: Centre for Economic and Policy Research.

Truex, Rory. 2014. "Who Believes the *People's Daily*? Bias and Credibility in Authoritarian Media." Paper presented at the annual meeting of the American Political Science Association, San Francisco, November.

Turney, Peter D., and Michael L. Littman. 2003. " Measuring Praise and Criticism: Inference of Semantic Orientation from Association." *ACM Transactions on Information Systems* 21, no. 4: 315–346.

Umland, Andreas. 2012. *Could Russia's Ultranationalists Subvert Pro-Democracy Protests?.* ETH Zürich: Center for Security Studies.

Watanabe, K. 2018. "Newsmap: A semi-supervised approach to geographical news classification." *Digital Journalism* 6, no. 3: 294–309. https://doi.org/10.1080/21670811.2017.1293487.

Weiss, Jessica. 2013. "Authoritarian Signaling, Mass Audiences, and Nationalist Protest in China." *International Organization* 67, no. 1: 1–35. doi: 10.1017/s0020818312000380.

White, Stephen, Sarah Oates, and I. A. N. McAllister. 2005. "Media Effects and Russian Elections, 1999–2000." *British Journal of Political Science* 35, no. 2: 191–208. doi: 10.1017/s0007123405000116.

Wilkinson, Steven I. 2004. *Votes and Violence: Electoral Competition and Ethnic Riots in India*. New York: Cambridge University Press.

Zald, Mayer N. 1996. "Culture, Ideology, and Strategic Framing." In *Comparative Perspectives on Social Movements*, ed. Doud McAdam, John D. McCarthy and Mayer N. Zald, 261–274. New York: Cambridge University Press.

Law and Labor

7 }

A Tale of Two Laws

MANAGING FOREIGN AGENTS AND OVERSEAS NGOS IN
RUSSIA AND CHINA

Elizabeth Plantan

In the wake of the color revolutions and the Arab Spring, authoritarian leaders have become more attuned to potential foreign and domestic threats within their borders. Given the prominent role of civil society and external democracy promotion in these waves of democratization (Beissinger 2007; Bunce and Wolchik 2011; Saari 2009; Stewart 2009a, 2009b; Kudlenko 2015), some countries, such as Russia and China, have focused specifically on management of this sector as one way to "diffusion-proof" the regime (see Chapter 4 in this volume). This has resulted in a series of legislative changes to further define and manage domestic NGO activity, not only in Russia and China but also in other regimes around the world (Christensen and Weinstein 2013). This repressive global legal trend suggests that authoritarian leaders "fear an active, engaged, and empowered nongovernmental sector," especially one that has been aided from abroad (Christensen and Weinstein 2013, 87).

In Russia and China in particular, several recent legal changes have codified each state's position with respect to international influence on their domestic civil societies. In Russia, the 2012 law on "foreign agents" stipulates that any domestic Russian non-governmental organization (NGO) that receives foreign funding and engages in ambiguously defined "political" activity must register as a foreign agent or face steep fines and even closure. This was followed by a 2015 law on "undesirable" organizations that gives prosecutors the ability to declare any foreign or international organization as undesirable and force it to shut down. In China, a new law on the management of overseas NGOs that came into effect on January 1, 2017, tightens the regulations for foreign NGO registration and operation in mainland China. It was preceded by the 2016 Charity Law, which encourages domestic charitable giving and simplifies the registration process for domestic Chinese organizations. These laws have increased state control over foreign and domestic funding to civil society, partnerships between international and domestic organizations, and the operations of international organizations within Russian and Chinese borders.

These parallel sets of laws in Russia and China provide an opportunity to compare their development, their overall effect on domestic and international NGOs operating in these countries, and the broader trend toward anti-foreign framings in two different authoritarian regimes. This chapter uses evidence from open sources and from original interviews conducted by the author from 2015 to 2017 with over 140 respondents from more than 80 different international and domestic organizations operating in Russia and China. While not all interviews are cited here, they all provided important background information for this research. The interview responses have been de-identified.

Using this data, I find that the main similarities between the two countries' approaches to these types of laws are in their timing and motivations for national security, their intentions to shape civil society to meet state goals, and their use of ambiguity or uncertainty as a tool of authoritarian governance. They differ, however, in the speed and creation of the laws, their choice of public versus private record, and their approach to implementation and punishment. This points to an important divergence in governance between the two regimes, where China has chosen a more deliberative and consultative form of authoritarianism while Russia more often excludes societal actors from governance.

Despite the differences in governance and approach to NGO management, the laws have had strikingly similar effects on domestic and international civil society actors by chilling the atmosphere for domestic-international civil society partnership and increasing bureaucratic burden amid uncertainty, which has driven some international organizations to leave and some domestic organizations to shut down. However, although foreign connections could be seen as threatening, both Russia and China have stopped short of barring all international connections to their domestic civil societies. This highlights the tension between repression and liberalization noted in Chapter 1 of this volume. Rather than repress all groups that receive foreign funding or block all foreign groups from operating, Russian and Chinese leaders have crafted laws that can be used (directly or indirectly) to repress some groups while allowing others, striking a balance between liberalization and repression.

Background: Foreign Assistance to Civil Society in Russia and China

The growth and development of Western-style civil society organizations in Russia and China follow similar trajectories, heavily aided by foreign funding in the 1990s. Spurred by beliefs about the potential benefits of democracy promotion (Mansfield and Snyder 1995; Russett 1994; Owen 1994) and connecting a strong civil society to democratic outcomes (de Tocqueville [1835] 1994; Putnam 1993; Linz and Stepan 1996; Diamond 1994; Keane 1998), many Western democracies began to pour money into civil society assistance around the world. While estimates of foreign aid to organizations in either Russia or China are imperfect, there are data available to suggest its scale. Focusing on aid from the United States, some estimates show that U.S. government democracy assistance to Russia totaled $860 million between 1990 and 2002 (Sundstrom 2006, 12). This assistance continued into the 2000s. In 2008, the U.S. Agency for International Development (USAID) gave $40.1 million (49.5 percent of its total Russia program budget) under the "Governing Justly and Democratically" program area, which includes rule of law, human rights, good governance, and civil society (USAID 2010, 374).[1] For China, a Congressional Research Service report found that between 2001 and 2014, the U.S. government allocated $390 million for Department of State and USAID programs in China, including those focused on human rights, democracy, and the environment (Lum 2014). In addition, drawing on data from the Foundation Center, Spires (2012) finds that U.S. foundations contributed more than $442 million in grants to China from 2002 to 2009. These figures give a glimpse into the high volumes of foreign aid that flow into China and Russia as a part of a larger commitment to democracy promotion.

Despite the underlying goal of democracy promotion, this international assistance to civil society went largely unchecked during the 1990s, especially as it often filled in gaps in government capacity for public service provision (Jakobson and Sanovich 2009; Henderson 2011; Spires 2011; Hildebrandt 2013; Richter and Hatch 2013). This changed in the mid-2000s after the events of the color revolutions in Eastern Europe and Central Asia. In assessments of these events, civil society and its external support were key for explaining regime collapse throughout the region (Beissinger 2007; Stewart 2009a, 2009b; Saari 2009; Bunce and Wolchik 2011; Kudlenko 2015). Not blind to this influence, Russian and Chinese authorities began to consider the threat posed by foreign assistance programs to groups within their borders. Lawmakers in increasingly authoritarian Russia amended existing legislation that had left NGOs in a state of "benign neglect" under Yeltsin (Henderson 2011, 18) to assert control over the third sector. In 2006, the Russian Duma passed amendments that impacted the civil code and the 1990s-era laws On Public Associations, On Non-Commercial Organizations, and On Closed Administrative Territorial

Formations. These amendments required NGOs to submit to annual audits and to report foreign funding, and they also allowed the authorities vague reasons under which they could deny registration, prohibit foreign NGOs from implementing programs or transferring funds to their branch offices, and ban certain foreign nationals and other "undesirable" persons from founding an NGO in Russia (Machleder 2006; Machalek 2012). The 2006 amendments to the laws governing NGOs significantly increased the bureaucratic burden for NGOs and, as some scholars argue, reduced NGO activity (Crotty et al. 2014).

While Russia's leaders clamped down on civil society during the mid-2000s, Chinese leaders largely stalled on revising their existing regulations amid disagreements on the degree of political liberalization (Wilson 2009, 376). In comparison with Russia, however, Chinese third sector management has been more stringent from the beginning. In 1998, government regulations required NGOs to formally register with the Ministry of Civil Affairs and with a separate sponsoring government agency. This also included stipulations under which registration could be refused (including perceived harm to national unity, security, or national interests), barred NGOs from establishing official branch offices, and discouraged other horizontal linkages between organizations (Schwartz 2004). As Richter and Hatch (2013) point out, these initial regulations on the third sector could be considered more restrictive than the 2006 changes to regulations governing NGOs in Russia.

Although the color revolutions illustrated potential threats from civil society, the influx of foreign funding in the 1990s also demonstrated the benefits of civil society to the regime. For instance, civil society organizations can strengthen state capacity by providing vital public services (Spires 2011) or by monitoring and enforcing government policies to improve local governance and identify corrupt officials (Richter and Hatch 2013, 325; Wilson 2009, 386). For this reason, at the same time that some measures were taken to constrain civil society, other policies increased government funding to civil society or created new pathways for (controlled) civic participation in governance. In Russia, this included the creation of the Public Chamber and the Presidential Council for Civil Society and Human Rights (Evans 2008; Richter 2009a, 2009b; Henderson 2011; Richter and Hatch 2013). It also culminated in amendments to the NGO law in 2009 that decrease the audit frequency from annually to once every three years, remove language about denying registration based on threat to national interest, and simplify the registration process (Machalek 2012). During his presidency, Medvedev also elevated the role of the Presidential Council for Civil Society and Human Rights, sending a signal that the government might sometimes want to work with civil society groups in a consultative relationship (Flikke 2016). The Russian government tackled the challenge posed by the color revolutions by pulling NGOs closer underneath the state umbrella while still allowing them to operate. Wilson (2010, 26) argues that the Russian government has adopted a "paternalistic model of civil society" in which NGOs continue to operate under the "protective wing of government scrutiny."

In China, despite the tighter initial 1998 regulations, there have also been some positive developments toward increasing the role of civil society in governance. Politics in China has become increasingly pluralized, with many new non-state actors becoming involved in policymaking as "policy entrepreneurs" (Mertha 2008, 2009). For example, after the 2008 Wenchuan earthquake in Sichuan province, local government officials learned how civil society organizations could assist with vital disaster relief (Teets 2009). Recognizing the potential overlap between state goals and civil society in China has opened an area of scholarship focusing on relatively autonomous civil society groups that can engage in cooperation, collaboration, and learning with state actors (Lu 2007; He 2011; Hildebrandt 2013; Koesel 2014; Teets 2014). In this new consultative authoritarian model (Teets 2014), Chinese civil society organizations and the government can find mutually beneficial relationships, despite the regulatory environment that emphasizes strict control and management.

However, in response to the Arab Spring, state-society relations in Russia and China took a more restrictive turn. These events, which manifested in the 2011–2012 election protests in Russia and the 2011 pro-democracy protests in China, also coincided with major leadership successions in both countries, a time when regimes are more susceptible to popular uprisings (Hess 2016; Trejo 2012; McAdam and Tarrow 2010; Bunce 1981). The 2011–2012 Russian protests were a reaction to leadership turnover, erupting after allegations of electoral fraud in the December 2011 Duma elections, but also reinforced by dissatisfaction and backlash against the earlier announcement in September that Medvedev and Putin planned to trade places in their positions of power (Koesel and Bunce 2012; Lipman and Petrov 2012; Gel'man 2013). Although not centered around national elections, the timing of the Arab Spring protests and the threat of their diffusion also coincided with a leadership transition in China, which caused a tightening of political space (Dickson 2011). After a year marked by political scandals, the Eighteenth National Congress of the Chinese Communist Party in November 2012 unveiled the transfer of power over the Party between Hu Jintao and Xi Jinping, made complete by Xi's election to the presidency in March 2013 at the Twelfth National People's Congress. Xi's rise to power in late 2012 and Putin's return to the presidency earlier that same year set the stage for a tightening of restrictions on civil society in Russia and China. It is against this background of foreign aid to civil society, waves of revolution, and leadership transition that the most recent laws governing foreign influence on civil society have developed.

Case Study: Comparing Recent Laws on Foreign Support to Civil Society

Shaped by the events of the color revolutions and the Arab Spring, Russian and Chinese leaders have developed a similar view of state-society relations and a "shared perspective regarding interactions with the Western powers, most notably the United States" (Wilson 2009, 369–370). This convergence of views has led both regimes to enact similar policies for the management of foreign influence to civil society in the 2010s: the 2012 foreign agent law (and the accompanying 2015 law on undesirable organizations) in Russia and the 2017 Overseas NGO Management Law in China. The following sections consider each of these new laws in turn. Perceptions, evaluations, and comments on these new regulations are drawn from interviews conducted from 2015 to 2017 with over 140 respondents from more than 80 different international and domestic organizations currently or formerly operating in Russia and China. The majority of interviewees are from the field of environmental civil society. Environmental civil society groups in both Russia and China are widely considered some of the strongest organizations in these countries, with a long history and a large contribution to civil society development (Henry 2010; Crotty et al. 2014; Ho 2001; Schwartz 2004; Hildebrandt 2013). In addition to environmental organizations, interviews were conducted with journalists, researchers, foreign and domestic government officials, international and domestic grant-making organizations, and other domestic civil society groups (for example, indigenous organizations, media freedom organizations, and grassroots park movements). All interviews were conducted by the author in the language of the interviewee's preference (Russian or Mandarin, or in a handful of cases English). These interviews have been de-identified to protect the individual respondents and their organizations.[2] A list of cited interviews follows this chapter.

RUSSIA: THE 2012 FOREIGN AGENT LAW

After the 2011 Russian election protests, the discussion of the role of foreign funding of civil society groups in exacerbating threats to state stability resurfaced, culminating in the creation of the law on foreign agents. The first mention of the planned regulations was in February 2012 during a Duma roundtable, where members of United Russia, the Liberal Democratic Party (LDPR), and the Communist Party (KPRF) emphasized the importance of increasing control over foreign funding to Russian NGOs (Lenta.ru 2012; Ivanov and Granik 2012). The Duma deputies discussed plans for increased reporting requirements, unscheduled audits, and a determination of whether the organization took part in political activity. Public support for the initiative arose in March 2012 as part of an Internet campaign on Podkontrol.ru, where Putin declared that any petition with more than 100,000 signatures would be given consideration by the State Duma (Infox.ru 2012). Duma deputy Alexander Sidyakin sponsored the legislation, officially introducing it as a draft bill on June 29, and although the Presidential Council for Civil Society and Human Rights met with Putin on July 10 to discuss its concerns, the Duma approved the legislation on July 13 (Kuz'menkova and Artem'ev 2012; Flikke 2016, 110–111). On July 20, Putin signed the law on foreign agents (amendments to Federal Law No. 121-FZ), thereby requiring any Russian NGO that accepts foreign funding and engages in ambiguously defined political activity to register as a foreign agent with the Russian Ministry of Justice or face heavy fines.

This fast-track approach to the creation of the law on foreign agents led to several problems at various stages of implementation. Although the law went into effect in November 2012, it was not broadly enforced until the following spring. In the early months of 2013, nearly ninety-four organizations were subjected to unplanned audits in more than twenty-eight regions across Russia (Davidoff 2013). Groups found in violation of the law for not previously registering as foreign agents were ordered to pay steep fines, and many organizations were consequently shut down. At first the law required organizations to voluntarily register themselves as foreign agents, and most organizations refused. The law had to be amended in June 2014 to allow the Ministry of Justice to add groups to the register of foreign agents without their consent (Interfax 2014). But since there was no corresponding mechanism to remove organizations from the list, the law was amended again to provide for their removal (RFERL 2015). However, once removed, the organization remained on the online register on the Ministry of Justice website, with a column indicating the date the foreign agent status was "suspended." This practice continued to stigmatize organizations that were legally removed from the register. After organizations lobbied, this was changed in January 2017, so those organizations with suspended status could be removed from the online list entirely. The necessity of making so many changes to the law during its implementation is a consequence of the rushed nature of passing the legislation without proper input from civil society, experts, or practitioners.

According to Ministry of Justice data available as of April 3, 2019, seventy-four organizations are on the register of organizations fulfilling the function of foreign agents, with 181 having been affected by the label at some point.[3] A handful of organizations have voluntarily registered, but the Ministry of Justice has added the majority without their consent following the June 2014 amendment. Out of the 181 organizations that have ever been on the list, at least 107 of them have been removed from the list either because of liquidation of legal status or because they successfully contested their inclusion on the list. Organizations that have been removed typically file a lawsuit arguing that they have ceased receiving foreign funds and/or no longer engage in political activity. For example, the Soldiers' Mothers organization of St. Petersburg was finally taken off the register after returning a foreign grant (*Moscow Times* 2015). But many other organizations have decided to liquidate their legal status. Reasons for an organization's decision to shut down may include not being able to pay the fine for non-compliance with the law, not wanting to pay legal fees to fight the label in court, facing bankruptcy after returning foreign funding, or a combination of these and other reasons. Organizations that remain on the list are subject to increased reporting requirements, can be the target of an unlimited number of unscheduled audits, and must label all their materials as being produced by a foreign agent. Besides the stigma of having to use the label "foreign agent" on all published material, the increased reporting requirements and audits are prohibitively time and resource intensive and would distract the organization from its normal operations.

Furthermore, in 2015 the law on undesirable organizations was passed, which gives authorities the discretion to shut down any international organization that threatens national security. This move was interpreted both as a follow-up to the foreign agents law and as a precaution leading up to the 2016 Duma elections (Luhn 2015). As of November 27, 2019, there are nineteen organizations on this list, including the National Endowment for Democracy, George Soros's Open Society Foundation and Open Society Institute Assistance Foundation, the National Democratic Institute, and the International Republican Institute.[4] These organizations have been barred from Russia, but many others that thought they might end up on the list left Russia preemptively, including the MacArthur Foundation and the Charles Stewart Mott Foundation.[5] This has further restricted funding options for domestic Russian civil society organizations, since these major international foundations have indefinitely suspended their grant-making to Russia.

RUSSIAN NGO REACTIONS TO THE FOREIGN AGENT LAW

Interviews with NGO leaders from domestic and international organizations operating (or formerly operating) in Russia provide more information on the law's direct and indirect effects. In terms of direct impacts on civil society, many interviewees expressed concern that the foreign agent law has significantly constrained their available funding sources (Interview 11; Interview 21; Interview 41).[6] One interviewee emphasized the lack of domestic funding for civil society in Russia, arguing that the meager presidential grants were not enough to replace foreign funding sources (Interview 82). For those who have been labeled foreign agents, trying to fight the label in court buries the NGOs in paperwork and distracts from their ability to do their normal everyday work (Interview 14; Interview 17; Interview 19; Interview 23). Many also had to raise funds to be able to pay the fine for not registering in the first place, which often took the form of collecting donations from members or a public crowd-funding campaign (Interview 17). Furthermore, after being labeled a foreign agent, organizations are required to include a warning on any of their published materials, including their website, to let readers know that the material has been prepared by a foreign agent. For some organizations, having to include this label is unbearable. Instead, some have decided to voluntarily take down their websites or suspend new postings while they fight the label in court, which obviously makes it difficult to continue to organize and spread information (Interview 23).

There are also ripple effects from the law for the entire NGO community, even for those NGOs that have not been added to the list of foreign agents or undesirable organizations or for those trying to work with them. For example, one organization was audited, but although the organization received foreign funding, it was not ultimately labeled as a foreign agent as result of that audit (Interview 29). Although this interviewee seemed relieved, they also noted that the organization has decided to lie low and try not to attract attention, for fear that something might be interpreted as political activity in the future (Interview 29). Another interviewee at an international organization observed that some domestic partner organizations had cooled relations, either not wanting to receive funding from abroad or not wanting to have any formal ties with international organizations (Interview 86). Confirming this, one interviewee at a domestic environmental organization mentioned that they were afraid to work with international organizations at all, let alone accept funding from abroad (Interview 99). This evidence indicates some amount of self-censorship at the level of domestic organizations in Russia, limiting their behavior in order to not trigger the negative consequences of either law.

However, some interviewees at domestic Russian organizations saw a silver lining in the law. One mentioned that the law could incentivize domestic Russian organizations to pay more attention to simpler, local issues that directly affect the population, rather than going after international grants that tend to finance abstract or broader-reaching campaigns (Interview 16). Others agreed with the basic sentiment of the law and thought that Russian organizations should not be depending on foreign money to conduct their work domestically (Interview 36; Interview 38). The problem, of course, is that these groups often do not have access to alternative domestic funding sources.

One interviewee mentioned that they are getting creative about solutions to the law, such as registering as a commercial, for-profit organization (Interview 21). They are also looking for ways to increase crowdfunding or donations from private citizens in Russia as a way to replace the now-stigmatized foreign funding (Interview 21). Another interviewee mentioned that if the organization were to formally close (it eventually did), it was likely to open in a different form, finding a way to "change its skin like a snake" (Interview 38). Some other activists mentioned that their group decided not to formally register as an official organization or seek legal status (which is necessary for receiving grants, whether domestic or foreign) because formal organizations can more easily be closed down by the authorities (Interview 11). A representative of a different organization explained that they decided not to register formally in part because of the new law (Interview 32). Another said that they are trying to move away from a legal structure with one clear leader to a mass movement without a discernible leader (Interview 21).

In short, interview material confirms that the foreign agent and undesirable organizations laws present a significant challenge for domestic Russian civil society organizations, decreasing both the supply of and the demand for foreign funding. Although some international organizations will continue to operate in Russia, the demand for their partnership has lessened. Without foreign funding, it will be difficult for some of the most well-developed and long-standing organizations to secure funding for their operational costs and program budgets. Furthermore, although the law may be discouraging formal registration in favor of leaderless, informal grassroots movements that are harder for the state to control, these groups would have even less access to funding (most groups registered in the first place to be eligible to receive grants, both foreign and domestic) and fewer opportunities to engage formally with government officials as professionals or experts on public policies. These impacts on civil society in Russia from the foreign agent law may be helpful to consider when evaluating similar legislation passed in 2017 in China.

CHINA: THE 2017 OVERSEAS NGO LAW AND 2016 CHARITY LAW

After years of stalling on clarifying regulations for both domestic and international civil society organizations operating in China, the Chinese government passed two significant new laws governing the third sector within months of each other. The first is the Charity Law, passed in March 2016 and implemented in September 2016, which decreases registration requirements for domestic Chinese NGOs and increases incentives for domestic charitable giving. While the 2016 Charity Law has been widely lauded for helping domestic Chinese civil society, the 2017 Law on the Management of Overseas Non-Governmental Organizations' Activities within Mainland China (referred to here as the Overseas NGO Law for simplicity) has largely been described by international media outlets as a "crackdown" on foreign influence in Chinese civil society since its passage in April 2016 (Wong 2016), although some scholars have tempered this assessment (Hsu and Teets 2016; Shieh 2017).

Both laws align with Xi Jinping's commitment to law-based governance (*yifa zhiguo*, 依法治国), but the 2017 Overseas NGO Law also carries with it a renewed attention to national security. The first draft of the Overseas NGO Law was not made public, but the second draft of the law was opened for public comment from May to June 2015 (China Development Brief 2015). One of the major concerns was the transfer of foreign NGO management from the Ministry of Civil Affairs to the Ministry of Public Security, which was widely interpreted as a signal of the state's underlying assumptions about foreign NGO activity (Gan 2016). The law also requires foreign NGOs and their partners to reregister with the Ministry of Public Security and a new professional supervisory unit (PSU) from an approved list. Once registered, organizations must annually report their planned activities for the year ahead to these authorities. The law was somewhat amended after the period of public comments, but the main reporting and registration requirements under the Ministry of Public Security remained. Overall, the process of passing the Overseas NGO Law took about sixteen months (Shieh 2017). Despite the national security undertones and a closely guarded first draft, the second draft and subsequent final text of the law carried with it the hallmarks of the CCP's increasingly deliberative authoritarian process.

Furthermore, the 2017 Overseas NGO Law has roots in earlier experimental legislation in Yunnan province. As a part of China's decentralization policies, local and regional policy experimentation became commonplace (Montinola, Qian, and Weingast 1995; Heilmann 2008). Yunnan province has historically attracted international development aid since the 1990s, and for a long time it was considered one of the most open provinces for civil society work (Hildebrandt 2013; Cooper 2006; Ho 2001). Although regional and local government officials in Yunnan province may have learned some positive lessons from civil society cooperation for disaster relief or poverty alleviation (Teets 2009), they also had some clashes, including over hydroelectric dams on the Nu River (Mertha 2008). This led the provincial authorities to enact their own, more stringent regulations on foreign NGOs operating within Yunnan province (Hsu and Teets 2016). The regulations required a similar system of dual registration (although under the Ministry of Civil Affairs, not Public Security), reporting requirements, and reregistration every two years. Despite the stricter requirements, Hsu and Teets (2016) find that few overseas and domestic NGOs were adversely affected, and by December 2010, approximately 140 overseas NGOs had been successfully registered under the new regulations (Shieh 2017). The policy experimentation in Yunnan set the stage for national-level legislation, adding another layer of careful deliberation to the lawmaking process in China.

However, even the slow process by which the law was developed did not rescue it from problems of implementation. The Ministry of Public Security, now tasked with presiding over foreign NGO management, significantly delayed information that organizations needed in order to register, including guidelines on the law and a list of official PSUs, which came out in the last few weeks of 2016 (Hancock 2016). When the law went into effect on January 1, 2017, no international NGOs had yet successfully registered. Instead, the registrations slowly trickled in, with thirty-two high-profile organizations—mostly trade and business associations—registering in late January 2017 (Lu 2017). According to the Ministry of Public Security, as of November 25, 2019, a total of 410 international organizations have successfully registered 499 representative offices under the new law, which is a drop in the bucket compared to the 7,000 international organizations that are estimated to operate in China (Wu 2017).[7] At the time of writing, at least one organization—the American Bar Association—has decided to preemptively cease its operations in mainland China, moving its office to Hong Kong (Cassens Weiss 2017). However, most other organizations have decided to remain in mainland China to wait out the regulatory uncertainty.

CHINESE NGO REACTIONS TO THE OVERSEAS NGO LAW AND CHARITY LAW

When asked about the Overseas NGO Law in 2016, most interviewees expressed uncertainty about the new law and how it would affect them (Interview 69; Interview 78; Interview 107; Interview 110; Interview 116). On the one hand, interviewees mentioned that having a legal structure and clear laws to govern the activities of international organizations in China was an important step (Interview 52; Interview 110). This is because for years international NGOs have operated in a legal gray area. On the other hand, others mentioned that this gray area gave foreign organizations some space to maneuver, and that as long as they didn't do anything too sensitive, they could continue their work relatively unhindered (Interview 52). Some interviewees felt that the Overseas NGO Law will change this atmosphere of relaxed understanding and make it clear what will and will not be tolerated.

Even after January 1, 2017, organizations continued to express uneasiness about the atmosphere of uncertainty. Many international organizations were still struggling to find a PSU in order to legally register (Interview 140). Interviewees complained that even those government agencies on the list of approved PSUs were reluctant to partner with any organizations, especially because they have no incentive to do so and because they would bear all the responsibility if an NGO were to go "rogue" (Interview 130; Interview 139). Some international NGOs have front-loaded their funding during 2016 to make up for their period of inactivity in 2017 before obtaining reregistration; others are considering reregistering as businesses; still another is now funneling money to domestic grantee organizations through domestic Chinese foundations (Interview 130; Interview 127). Some domestic organizations mentioned that they felt deterred from working with foreign partners or taking money directly from international foundations during this uncertain period in the early part of the year (Interview 127). International organizations also noted that some of their grantees had already been "taken out for tea" and questioned by the authorities, which may deter them from applying for the international NGOs' grants in the future (Interview 140).

Several interviewees also noted that domestic NGOs and international NGOs were receiving two completely different sets of messages from the relevant authorities. While international NGOs were being told that they would be registered and just need to wait, domestic NGOs were already being told explicitly which international NGOs not to accept funding from or otherwise partner with (Interview 139; Interview 141). While the implementation of the law involves a public whitelist on the Ministry of Public Security's website, in practice, there may be an informal or internal blacklist of organizations that domestic NGOs are being warned to avoid. This suggests that the Chinese government potentially intends to freeze out organizations by delaying their registration and deterring domestic partners, instead of creating a public record of their rejection. Whether or not this is true, the law has certainly created a chilling effect for foreign NGOs operating in China (Interview 130).

Interviewees agree that the strongest signal international organizations received was that the management of overseas NGOs would be transferred from the Ministry of Civil Affairs to the Ministry of Public Security (Interview 107; Interview 116). This transfer has signaled to international organizations that the underlying assumption about their activities has changed. Instead of being perceived as "good" organizations helping China, they are now seen as doing something suspicious that could undermine the stability of the country (Interview 110; Interview 116). There are also perceptions that the law will cause international NGOs to cut funding to their programs in China or leave China entirely, so foreign funding might become more limited in the future (Interview 73; Interview 107). Some international organizations have already considered the potential administrative burden from the new law and have discussed decreasing funding for programs in China or stopping activities in China entirely (Interview 78). One interviewee, a former employee at an international environmental organization in Beijing, said that the Overseas NGO Law was a key factor in deciding to leave the organization for a job at a domestic Chinese think tank (Interview 109). One interviewee predicts that if international funding opportunities shrink, there will be a gap in funding for civil society organizations, since Chinese foundations are in an earlier stage of development and will not be able to immediately replace the lost funding from abroad (Interview 107).

Some organizations see a silver lining in the new law. One interviewee hoped that these changes would encourage the Chinese business sector to invest more in local domestic NGOs (Interview 78). This same interviewee also thought that if international NGOs leave China, then their professionals might have to switch to jobs at domestic organizations, which would help to build professional capacity at domestic NGOs (Interview 78). There are also hopes that the new Charity Law will help encourage the development of domestic Chinese foundations and increase the sources of domestic funding from the private sector. Several interviewees were optimistic about the new Charity Law (Interview 52; Interview 107; Interview 128). Another interviewee at a domestic foundation thought that the law was encouraging; Chinese foundations had learned as much as they could from international ones, and now domestic foundations were ready to take over as the primary donors to Chinese civil society (Interview 133). However, similar to the Russian foreign agent law that ambiguously defines political activity, there is also a line in the new law prohibiting organizations that "undermine social stability and national security." This ambiguous language has worried some interviewees, since it is unclear how it will be interpreted, and it could be used to selectively prosecute those NGOs that are seen as "troublemakers" (Interview 52).

Because some of the changes to regional law on civil society management in Yunnan province in 2010 have been incorporated into the new law, interviews with organizations in Yunnan were able to give a fuller long-term perspective. Organizations there have already described some problems with these changes, including having the government refuse to approve a joint program with an international donor (Interview 114). Furthermore, over the past few years many international organizations have left Yunnan province, which was once a hub for international NGOs, particularly environment and development organizations. For one interviewee, the reason many international NGOs left Yunnan was because of the change in regulations, which shifted the province from a particularly accommodating region to one that was more difficult to work in than other parts of China (Interview 116). Another interviewee, however, thought that international organizations were leaving the province because of funding issues, not because of political pressure or bureaucratic red tape (Interview 115).

Overall, the perceived impacts of the Overseas NGO Law have some similarities to the actual impacts of the Russian laws on foreign agents and undesirables. First, organizations fear a decrease in foreign funding, especially if many international organizations choose to leave China entirely. NGO leaders are also expecting a funding gap, since Chinese foundations might not be developed enough to replace the lost funding. In addition, international organizations and domestic organizations wishing to work with them think the law will bring some level of increased bureaucratic burden. As a final important difference, although the Overseas NGO Law may be worrying, many interviewees are simultaneously optimistic about the positive impacts associated with the new Charity Law. There is also the sense that, because of the nature of the law, many international organizations will be able to register and continue operating in China, even as a few more sensitive groups are quietly shut out from registration.

Discussion: The Laws in Comparative Perspective

The background on the development of the laws confirms that Russian and Chinese leaders share similar motivations and intent. The laws were formulated after the events of the color revolutions and the Arab Spring, and their timing coincided with leadership transitions in both countries. The language of the laws also underscores national security concerns, and their implementation makes use of uncertainty and ambiguity. Both laws have vague language about political activity or harming national interest that could be used to selectively prosecute those civil society actors deemed troublesome. Furthermore, the uncertain atmosphere created by uneven or incomplete implementation of the laws has succeeded in getting some organizations to preemptively shut themselves down or move operations, while other organizations might choose to self-censor their activities or partnerships to avoid state repression. Finally, because both laws fall short of completely ousting foreign organizations or their funding, Chinese and Russian leaders can use the laws to shape civil society to their liking, recognizing some utility to having an active civil society in certain areas.

In terms of concrete impacts, the laws in both countries constrain the funding available for domestic civil society organizations. For some organizations, this will create a funding gap, since domestic charitable giving might not immediately be developed enough to replace the loss in international grants. China has a more hopeful situation with respect to domestic charitable foundations, especially with increased incentives under the new Charity Law. However, groups operating in the most sensitive issue areas (human rights, for example) that have been largely dependent on foreign funding will be the most vulnerable, since it may be difficult for them to convince a domestic charity to support their programming.

Fighting the new regulations or waiting to be legally in compliance with them has also distracted or stalled organizations from working on their primary goals. Although Russian organizations are more visibly and directly dealing with the effects of the law through court cases, paperwork, and fines, international NGOs in China are unable to make new grants or continue their activities while they wait for registration. Furthermore, as some of the interviews implied, there may be organizations that the Chinese government never intends to register that will slowly lose their ability to operate in China as they are isolated from domestic partners. Even though some international organizations will continue to operate and fund domestic groups in both countries, the laws have caused ripple effects throughout Russian and Chinese civil society, chilling the atmosphere for domestic-international NGO partnership.

There are also important differences that can be seen by putting the two laws, their development, and their implementation in comparative perspective. First, the Russian foreign agent law was conspicuously rushed through the Duma without public comment and without much input from practitioners or experts. By contrast, the Chinese law took a total of sixteen months to pass, with several drafts, a period of public comments, and amendments to the draft before it passed. This highlights a key difference in governance strategies between Russia and China: while China has chosen a deliberative authoritarian path, Russia tends to exclude public participation in governance or carefully control it through institutions such as the Public Chamber and the Presidential Council for Civil Society and Human Rights. Second, there is a difference in each law's approach to public records. In Russia, the Ministry of Justice has maintained two public blacklists on its website: one with undesirable foreign organizations and, until recently, one with domestic foreign agents. This decision stigmatizes the organizations, and these labels are often reported in state-controlled media with an underlining goal of shaming the organizations, but it can also draw negative feedback from the international community.

In China, however, the Ministry of Public Security keeps a public whitelist of international organizations that have successfully registered, highlighting and rewarding groups whose interests happen to align with state goals while quietly "freezing out" those organizations whose interests do not. This may be a strategy intended to deter criticism from abroad and perhaps a sincere indication that China is still open to most international collaboration. It could also signal a higher degree of uncertainty about state intentions among the NGO community, which is clear from interviewees' worries about an internal blacklist that would mean certain "troublesome" international groups will find it difficult to secure registration. In any case, the Chinese approach to the 2017 Overseas NGO Law has been more cautious and deliberative than the haphazard Russian approach to the 2012 law on foreign agents and 2015 law on undesirable organizations.

Conclusions and Broader Implications

Recent laws on the management of foreign NGOs and foreign funding to domestic civil society in Russia and China provide a window into parallel state motivations, strategies for shaping civil society, and methods of authoritarian governance. It also shows how these laws have similarly affected civil society organizations by dampening (but not ruining) the atmosphere for international-domestic partnership, decreasing the ease of obtaining funding from abroad, and increasing bureaucratic burden. Key differences in the laws can be seen in their development (fast-tracked versus deliberative), the decisions about public records (blacklist versus whitelist), and methods of punishment (direct impact versus freezing out). In this concluding section, I examine three final areas: (1) public opinion regarding the laws and anti-foreign sentiment in general, (2) unintended consequences of the law, and (3) evidence for governing between repression and liberalization in authoritarian regimes.

First, these laws are not isolated or unsupported actions by the regime to curtail foreign influence; they are supported both by donor-driven funding priorities and by broader trends in negative views of influence from abroad. After the color revolutions and the Arab Spring, Russian and Chinese leaders used negative framing of the events to dissuade domestic demand for similar movements (see Chapter 4). This negative framing could more easily apply to domestic professional NGOs that had received foreign assistance because their local communities were less familiar with their work or goals. As scholars of both countries have noted, civil society assistance tended to focus on the donor-driven priorities of professionalization and capacity building, which were often divorced from local needs and bottom-up demand (Henderson 2003; Sundstrom 2006; Spires 2012). This created civil society organizations that, while professionalized, were less connected to their local communities, which may undermine public support for these organizations. Furthermore, a negative framing of foreign influence on civil society as undermining the Russian and Chinese regimes resonates with public opinion in both countries. In a recent poll, 81 percent of Russians reported having an unfavorable view of the United States (Pew Research Center 2015). Similarly, 77 percent of Chinese respondents agreed that "our way of life needs to be protected against foreign influence" (Pew Research Center 2016). The combination of a primed public and a misunderstanding of and disconnect from the role of professionalized civil society organizations has led to domestic support for these types of laws.

However, although these publicly supported laws have made foreign assistance to civil society more difficult in both countries, there are also some hints of unintended consequences for the regime. In Russia, the law is dissuading informal grassroots movements from formally registering. It is also causing some formally registered organizations that end up on the foreign agent list to liquidate their formal legal status but continue to operate. These types of organizations or movements are much harder for the state to control through formal laws and regulations. In both countries, dissuading formal organizations from taking foreign funding may also help already professionalized organizations reconnect to their communities, solving some of the problems of donor-driven priorities mentioned in the literature and in the interview material presented earlier.

A final important takeaway is that these trends in civil society management in hybrid and authoritarian regimes such as Russia and China show how these regimes must find a balance between the pressures of liberalization and repression (as highlighted in Chapter 1). Sensing a threat from international support of domestic civil society, both Russia and China have made moves to further restrict and control international funding and international influence within their borders. However, neither regime has completely blocked foreign funding or foreign organizations. Instead, these laws are being used (directly or indirectly) to repress certain troublesome organizations while allowing others. Importantly, however, although many international groups still operate in Russia and make grants to civil society, the Russian authorities have made the repressive parts of the laws forward-facing, stigmatizing the foreign agents and undesirable organizations. Meanwhile, while many international organizations will be able to register under the new law in China, some organizations will struggle to register or may be quietly denied. Whether publicly or privately repressing some groups, both regimes strike a balance between complete liberalization and full repression. These findings reflect the somewhat contradictory trends that others have found in this volume (Chapters 3 and 5), where repression can coexist alongside critical voices. Even when managing the foreign, both regimes are balancing the threats and benefits to their rule.

Notes

1. USAID maintained a similar level of annual aid to Russia until the Russian government forced it to close operations in 2012. Archived congressional budget justifications for USAID with exact funding amounts can be found on USAID's website: https://www.usaid.gov/results-and-data/budget-spending/congressional-budget-justification.

2. Some individuals interviewed gave the author permission to use their names or the names of their organizations. However, since this is such a small community, all respondents are de-identified to deter identification of other interviewees (who explicitly asked for confidentiality) through a process of elimination.

3. As of April 3, 2019, according to the list on the Ministry of Justice website (in Russian): http://unro.minjust.ru/NKOForeignAgent.aspx. The author used this list to create her own database of organizations listed as foreign agents. The list used to be accessible without registration, but in April 2019 the information platform now requires registration and is only accessible to Russian citizens or registered organizations. The author retains archived data from the previous publicly accessible list updated through April 3, 2019.

4. As of November 27, 2019, according to the Ministry of Justice's official list: http://minjust.ru/ru/activity/nko/unwanted. This list is still publicly available as of November 27, 2019, without registration.

5. Both foundations published statements explaining their decision to leave Russia: MacArthur Foundation, "Statement of MacArthur President Julia Stasch on the Foundation's Russia Office," July 21, 2015, https://www.macfound.org/press/press-releases/statement-macarthur-president-julia-stasch-foundations-russia-office; Charles Stewart Mott Foundation, "Statement on Foundation's Grantmaking in Russia," July 24, 2015, https://www.mott.org/news/articles/statement-on-foundations-grantmaking-in-russia.

6. Interviews are numbered according to the order in which they occurred during the study period. A list of cited interviews with more information is included at the end of this chapter.

7. Information on registered representative offices for Overseas NGOs is regularly updated on the Ministry of Public Security website (in Mandarin) and compiled in English by China File's NGO Project. For the latest data, see http://www.chinafile.com/ngo/registered-foreign-ngo-offices-map-full-screen.

References

Beissinger, Mark. 2007. "Structure and Example in Modular Political Phenomena: The Diffusion of Bulldozer/Rose/Orange/Tulip Revolutions." *Perspectives on Politics* 5, no. 2: 259–276.

Bunce, Valerie. 1981. *Do New Leaders Make a Difference? Executive Succession and Public Policy Under Capitalism and Socialism*. Princeton: Princeton University Press.

Bunce, Valerie, and Sharon Wolchik. 2011. *Defeating Authoritarian Leaders in Postcommunist Countries*. Cambridge: Cambridge University Press.

Cassens Weiss, Debra. 2017. "ABA Initiative Pulls Out of Beijing Amid Uncertainty Caused by Law Regulating Foreign Nonprofits." *ABA Journal*, January 3.

China Development Brief. 2015. "Draft Overseas NGO Law Released Online for Public Consultation." May 6. http://chinadevelopmentbrief.cn/news/foreign-ngo-law-released-online-for-public-consultation.

Christensen, Darin, and Jeremy M. Weinstein. 2013. "Defunding Dissent: Restrictions on Aid to NGOs." *Journal of Democracy* 24, no. 2: 77–91.

Cooper, Caroline M. 2006. "'This Is Our Way In': The Civil Society of Environmental NGOs in South-West China." *Government and Opposition* 41, no. 1: 109–136.

Crotty, Jo, Sarah Marie Hall, and Sergej Ljubownikow. 2014. "Post-Soviet Civil Society Development in the Russian Federation: The Impact of the NGO Law." *Europe-Asia Studies* 66, no. 8: 1253–1269.

Davidoff, Victor. 2013. "The Hunt for Foreign Agents Has Begun." *Moscow Times*, April 1.

Diamond, Larry. 1994. "Rethinking Civil Society: Toward Democratic Consolidation." *Journal of Democracy* 5, no. 3: 4–17.

Dickson, Bruce. 2011. "No 'Jasmine' for China." *Current History* 110, no. 737: 211–216.

Evans, Alfred B. Jr. 2008. "The First Steps of Russia's Public Chamber: Representation or Coordination?" *Demokratizatsiya* 16: 345–362.

Flikke, Geir. 2016. "Resurgent Authoritarianism: The Case of Russia's New NGO Legislation." *Post-Soviet Affairs* 32, no. 2: 103–131.

Gan, Nectar. 2016. "China's Controversial New Law on Foreign NGOs to Include Greater Police Oversight, Stricter Financial Scrutiny." *South China Morning Post*, April 26.

Gel'man, Vladimir. 2013. "Cracks in the Wall." *Problems of Post-Communism* 60, no. 2: 3–10.

Hancock, Tom. 2017. "Chinese Police Given Sweeping Powers over Foreign NGOs." *Financial Times*, December 30.

He, Baogang. 2011. "Civic Engagement Through Participatory Budgeting in China: Three Different Logics at Work." *Public Administration and Development* 31, no. 2: 122–133.

Heilmann, Sebastian. 2008. "From Local Experiments to National Policy: The Origins of China's Distinctive Policy Process." *China Journal* 59: 1–30.

Henderson, Sarah L. 2003. *Building Democracy in Contemporary Russia: Western Support for Grassroots Organizations*. Ithaca, NY: Cornell University Press.

Henderson, Sarah L. 2011. "Civil Society in Russia: State-Society Relations in the Post-Yeltsin Era." *Problems of Post-Communism* 58, no. 3: 11–27.

Henry, Laura. 2010. *Red to Green: Environmental Activism in Post-Soviet Russia.* Ithaca, NY: Cornell University Press.

Hess, Steve. 2016. "Sources of Authoritarian Resilience in Regional Protest Waves: The Post-Communist Colour Revolutions and 2011 Arab Uprisings." *Government and Opposition* 51, no. 1: 1–29.

Hildebrandt, Timothy. 2013. *Social Organizations and the Authoritarian State in China.* Cambridge: Cambridge University Press.

Ho, Peter. 2001. "Greening Without Conflict? Environmentalism, NGOs and Civil Society in China." *Development and Change* 32, no. 5: 893–921.

Hsu, Carolyn, and Jessica Teets. 2016. "Is China's New Overseas NGO Management Law Sounding the Death Knell for Civil Society? Maybe Not." *Asia-Pacific Journal* 14, no. 4: 1–17.

Infox.ru. 2012. "Granty i garanty" [Grants and guarantors]. March 28. http://www.infox.ru/authority/state/2012/03/28/Grantyy_i_garantyy_print.phtml.

Interfax. 2014. "Putin uprostil protseduru vklyucheniya NKO v reestr inostrannykh agentov" [Putin simplified the procedures for including NGOs on the register of foreign agents]. June 4. http://www.interfax.ru/russia/379650.

Ivanov, Maksim, and Irina Granik. 2012. "Nekommercheskii vybor Rossii" [Russia's non-commercial choice]. *Kommersant,* February 3. https://www.kommersant.ru/doc/1864484.

Jakobson, L. I., and C. V. Sanovich. 2009. "Smena modelej rossijskogo tret'ego sektora: faza Importozameshcheniia" [Changing models of the Russian third sector: the phase of import substitution]. *Obshchestvo i Reformy* 4: 21–34.

Keane, John. 1998. *Civil Society: Old Images, New Visions.* Stanford, CA: Stanford University Press.

Koesel, Karrie J. 2014. *Religion and Authoritarianism: Cooperation, Conflict, and the Consequences.* Cambridge: Cambridge University Press.

Koesel, Karrie J., and Valerie Bunce. 2012. "Putin, Popular Protests, and Political Trajectories in Russia: A Comparative Perspective." *Post-Soviet Affairs* 28, no. 4: 403–423.

Koesel, Karrie J., and Valerie Bunce. 2013. "Diffusion-Proofing: Russian and Chinese Responses to Waves of Popular Mobilizations Against Authoritarian Rulers." *Perspectives on Politics* 11, no. 3: 753–768.

Kudlenko, Anastasiia. 2015. "From Colour Revolutions to the Arab Spring: The Role of Civil Society in Democracy Building and Transition Processes." *Journal of Contemporary Central and Eastern Europe* 23, nos. 2–3: 167–179.

Kuz'menkova, Ol'ga, and Alexander Artem'ev. 2012. "Sidyakin raskryl 'inostrannykh agentov'" [Sidyakin uncovered "foreign agents"]. *Novaya Gazeta,* June 29. https://www.gazeta.ru/politics/2012/06/29_a_4650205.shtml.

Lenta.ru. 2012. "'Edinaya Rossiya' reshila 'fil'trovat'' rabotu NKO" [United Russia decided to "filter" the work of NGOs]. February 3. https://lenta.ru/news/2012/02/03/nko.

Linz, Juan J., and Alfred Stepan. 1996. *Problems of Democratic Transition and Consolidation: Southern Europe, South America and Post-Communist Europe.* Baltimore: Johns Hopkins University Press.

Lipman, Maria, and Nikolay Petrov. 2012. "What the Russian Protests Can—and Can't—Do: Why Putin's Grasp on Power Remains Firm." *Foreign Affairs*, February 9.

Lu, Yiyi. 2007. "The Autonomy of Chinese NGOs: A New Perspective." *China: An International Journal* 5, no. 2: 173–203.

Lu, Joanne. 2017. "32 Organizations Register with Police Under China's New Foreign NGO Law." *Humanosphere*, January 27. http://www.humanosphere.org/world-politics/2017/01/32-organizations-register-police-chinas-new-foreign-ngo-law.

Luhn, Alec. 2015. "Russia Bans 'Undesirable' International Organizations Ahead of 2016 Elections." *Guardian*, May 19.

Lum, Thomas. 2014. "U.S. Assistance Programs in China." Congressional Research Service. May 9. http://www.fas.org/sgp/crs/row/RS22663.pdf.

Machalek, Katherin. 2012. "Factsheet: Russia's NGO Laws." Freedom House. https://freedomhouse.org/sites/default/files/Fact%20Sheet_0.pdf.

Machleder, Josh. 2006. "Contextual and Legislative Analysis of the Russian Law on NGOs." INDEM Foundation. March 16. http://www.indem.ru/en/publicat/Russian_NGO_Law_03252006.pdf.

Mansfield, Edward D., and Jack Snyder. 1995. "Democratization and the Danger of War." *International Security* 20, no. 1: 5–38.

McAdam, Doug, and Sidney Tarrow. 2010. "Ballots and Barricades: On the Reciprocal Relationship Between Elections and Social Movements." *Perspectives on Politics* 8, no. 2: 529–542.

Mertha, Andrew. 2008. *China's Water Warriors: Citizen Action and Policy Change*. Ithaca, NY: Cornell University Press.

Mertha, Andrew. 2009. "Fragmented Authoritarianism 2.0: Political Pluralization in the Chinese Policy Process." *China Quarterly* 200: 995–1012.

Moscow Times. 2015. "Soldiers' Mothers NGO Removed from 'Foreign Agents' List." October 29.

Montinola, Gabriella, Yingyi Qian, and Barry R. Weingast. 1995. "Federalism, Chinese Style: The Political Basis for Economic Success in China." *World Politics* 48, no. 1: 50–81.

Owen, John M. 1994. "How Liberalism Produces Democratic Peace." *International Security* 19, no. 2: 87–125.

Pew Research Center. 2015. "Russian Public Opinion: Putin Praised, West Panned." June 10. http://www.pewglobal.org/2015/06/10/2-russian-public-opinion-putin-praised-west-panned.

Pew Research Center. 2016. "Chinese Public Sees More Powerful Role in the World, Name U.S. as Top Threat." October 5. http://www.pewglobal.org/2016/10/05/chinese-public-sees-more-powerful-role-in-world-names-u-s-as-top-threat.

Putnam, Robert. 1993. *Making Democracy Work*. Princeton: Princeton University Press.

RFERL. 2015. "Putin Proposes Conditions for Removing NGOs from 'Foreign Agents' List." Radio Free Europe Radio Liberty. February 5. http://www.rferl.org/content/russia-ngo-foreign-agents-law/26831174.html.

Richter, James. 2009a. "Putin and the Public Chamber." *Post-Soviet Affairs* 25: 40–66.

Richter, James. 2009b. "The Ministry of Civil Society? The Public Chambers in the Regions." *Problems of Post-Communism* 56, no. 6: 7–20.

Richter, James, and Walter F. Hatch. 2013. "Organizing Civil Society in Russia and China: A Comparative Approach." *International Journal of Politics, Culture, and Society* 26: 323–347.

Russett, Bruce. 1994. *Grasping the Democratic Peace: Principles for a Post-Cold War World.* Princeton: Princeton University Press.

Saari, Sinikukka. 2009. "European Democracy Promotion in Russia Before and After The 'Colour' Revolutions." *Democratization* 16, no. 4: 732–755.

Schwartz, Jonathan. 2004. "Environmental NGOs in China: Roles and Limits." *Pacific Affairs* 77, no. 1: 28–49.

Shieh, Shawn. 2017. "The Origins of China's New Law on Foreign NGOs." *China File*, January 31.

Spires, Anthony. 2011. "Contingent Symbiosis and Civil Society in an Authoritarian State: Understanding the Survival of China's Grassroots NGOs." *American Journal of Sociology* 117, no. 1: 1–45.

Spires, Anthony. 2012. "Foreign Influences on China's Emerging Civil Society." *China Journal* 68: 125–146.

Stewart, Susan. 2009a. "Democracy Promotion Before and After the 'Color Revolutions.'" *Democratization* 16, no. 4: 645–660.

Stewart, Susan. 2009b. "The Interplay of Domestic Contexts and External Democracy Promotion: Lessons from Eastern Europe and the South Caucasus." *Democratization* 16, no. 4: 804–824.

Sundstrom, Lisa M. 2006. *Funding Civil Society: Foreign Assistance and NGO Development in Russia.* Stanford, CA: Stanford University Press.

Teets, Jessica C. 2009. "Post-Earthquake Relief and Reconstruction Efforts: The Emergence of Civil Society in China?" *China Quarterly* 198: 330–347.

Teets, Jessica C. 2014. *Civil Society Under Authoritarianism: The China Model.* Cambridge: Cambridge University Press.

Tocqueville, Alexis de. [1835] 1994. *Democracy in America, First Part.* London: Everyman's Library.

Trejo, Guillermo. 2012. *Popular Movements in Autocracies: Religion, Repression, and Indigenous Collective Action in Mexico.* New York: Cambridge University Press.

USAID. 2010. "Russia: Foreign Assistance Program Overview." U.S. Agency for International Development, Congressional Budget Justification. http://pdf.usaid.gov/pdf_docs/PCAAB894.pdf.

Wilson, Jeanne L. 2009. "Coloured Revolutions: The View from Moscow and Beijing." *Journal of Communist Studies and Transition Politics* 25, no. 2: 369–395.

Wilson, Jeanne L. 2010. "The Legacy of the Color Revolutions for Russian Politics and Foreign Policy." *Problems of Post-Communism* 57, no. 2: 21–36.

Wong, Edward. 2016. "Clampdown in China Restricts 7,000 Foreign Organizations." *New York Times*, April 28.

Wu, D. D. 2017. "More than 7,000 Foreign NGOs in China: Only 91 Registered So Far." The *Diplomat*, June 2.

Appendix 7.1 List of Cited Interviews (Russia)

(Interview number, date, description, location*)
The "foreign agent" designation in parentheses means the organization has at some time been listed as such by the Ministry of Justice.

1. Interview 5, October 2015, international environmental NGO, Moscow
2. Interview 11, October 2015, domestic environmental movement, Moscow
3. Interview 14, October 2015, international environmental NGO, Moscow
4. Interview 16, October 2015, international environmental NGO, St. Petersburg
5. Interview 17, October 2015, domestic free press NGO (*foreign agent*), St. Petersburg
6. Interview 19, October 2015, international environmental NGO (*foreign agent*), St. Petersburg
7. Interview 21, October 2015, domestic environmental NGO, Moscow
8. Interview 23, November 2015, domestic environmental NGO (*foreign agent*), eastern Siberia
9. Interview 29, November 2015, domestic environmental NGO, St. Petersburg
10. Interview 32, November 2015, domestic environmental movement, St. Petersburg
11. Interview 33, November 2015, domestic environmental NGO (*foreign agent*),** eastern Siberia
12. Interview 36, November 2015, domestic environmental NGO (*foreign agent*),** eastern Siberia
13. Interview 38, November 2015, domestic environmental NGO (*foreign agent*),** eastern Siberia
14. Interview 41, November 2015, domestic environmental NGO, eastern Siberia
15. Interview 42, November 2015, domestic environmental NGO, western Russia
16. Interview 45, November 2015, domestic environmental NGO (*foreign agent*), northern Russia
17. Interview 82, July 2016, domestic environmental NGO, Moscow
18. Interview 86, July 2016, international environmental NGO, St. Petersburg
19. Interview 87, July 2016, international environmental NGO, St. Petersburg
20. Interview 99, August 2016, domestic environmental NGO, western Siberia

* To preserve confidentiality, outside of St. Petersburg and Moscow I use an approximate geographical location. (I do this instead of a region's name since each region often only has one "foreign agent").

**Different individual interviews with representatives of the same organization.

Appendix 7.2 List of Cited Interviews (China)

(Interview number, date, description, location*)

1. Interview 52, February 2016, domestic civil society NGO in Beijing (former employee), Hong Kong
2. Interview 57, March 2016, domestic environmental NGO, Beijing
3. Interview 69, May 2016, international environmental NGO, Beijing
4. Interview 73, May 2016, domestic environmental NGO, Shanghai
5. Interview 78, May 2016, international environmental NGO, Beijing
6. Interview 107, August 2016, domestic civil society NGO, Beijing
7. Interview 109, August 2016, international environmental NGO (former employee), Beijing
8. Interview 110, August 2016, international environmental NGO, Beijing
9. Interview 114, August 2016, domestic environmental NGO, Yunnan

10. Interview 115, August 2016, international environmental NGO (former employee), Yunnan
11. Interview 116, August 2016, international environmental NGO, Yunnan
12. Interview 127, January 2017, domestic environmental NGO, Guangdong
13. Interview 128, January 2017, university-based civil society expert, Guangdong
14. Interview 130, January 2017, official at a foreign consulate, Guangdong
15. Interview 133, January 2017, domestic charitable foundation, Guangdong
16. Interview 139, January 2017, international environmental NGO, Beijing
17. Interview 140, January 2017, international NGO, Beijing
18. Interview 141, January 2017, official at a foreign embassy, Beijing

* To preserve confidentiality, I have listed the province instead of the exact city outside of Beijing and Shanghai.

8 }

Holding the Government's Attention
STATE SECTOR WORKERS IN CHINA
Manfred Elfstrom

Labor activism has played an important if underappreciated role in the politics of China and Russia. Workers in both countries took to the streets in 1989. Their mobilization since then has converged and diverged. In this chapter, I focus on China and argue that labor there has powerful leverage over the state for several reasons, including its crucial role in the Chinese development model, the constant threat that labor protests will spread to other segments of society, and labor's symbolic function in a country that has largely embraced markets but retained elements of the ideological apparatus from its previous planned economy. Workers in state-owned enterprises (SOEs), in particular, while relatively quiescent today compared to others, especially migrant workers in private enterprises, present an added challenge: they are now concentrated in a few heavy and extractive industries and dominate inland company towns; they include a group of savvy organizers inherited from previous struggles; they are employed by government-run corporations, making their mobilization inherently politically loaded; and they have the weakened but still persuasive normative claim of being the old state socialist vanguard class. With a brief statistical analysis and some illustrative examples drawn from the news, I show that the government tends to react in a similar if not more forceful manner—in both coercive and conciliatory ways—to activism by employees of SOEs than to activism by employees of foreign-owned enterprises, who have received more attention lately. As other chapters in this volume demonstrate in various ways, the Chinese government, although lacking an organized opposition, must constantly attend to popular claims. And workers, especially those in the state sector, can hold the state's attention to a remarkable degree. Structures, norms, and experiences of protest inherited from the past still exert a powerful pull. This pull, I hypothesize, subtly shapes Chinese policymaking across a range of issues. It reveals much about governance not only in China but also in other post-state-socialist autocracies, including Russia.

Chinese and Russian Labor

In the spring and summer of 1989, workers took the streets in both the Soviet Union and the People's Republic of China in massive numbers. In Beijing and elsewhere in China, they formed workers' autonomous federations (WAFs) and decried the corruption, inflation, and new managerial prerogatives that came with Deng Xiaoping's market reforms, while supporting the calls for a political opening made by student protesters gathered in Tiananmen Square (despite the latter's elitism, which led student leaders to frequently marginalize the workers) (Perry 2002, ch. 10; Sheehan 1998, ch. 7; Walder and Gong 1993). Coal miners in Russia as well as other parts of the USSR, such as Ukraine, went on strike and, between 1989 and 1991, escalated from narrow economic claims into demands for the abolition of state socialism altogether (the system was viewed by many workers as benefiting only a small group of parasitic state managers) and the independence of the Soviet republics (even as steelworkers and others notably stayed on the job) (Crowley 1997). More than 400,000 miners took part in these actions, and they formed an independent miners union. They were joined by employees in oil and gas, transport, and the public sector (Vinogradova, Kozina, and Cook 2012, 220).

As noted by others in this volume, the two governments and their societies then deviated in crucial regards, though they retained important similarities. Chinese authorities massacred workers in Beijing—workers were treated much more harshly than students, by most accounts—and arrested WAF leaders including Han Dongfang (who eventually founded the advocacy group China Labour Bulletin in exile in Hong Kong) (on the repression, see Sheehan 1998, 221–222). Russian labor, in contrast, was part of a great working-class insurgency that had been growing in other parts of the Soviet bloc, especially Poland, for two decades. This insurgency, while sometimes repressed, spawned offshoot movements by intellectuals, farmers, and others, and ultimately helped bring about political liberalization across Eastern Europe and the breakup of the Soviet Union itself (on Poland, see Kubik 2000; Laba 1991; Ost 1990; Touraine et al. 1983). But democratization in the political arena was accompanied by disarray in the economic arena, with state assets looted by new oligarchs and workers going for long periods without pay or pensions. Moreover, in Russia especially, the new government retained or reacquired authoritarian characteristics, making it a hybrid regime or electoral autocracy (as explored in greater detail by others in this volume). Chinese labor, meanwhile, was left to soldier on under Chinese Communist Party (CCP) rule, as before. However, although China did not embark on "shock therapy" marketization, it nonetheless significantly restructured its SOEs over the coming decades, throwing millions of their employees out of work, like their Russian counterparts, something I will return to in later sections of this chapter (Lee 2007; Hurst 2009; Cai 2006).

Since this partial inflection point, workers in Russian and Chinese workers have alternately converged and diverged in their mobilization. In the 1990s, Russian labor organized into militant alternative unions outside of the (misnamed) Federation of Independent Trade Unions of Russia (FNPR), the successor to the Communist Party–controlled General Confederation of Trade Unions of the Soviet Union—a development hard to imagine in the Chinese context, despite the brief existence of WAFs. Unpaid wages and pensions led to a wave of activism at the end of the decade, even if difficulty attributing blame for the arrears prevented the wave from becoming bigger than it did (Javeline 2003; Robertson 2011). At points, workers' aims overlapped with those of local political elites, who used strikes to bargain with Moscow (Robertson 2007). But a new labor law in 2002 narrowed the legal space for striking and helped the FNPR reassert dominance (Pringle and Clarke 2011). This, combined with the rise of Vladimir Putin and changed patterns of elite competition, brought down protest numbers in the early 2000s (Robertson 2011; Pringle and Clarke 2011). In China, meanwhile, the official All China Federation of Trade Unions (ACFTU), which in the aftermath of Tiananmen backed away from the modest bids for greater autonomy it had made in the 1980s (see China Labour Bulletin 2009b), facilitated through its weakness (and in many instances its complete absence) a burst of wildcat strikes and marches by laid-off SOE workers in old heavy industries in the late 1990s and early 2000s, at the same time as Russian workers were protesting, and labor actions by migrant workers in the country's export-oriented sweatshops from the early 2000s onward (Solinger 2009; Hurst 2009; Lee 2007; Cai 2006; Chan 2001). This activism only grew through the early 2010s, with the ACFTU struggling to stay relevant and the government attempting to corral workers into safer legal channels of dispute resolution, with only partial success (Friedman 2014; Pringle 2011; Gallagher 2017; C. K. Chan 2010; Hui 2018; Elfstrom and Kuruvilla 2014). As Russian worker militancy began to fade, in other words, Chinese workers were just getting started.

Today, Chinese workers present a more serious challenge to their government than their Russian counterparts do to theirs. Scholars have described China as an "emerging epicenter" and even as "*the* epicenter" of global labor unrest (Silver and Zhang 2009; Friedman 2012). Unofficial strike counts by China Labour Bulletin and my own China Strikes map show a steady increase in industrial conflict over the past decade. In 2008, formally adjudicated employment disputes nearly doubled from 350,182 to 693,495—and they have gradually risen further since (PRC Department of Population and Employment Statistics 2009). And unrest is not just becoming more intense in quantitative terms. Workers in the country are increasingly seen as moving beyond bare legal claims and toward more ambitious demands for higher wages irrespective of the law and a greater voice on the shop floor—or at least this was the case until the current economic slowdown (Elfstrom and Kuruvilla 2014; Chan and Hui 2013; Chang and Brown 2013). In contrast, the relative quiescence of Russian workers—along with that of workers elsewhere in the old Soviet bloc, such as Poland, and even places such as independent-minded Yugoslavia, which had allowed much greater worker participation in factory management— has been the subject of a small but fascinating body of research (Crowley 1997; Ost 2015; Grdešić 2015; Vinogradova, Kozina, and Cook 2012; Javeline 2003). Nonetheless, there are fresh signs of discontent in the Russian work- force. Similar to the Chinese trends noted earlier, Vinogradova, Kozina and Cook (2012, 223–225) envisioned a shift under way in 2006–2008 toward more "classical" strikes "aimed at better wages and working conditions" rather than protecting minimal living standards. This shift, they said, was reversed during the global financial crisis, when the focus shifted back to defensive claims. But recent years have seen an uptick in fairly ambitious strikes by Russian factory workers and teachers (Kramer 2015), truck drivers (MacFarquhar 2015), and others. In the next sections, I will discuss possible reasons for the Chinese government to be anxious about labor activism, focusing on why it might be especially concerned about SOE employees. In the conclusion, I will draw lessons from China for Russia and other similarly situated regimes.

The Challenge of Labor for Chinese Authorities

There are many reasons that labor presents a challenge for Chinese authorities. Most basically, workers occupy a special structural position in China's development model. Of course, in theory, labor anywhere has an incredible weapon at its disposal: as Brecher (1972, viii) writes of workers, "If they refuse to work, the country stops. . . . [I]f they take control of their own activity, their own work, they thereby take control of society." But Chinese labor ac- tivism packs an additional punch. Although they lack unions of their own, or what Wright (2000) calls "associational power," workers in China possess a high degree of both "marketplace bargaining power" and "workplace bar- gaining power" (see also Silver 2003, 13–16). The Chinese model, despite de- termined attempts to move up the value-added ladder, is still heavily reliant on labor-intensive exports: textiles, apparel, and furniture, as well as electronics assembly (Berger and Martin 2011).[1] Moreover, activism is spreading to the new, technology-enabled areas of the economy in which the Chinese lead- ership has placed its hopes for future growth, with strikes occurring among app-based delivery workers and subversive rumblings heard among software engineers meeting virtually on Github (China Labour Bulletin 2018; Feng 2019). This all gives workers workplace bargaining power. Meanwhile, a labor shortage on the country's coast that started around 2004 has persisted even as the economy has slowed down, leading some to speculate that the country has reached its Lewis turning point early (and others to blame China's restrictive household registration system) (K. W. Chan 2010; Barboza 2006; Curran 2015). Here, workers derive marketplace bargaining power. Given this unique leverage possessed by workers, in order for China to meet its goals of creating a "moderately prosperous society" (*xiaokang shehui*), it must satisfy labor.

Worker activism additionally continually threatens to spill over into other spheres. Workers are, by definition, concentrated in cities. Unlike farmers, they have easy access to foreign and domestic media outlets and have potential allies close at hand, like the lower middle class (on the dangers of urban insurrection, see Wallace 2014). Over the past decade, Chinese student activists have worked undercover in Coca-Cola bottling plants and the Foxconn electronics company to document abuses (China Labor News Translations 2009; Pun et al. 2014). These solidarity efforts took a more dramatic form in 2018, when leftist student groups around the country organized in support of striking workers at the Jasic electronics factory in Shenzhen. The government reacted by raiding apartments used by the students, detaining student leaders near their elite campuses in broad daylight, and forcing key activists to appear in confession videos shown to their classmates (Yang 2019). Below the radar, feminist organizers have built important relationships with labor: it was no accident that when the "Feminist Five" were arrested in 2015, workers showed them support (Fincher 2018, ch. 7). So, too, have veteran democracy campaigners and religious groups. Chinese authorities have long kept popular mobilization firmly segmented within the walls of a social "honeycomb" (Shue 1990). Workers have protested—and have sometimes even been encouraged to protest—but have always done so with other workers, just as farmers have rallied with farmers and students with students (Perry 2008; Wright 2010). Recent breaches in these boundaries are deeply alarming for Beijing.

Finally, workers also enjoy a strong normative position. They were once, after all, the vanguard class under state socialism. Article 1 of the current (2004) Chinese constitution—not the Party constitution but the country's constitution—still reads, "The People's Republic of China is a socialist state under the people's democratic dictatorship led by the working class and based on the alliance of workers and peasants." Workers possess their own "mass organization" on the old transmission belt model in the form of the ACFTU. The union, as noted, has shown itself to be woefully unprepared for its new role in a market economy, whether that role is understood as protecting workers' rights or simply keeping peace for the Party. This is despite various reform initiatives it has embarked upon (Friedman 2014; Howell 2008; Pringle 2011;

Liu 2010). But farmers do not have a body of this sort. The country even continues to award exemplary citizens with the title "Model Worker"! China's leadership has adapted its institutions to accommodate private businesspeople and has fitfully tried to reframe its mission as serving the "most advanced forces of production" and building out the "middle stratum" (the word "class" being now too sensitive) (Dickson 2003; Tsai 2007; Goodman 2014). But it has found itself unable to close the door on its past egalitarian commitments, which constitute something of a double-edged sword (Perry 2012, 292–293). These factors all make the state's relationship to workers a thorny issue. But SOE workers, in particular, pose an extra challenge.

The Special Challenge of State Sector Workers

Workers in the state sector raise special concerns for the government. The first concern is again structural. State firms are not a major contributor to exports (Hubbard 2016). However, concentrated as they are in heavy and extractive sectors, SOEs can have massive workforces. For example, in 2014, China's largest state-owned mining company, Longmay, employed 240,000 workers across four cities and was responsible for another 180,000 pensioners (it currently plans to lay off 100,000; see Chang 2015). In many places, state firms and their spin-off businesses are virtually synonymous with their surrounding cities, like Soviet *monogorads*. Workers are residents and residents are workers. Given that most employees in such places are locals, they are enmeshed in local political structures in a way that migrant workers will never be (on the different access enjoyed by local versus migrant workers, see Liu, Yong, and Shu 2011; Paik 2014).[2] Workers living together in company housing naturally develop a strong sense of solidarity. The housing, often sold at low rates to tenants during reforms, also provides a safety net—and a physical base for organizing (Lee 2007, chs. 3–4). In SOEs, there are also a number of individuals with leadership experience and a keen knowledge of the Chinese system who are willing to serve as organizers. These include former Cultural Revolution rebels, military veterans, and sometimes even current and former managers (Cai 2002, 332–337; Lin 2009). Most importantly, the fact that state firms are extensions of the state—enterprise bosses are appointed by the government and in turn enjoy prominent positions in national political bodies, especially now, under Xi Jinping (Zhai 2017)—means that workplace conflicts in SOEs are inescapably political. Officials are parties to the disputes from the get-go.

Second, state sector workers have a unique normative claim on the Party. In the Mao era, compared to peasants and even the employees of collective firms, SOE employees enjoyed a privileged place in society, with virtually guaranteed jobs (the "iron rice bowl") and benefits ranging from company housing to company daycare and company theaters (Bian 1994). They were the vanguard within the vanguard class. It was not unknown for young people to pass up college for the chance of service in a state-owned factory (Blecher 2002, 286). Even today, as a study of a Harbin neighborhood by Cho (2013) shows, former SOE employment confers a greater sense of being of "the people" than other personal histories. In the past, if state workers were often constrained by their patron-client relationships with shop floor Party cadres (Walder 1988), forums such as the Staff and Workers Representative Congresses provided a thin degree of voice (Zhu and Chan 2005; Estlund 2013). This fortunate position, workers believed, was only fair: they sacrificed their health—and even sometimes their lives—in massive production drives, and benefits aside, they generally lived simply. But market reforms diffused private sector human resources practices to SOEs (Gallagher 2005). Then, between 1993 and 2002, roughly 63 million SOE employees lost their jobs, sometimes as a result of crude layoff quotas handed down by bureaucrats (Hurst 2009, 16, 55–56). In just the year 1997 alone, 13 million people found themselves suddenly out of work and 39 percent of urban households experienced a drop in income (Hassard et al. 2007, 86–87, 157). As Solinger (2004) put it, workers went from "master to mendicant" in a heartbeat. Today, many workers in gutted companies continue to be stuck in a gray zone between employment and unemployment (Li 2015). In the healthier state firms, jobs are now being taken up by employees hired through labor dispatch companies and production lines are speeding up, forcing the quality of life of fully employed SOE workers to converge downward with that of migrant workers (Lin 2015; on work in state-owned auto plants, in particular, see Zhang 2015). All this amounts to a dramatic betrayal of the country's "moral economy" (Hurst and O'Brien 2002) and "socialist social contract" (Lee 2007).

Finally, state sector workers have a history of militancy. At the height of SOE restructuring in the late 1990s and early 2000s, workers marched, blocked railways, and to a very limited degree also broke a long-standing taboo and linked up across factories. For instance, when Liaoyang Ferro-Alloy factory workers protested their company's bankruptcy between 2000 and 2002, they were joined by workers from "a textile mill, a piston ring factory, an instrument and meter plant, a leather plant, and a precision component factory" (Au and Bai 2010, 494). Importantly, too, SOE workers in this period framed their dissent in ways that cut to the core of the CCP's founding narrative. Gatherings featured portraits of Chairman Mao, boom boxes blaring "The Internationale," and poems in memory of model workers (Weston 2004; Lee 2002; Hurst 2009). Some activists directly charged the Party with abandoning its founding principles, as the "Zhengzhou Four" did in a widely read pamphlet that landed them in prison in 2001 (see Weil 2006). Since this period, state sector mobilization has taken a backseat to protests by migrant workers (C. K. Chan 2010). Nonetheless, SOEs can still be the sites of intense conflict. For example, a privatization scheme at the Tonghua steel mill in Jilin province in 2009 resulted in mass demonstrations and the beating to death of the mill's new general manager (Bradsher 2009). Li (2011) reports that an older worker with experience in the Mao-era planned economy led the resistance at Tonghua by making it "clear to the workers that the real issue was not about any particular problem, but about 'the political line of privatization.'" More recently, in 2012, workers at the restructured Jiannanchun liquor factory in Sichuan protested over company attempts to take back employee-held shares at cut rates; when activists were beaten, the workers blocked roads (for an overview, see iFeng.com 2012). The white-collar employees of state commercial banks have even begun linking up nationwide for protests in Beijing over layoffs (Libcom.org 2010; Boxun 2007; RFA 2012a). Figure 8.1 shows the number of conflicts involving SOE workers between 2004 and 2015 based on the Global Hub Labour Conflicts dataset (more on this source and its strengths and weaknesses later). With the exception of a dip around 2012, the trend is up and up and up—again, not as much as for other workers, perhaps, but rising all the same. State sector employees present challenges along several dimensions at once.

State Reactions to State Sector Worker Protests

The Chinese government's intense concern about SOE worker activism can be seen in how it reacts to protests in state firms compared to other firms. Elsewhere I have shown that, in general, increases in worker resistance push authorities toward both greater repression and responsiveness—or, more accurately, increased repressive and responsive capacity. Specifically, more

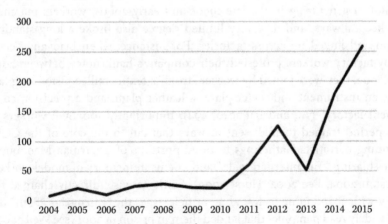

FIGURE 8.1 Strikes, Protest, and Riots by SOE Workers 2004–2015

Source: Sjaak Van der Velden, Micro Labour Conflicts Dataverse, 2016, https://datasets.socialhistory.org/dataset. xhtml?persistentId=hdl:10622/EAASRV.

unrest in a given place means more investment in the paramilitary police, on the one hand, and a greater ability to overcome the objections of powerful local employers and rule in employees' favor in mediation, arbitration, and court, on the other (Elfstrom 2019). In other words, the two responses are not mutually exclusive. In the next sections, I will use a brief statistical analysis to show that incidents at SOEs are more likely to result in both coercive and conciliatory reactions by the state than are incidents that occur at domestic private companies. Moreover, state sector activism has roughly the same or higher likelihood of drawing these responses as do incidents at foreign-invested companies. This is despite the fact that, again, SOE workers account for a minority of labor protests. And it contrasts with the popular impression that the Chinese government is more lenient toward workers protesting against non-Chinese bosses (see, for example, Wasserstrom 2010). If worker protests generally are a concern for the government and push it to go all out, using all of its tools at once to restore order, then SOE protests drive authorities yet further in this direction. In the next section I document this statistically.

Data on Strikes and State Reactions

My source for data on strikes, protests, and riots (hereinafter all referred to as "strikes") is the 2016 version of the Global Hub Labour Conflicts (GHLC) dataset, which, after the data are cleaned up, covers 6,161 incidents in mainland China occurring between 2004 and 2015 (available at http://hdl.handle.net/10622/EAASRV).[3] The GHLC, which is maintained by the Global Labour History program of the International Institute of Social History in Amsterdam, combines two other datasets: the 2014 version of my own China Strikes map of incidents occurring between 2004 and 2012 (https://chinastrikes.crowdmap.com) and the newer China Labour Bulletin (CLB) strike map (http://maps.clb.org.hk/strikes/en), which covers an overlapping period, from mid-2011 through the present. Both China Strikes and CLB's map draw on state media, social media, and websites of dissidents and advocacy groups.

The GHLC dataset is preferable to both of these sources individually because of its longer time frame and therefore larger strike count. But it is very much a work in progress. New incidents are added as they are found and old incidents are edited when new information becomes available (this is true, too, for its two underlying sources). The GHLC attempts to merge the coding systems of CLB and my maps, resulting in competing categorizations in places. This can be resolved by generating consistent codes based on searches for certain keywords in the incident descriptions (as I have done). But the process is rough. The GHLC coding is based, in the first place, on English-language summaries of the incidents in question and therefore relies on the shorthand employed by each of its sources. Because of this, it lumps together diverse worker tactics at points. Nonetheless, despite these shortcomings, the dataset provides a rough overall guide to what is happening on China's shop floors.

More seriously, there are likely geographic biases in the information captured by any attempt to use media to track protest in China. Some parts of the country have more open domestic news environments; others are more accessible to foreign reporters. Nonetheless, the GHLC and its two main sources capture activism across a remarkable swath of the country, from strikes by tour bus operators in remote Yunnan province to stoppages by truck drivers at Shanghai's port to rebellions in the production corps on the frontier in Xinjiang. The spatial concentration of the incidents documented also roughly matches that of the formally adjudicated employment disputes documented by China's *Labour Statistical Yearbooks*. Seasonal fluctuations in the GHLC's reports furthermore match expectations: there are more reports from right before Spring Festival, when migrant workers return home to celebrate with families and must be paid, fewer during the festival itself and in the early part of the year.

Coercion is relatively straight forward to track. Davenport (2005) and Greitens (2016) both argue convincingly that repression should be understood to include a wide range of state actions: non-state violence (e.g., by hired thugs or more spontaneous mobs), surveillance, even media portrayals of particular groups. Nonetheless, arrests are an especially clear form. They are also comparatively easily documented. Dissident sources—blogs, social media, and the reports of advocacy groups—are the most likely sources to report arrests. They are certainly the ones most likely to accompany their reports with documentation in the form of photos and videos. However, state media may (more rarely) mention arrests as a warning. For example, when taxi drivers went on strike in Xining, Qinghai province, in 2009, the *Xining Evening Post* announced that "the city's public security apparatus detained 50 people who had engaged in illegal activities such as taking the opportunity to cause a disturbance, agitating people to cause trouble, threatening and intimidating, and blocking traffic" (China Labour Bulletin 2009a). Both CLB and my strike maps, and therefore the GHLC, code incidents for arrests.

Conciliatory gestures are harder to nail down. Increasingly, teams of government cadres are sent directly to the scene of labor conflicts to mediate. These sorts of interventions often include not only the expected personnel from the Ministry of Human Resources and Social Security but also cadres from judicial organs (Chen and Xu 2012). Workers, anticipating this possibility, actively try to draw in officials and use the "street as courtroom" (Su and He 2010). This phenomenon provides a clue as to the general character of official intervention: it is generally conciliatory (if not always sincere or effective). Cadres typically show up not to harangue workers but to win them over. State and dissident sources alike note the presence of officials at protests (though the former do more). The GHLC, based on its two underlying sources, codes for such interventions, although the codes must be checked. Before discussing my findings with this dataset, I will explain my controls.

Confounding Factors

Various factors may complicate the relationship between what workers do and the state's reactions to the same. In my analysis I try to control for these confounding variables. First, it may be the case that the tactics employed by activists are what is most important for authorities, and these tactics just happen to cluster around certain kinds of enterprises. I therefore code incidents as involving strikes (halting production), protests (marches and other public gatherings), or blockades (of factory entrances, highways, or railroads). Second, it is possible that certain demands are especially disruptive and, like tactics, correlate with ownership. I thus include controls for whether incidents feature offensive wage demands (for higher wages, not for the observation of legal minimums or the payment of arrears). These are only one of the many different kinds of demands that may be made, but they have risen in frequency in China in recent years (Elfstrom and Kuruvilla 2014) and mark one end of the spectrum of worker activism (Tilly 1995; for discussions of offensive and defensive demands, see Knowles 1952). Third, the government may be most sensitive about activism in certain sectors of the economy, whether because of those sectors' visibility or because of their importance to growth. State ownership is, as already discussed, also concentrated in certain areas, such as heavy industries and extractive industries. Thus I include broad controls for manufacturing, services, construction, extractive industries and utilities, and transportation. Finally, the number of workers involved may be key. Bigger protests mean bigger problems for authorities. Activists certainly understand this dynamic. I therefore control for the size of incidents, too. Table 8.1 displays summary statistics for each of the variables I will use in my analysis: incident outcomes, specifically arrests and official interventions; economic sectors; ownership types; worker tactics; worker demands, specifically whether they made offensive wage claims; and the number of workers involved in a dispute (necessarily very rough estimates).[4] Note that SOEs account for only 13 percent of all incidents. Again, the state sector is not the most active area of the economy when it comes to unrest—it just draws special concern. Offensive demands also feature only in a small portion of the incidents, despite their increase over the past decade. Manufacturing dominates conflict, followed by construction and transportation. Protests and strikes, finally, are the most common form of collective action. All these factors demand consideration.

Model and Results

To capture the relationship between enterprise ownership type and state reactions to protests, I estimate a series of logistic regressions with either arrests of activists or official interventions following disputes (both binary variables) as the outcomes. Figures 8.2 and 8.3 display the odds ratios of arrests being made

TABLE 8.1 } Strikes, Protests, and Riots by SOE Workers 2004–2015: Summary Statistics

Variable	Number	Total Observations	Mean	Standard Deviation
Arrests	553	6,161	.0897582	.2858582
Official Interventions	1,586	6,161	.2574257	.4372514
Privately Owned	2,697	6,161	.4377536	.4961505
Self-Employed	36	6,161	.0058432	.0762234
Foreign-Invested	548	6,161	.0889466	.2846898
State-Owned	811	6,161	.1316345	.3381204
Services	1,036	6,161	.1681545	.3740338
Construction	1,374	6,161	.2230157	.4163026
Manufacturing	2,355	6,161	.3822431	.485975
Extractive and Utilities	174	6,161	.0282422	.1656774
Transportation	1,040	6,161	.1688038	.3746089
Strike	2,522	6,161	.4093491	.4917537
Protest	2,376	6,161	.3856517	.4867884
Blockade	691	6,161	.1121571	.3155853
Offensive Wage Demands	791	6,161	.1283882	.3345488
Number of Workers	*	5,344	350.2461	2041.909

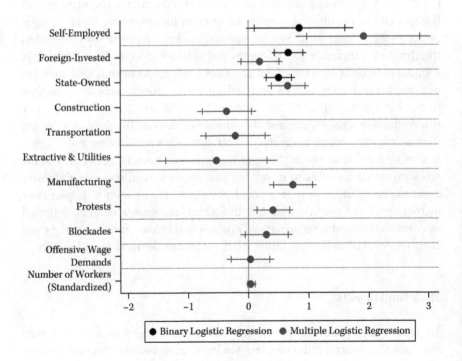

FIGURE 8.2 Odds Ratios of Arrests Being Made During Labor Conflicts

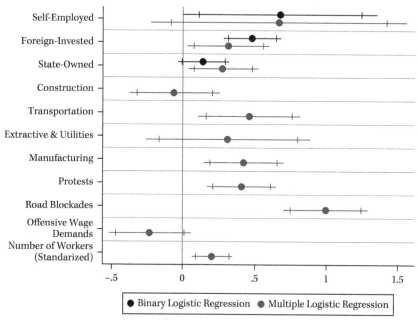

FIGURE 8.3 Odds Ratios of Officials Intervening During Labor Conflicts

Note: The omitted variable for enterprise ownership type is domestic-private; for worker tactics, strikes; and for economic sector, service. Ninety and 95 percent confidence intervals shown. Provincial fixed effects used throughout.

Source: Sjaak Van der Velden, Micro Labour Conflicts Dataverse, 2016, https://datasets.socialhistory.org/dataset.xhtml?persistentId=hdl:10622/EAASRV.

and officials intervening, respectively, along with their 90 percent and 95 percent confidence intervals. The figures include models with and without controls. In the full models, provincial fixed effects are employed. These are intended to control for the sorts of biases in reporting that might conceivably exist between different parts of China, noted earlier. Note that the omitted category for enterprise ownership type is domestic private firms; for worker tactics, strikes; and for sectors, the service sector. The one worker claim measured—offensive wage demands—is a simple binary variable. My measure of an incident's number of workers involved is standardized for easy comparison.

The two figures confirm that the state is more concerned with unrest in state-owned enterprises than in private enterprises and, in some cases, more than in foreign firms. Specifically, with full controls, arrests are 22 percent more likely if a firm is foreign-owned than if it is a domestic private company, but the likelihood of arrests is *94 percent* more likely if the firm is state-owned. (Self-employed workers—in the dataset, these are mostly taxi drivers—are nearly seven times as likely to meet with arrests, but such disputes are relatively rare.) It should be noted that if only my China Strikes dataset is used, with its shorter time span, the relationship between coercion and ownership type is significant and in the same direction but different in size. Similar but somewhat less dramatic relationships are found when the outcome in question is interventions by government officials. Foreign-invested and state-owned firms run neck and neck here. Interventions are 37 percent more likely for foreign-invested firms than for domestic private firms and 32 percent more likely for SOEs than for domestic private firms (here my China Strikes dataset alone offers no backing). Despite the fact that state worker activism accounts for only a small percentage of incidents, this form of activism is clearly a political priority.

Some of the ancillary results of my analysis are also interesting. The strike is being honed as a tool of bargaining by China's migrant workers (Lyddon et al. 2015; C. K. Chan 2010; Chan and Hui 2013). This is typically seen as an advance in organizing capacity. However, strikes are the least likely to result in arrests or official interventions: protests are significantly more likely to result in arrests, and both protests and blockades are significantly more likely to result in official interventions. This may be a result of either the fact that the government has a harder times suppressing such activity (as Polish workers found during the Solidarity trade union movement; see Laba 1991). More likely, though, it shows the intense concern that officials feel about activism spreading to other groups. At any rate, the tactics most often used by SOE workers, blockades and protests, are the most likely to draw a reaction. Worker demands do not seem to have a significant effect. The number of workers involved raises the likelihood of official interventions but not arrests. In terms of sectors, only manufacturing shows a consistently significant, positive correlation with particular state actions. Enterprise ownership type clearly plays a key role in determining state reactions, even as it interacts with other factors.

Examples of State Reactions to SOE Worker Activism

Some examples of individual incidents from the GHLC dataset illustrate what these aggregate findings can mean on the ground. In January 2012, workers at the state-owned Pangang Group Chengdu Steel and Vanadium (hereinafter Pangang Steel) factory went on strike for higher wages. The New York–based group China Labor Watch reported that Pangang Steel paid only 1,200 RMB per month as a base monthly salary, not much above the local legal minimum of 850 RMB and much below the earnings of plant managers, who earned as much as 100,000 RMB per year. When employees of the nearby Sichuan Chemical stopped production and won a raise of 400 RMB per month and a 3,000 RMB annual bonus, Pangang Steel employees were encouraged. The Pangang workers then used common tactics: they struck and blocked a section of the Chengdu-Mianyang Highway, and in response, police used pepper spray on the strikers and arrested five activists (China Labor Watch 2012). But the plant encouraged the police to release them and, presumably acting on the advice of intervening government officials, further agreed to both a modest wage increase of 260 RMB and a freeze on managerial pay (*Economist* 2012). In August the same year, four to five hundred retired and laid-off workers from the Sinosteel Ferroalloy Factory in Jilin protested at the plant gates, waving a banner demanding respect, wages, and jobs. When Radio Free Asia interviewed the protesters, they had just lost contact with their leader and presumed he had been detained. Someone who answered the phone at the factory, though, said that the provincial government had intervened and organized a "working group" to deal with the issues raised by employees (RFA 2012b). Earlier, in 2003, the *New York Times* reported on the protests of laid-off workers from a state textile mill and pulp mill in Jiamusi city, in Heilongjiang province. The workers regularly blocked roads and rail lines; on at least one occasion, they lay down across an airport runway (Ibid.). Some organizers were detained. But officials met with the textile workers for three straight days in a theater and ended up offering them a $15 monthly living stipend, while the pulp workers, who were the ones who had blocked the runway, won $30 (Rosenthal 2003). These examples do not show the government to be entirely at the mercy of state sector workers. The gains made by protesters, including modest wage increases, working groups to discuss their problems, and so on, are not major concessions. And, of course, any gains are matched by repression—often targeted at key individuals, but repression all the same. Nonetheless, authorities' anxiousness to get the situation under control in each instance is pronounced. They are throwing all their resources at this group.

The Pull of the Past

The extra concern drawn by state sector workers speaks to the powerful pull of the past. The Chinese government is sometimes portrayed as unfettered, especially compared to its counterparts in the United States and Europe, which appear mired in intractable social conflicts today. However, the economic structures and normative commitments that the government has inherited from the past bind it in important ways. China's decision to focus on labor-intensive exports helped spur an unprecedented period of economic growth. It also meant that when workers stirred, their actions would have powerful repercussions. The country's legacy household registration system distorts its labor market and brutalizes migrants but also gives labor power through its scarcity. Perhaps equally importantly, the Mao-era promises of the CCP to elevate the dignity of work, never fully fulfilled, continue to haunt the Party. For state sector workers especially, particular structures come into play—crucial heavy industries, company towns, the politics-business nexus, et cetera—along with yet more powerful chains of moral obligation. Added to these factors are a history of SOE mobilization that hangs in the memory of officials whose careers traversed the late 1990s and early 2000s. This all means that despite its image as the new paradise of the "Davos Man" and "Davos Woman," Beijing must constantly negotiate and renegotiate its major initiatives with the people who build its skyscrapers, stoke its furnaces, and assemble its technology. This likely shapes policymaking in subtle ways, far beyond the immediate government reactions to outbreaks of unrest discussed earlier.

Policy Implications of the Government's Fear of SOE Worker Activism

There are many areas where we might be witnessing the effect of the governments' fear of SOE worker activism. First, these fears may serve a brake on efforts to advance market reforms. For example, the current Xi Jinping administration has repeatedly stated a commitment to cutting excess capacity in state firms, particularly in the coal and steel industries. Media commentary frequently portrays this drive as stymied by bureaucratic interests. Yet worker pressures are clearly also a factor. For example, in March 2016, the governor of Heilongjiang province, Lu Hao, seeking to demonstrate his success in responsible downsizing, boasted to the annual meeting of China's National People's Congress that his province's struggling mining company, Longmay, was "not a penny overdue" in paying its workers. Thousands of the company's miners in the city of Shuangyashan protested, calling the claim a line. The governor quickly apologized and sought ways to pay the workers (Huang 2016). Cutting excess capacity in mining, in particular, has made little progress since then.

Second and relatedly, concern about SOE worker activism is likely a significant spur to government spending. The recent push to cut coal and steel overcapacity, for example, has been accompanied by promises of at least $23 billion to care for laid-off workers, which will be spent on unemployment benefits and retraining. Interestingly, this allotment was announced before any plans were made to provide money to cover the firms' bad debts (Lim, Miller, and Stanway 2016). As already noted, the late 1990s and early 2000s round of SOE activism brought a dramatic expansion of the country's overall social safety net (Cai 2010, ch. 8; Solinger 2009). Meanwhile, fears about protests contribute to hikes in China's skyrocketing domestic security budget, which has repeatedly exceeded its defense budget (MacLeod 2013; Blasko 2012). Wang (2014) shows that reductions in SOE employment, in particular, are correlated with higher police spending. In other words, pushed by worries of popular discontent, the government is growing—in ways that both benefit citizens and threaten them.

Third, concern about protests complicates yet more tangentially related policies, sometimes pitting central and local authorities against each other. For example, air pollution has become a flash point for urbanites. In December 2016, President Xi Jinping declared, "The goal of achieving an ecological civilization is a key part of China's overall development strategy, and governments at all levels should remember that clear waters and green mountains are invaluable assets" (Reuters 2016). But resolving pollution would mean shuttering state-owned factories and laying off workers. When a controversial chemical plant project was halted in Xiamen in 2007 following a massive middle-class mobilization, workers affected by the cancellation protested (Ansfield 2008). Graded by superiors on their ability to maintain growth *and* stability, regional governments are in a dilemma (Wang and Minzner 2013; Lee and Zhang 2013). Thus air pollution policies come and go but smokestacks keep churning out particulate matter.

In sum, as it attempts to steer its economy and society forward, the Chinese government confronts a potential tangle of different interests. Often, the trade-offs assumed are not the most important ones. The challenge of labor, especially SOE workers, adds a crucial but sometimes hidden element to the mix. It means that there are negotiations all the way down, not just at the top. Given that workers do not enjoy meaningful formal representation in state affairs— the ACFTU leadership is not actually elected by workers, and the number of worker-delegates in the National People's Congress and other bodies has fallen dramatically since the Mao era or even the early reform era—this negotiation cannot occur through actual deals, where two sides exchange concessions. Instead, it must happen at a remove: going slow on a national reform, spending more here or there, locals undermining some central policy, all with the hope of defusing workplace opposition. The Chinese government may appear enviably unimpeded by interest groups—or constrained only by its own internal divisions. But this freedom is a mirage.

China in a Broader Context

Although this chapter has focused on China, similar dynamics may be found in many other post-state-socialist authoritarian states. For example, in Vietnam, dramatic protests by workers over a new social insurance law forced the country's government to backtrack in 2015 (Minh 2015). This echoes a previous round of labor unrest in the country in 2006 that succeeded in expanding the legal right to strike (even as lawyers and others allied with workers were imprisoned) (Kerkvliet 2011; Human Rights Watch 2009). Also in 2015, Zimbabwe promised to amend new labor legislation when unions pushed back but detained union leaders ahead of planned protests (Dzirutwe 2015; ITUC 2015). In Belarus, authorities delayed a new tax on the unemployed in the face of massive demonstrations in 2017, even as the government chased down critics (BBC 2017; Erickson 2017). Russia is no exception. By his actions, Putin has shown he is quite sensitive to labor grievances—especially, again, the claims of SOE workers. For example, in 2009, he helicoptered into the *monogorad* of Pikalevo to harangue factory managers delinquent on salary payments to their workers (Barry 2009). And when workers constructing a new space center protested during a visit by Putin in 2016, he quickly promised full payment of what they were owed (Parfitt 2015). Recently, the Russian government compromised on a new toll system for trucks following blockades and other actions by drivers, although the drivers were harassed (Coalson 2016; Filipov 2017; MacFarquhar 2015). The structures involved are different. Russia is much more reliant on extractive industries than manufacturing-export-led China. Beijing has never made a clean ideological break with its past, as Russia did. However, although China and Russia—along with other post-state-socialist societies—have seen rises and falls in worker militancy, their states appear to share a vulnerability to labor's claims. This will probably continue to shape their leaders' choices going forward.

Notes

1. And although domestic consumption in China has risen remarkably in recent years, exports account for nearly twice as much of China's GDP as America's (World Bank 2016).

2. As a police officer in Benxi, a small Liaoning city that is dominated by the state-owned Benxi Steel Corp., said to Hurst (2009, 123), "The laid off workers who make disturbances are neighbors and classmates, our parents and relatives. How could we repress them?"

3. I eliminate all the reports with unclear locations and dates, as well as those that appear to occur outside of an industrial setting (agricultural disputes).

4. Tactics are most accurately documented for later years, as CLB tracks this but China Strikes does not, leaving GHLC's administrators to try to infer the tactics for early years on their own, based on the headings of incidents.

References

Ansfield, Jonathan. 2008. "PX Workers Protest, No One Notices (Updated)." *China Digital Times*, January 24.

Au, Loong-Yu, and Ruixue Bai. 2010. "Contemporary Labor Resistance in China, 1989–2009." *WorkingUSA* 13: 481–505.

Barboza, David. 2006. "Labor Shortage in China May Lead to Trade Shift." *New York Times*, April 3.

Barry, Ellen. 2009. "Putin Plays Sheriff for Cowboy Capitalists." *New York Times*, June 5.

BBC. 2017. "Hundreds Arrested in Belarus Protests." BBC News, March 25, 2017.

Berger, Brett, and Robert F. Martin. 2011. "The Growth of Chinese Exports: An Examination of the Detailed Trade Data." Board of Governors of the Federal Reserve System. Washington, DC.

Bian, Yanjie. 1994. *Work and Inequality in Urban China*. Albany: State University of New York Press.

Blasko, Dennis J. 2012. "Politics and the PLA: Securing Social Stability." *China Brief* 12, no. 7: 5–8.

Blecher, Marc. 2002. "Hegemony and Workers' Politics in China." *China Quarterly* 170: 283–303.

Boxun. 2007. "2007 nian 6 yuefen Zhongguo minquan, renquan xiangguan qunti shijian huigu" [Review of Chinese mass incidents from June 2007]." http://blog.boxun.com/hero/2007/hewh/91_2.shtml.

Bradsher, Keith. 2009. "Bowing to Protests, China Halts Sale of Steel Mill." The New York Times, August 17.

Brecher, Jeremy. 1972. *Strike!* San Francisco: Straight Arrow Books.

Cai, Yongshun. 2002. "The Resistance of Chinese Laid-off Workers in the Reform Period." *China Quarterly* 170: 327–344.

Cai, Yongshun. 2006. *State and Laid-Off Workers in Reform China: The Silence and Collective Action of the Retrenched.* Abingdon: Routledge.

Cai, Yongshun. 2010. *Collective Resistance in China: Why Popular Protests Succeed or Fail.* Stanford, CA: Stanford University Press.

Chan, Anita. 2001. *China's Workers Under Assault: The Exploitation of Labor in a Globalizing Economy.* London: M. E. Sharpe.

Chan, Chris King-chi. 2010. *The Challenge of Labour in China: Strikes and the Changing Labour Regime in Global Factories.* Abingdon: Routledge.

Chan, Chris King-chi, and Elaine Sio-ieng Hui. 2013. "The Development of Collective Bargaining in China: From 'Collective Bargaining by Riot' to 'Party State-Led Wage Bargaining.'" *China Quarterly* 217: 221–242.

Chan, Kam Wing. 2010. "A China Paradox: Migrant Labor Shortage Amidst Rural Labor Supply Abundance." *Eurasian Geography and Economics* 51, no. 4: 513–530.

Chang, Kai, and William Brown. 2013. "The Transition from Individual to Collective Labour Relations in China." *Industrial Relations Journal* 44, no. 2: 102–121.

Chang, Lyu. 2015. "Longmay to Cut 100,000 Coal Jobs." *China Daily*, September 26.

Chen, Feng, and Xin Xu. 2012. "'Active Judiciary': Judicial Dismantling of Workers' Collective Action In China." *China Journal* 67: 87–108.

China Labor News Translations. 2009. "Chinese Students Go Undercover to Investigate Coca Cola." http://www.clntranslations.org/article/41/chinese-students-go-undercover-to-investigate-coca-cola.

China Labor Watch. 2012. "Chengdu Steel Factory Workers Strike for More Pay." China Labor Watch. http://www.chinalaborwatch.org/news/new-410.html.

China Labour Bulletin. 2009a. "In Handling of Taxi Strikes, Xining and Chongqing Provide Stark Contrasts." http://www.clb.org.hk/en/content/handling-taxi-strikes-xining-and-chongqing-provide-stark-contrasts.

China Labour Bulletin. 2009b. "Protecting Workers' Rights or Serving the Party: The Way Forward for China's Trade Unions." http://www.clb.org.hk/en/files/share/File/research_reports/acftu_report.pdf.

China Labour Bulletin. 2018. "Food Delivery Workers in China Strike over Pay Cuts and Unfair Work Practices." June 5. http://www.clb.org.hk/content/food-delivery-workers-china-strike- over-pay- cuts-and-unfair-work-practices.

Cho, Mun Yong. 2013. *The Specter of "the People": Urban Poverty in Northeast China.* Ithaca, NY: Cornell University Press.

Coalson, Robert. 2016. "Russian Truckers Resume Protests Against Controversial Toll System." Radio Free Europe Radio Liberty, November 11. http://www.rferl.org/a/russian-truckers-resume-protests-toll-system/28110513.html.

Crowley, Stephen. 1997. *Hot Coal, Cold Steel: Russian and Ukrainian Workers from the End of the Soviet Union to the Post-Communist Transformations*. Ann Arbor: University of Michigan Press.

Curran, Enda. 2015. "China's Manufacturing Hub Faces Labor Shortage and Higher Wages." Bloomberg, May 7. https://www.bloomberg.com/news/articles/2015-05-07/china-s-manufacturing-hub-faces-labor-shortage-and-higher-wages.

Davenport, Christian. 2005. "Repression and Mobilization: Insights from Political Science and Sociology." In *Repression and Mobilization*, ed. Christian Davenport, Carol Mueller, and Hank Johnston, vii–xli. Minneapolis: University of Minnesota Press.

Dickson, Bruce J. 2003. *Red Capitalists in China: The Party, Private Entrepreneurs, and Prospects for Political Change*. New York: Cambridge University Press.

Dzirutwe, Macdonald. 2015. "Zimbabwe Union Says 20,000 Jobs Lost, Government to Amend Labor Law." Reuters, August 16.

Economist. 2012. "A Dangerous Year: Unrest in China." January 28.

Elfstrom, Manfred. 2019. "Two Steps Forward, One Step Back: Chinese State Reactions to Labour Unrest." *China Quarterly* 240: 855–879.

Elfstrom, Manfred, and Sarosh Kuruvilla. 2014. "The Changing Nature of Labor Unrest in China." *Industrial and Labor Relations Review* 67, no. 2: 453–480.

Erickson, Amanda. 2017. "Belarus Wanted to Tax Its Unemployed 'Parasites.' Then the Protests Started." *Washington Post*, March 10.

Estlund, Cynthia L. 2013. "Will Workers Have a Voice in China's 'Socialist Market Economy'? The Curious Revival of the Workers Congress System." Public Law and Legal Theory Research Paper Series no. 13-80. New York University School of Law.

Feng, Emily. 2019. "GitHub Has Become a Haven for China's Censored Internet Users." NPR, April 10.

Filipov, David. 2017. "The Latest Protest Moscow Is Trying to Ignore: Thousands of Angry Truckers." *Washington Post*, April 21.

Fincher, Leta Hong. 2018. *Betraying Big Brother: The Feminist Awakening in China*. New York: Verso Books.

Friedman, Eli. 2012. "China in Revolt." *Jacobin*, nos. 7–8 (August 1).

Friedman, Eli. 2014. *Insurgency Trap: Labor Politics in Postsocialist China*. Ithaca, NY: Cornell University Press.

Gallagher, Mary E. 2005. *Contagious Capitalism: Globalization and the Politics of Labor in China*. Princeton: Princeton University Press.

Gallagher, Mary E. 2017. *Authoritarian Legality in China: Law, Workers, and the State*. New York: Cambridge University Press.

Goodman, David S. G. 2014. *Class in Contemporary China*. Malden, MA: Polity Press.

Grdešić, Marko. 2015. "Exceptionalism and Its Limits: The Legacy of Self-Management in the Former Yugoslavia." In *Working Through History: Labor and Authoritarian Legacies in Comparative Perspective*, ed. Teri L. Caraway, Maria Lorena Cook, and Stephen Crowley, 103–121. Ithaca, NY: Cornell University Press.

Greitens, Sheena Chestnut. 2016. *Dictators and Their Secret Police*. New York: Cambridge University Press.

Hassard, John, Jackie Sheehan, Meixiang Zhou, Jane Terpstra-Tong, and Jonathan Morris. 2007. *China's State Enterprise Reform: From Marx to the Market*. New York: Routledge.

Howell, Jude. 2008. "All-China Federation of Trades Unions Beyond Reform? The Slow March of Direct Elections." *China Quarterly* 196: 845–863.

Huang, Joyce. 2016. "Unpaid Chinese Coal Miners in Heilongjiang Stage Protests." Voice of America, March 14.

Hubbard, Paul. 2016. "China's Global Economic Impact Is No Longer State-Owned." East Asia Forum, May 4.

Hui, Elaine Sio-Ieng. 2018. *Hegemonic Transformation: The State, Laws, and Labour Relations in Post-Socialist China*. New York: Palgrave Macmillan.

Human Rights Watch. 2009. "Not Yet a Workers' Paradise: Vietnam's Suppression of the Independent Workers' Movement." May 4. https://www.hrw.org/report/2009/05/04/not-yet-workers-paradise/vietnams-suppression-independent-workers-movement.

Hurst, William. 2009. *The Chinese Worker After Socialism*. New York: Cambridge University Press.

Hurst, William, and Kevin O'Brien. 2002. "China's Contentious Pensioners." *China Quarterly* 170: 345–360.

iFeng.com. 2012. "Jiannanchun ni jianjia shouhui 10 yi yuangong chigu, zai bagong kangyi" [Jiannanchun plans to take back 100 million shares held by employees, meets with strike and protests]." 2012. http://biz.ifeng.com/huanan/special/jiannancunbg.

ITUC. 2015. "Zimbabwe: Trade Union Leaders Arrested Ahead of Planned Demonstration." International Trade Union Confederation. August 10. http://www.ituc-csi.org/zimbabwe-trade-union-leaders-16406.

Javeline, Debra. 2003. *Protest and the Politics of Blame: The Russian Response to Unpaid Wages*. Ann Arbor: University of Michigan Press.

Kerkvliet, Benedict J. Tria. 2011. "Workers' Protests in Contemporary Vietnam." In *Labour in Vietnam*, ed. Anita Chan, 160–210. Singapore: ISEAS Publishing.

Knowles, K. G. J. C. 1952. *Strikes: A Study in Industrial Conflict*. Oxford: Basil Blackwell.

Kramer, Andrew E. 2015. "Unpaid Russian Workers Unite in Protest Against Putin." New York Times, April 22.

Kubik, Jan. 2000. "Between the State and Networks of 'Cousins': The Role of Civil Society and Noncivil Associations in the Democratization of Poland." In *Civil Society Before Democracy: Lessons from Nineteenth Century Europe*, ed. Nancy Bermeo and Philip Nord, 181–207. Lanham, MD: Rowman & Littlefield.

Laba, Roman. 1991. *The Roots of Solidarity: A Political Sociology of Poland's Working-Class Democratization*. Princeton: Princeton University Press.

Lee, Ching Kwan. 2002. "From the Specter of Mao to the Spirit of the Law: Labor Insurgency in China." *Theory and Society* 31, no. 2: 189–228.

Lee, Ching Kwan. 2007. *Against the Law: Labor Protests in China's Rustbelt and Sunbelt*. Berkeley: University of California Press.

Lee, Ching Kwan, and Yonghong Zhang. 2013. "The Power of Instability: Unraveling the Microfoundations of Bargained Authoritarianism in China." *American Journal of Sociology* 118, no. 6: 1475–1508.

Li, Ju. 2015. "From 'Master' to 'Loser': Changing Working-Class Cultural Identity in Contemporary China." *International Labor and Working-Class History* 88: 190–208.

Li, Minqi. 2011. "The Rise of the Working Class and the Future of the Chinese Revolution." *Monthly Review* 63, no. 2: 38–51.

Libcom.org. 2010. "Laid-Off Bank Workers Protest in Beijing." April 21. http://libcom.org/news/laid-bank-workers-protest-beijing-21042010?quicktabs_1=0.

Lim, Benjamin Kang, Matthew Miller, and David Stanway. 2016. "Exclusive: China to Lay Off Five to Six Million Workers, Earmarks at Least \$23 Billion." Reuters, March 1.

Lin, Kevin. 2015. "Recomposing Chinese Migrant and State-Sector Workers." In *Chinese Workers in Comparative Perspective*, ed. Anita Chan, 69–84. Ithaca, NY: Cornell University Press.

Lin, Kun-Chin. 2009. "Class Formation or Fragmentation? Allegiances and Divisions among Managers and Workers in State-Owned Enterprises." In *Laid-Off Workers in a Workers' State: Unemployment with Chinese Characteristics*, ed. Thomas B. Gold, William J. Hurst, Jaeyoun Won, and Qiang Li, 61–92. New York: Palgrave Macmillan.

Liu, Linping, Xin Yong, and Fenfen Shu. 2011. "Laodong quanyide diqu chayi: jiyu dui Zhusanjiao he Changsanjiao diqu wailaigongde wenjuan diaocha [Regional differences in labor rights: a survey investigation of the Pearl River Delta and Yangtze River Delta regions' migrant workers]." *Zhongguo Shehui Kexue* 2: 107–124.

Liu, Mingwei. 2010. "Union Organizing in China: Still a Monolithic Labor Movement?" *Industrial and Labor Relations Review* 64, no. 1: 30–52.

Lyddon, Dave, Xuebing Cao, Quan Meng, and Jun Lu. 2015. "A Strike of 'Unorganised' Workers in a Chinese Car Factory: The Nanhai Honda Events of 2010." *Industrial Relations Journal* 46, no. 2: 134–152.

MacFarquhar, Neil. 2015. "Russian Truckers, Irate over New Tolls, Block Roads Near Moscow." *New York Times*, December 4.

MacLeod, Calum. 2013. "China Boosts Military and Domestic Security Spending." *USA Today*, March 5.

Minh, Tran Van. 2015. "Thousands of Workers Strike for 6th Day at Nike, Adidas Factory in Vietnam." *Globe and Mail*, April 1.

Ost, David. 1990. *Solidarity and the Politics of Anti-Politics*. Philadelphia: Temple University Press.

Ost, David 2015. "The Peculiarities of Communism and the Emergence of Weak Unions in Poland." In *Working Through History: Labor and Authoritarian Legacies in Comparative Perspective*, ed. Teri L. Caraway, Maria Lorena Cook, and Stephen Crowley, 82–102. Ithaca, NY: Cornell University Press.

Paik, Wooyeal. 2014. "Local Village Workers, Foreign Factories and Village Politics in Coastal China: A Clientelist Approach." *China Quarterly* 220: 955–967.

Parfitt, Tom. 2015. "Russian Space Centre Workers Launch Hunger Strike After Vladimir Putin Promises Fail." *Telegraph*, April 22.

Perry, Elizabeth J. 2002. *Challenging the Mandate of Heaven: Social Protest and State Power in China*. Armonk, NY: M. E. Sharpe.

Perry, Elizabeth J. 2008. "Permanent Rebellion? Continuities and Discontinuities in Chinese Protest." In *Popular Protest in China*, ed. Kevin J. O'Brien, 205–215. Cambridge, MA: Harvard University Press.

Perry, Elizabeth J. 2012. *Anyuan: Mining China's Revolutionary Tradition*. Berkeley: University of California Press.

PRC Department of Population and Employment Statistics. 2009. *China Labour Statistical Yearbook 2009*. Beijing: China Statistics Press.

Pringle, Tim. 2011. *Trade Unions in China: The Challenge of Labour Unrest.* Abingdon: Routledge.

Pringle, Tim, and Simon Clarke. 2011. *The Challenge of Transition: Trade Unions in Russia, China and Vietnam.* New York: Palgrave Macmillan.

Pun, Ngai, Yuan Shen, Yuhua Guo, Huilin Lu, Jenny Chan, and Mark Selden. 2014. "Worker-Intellectual Unity: Trans-Border Sociological Intervention in Foxconn." *Current Sociology* 20, no. 10: 1–14.

Reuters. 2016. "China's Xi Promises New Measures to Fight Pollution." Voice of America, December 3.

RFA. 2012a. "Hunansheng nonhang qiangtui maiduan gongling zao yuangong qianglie kangyi" [Hunan province agricultural bank employees who were forced into retirement and had their seniority bought out protest]. Radio Free Asia, September 27.

RFA. 2012b. "Jilin shubai xiagang ji tuixiu gongren qingyuan Guangdong dianchang gaizhi gongren jingzuo duo ri" [Several hundred laid off and retired workers petition in Jilin; workers from a restructured power plant in Guangdong stage a sit-in for several days]. Radio Free Asia, August 21.

Robertson, Graeme B. 2007. "Strikes and Labor Organization in Hybrid Regimes." *American Political Science Review* 101, no. 4: 781–798.

Robertson, Graeme B. 2011. *The Politics of Protest in Hybrid Regimes: Managing Dissent in Post-Communist Russia.* New York: Cambridge University Press.

Rosenthal, Elisabeth. 2003. "Workers' Plight Brings New Militancy in China." *New York Times*, March 10.

Sheehan, Jackie. 1998. *Chinese Workers: A New History.* London: Routledge.

Shue, Vivienne. 1990. *The Reach of the State: Sketches of the Chinese Body Politic.* Stanford, CA: Stanford University Press.

Silver, Beverly J. 2003. *Forces of Labor: Workers' Movements and Globalization Since 1870.* New York: Cambridge University Press.

Silver, Beverly J., and Lu Zhang. 2009. "China as an Emerging Epicenter of World Labor Unrest." In *China and the Transformation of Global Capitalism*, ed. Ho-fung Hung, 174–187. Baltimore: Johns Hopkins University Press.

Solinger, Dorothy. 2004. "The New Crowd of the Dispossessed: The Shift of the Urban Proletariat from Master to Mendicant." In *State and Society in 21st Century China: Crisis, Contention and Legitimation*, ed. Peter Hays Gries and Stanley Rosen, 50–66. New York: Routledge Curzon.

Solinger, Dorothy. 2009. *State's Gains, Labor's Losses: China, France, and Mexico Choose Global Liaisons, 1980–2000.* Ithaca, NY: Cornell University Press.

Su, Yang, and Xin He. 2010. "Street as Courtroom: State Accommodation of Social Protest in China." *Law and Society Review* 44, no. 1: 157–184.

Tilly, Charles. 1995. *Popular Contention in Great Britain: 1759–1834.* Cambridge, MA: Harvard University Press.

Touraine, Alain, François Dubet, Michel Wieviorka, and Jan Strzelecki. 1983. *Soldarity: Poland 1980–1981.* London: Cambridge University Press.

Tsai, Kellee S. 2007. *Capitalism Without Democracy: The Private Sector in Contemporary China.* Ithaca, NY: Cornell University Press.

Vinogradova, Elena, Irina Kozina, and Linda Cook. 2012. "Russian Labor: Quiescence and Conflict." *Communist and Post-Communist Studies* 45, nos. 3–4: 219–231.

Walder, Andrew. 1988. *Communist Neo-Traditionalism: Work and Authority in Chinese Industry*. Berkeley: University of California Press.

Walder, Andrew, and Xiaoxia Gong. 1993. "Workers in the Tiananmen Protests: The Politics of the Beijing Workers' Autonomous Federation." *Australian Journal of Chinese Affairs* 29: 1–29.

Wallace, Jeremy L. 2014. *Cities and Stability: Urbanization, Redistribution, and Regime Survival in China*. New York: Oxford University Press.

Wang, Yuhua. 2014. "Coercive Capacity and the Durability of the Chinese Communist State." *Communist and Post-Communist Studies* 47, no. 1: 13–25.

Wang, Yuhua, and Carl F. Minzner. 2013. "The Rise of the Chinese Security State." *China Quarterly* 222: 339–359.

Wasserstrom, Jeffrey. 2010. "Historical Precedents for the Strike Wave by Chinese Workers at Honda Plants." *Huffington Post*, May 30.

Weil, Robert. 2006. "Conditions of the Working Classes in China." Monthly Review, June.

Weston, Timothy B. 2004. "The Iron Man Weeps: Joblessness and Political Legitimacy in the Chinese Rust Belt." In *State and Society in 21st Century China: Crisis, Contention and Legitimation*, ed. Peter Hays Gries and Stanley Rosen, 67–86. New York: Routledge Curzon.

World Bank. 2016. "Exports of Goods and Services (% of GDP)." http://data.worldbank.org/indicator/NE.EXP.GNFS.ZS?locations=CN-US.

Wright, Erik Olin. 2000. "Working-Class Power, Capitalist-Class Interests, and Class Compromise." *American Journal of Sociology* 105, no. 4: 957–1002.

Wright, Teresa. 2010. *Accepting Authoritarianism: State-Society Relations in China's Reform Era*. Stanford, CA: Stanford University Press.

Yang, Yuan. 2019. "Inside China's Crackdown on Young Marxists." *Financial Times*, February 13.

Zhai, Keith. 2017. "China's Xi Mines State Firms for Political Jobs Before Reshuffle." Bloomberg, June 21.

Zhang, Lu. 2015. *Inside China's Automobile Factories: The Politics of Labor and Worker Resistance*. New York: Cambridge University Press.

Zhu, Xiaoyang, and Anita Chan. 2005. "Workplace Democracy or an Arena of Management-Labor Contestation: The Chinese Staff and Workers' Representative Congress." In *China's Experience: Workplace Governance and Workers Democratic Participation in Transitional Economy*, ed. Feng Tongqing, 21–57. Beijing: Social Sciences Academic Press.

Building Public Support

9 }

The Logic of Vladimir Putin's Popular Appeal
Aleksandar Matovski

Ever since his emergence in 1999, Russia's Vladimir Putin has been perceived in the West as a riddle wrapped in a mystery inside an enigma, as Winston Churchill famously quipped about his country. Looking for clues to Putin's motives and behavior, analysts have resorted to everything from psychological profiling and deep personality analyses to esoteric interpretations of Russia's geopolitical doctrines and historical visions that he supposedly channels. However, relatively scant attention has been paid to one of the most vital and vexing aspects of his rule: the roots of his popular appeal in Russia.

Vladimir Putin's popularity has been as sudden as his rise and as steadfast as the grip he managed to establish on power. When Putin was first appointed as acting prime minister in August 1999, he was virtually unknown and had negative approval ratings. A month later, in September 1999, a string of terrorist attacks and Russia's decisive military response in the breakaway region of Chechnya turned him into an instant star. In the eyes of the crisis-weary Russian public, the brutal prosecution of the second Chechen war made Putin appear like the man who can reverse Russia's seemingly unstoppable post-Soviet decline. Unlike the other leadership alternatives at the time—the frail and erratic outgoing president, Boris Yeltsin; the leader of the unreformed Russian Communist Party, Gennady Zyuganov; and the septuagenarian presidential wannabe Yevgeny Primakov—the forty-seven-year-old Putin appeared youthful, vigorous and promising (Colton and McFaul 2003).

Putin's approval ratings, shown in Figure 9.1, jumped from practically zero to 80 percent from August to November 1999. And they stayed high ever since. Across the entire period between 2000 and mid-2018, Vladimir Putin's popular approval averaged at about 76 percent, hovering around this level during his two presidencies and the four-year stint as prime minister in between. In the wake of his controversial return to the presidency in 2012 and the protest wave

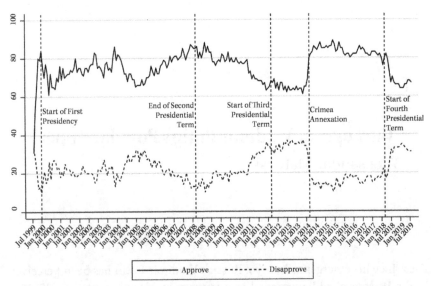

FIGURE 9.1 Percentage Approving and Disapproving of Vladimir Putin's Performance in Office

Note: Created by author using data from Levada Center Surveys.

that ensued, Putin's approval ratings dropped to an all-time low of 62 percent in 2013. But it rebounded in 2014, after the war in Ukraine—reaching a peak of 89 percent and an average of 83 percent in the four years since the annexation of Crimea in February 2014.

Such consistently high approval ratings are virtually unachievable for the leaders of stable democracies. The average popular approval of the U.S. presidents since 1968, for instance, was 51 percent, and has ranged between 45 percent (for President Jimmy Carter) to 61 percent (for President George H. W. Bush). Moreover, the popularity of U.S. presidents was far more variable than Vladimir Putin's. President George W. Bush, for example, had both the highest (90 percent in September 2001) and lowest approval rating (25 percent in October 2008). The seven other presidents that served since 1968 all had lows of popular approval percentages in the 20s and 30s during their terms in office—much worse than Putin's record low approval rating of 62 percent.[1]

Democratic leaders also tend to become less popular over time. Vladimir Putin, on the other hand, did not seem to suffer from this problem for a long time. We can see this in Figure 9.2, which compares Putin's and U.S. presidential approval by months in office. While most American presidents experienced declining or relatively flat ratings over time, Putin's ratings gradually increased in both his first and second terms.[2]

It is hard to overstate just how essential this unrelenting popularity of Vladimir Putin has been for the regime he established. Above all, it allowed him to achieve towering electoral dominance without egregious vote fraud—a feature that discouraged opposition and bestowed a veneer of democratic legitimacy on his rule. Also, far more than any other resource at his disposal,

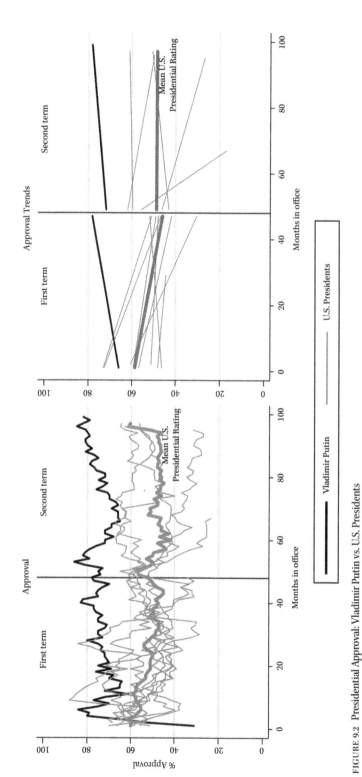

FIGURE 9.2 Presidential Approval: Vladimir Putin vs. U.S. Presidents

Note: Created by author using data from Levada Center and Gallup Surveys.

popularity enabled Putin to rein in Russia's quasi-feudal, self-serving, and notoriously capricious bureaucracy, as well as the country's political, economic and regional elites. The reason is simple: Putin's popular appeal meant that he would only emerge stronger from confrontations with any of Russia's widely despised officials, local bosses, and robber baron oligarchs, while they would essentially be destroyed. Hence, members of the Russian elite quickly learned to fall in line to avoid the fate of Mikhail Khodorkovsky, Boris Berezovsky, and others who challenged Putin's authority (Rogov 2015).

Putin's popular appeal had an even deeper and more perverse effect. Russian bureaucrats, regional bosses, and oligarchs did not just fear Putin's popularity: they became utterly dependent on it. As long as Putin stayed popular and they remained in his good graces, Russia's elites could be sure that their unchecked power and ill-gotten wealth would be safe from expropriation by anyone, ranging from resurgent Communists to the angry masses rising in rebellion. Totally lacking any legitimacy of their own, Russia's unaccountable, kleptocratic officialdom and oligarchy could be sustained only by aligning themselves with someone of Putin's popular stature. This makes Putin's towering popularity essential for the day-to-day functioning of the Russian system of government. Without it, Russia's otherwise unchecked bureaucrats would have no credible signal that Putin will hold power long enough to reward their compliance, punish their transgressions, and protect them from reprisals. Without Putin's high ratings to anchor their expectations of the future, they will almost certainly become unwilling to carry out orders on a whole host of issues, ranging from mundane tasks of government to perilous assignments, like repressing the opposition or committing electoral fraud (on this dynamic, see, e.g., Rundlett and Svolik 2016; Gehlbach and Simpser 2015).

But the most sinister effect of Putin's appeal has manifested beyond Russia's borders. For its ability to command unprecedented popular support even as it transformed Russia into a bastion of authoritarianism, Putinism became a role model for authoritarian leaders and forces across the world, who sought to achieve the same in their countries. So much so that the leaders of EU and NATO member Hungary and NATO member Turkey—who have taken decidedly authoritarian turns in recent years—have openly praised Vladimir Putin's style of governing as an inspiration (Caryl 2015; Orban 2014). And amid the rising political turmoil and anti-establishment sentiments, it appears that admirers of Putinism could assume power in some of the established Western democracies (Foa and Mounk 2016; Kelemen 2016).

The Puzzle of Putin's Popularity

How did Vladimir Putin become and stay so popular? The simplest explanation for his broad popular acclaim is that it is not real, whether because pollsters have falsified survey results or because Russian respondents lie to pollsters that they approve of their authoritarian leader because of fear and intimidation. But these assumptions are wrong. First, there is broad consensus that Russia's most highly regarded pollsters have not tampered with their surveys to paint a rosier picture of Putin's popularity. The prime example is Russia's independent Levada Survey Center, which has been known for its professionalism since Soviet times and has been relentlessly pressured by the Putin regime because of its objective analysis (see Treisman 2013). Second, there is mounting evidence that Russians have not falsely professed adoration for their leaders (for an overview, see, e.g., Rose 2007). The most recent and methodologically sophisticated confirmation that Putin's popularity is genuine is provided by two studies conducted in 2012 and 2015 (see Colton and Hale 2014 and Frye et al. 2017). Using the list experiment technique, which allows surveyed individuals to provide anonymous responses on sensitive issues, these analyses estimate that only about 6–9 percent of survey respondents have falsely claimed they support Putin when asked a direct question—a proportion that is small relative to Putin's overall approval, and close to the estimation error for the list experiment technique.

But the most compelling indication that Russians have not held back their true feelings about Vladimir Putin is far more straightforward: their responses to other survey questions about him. Despite approving of Putin's overall conduct, Russian survey respondents have been remarkably critical of Putin's actual achievements in office. I illustrate this in Figure 9.3, which shows popular evaluations of Vladimir Putin's achievements in eight key issue areas on the eve of his reelection in 2012.[3] A clear majority (about 60 percent) say that there have been improvements in only one major issue area during Putin's reign: the global influence of Russia. On the other hand, fewer than 50 percent of respondents believed that Russia's political stability and the stability of the North Caucasus—two of Putin's most touted achievements—increased during his rule, 71 percent of the respondents found that income inequality increased under Putin, and a majority of 51 percent deemed that corruption worsened in his time in office. Only 33 percent detected improvements in the standard of living—the other showcased accomplishment of Putin's rule—as opposed to 34 percent who thought that living standards actually worsened. Yet in the end, despite these bleak evaluations, a full 66 percent of respondents in the same survey said they voted for Putin in the 2012 election.

Contrary to some interpretations (see, e.g., Pipes 2004), Russians did not harbor any inborn cultural predispositions or habituated fondness for authoritarian rule that might have explained this behavior. Indeed, Russian citizens have voiced their dislike of the Putinist system in this regard too: by accurately assessing it as semi-authoritarian, and by expressing a desire to live in a considerably more democratic society. I depict these outlooks in Figure 9.4, which records the average assessments Russians gave their actual and desired political systems on a 1–10 scale, ranging from closed authoritarianism to full

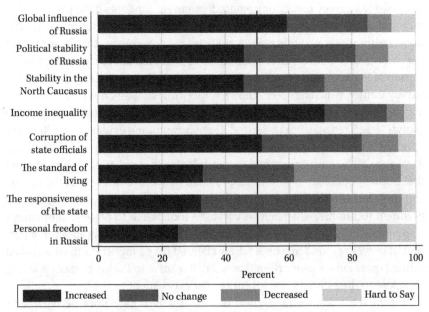

FIGURE 9.3 In the Last 12 Years Since Putin First Became President, Have the Following Things Increased, Decreased, or Remained Unchanged?

Note: Created by author using data from Russia Election Study, Colton et al. (2014).

democracy.[4] This graph shows that throughout the first ten years of Putin's rule, Russian citizens, on average, gave their current regime a remarkably accurate grade of slightly above 5 on this scale—the midpoint between democracy and full dictatorship. At the same time, they consistently expressed a desire to live in a system that is about 2 points higher on this scale—substantially closer to the Western standard of democracy.

The Logic of the Strongman Authoritarian Appeal

The real puzzle of Putin's popularity, as these sentiments suggest, is not whether it is real or faked, but how it was even possible when people had such poor evaluations of his performance and desired to live in a more democratic system than the one he maintained. The key to understanding this phenomenon, I argue, lies in Russia's cataclysmic decade of post-Communist transition and its traumatic effects on Russian mass opinion.

Following the Soviet collapse, Russia experienced what amounts to the biggest peacetime decline in history. The Russian population not only witnessed their country lose its superpower status and control of vast amounts of its territory but also endured a socioeconomic decline twice as intense as the Great Depression of the 1930s.[5] The scope of this cataclysm was so immense

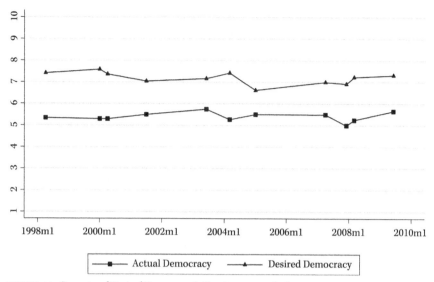

FIGURE 9.4 Current and Desired Democracy in Russia on a 1–10 Scale

Note: Created by author using data from New Russia Barometer Surveys, Rose (2010).

that it is best captured not by economic measures but by population decline—a drop of about three-quarters of a million people per year throughout the 1990s (Balzer 2002).

The reaction of the Russian public has been likened to post-traumatic stress disorder (Guillory 2014). After a brief outpouring of enthusiasm about liberalization in the late 1980s, the bulk of the Russian population adopted exceptionally gloomy and anxious outlooks. Fearing for their own and Russia's survival, people completely reversed their views about Russia should be governed. I show this in Figure 9.5. Right before the fall of the Berlin Wall in November 1989, a solid plurality of about 45 percent of Russians held the liberal view that executive power should never be put in the hands of one person. On the other hand, a quarter of the population insisted their country always needs to be run by a strong leader, and another 15 percent believed that the current situation warrants one. This shows once again that the Russian population did not harbor any innate or habituated pro-authoritarian tendencies at the end of the Cold War, despite spending the previous seventy-one years under a totalitarian dictatorship. Quite the opposite: they seem to have demonstrated a budding enthusiasm for Russia's liberalization.

But then came the catastrophe. The dissolution of the Soviet Union in 1991 was followed by "shock therapy" market reforms, the rise of crony capitalism, economic collapse, and a political and constitutional crisis that culminated with the shelling of Parliament in October 1993 (these events are represented by the gray vertical lines in Figure 9.5). By 1995, the Russian economy had dwindled to half its size from before the Soviet collapse. To top things off, the

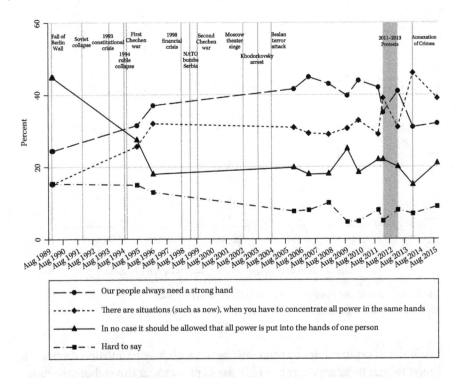

FIGURE 9.5 Are There, in Your Opinion, Situations in Our Nation When the People Need a Strong and Imperious Leader, a "Strong Hand"?

Note: Created by author using data from Levada Center surveys.

disastrous first invasion of Chechnya made it seem as though Russia would it-self soon disintegrate in a bloody civil war. These experiences sharply reversed popular sentiments about the type of leadership most appropriate for Russia. If liberal outlooks were dominant in 1989, a solid majority of 60 percent supported temporary or permanent strong-arm rule by 1995. Only 28 percent rejected calls for concentration of power. Thus, well before the rise of Putinist propaganda and media control, extreme hardship compelled most Russians to think that only a strongman could rescue Russia.

Rising against this backdrop, Vladimir Putin became wildly popular, as he fit the image of the tough leader that Russia needed. This appeal, paradoxi-cally, allowed him to be liked even without doing much to resolve Russia's un-derlying problems. Instead, Putin's popularity has been predominantly based on hope and fear, a pattern I illustrate in Figure 9.6. Asked why people trust Putin, only about 15–30 percent of Russians in the 2001–2015 period said this is because he adequately tackles the country's problems. A combined total of between 65 and 80 percent believed that people have faith in Putin either be-cause they hope he will deal with Russia's problems in the future or because they see no other reliable alternative—a sentiment reflecting fears the country

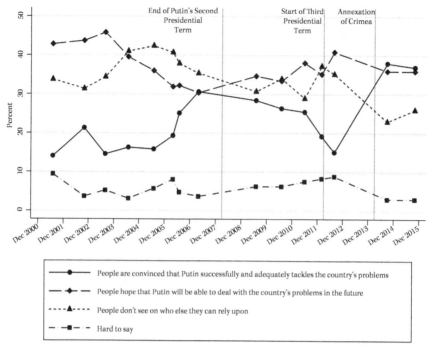

FIGURE 9.6 Why Do You Think Many People Trust Vladimir Putin?

Note: Created by author using data from Levada Center surveys.

will slip back to the chaos of the 1990s if Putin is replaced. The great majority of Russians, in other words, thought their compatriots embraced Putin not for what he achieved but for what they thought he prevents and for what they hoped he might eventually deliver.

And in responding to the question about why people trust Vladimir Putin in Figure 9.6, Russians did not simply rationalize the behavior of compatriots with whom they did not necessarily agree. Instead, they seemed to project their own reasons for supporting Putin. We see evidence of this if we examine only the responses of Russians who themselves had positive appraisals of Putin. Looking at the 2000–2013 period (for which data for cross-tabulations are available), an average of only about 27 percent of Levada Center survey respondents who approved of Vladimir Putin's performance said he was trusted because he successfully tackled Russia's problems. In turn, 41 percent on average said that people trusted him because they hoped he will do so in the future, and 29 percent of those approving his performance said Putin is trusted because people see no better alternatives. In other words, 70 percent of Russians who approved of Putin's performance said that he is trusted because of the hope he inspired or the lack of better alternatives.

This logic of delayed and suspended accountability raises a crucial question: did it allow Putin to maintain support among dissatisfied citizens who under different circumstances might have voted him out of office? To examine this, I estimate multinomial logit models of responses to the question of why people trust Putin using data from the fifteen available Levada Center surveys that contain this question. These models account for the effects of respondent characteristics such as age, gender, social class, education, and size of the settlement where respondents live, as well as two key politically relevant outlooks—belief that things in Russia are going in the right direction, and the respondent's party sympathies.[6]

In Figure 9.7, I depict the estimated effects of these variables on the odds of a response other than the baseline category "People trust Putin because they believe he successfully and adequately tackles Russia's problems."[7] The left panel in the graph covers all fifteen surveys that contain this question in the 2001–2014 period, and the one to the right includes estimates using surveys only for 2001–2007, which also contain data on the respondents' party sympathies. The top part of each of these panels displays the estimated odds of choosing the "People trust Putin because they hope he will tackle Russia's problems in the future" response as opposed to the baseline category. The bottom part shows the relative odds of choosing the "People trust Putin because they see no one else they can depend on" response. The odds are shown with 95 percent confidence intervals derived from robust standard errors. Point estimates above 1 suggest that increases in the given variable correlate with an increase in the odds of choosing that response relative to the baseline category. The opposite is true for odds ratios estimates below 1.

If people's hopes about Putin's leadership and their perceived lack of better alternatives did indeed help him maintain the support of dissatisfied Russians, beliefs that things in Russia are going in a bad direction should significantly increase the odds of choosing these reasons for why people trust Putin. In other words, respondents with negative assessments of the general circumstances in Russia should be more likely to rationalize trust in Putin in terms of future hopes and lack of alternatives.

The estimates shown in Figure 9.7 strongly support these claims. The perception that things in Russia are going in a bad direction is the strongest predictor of responses that Putin is trusted due to hopes of future improvements or lack of alternatives, rather than actual achievements. This effect holds both for the model covering the entire 2001–2014 period in the left panel of Figure 9.7 and for the model covering 2001–2007 in the right panel, which includes controls for party sympathies. Indeed, it is striking that negative assessments of Russia's direction have an effect just as great as sympathies for the major oppositional parties. Thus, according to the estimates in the right panel of Figure 9.7, pessimistic evaluations of Russia's general direction increase the odds that respondents will ascribe Putin's popularity to hope or lack of alternatives by more than 1.5 and 2.5 times, respectively—just as much as the difference between sympathizing with the main opposition parties instead of with the

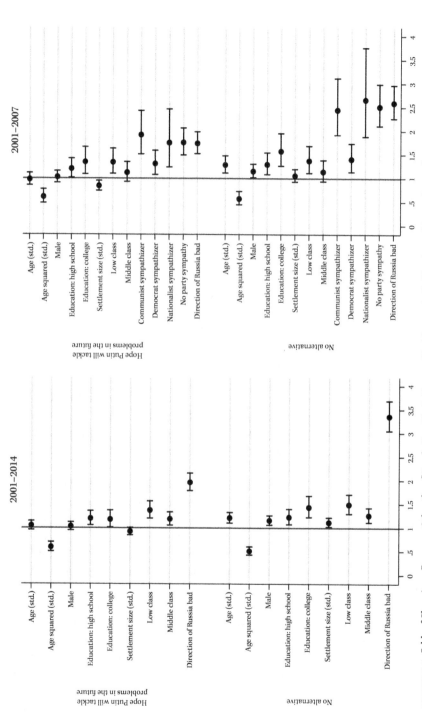

FIGURE 9.7 Odds of Choosing a Response Other than "People Trust Putin Because He Adequately Tackles the Problems of Russia"

Note: Created by author using data from Levada Center surveys.

pro-regime ones. This suggests that hope in Putin's leadership and the perceived lack of alternatives—sentiments stemming from the trauma of Russia's post-Communist crisis—allowed Putin to maintain support not only among Russia's generally dissatisfied majority but also among citizens with pro-oppositional outlooks. And as I show in Figure 9.A.1 in the appendix, negative appraisals of Russia's general direction are the best predictor of beliefs that Putin is trusted because of hope and fear even among respondents who approve of Putin's performance in office, though the effect is somewhat smaller.[8] Once again, this indicates that the estimates in Figure 9.7 largely reflect people's own reasons for trusting Putin, which they have projected onto other Russians.

The behavior of the other variables with significant effects in the models displayed in Figure 9.7 and Figure 9.A.1 is in line with these conclusions. In particular, low social class significantly increases the odds that a respondent would say that people trust Putin because of hope and lack of other choices rather than because of his actual achievements. The same is true for respondents with higher education—particularly college-educated individuals—and for middle-aged individuals. I depict the latter effect, captured by the significant squared age term, in Figure 9.A.2 in the appendix. These graphs suggest that the probability of responding that people trust Putin because of his achievements declines by up to one-third for respondents around the age of fifty when all other variables are held at their means. The likelihood of the "hope" and particularly the "no alternative" responses for this age group increases correspondingly.

Taken together, these results indicate that poorer, more highly educated, and middle-aged Russians, those dissatisfied with Russia's direction, and sympathizers of opposition parties were significantly more likely to justify trust in Putin in terms of hope and lack of alternatives rather than his actual performance. For this diverse group, jointly making up to two-thirds of Putin's support, hope and fear of alternatives were the psychological mechanisms that enabled what Rose, Mishler, and Munro (2004) called the "resigned acceptance" of Putinist autocracy. When the system performed well, they supported its leader. When the system performed badly, they were still willing to support Putin, however reluctantly, as the recent trauma of Russia's post-Communist decline has taught them there is little else to hope for and much to fear from change. The bulk of Putin's support, in other words, was not driven by a "What have you done for me lately?" economic voting logic, as in stable democracies. Instead, it became captive to a "Would all hope be lost and would things become worse without Putin?" outlook.

This rationale helps clarify why one of the most prominent explanations of Putin's popularity—that it was driven by Russia's economic performance under his reign (see, e.g., Treisman 2011)—has produced inconsistent results (Treisman 2014). Putin's approval ratings and popular perceptions of the economy, as I illustrate in Figure 9.8, appeared to be closely aligned

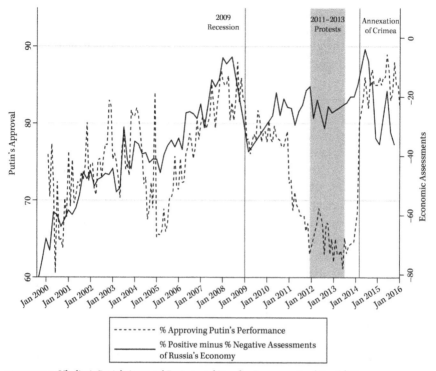

FIGURE 9.8 Vladimir Putin's Approval Ratings and Popular Assessments of Russia's Economy

Note: Created by author using data from Levada Center surveys.

throughout the 2000–2009 period. These nine years of continuous growth yielded the greatest economic success of Putin's rule: restoring Russia's real per capita GDP to the level of 1989, just before the Soviet collapse. As aggregate economic assessments shifted from very bad to almost neutral, Putin's approval ratings soared by another 15–20 percentage points from the starting level—about the same amount as perceptions that people trust Putin because of his achievements in resolving Russia's problems, depicted in Figure 9.6. Thus, the economic improvements throughout the 2000s may have justified support for Putin among Russians who endorsed him for his performance. But at best, they contributed about 20 percent to his overall ratings. At least 60 percent of Putin's approval was not directly affected by evaluations of his actual performance, economic or otherwise. Rather, it was sustained by hope that Vladimir Putin's leadership will bring future improvements, and fears that replacing him could have the same effect as letting the Soviet Union collapse.

Putin could attract such broad popular support on hope and fear alone because people believed he was uniquely qualified to complete a crucial but essentially narrow and transient mission: reversing Russia's decline. This is why Putin's popularity began to slip, ironically, right after people's perceptions of the Russian economy peaked. This process, as we can see in Figure 9.8, began after

Russia's spillover recession from the global economic crisis in 2009. At first Putin's ratings stayed relatively flat even as economic assessments recovered from this crisis. Then, in early 2011, his approval took a sharp plunge of 15–20 percentage points, foreshadowing the unprecedented wave of anti-regime protests in 2011–2013.

This highlights a key lesson for the nature of strongman popularity. Putin's popular support declined after 2011 because the mission he was endorsed to perform—reversing Russia's post-Soviet decline—was essentially completed. As the economy gradually returned to pre-transition levels, people's priorities began to shift from basic survival and consumption to resolving Russia's structural problems in areas such as healthcare, education, rule of law, and control of corruption (Belanovsky and Dmitriev 2013). These are issues that an unaccountable authoritarian system, designed to guarantee stability, could not address. To compensate, Putin initially championed the ostensibly reformist technocrat lawyer Dmitry Medvedev as his successor in the presidency, while he took the backseat as prime minister. But it quickly became apparent that this transition was a sham. Frustration seeped in and approval ratings began to drop among those who supported Putin for his performance and desired change.[9] Then, to add insult to injury, Putin announced in September 2011 that he would return to the presidency the next year, ending hopes of meaningful change in the foreseeable future. The wave of protests, dominated by reform-minded, middle-class, highly educated urbanites, erupted soon after.[10]

"Making Russia Great Again" to Survive Politically: The Path to the Ukraine War

Leaders rise and fall with the popularity of the public images they project: once they are identified with a particular role, it tends to become anchored in the collective consciousness of the nation. Thus when circumstances change, people can turn their backs on even highly revered leaders who do not seem to be cut out for the times. Winston Churchill's landslide electoral defeat in 1945—coming just after he had heroically steered Britain throughout its greatest ordeal in history—is a case in point.

Vladimir Putin faced a similar prospect in 2013, but in the much higher-stakes political environment of Russia. A decade before, by crushing Chechen rebels and unfettered oligarchs, he assumed the mantle of the competent strongman that Russia craved. But as the country stabilized from the post-Soviet crisis, the image of a bare-chested, take-charge tough-guy president toiling to "raise Russia from its knees" was becoming stale. Worse still, people began to realize that the particular brand of authoritarianism that he had created—the security-services-dominated crony capitalist system, designed to maximize loyalty and control—stood in the way of Russia's further progress.

The only reason Putin's approval did not plunge below 60 percent in the face of the 2011–2013 protest wave was because a third of the population still hoped that he could refashion himself into Russia's modernizer, and another third still feared that without him the country would slip back into chaos. For the time being, only the performance-motivated trust in Putin declined, as we can see in Figure 9.6. But over the long run, hope and fear are perishable commodities. They need to be refreshed by tangible achievements and credible threats.

And Putin's regime provided exactly the opposite signals. The shock of the 2009 recession, which despite the Kremlin's assurances to the contrary hit Russia particularly hard, shattered the regime's image as an indispensable guarantor of stability (see, e.g., Chaisty and Whitefield 2012). And as result of Russia's increasingly apparent economic stagnation and corrupt political system, hope was starting to wear thin. By 2013, about 60 percent of respondents to Levada Center surveys said they fully or mostly agreed that people have grown tired of waiting for Vladimir Putin to produce positive changes in their lives.[11] Worse still, there were early signals that such sentiments and feelings of discontent were spreading beyond the more sophisticated urban population, which formed the core of the 2011–2012 protest wave, to Russia's more conservative, blue-collar majority living in the provinces (Dmitriev and Treisman 2012).

With his brand in terminal decline, Putin saw little choice but to resort to radical measures. To stay in power, he had to refocus popular attention back on issues that favored him: battling Russia's "threats" and ensuring its stability. Staged against this backdrop, the interventions in Ukraine and beyond were part of a last-ditch effort to salvage his authoritarian regime. By placing the country on a war footing, Putin effectively changed the terms of reference Russians used to evaluate the performance of their leadership. If attempts to modernize Russia exposed the weaknesses of his regime and were gradually turning Putin into a villain, the campaigns in Ukraine and Syria resurrected his strongman savior image.

They also reshuffled the perspectives and priorities of ordinary Russians in ways favorable to the Kremlin. In Russia's public consciousness, these foreign interventions essentially reset the clock back to the period before 1989. This was a time when Russians were poor but lived in a superpower that provided stability and a sense of pride. And for most Russian citizens, giving up this status in the 1990s resulted in far greater hardship and humiliation than anything they had to endure under the Soviet dictatorship. To put it differently, for ordinary people in Russia who lived through the 1990s, great-power nationalism and Soviet nostalgia are not just attractive myths; they also had tangible economic repercussions.[12] The last time that Russians traded their guns for more butter, they pretty soon lost all the butter too.

This is why the ability to restore Russia's great-power status had always been a key criterion the Russian voters used to evaluate their potential leaders. As

I show in Table 9.1, the main expectation Russian voters had from presidential candidates was to "make Russia a great, respected power again." Over 50 percent of respondents consistently chose this option in each election year since 1996, when Putin was still a provincial bureaucrat far from the Kremlin's levers of power. This was 10–20 percent more than the share of voters who demanded a fair distribution of incomes or compensation for their losses during Russia's catastrophic post-Communist transformation—issues one might expect that the degraded and impoverished Russians would hold closer to heart. Again, this was not because Russian citizens were willing to sacrifice their well-being for the Russian nation's greatness.[13] They emphasized restoring Russia's great-power status because they believed this was the best (and only) way to ensure their well-being and to guarantee order and stability in the country.

Tapping into these sentiments, Russia's interventions in Ukraine and Syria resurrected both the greatest hope and the deepest fear of post-Soviet Russia. The hope was that, having decisively pushed back against the West for the first time since 1989, Russia would finally be able to reclaim its lost stature and opportunity to pursue its own path to development. And the fear was that now that Russia was on its feet again, its citizens would risk reliving the Soviet collapse and making their lives much worse if they embraced another liberalization and rejected the Putinist authoritarian system that guaranteed a semblance of order at home and "made Russia great" abroad.

This diversionary conflict strategy has been paying off handsomely for the Kremlin in the past few years. After the Crimea annexation, Putin instantaneously reclaimed his status as the indispensable leader, "raising Russia from its knees." As we can see in Figure 9.1, his popularity bounced back to around

TABLE 9.1 } What do You Expect Most of All from a President Who You Are Prepared to Vote for? (respondents can choose multiple answers)

	Jan. 1996	Jan. 2000	Jan. 2004	Jan. 2008	Jan. 2012
Make Russia a great, respected power again	54	55	58	51	57
Strengthen law and order	58	54	45	45	51
Strengthen role of the state in the economy	37	37	39	34	37
Fair distribution of incomes for ordinary people	37	43	48	41	49
Continue reforms, but with more social protection	35	35	38	37	34
Give ordinary people the means the lost during reform	38	38	41	28	29
Finish the war in Chechnya	59	56	43	23	18
Keep Russia on the path of reform	13	12	11	15	16
Set the course for reunification with the former Soviet republics	13	10	12	9	9
Continue rapprochement with the West	6	8	7	6	5
Other	1	2	1	2	3
Don't know	5	3	2	3	3

Source: Levada Center Surveys

85 percent in early 2014 and hovered around this level until late 2018, in spite of sanctions and Russia's greatest decline in living standards since the 1990s. Even Putin's performance-based evaluations soared upward: the share of Russians who believed their leader is trusted due to his achievements rose from 15 percent in mid-2012 to a record high of almost 40 percent at the end of 2014, according to Figure 9.6. Performance-motivated support for Putin was reset from "It's the economy, stupid!" to "It's the stability, stupid!"

Crucially, Russia's newly assertive posture restored Putin's staying power in politics before his reelection to his fourth presidential term in 2018. As I illustrate in Figure 9.9, 41 percent of Russians in early 2013 said that they would like to see Vladimir Putin replaced in the next election by someone who would pursue different solutions to Russia's problems, while a combined 40 percent wished to see another Putin presidency or his replacement by someone who would continue his policies. The writing on the wall was clear: Putin's brand as an indispensable strongman was in terminal decline. After the annexation of Crimea and the war in Ukraine, these sentiments completely reversed. By June 2015, a full 66 percent wanted Putin himself to stay in power, while only 15 percent thought that he should be replaced by a president who will follow a different course. The crusade to make Russia a great power again clearly gave

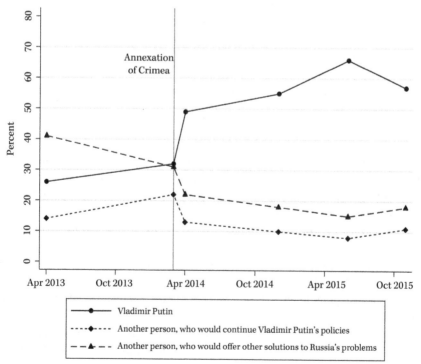

FIGURE 9.9 Who Would You Like to See as President After the Next Elections?
Note: Created by author using data from Levada Center surveys.

Putin's regime a new lease on life. But how long can this last? And how will it shape the Kremlin's behavior?

The Strategy of the Cornered Rat

Regimes that stake their legitimacy on a quest of tackling foreign threats and safeguarding stability at home, as Huntington (1991) pointed out, become redundant both if they succeed and if they fail in their mission. To survive, they must juggle two incompatible goals: they must sustain or even manufacture the crises and threats that justify their rule, while also appearing to be successful in addressing them. The proverbial dragon-slaying knight in shining armor is the undisputed hero of the realm only as long as there are dragons to slay and he appears to be good at it. Having fully committed to this role with the Ukraine intervention, Vladimir Putin has three crucial imperatives for sustaining his popular support. First, he cannot afford to suffer a humiliating defeat or a bloody quagmire while pursuing a crusade to reassert Russia's great-power status. Second, he cannot compromise and bargain away the gains of this struggle (like Crimea and other Russian-controlled parts of Ukraine) or allow further infringements into Russia's "sphere of influence" (think potential color revolutions in other countries in the former Soviet Union) without losing credibility. Finally, and most importantly, he cannot afford peace for long. Too much time off from the struggle for Russia's rightful place in the world will divert public attention from an area where Putin is perceived to be at his best (foreign affairs) back to festering domestic issues (like fixing the economy or tackling corruption and inequality), where he is bound to be seen as a failure.

The clearest indication that Putin's renewed popular support is highly dependent on the existence of a "clear and present danger" to Russia is provided by the shifts in popular attitudes toward strong-arm rule in the wake of the Crimea annexation. As we can see from Figure 9.5, between March 2013 and March 2014 the share of respondents who believed that "there are times (such as now) when it is necessary to concentrate all power in the same hands" sharply increased, from 31 to 46 percent of the total. The Ukraine war made this group of "contingent authoritarians" dominant for the first time since 1989—garnering 15 percentage points more than the unreserved authoritarian outlook ("Russia always needs to be run by a strong leader") and 30 points more than the liberal view ("Power should never be concentrated in the hands of a single person").[14]

Most important of all, the rise of Russia's "contingent authoritarians" has accounted for the bulk of Putin's post-Crimea popularity boost. Of Putin's 17 percent rise in popular approval in this period, 14 percent (or more than four-fifths) came from the swelling ranks of Russians who believed their country needs a "strong hand" now, but not always. This attitude shift in the wake of the Ukraine conflict not only helped Putin restore his popularity but also seemed to demobilize the protest sentiments that threatened his rule. As I show in Figure 9.A.3 and Table 9.A.2 in the appendix, in March 2017 the respondents who provisionally supported strong-arm rule instead of the unconditional authoritarian view ("Our people always need a strong hand") tended to be residents of Moscow, of middle- and upper-class backgrounds, and dissatisfied with the general direction of Russia: the basic profile of the participants in the protest movement of 2011–2012. The Ukraine conflict clearly rallied these people behind the regime. But if they were to someday become convinced that the dangers Russia faces no longer require heavy-handed leadership, they could withdraw their support for Putin's rule, sending his approval ratings tumbling and raising the specter of renewed anti-regime protests. Thus, to maintain the loyalty of this new majority of contingent authoritarians, Vladimir Putin's regime will need to supply a steady stream of conflicts that will give them a credible enough reason to feel threatened.

Unless he is effectively challenged by the West, Putin can sustain this sort of diversionary conflict legitimation for a long time, despite Russia's severe and oft-cited limitations and weaknesses. First, to keep the fear of foreign enemies and instability at home alive—as well as the appearance of great-power status and sphere of influence in the former Soviet space—Putin does not need to occupy and control Russia's neighbors and other countries; he only needs to create enclaves and frozen conflicts that will destabilize them. Russia did this effectively when it was far weaker in the 1990s. Second, Putin's direct opponents in this campaign will be the dysfunctional and fragile former Soviet states, highly exposed to Russia's leverage. Finally, to maintain the appearance of challenging Western supremacy globally, Putin can resort to methods ranging from boastful intransigence at the UN to cyberattacks, airspace intrusions, provocative wargames, and acting as a spoiler in critical regions like the Middle East. These are essentially "trolling" tactics, designed to frustrate the West and delight Russians without much risk of open confrontation (Kornbluth 2015). Russia is quite capable of sustaining such activities for a long time.

Of course, this strategy carries a risk of unwanted escalations and failures that could damage rather than boost the regime's legitimacy. But Russia's strongman cannot back down and survive politically. The best-known story from Vladimir Putin's childhood is about a rat he chased into a corner; left with no choices, the rat jumped out at the startled young Putin, escaping in the process (Putin et al. 2000). Now, by staking his regime's credibility on the quest to restore Russia's fading glory and greatness, Putin has turned his regime into a cornered rat. It can survive only by startling the West, its neighbors, and the Russian population with aggressive audacity.

Sanctions and the economic woes they induce will not easily undermine the ability of Russia's autocracy to sustain itself in this fashion. Putin's predecessor Boris Yeltsin provides the clearest example of just how much economic ruin a Russian president can preside over and still stay in power. After leading Russia through the greatest peacetime economic decline in history, the frail and incoherent Yeltsin still managed to secure another term in 1996 with an approval rating of only 30 percent. And Yeltsin never effectively diverted attention away from economics by pursuing an aggressive confrontational policy beyond Russia's borders, as Putin did. Authoritarian regimes far less capable than Putin's Russia have sustained their rule by pursuing devastating conflicts, demobilizing domestic opposition through fear-mongering and nationalist-patriotic rhetoric, despite crippling economic circumstances, sanctions, and external pressure. The case in point is Serbia's Slobodan Milosevic, who, unlike Putin, ruled a small country with limited resources and no nuclear weapons, devastated by sanctions, and surrounded by U.S. friends and allies. Despite all this, Milosevic managed to cling to power for over a decade, with ruinous consequences for his country and the Balkans (Gagnon 2004).

In the ultimate analysis, a social and economic collapse in Russia never produced a democracy (Ioffe 2014). A sanctions-induced economic meltdown could lead not just to Putin's downfall but also to chaos and another, possibly even nastier autocracy. This leads us to one final point. When confronting the Kremlin's perilous use of aggression abroad to sustain domestic support, the West has largely assumed that it only has a "Putin problem," not a "Russia problem." But this is a dangerous assumption to make. The (dirty) truth about the image of the super-popular savior strongman, battling Russia's foreign and domestic detractors, is that it can be assumed by other ambitious politicians and bureaucrats waiting in the shadows. Putin himself is the ultimate proof: all it took to cast a complete—and initially awkward and reluctant—outsider into this role in 1999 was a deftly synchronized power transition and a small "victorious" war (in the form of the second Chechen war).

Putinism, to put things differently, is not only a supply-side problem but also a demand-side problem. As long as the specter of festering conflicts, humiliating economic cataclysms, or another collapse haunts the Russian population, majorities may be compelled to willingly—if reluctantly—support strong-arm rule as the least bad remedy. And because of this broad appeal, Putinism will also be embraced by Russia's kleptocratic, unaccountable, and widely despised political, bureaucratic, and business elites, who, as I have argued earlier, need a popular authoritarian patron to protect their ill-gotten wealth and power from expropriation. So if Putin is gone one day, Russia's elites and society might again feel compelled to support someone just like him. As Putin's own former spin doctor Gleb Pavlovsky put it: "It's impossible to say when this system will fall, but when it falls, it will fall in one day. And the one to replace it will be a copy of this one" (quoted in Ioffe 2014; see also Pavlovsky 2016).

Conclusion

This chapter examines the sources of Vladimir Putin's popularity in Russia—one of the most fundamental and distinctive features of his reign since 2000. Contrary to some existing preconceptions, the chapter argues that Russians have not supported their leader because they were bribed, brainwashed, and coerced into submission, or because they were somehow culturally predisposed to favor strong-arm authoritarian rule. Instead, I show that Russian citizens endorsed Putin's electoral authoritarian regime because they perceived it as the least bad alternative, capable of stabilizing their country after the cataclysmic post-Soviet decline. Hoping that Putin's stern leadership will eventually restore order and prosperity in Russia, and fearing that replacing it will bring back the chaos of the 1990s, ordinary Russians have also been remarkably willing to tolerate Putinist autocracy, despite its relatively poor record of achievement.

These sentiments allowed Putin to retain the bulk of his support in the wake of the protest wave against his rule in 2011–2012. But his legitimacy based on hope and fear was quickly becoming exhausted in this new context. As Russia recovered from its post-Communist decline, it became increasingly harder to hold its population captive to the belief that an authoritarian overlord is needed to prevent further instability, and more and more Russians realized that Putin's corrupt authoritarian regime stood in the way of future progress. Faced with terminal decline, Putin's strongman authoritarian regime had no other way to resuscitate its legitimacy except to push Russia toward another existential struggle by staging the interventions in Ukraine, Syria, and beyond. Tapping into the deepest traumas from the defeat in the Cold War and the subsequent Soviet collapse, these conflicts stifled appetites for liberalization and gave Putin a new lease on life. However, as popular opinion trends suggest, this newfound legitimacy is dangerously dependent on the regime's ability to supply a constant stream of threats, conflicts, and victories to justify Putin's heavy-handed rule. Lacking other sources of legitimacy and facing bleak economic prospects, Vladimir Putin has few other choices but to pursue this high-cost and high-risk diversionary conflict strategy to survive politically.

The ability of Putin's regime to maintain power in this fashion will have key implications not just for Russia and the regions most affected by it but also for other major autocracies. As a prototype of a robust post–Cold War authoritarian system, Putinist Russia and its future course will profoundly influence the behavior of non-democratic regimes across the world. In particular, the ability of Putin's regime to sustain its domestic legitimacy through diversionary conflicts could inspire other autocracies to pursue similar tactics when facing domestic challenges. In this sense, the fate of Putin's diversionary authoritarian legitimation is bound to have a crucial demonstration effect for the Chinese regime. If the objectively weaker Russian regime could get away with a territorial grab like Crimea or the intervention in Syria to prop up its domestic standing, why shouldn't China be able to perform analogous stunts in its "sphere of influence" in Asia?

Putin's brand of strongman authoritarianism has already been influencing the legitimation strategy of the Chinese regime for some time. Indeed, one of the most striking instances of convergence between Russian and Chinese regimes in recent years—the key theme of this volume—has been in the public image and appeal of their leaders. Ever since his rise, China's Xi Jinping has mirrored Putin's strongman appeal so systematically that one might argue that Putinism may be a key role model for Xi as he takes decisive steps toward more personalized rule, unconstrained by term limits. In particular, while much of the image that Xi is attempting to project is modeled on China's homegrown strongmen, of the past like Mao Zedong and Deng Xiaoping, Putinism has been the crucial contemporary reference point for this shift.

This becomes clear if we compare the trajectories of the two leaders. Much like Putin and in a sharp departure from his predecessors' low-key, technocratic leadership style, Xi assumed a strongman public persona from the outset of his reign. Domestically, the Chinese regime has become significantly more repressive under Xi, and doubly so after the abolishment of term limits—aggressively promoting dystopian strategies of social control, especially in troubled ethnic regions like Xinjiang province (*Economist* 2016, 2018). This, in many ways, has mirrored the tightening of domestic social control after Putin's disputed return for a third (and then fourth) presidential term, as well as his tough stance on Chechnya. Also like Putin, who consolidated power by eradicating powerful oligarchs who have become entrenched under his predecessor, Xi started his reign with an unprecedented anti-corruption purge of party elites previously deemed untouchable (Forsythe 2015).

Internationally, Xi has followed a trajectory of increasing assertiveness, reminiscent of his Russian counterpart's. Like Putin, Xi upped the ante on China's ambitious modernization of the military and has been aggressively using this buildup to project power and challenge China's neighbors and the United States (Myers 2018). Under Xi, China has yet to go as far as intervening militarily to prop up other autocracies the way Putin did in Syria, but it has heavily leveraged its economic power and initiatives like the "One Belt, One Road" to achieve much of the same throughout Asia and beyond. Most importantly, through its unprecedented expansion in the disputed waters of the South China Sea, the Chinese regime under Xi Jinping has been aggressively manufacturing a frozen conflict, which can perform a crucial regime-preserving function if necessary. Much like the frozen conflicts that Putin's regime keeps at a slow simmer in Ukraine and throughout the former Soviet space, the South China Sea standoff may be strategically escalated to rally nationalist sentiments, demobilize opposition, and divert attention from troubles at home. All of these policies are part of a nationalist domestic legitimation strategy that mobilizes old resentments, seeking to reclaim China's "rightful role" as a global leader after two centuries of foreign subjugation (Johnson 2017). It is hard not to draw a parallel here with Putin's trademark narrative of "lifting Russia from its knees" or the personalization of these policies around the regime's leader.

The similarities with the Putinist legitimation style have also been apparent in Xi's public demeanor. Again breaking with his far more cautious predecessors, Xi has shown off his strongman credentials, Putin style, by presiding over spectacular military parades while dressed either in a military uniform or in the traditional suit preferred by China's ultimate strongman, Mao Zedong (Buckley 2015, 2017). Also in line with Putin, Xi has balanced the strongman image with an aura of the relatable everyman who stands in contrast to aloof elites. Putin perfected this maneuver throughout his tenure with the use of folksy, down-to-earth language and jokes, participating in various popular and "humanizing" activities, and regularly mingling with ordinary people in casual clothing and manner (Cassiday and Johnson 2010; Wood 2016). Xi has nurtured a similar "man of the people" impression by embracing the affectionate nickname "Uncle Xi" since the start of his rule; he also broke with the strict suit-and-tie dress code of his predecessors, boasting a much humbler zippered windbreaker as he led China's anti-corruption campaign. More recently, Xi fashioned streaks of gray hair to portray himself as a hardworking servant of the people, also in stark contrast to the previous generation of technocratic leaders, who religiously dyed their hair (Hernandez 2019). This is reminiscent of Putin's trademark image of a tireless leader, wearing himself down to secure the good of the nation.[15]

This convergence of leadership appeals has been a natural consequence not only of Xi Jinping's unprecedented personalization of authoritarian power but also of the reaction to Putin among the Chinese population. From a pragmatic standpoint, it is highly convenient for Xi Jinping to emulate Vladimir Putin's image when the latter's approval rating in China has stood at over 90 percent, biographies of Russia's strongman have far outsold those of any other world leader, and he is commonly referred to as "Putin the Great" among Chinese citizens (Caryl 2015; Page 2014).

But what are the limits of this convergence in leadership legitimation strategies of the Russian and Chinese authoritarianism? How far can Xi push the strongman act in China? There are certainly significant historical, cultural, structural, and institutional constraints that prevent Xi Jinping from becoming a carbon copy of Vladimir Putin. However, even a partial shift toward the Putinist legitimation strategy can have significant consequences. Over the long run, Xi's embrace of the strongman formula threatens to put the Chinese regime into the same behavioral straitjacket as its Russian counterpart. A strongman autocracy, as the Russian case clearly demonstrates, is a prisoner of its self-appointed mission of national salvation and glory. It must never be seen as weak and conciliatory, and it must constantly produce the enemies that justify its existence.

For the time being, the Chinese regime can opt out of the strongman strait-jacket because it has a major alternative source of legitimacy: its (still) rela-tively robust economic performance (see, e.g., Wright 2010). This is a luxury that Vladimir Putin has not had for quite a while, and never to such an extent. As result, his credibility as a strongman ruler was always underwritten by the use of force—starting with the brutal second war in Chechnya in 1999 and continuing with the current interventions in Ukraine and Syria. Seen from this perspective, the crucial test of Xi's strongman shift will come if there is a significant slowdown of the Chinese economy or a major rise in domestic discontent. It remains to be seen whether circumstances like these will compel Xi—or a successor in his mold—to behave like the cornered rat from Putin's childhood and to lash out against China's minorities, its neighbors, or the West. But the urge and the incentives to do so may be strong.

Notes

The author would like to thank the Hoover Institution at Stanford University and the Davis Center for Russian and Eurasian Studies at Harvard University for their generous sup-port that has made the research for this chapter possible, as well as John Dunlop, Valerie Bunce, Michael McFaul, and Paul Gregory, as well as the participants at the Citizens and the State Workshops at Cornell University and the University of Notre Dame for their helpful comments to previous versions of this chapter.

1. Data drawn from Gallup presidential ratings surveys at www.gallup.com/poll/116677/presidential-approval-ratings-gallup-historical-statistics-trends.aspx.

2. And as depicted in Figure 9.1, after sixteen years of effectively holding power—the equivalent of four U.S. presidential terms—Putin's approval skyrocketed again in the wake of the annexation of Crimea in 2014 and then remained steady at over 80 percent until late 2018.

3. This data is from the Russia Electoral Study in 2012 (see Colton et al. 2014).

4. The data in Figure 9.4 are drawn from the New Russia Barometer surveys (Rose 2010) carried out by the Levada Center for the 2000–2009 period.

5. As Kotkin (2016, 3) illustrates: "With the breakup of the Soviet Union in 1991, Moscow lost some two million square miles of sovereign territory—more than the equiv-alent of the entire European Union (1.7 million square miles) or India (1.3 million). Russia forfeited the share of Germany it had conquered in World War II and its other satellites in Eastern Europe—all of which are now inside the Western military alliance."

6. In all models, I also include a squared term for age to capture the non-linear effect of this variable. For social class, I use low, middle, and upper class dummies (the low class dummy is left out of the models to serve as a reference category), derived from respondents' self-reported ability to purchase various goods. The party affiliation variable I use for the analysis records sympathies not for specific parties but for the most relevant party groups in Russia—the "Communists," "democrats," "patriots" (denoting nationalists), and "party of power" (i.e.,

incumbent). I leave out the dummy for "party of power" sympathizers in all models, so the effects of the other party affiliation dummies should be interpreted in relation to this category.

7. Table 9.A.1 in the appendix provides the full results from pooled multinomial logit models using all fifteen Levada center surveys that contain the question about why people trust Putin. The pooled model contains survey fixed effects to account for potential differences across the surveys that contain this question, and also employ robust standard errors. As an additional robustness check, I also estimate these models separately for each survey, to check whether the size and direction of these variables' effects differ over time. The results from this analysis (available on demand) are virtually identical to the ones presented in the paper.

8. In particular, the results in the right panel of Figure 9.A.1 suggest that the belief that Russia is headed in the wrong direction increases odds of responding that people support Putin because of a lack of better alternatives instead of his ability to tackle Russia's problems by 1.9 times among respondents who approved Putin's performance and by 3.4 times among all respondents. This discrepancy reduces considerably in the right panel of Figure 9.A.1, which includes controls for party sympathies.

9. We can see the performance-related nature of the decline in Putin's popular support by comparing Figures 9.6 and 9.8. The size and timing of the 15 percent drop in Putin's approval between early 2011 and early 2012 closely corresponds to the decline in the share of respondents who believed that people trust Putin because of his performance.

10. For the profile of the participants in the 2011–2012 protest movements, see the results of protest participant surveys conducted by the Levada Center (Levada Center 2011, 2012a, 2012b).

11. Calculated using Levada Center surveys downloaded from the Joint Economic and Social Data Archive at the Higher School of Economics in Moscow (http://sophist.hse.ru).

12. In this sense, opinion research has consistently shown that the economic consequences of the Soviet collapse were among the key drivers of Russian nostalgia for the former empire. Thus, the top response Russian citizens have consistently given as to why they regret the collapse of the USSR was "destruction of the common economic system," with "loss of a sense of belonging to a great power" as a close second (see Levada Center 2016b). Also, nostalgia for the USSR was considerably more pronounced among poorer Russian citizens, who suffered the most in the aftermath of the Soviet collapse. Thus, 77 percent of the poor respondents to Levada Center surveys in 2014 declared they regret the collapse of the USSR—almost 20 and 35 percent more than middle-class and upper-class respondents (see Levada Center 2014).

13. Quite the contrary; issues like price increases, poverty, unemployment and inequality consistently topped the list of concerns of Russian citizens in Levada surveys, far ahead of foreign policy and security concerns (see, e.g., Levada Center 2016a).

14. This shift in Russian attitudes about the propriety of heavy-handed rule actually began during the 2011–2012 protest wave, when the share of unconditional supporters of authoritarianism ("Our people always need a strong hand") began to decline. At the same time, the regime's efforts to portray the protests as an externally concocted threat to Russia's stability has created a general sense of crisis, which has induced more Russians to think the country needs emergency management for now. However, while negative propaganda against activists and protest actions like the Pussy Riot case slowed down the spread of anti-regime sentiments (Smyth and Soboleva 2014), these campaigns could not serve as a credible existential threat to rally the majority of increasingly skeptical citizens behind the

regime, even conditionally. Only the conflicts in Ukraine and Syria and the ongoing confrontation with the West provided a tangible enough threat to justify the regime's claims that strong-armed rule is necessary for the time being (on this mechanism of authoritarian support, see also Slater 2010).

15. In this sense, Putin once famously described himself as working as a "galley slave" to ensure the security and prosperity of Russia (Myers 2015, 339).

References

Balzer, Harley. 2002. "Human Capital and Russian Security in the Twenty-First Century." In *Russia After the Fall*, ed. Andrew Kuchins, 163–184. Washington, DC: Carnegie Endowment for International Peace.

Belanovsky, Sergey, and Mikhail Dmitriev. 2013. "Novoe jelektoral'noe ravnovesie: srednesrochnyj trend ili 'vremennoe zatish'e'?" [The new electoral equilibrium: a midterm trend or "temporary lull"?)." *Report of the Center for Strategic Research Foundation.*

Buckley, Chris. 2015. "Military Parade in China Gives Xi Jinping a Platform to Show Grip on Power." *New York Times*, September 4.

Buckley, Chris. 2017. "China Shows Off Military Might as Xi Jinping Tries to Cement Power." *New York Times*, July 30.

Caryl, Christian. 2015. "New Model Dictator: Why Vladimir Putin Is the Leader Other Autocrats Wish They Could Be." *Foreign Policy*, February 13.

Cassiday, Julie A., and Emily D. Johnson. 2010. "Putin, Putiniana and the Question of a Post-Soviet Cult of Personality." *Slavonic and East European Review* 88, no. 4: 681–707.

Chaisty, Paul, and Stephen Whitefield. 2012. "The Effects of the Global Financial Crisis on Russian Political Attitudes." *Post-Soviet Affairs* 28, no. 2: 187–208.

Colton, Timothy, Henry E. Hale, Mikhail Kosolapov, Elena Tonis, and Anna Prudnikova. 2014. *V1 Russian Post-Presidential Election Survey in 2012.* Harvard Dataverse. http://dx.doi.org/10.7910/DVN/24202.

Colton, Timothy, and Henry Hale. 2014. "Putin's Uneasy Return and Hybrid Regime Stability: The 2012 Russian Election Studies Survey." *Problems of Post-Communism* 61, no. 2: 3–22.

Colton, Timothy, and Michael McFaul. 2003. *Popular Choice and Managed Democracy: The Russian Elections of 1999 and 2000.* Washington, DC: Brookings Institution Press.

Dmitriev, Mikhail, and Daniel Treisman. 2012. "The Other Russia: Discontent Grows in the Hinterlands." *Foreign Affairs* 91, no. 5: 59–72.

Economist. 2016. "Big Data, Meet Big Brother: China Invents the Digital Totalitarian State." *Economist*, December 17.

Economist. 2018. "Apartheid with Chinese Characteristics: China Has Turned Xinjiang into a Police State like No Other." *Economist*, May 31.

Foa, Roberto Stefan, and Yascha Mounk. 2016. "The Democratic Disconnect." *Journal of Democracy* 27, no. 3: 5–17.

Forsythe, Michael. 2015. "Zhou Yongkang, Ex-Security Chief in China, Gets Life Sentence for Graft." *New York Times*, June 12.

Frye, Timothy, Scott Gehlbach, Kyle L. Marquardt, and Ora John Reuter. 2017. "Is Putin's Popularity Real?" *Post-Soviet Affairs* 33, no. 1: 1–15.

Gagnon, Valère Philip Jr. 2004. *The Myth of Ethnic War: Serbia and Croatia in the 1990s.* Ithaca, NY: Cornell University Press.

Gehlbach, Scott, and Alberto Simpser. 2015. "Electoral Manipulation as Bureaucratic Control." *American Journal of Political Science* 59, no. 1: 212–224.

Guillory, Sean. 2014. "Is Russia Suffering from Post-Traumatic Stress Disorder?" *New Republic*, April 23.

Hernandez, Javier C. 2019. "With Streaks of Gray Hair, Xi Jinping of China Breaks with Tradition." *New York Times*, March 7.

Huntington, Samuel P. 1991. *The Third Wave: Democratization in the Late Twentieth Century.* Norman: University of Oklahoma Press.

Ioffe, Julia. 2014. "Vladimir Putin Might Fall. We Should Consider What Happens Next." *New Republic*, August 6.

Johnson, Ian. 2017. "Xi Jinping and China's New Era of Glory." *New York Times*, October 13.

Kelemen, R. Daniel. 2016. "A Dark Age for European Democracy?" *Foreign Affairs*, December 7.

Kornbluth, Andrew. 2015. "Russia Is a 'Troll State,' Not a Rogue State." *Ukraine Alert* (blog), Atlantic Council, December 2. http://www.atlanticcouncil.org/blogs/new-atlanticist/russia-is-a-troll-state-not-a-rogue-state.

Kotkin, Stephen. 2016. "Russia's Perpetual Geopolitics: Putin Returns to the Historical Pattern." *Foreign Affairs* 95, no. 3: 2–9.

Levada Center. 2011. "Opros na Prospekte Saharova 24 Dekabrja" [Survey at the Saharov Prospect on December 24]. http://www.levada.ru/2011/12/26/opros-na-prospekte-saharova-24-dekabrya.

Levada Center. 2012a. "Opros na 'Marshe Millionov' v Moskve 15 Sentjabrja" [Survey at the "March of Millions" in Moscow on Sepbember 15). http://www.levada.ru/2012/09/17/opros-na-marshe-millionov-v-moskve-15-sentyabrya.

Levada Center. 2012b. "Opros na mitinge 4 Fevralja" [Survey at the February 4 rally]. http://www.levada.ru/2012/02/13/opros-na-mitinge-4-fevralya.

Levada Center. 2014. "Rossijane o raspade SSSR" [Russians on the collapse of the USSR]. http://www.levada.ru/2014/01/14/rossiyane-o-raspade-sssr-2.

Levada Center. 2016a. "Naibolee trevozhashhie problemy" [Most concerning problems]. http://www.levada.ru/2016/09/15/naibolee-trevozhashhie-problemy-2.

Levada Center. 2016b. "Raspad SSSR: prichiny i nostal'gija" [Collapse of the USSR: causes and nostalgia]. http://www.levada.ru/2016/12/05/raspad-sssr-prichiny-i-nostalgiya.

Myers, Steven Lee. 2015. *The New Tsar: The Rise and Reign of Vladimir Putin.* New York: Alfred A. Knopf.

Myers, Steven Lee. 2018. "With Ships and Missiles, China Is Ready to Challenge U.S. Navy in Pacific." *New York Times*, August 29.

Orban, Victor. 2014. "Prime Minister Viktor Orbán's Speech at the 25th Bálványos Summer Free University and Student Camp." http://www.kormany.hu/en/the-prime-minister/the-prime-minister-s-speeches/prime-minister-viktor-orban-s-speech-at-the-25th-balvanyos-summer-free-university-and-student-camp.

Page, Jeremy. 2014. "Why Russia's President Is 'Putin the Great' in China." *Wall Street Journal*, October 1.

Pavlovsky, Gleb. 2016. "Russian Politics Under Putin: The System Will Outlast the Master." *Foreign Affairs* 95, no. 3: 10–17.

Pipes, Richard. 2004. "Flight from Freedom: What Russians Think and Want." *Foreign Affairs* 83, no. 3: 9–15.

Putin, Vladimir, Nataliya Gevorkyan, Natalya Timakova, and Andrei Kolesnikov. 2000. *First Person: An Astonishingly Frank Self-Portrait by Russia's President Vladimir Putin.* New York: Public Affairs.

Rogov, Kirill. 2015. "Triumphs and Crises of Plebiscitary Authoritarianism." In *Putin's Russia: How It Rose, How It Is Maintained, and How It Might End,* ed. Leon Aron, 83–105. Washigton, DC: American Enterprise Institute.

Rose, Richard. 2007. "Going Public with Private Opinions: Are Post-Communist Citizens Afraid to Say What They Think?" *Journal of Elections, Public Opinion and Parties* 17, no. 2: 123–142.

Rose, Richard. 2010. *New Russia Barometer I–XVIII Trend Dataset, 1992–2009.* UK Data Service. SN: 6445. http://dx.doi.org/10.5255/UKDA-SN-6445-1.

Rose, Richard, William Mishler, and Neil Munro. 2004. "Resigned Acceptance of an Incomplete Democracy: Russia's Political Equilibrium." *Post-Soviet Affairs* 20, no. 3: 195–218.

Rundlett, Ashlea, and Milan Svolik. 2016. "Deliver the Vote! Micromotives and Macrobehavior in Electoral Fraud." *American Political Science Review* 110, no. 1: 180–197.

Slater, Dan. 2010. *Ordering Power: Contentious Politics and Authoritarian Leviathans in Southeast Asia.* Cambridge: Cambridge University Press.

Smyth, Regina, and Irina Soboleva. 2014. "Looking Beyond the Economy: Pussy Riot and the Kremlin's Voting Coalition." *Post-Soviet Affairs* 30, no. 4: 257–275.

Treisman, Daniel. 2011. "Presidential Popularity in a Hybrid Regime: Russia Under Yeltsin and Putin." *American Journal of Political Science* 55, no. 3: 590–609.

Treisman, Daniel. 2013. "Why the Kremlin Hates Levada Center." *Moscow Times,* May 23.

Treisman, Daniel. 2014. "Putin's Popularity Since 2010: Why Did Support for the Kremlin Plunge, Then Stabilize?" *Post-Soviet Affairs* 30, no. 5: 370–388.

Wood, Elizabeth A. 2016. "Hypermasculinity as a Scenario of Power: Vladimir Putin's Iconic Rule, 1999–2008." *International Feminist Journal of Politics* 18, no. 3: 329–350.

Wright, Teresa. 2010. *Accepting Authoritarianism: State-Society Relations in China's Reform Era.* Stanford, CA: Stanford University Press.

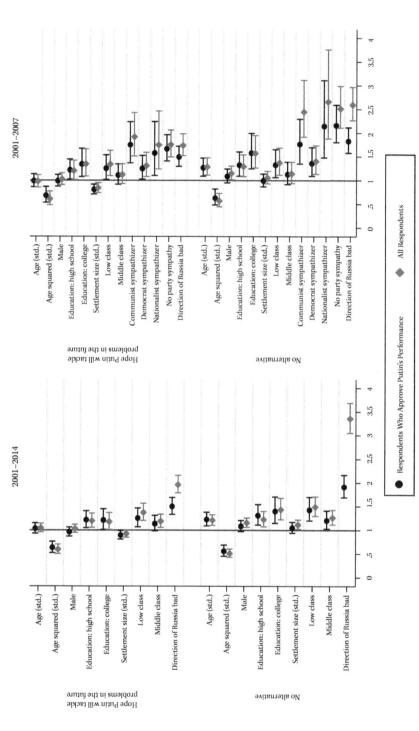

FIGURE 9.A.1 Odds of Choosing a Response Other than "People Trust Putin Because He Adequately Tackles the Problems of Russia" (Respondents Who Approve of Putin's Performance vs. All Respondents)

Note: Created by author using data from Levada Center surveys.

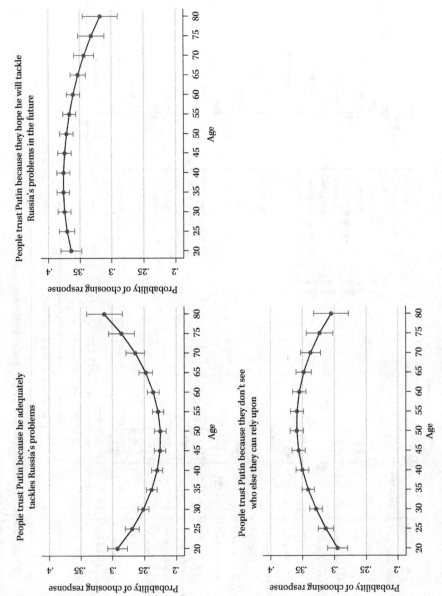

FIGURE 9.A.2 Predicted Probability of Choosing a Response to the "Why People Trust Putin" Question, by Age

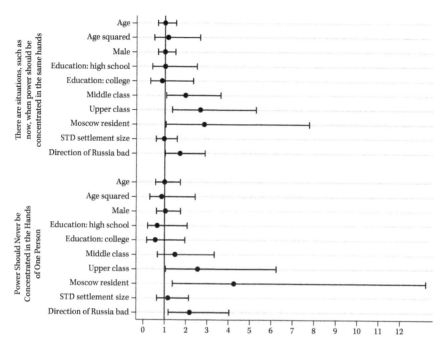

FIGURE 9.A.3 Odds of Choosing a Response Other than "Our People Always Need a Strong Hand" (March 2014)

Note: Created by author using data from Levada Center surveys.

TABLE 9.A.1 } Multinomial Logit Estimates of Responses About Why People Trust Putin ("People Trust Putin Because He Adequately Tackles Russia's Problems" Response as Base Category)

	2001–2014			2001–2007		
	Hope he will tackle in the future	No alternative	Don't know	Hope he will tackle in the future	No alternative	Don't know
Age (std.)	0.05 (0.05)	0.19 (0.05)**	0.17 (0.09)*	-0.02 (0.07)	0.25 (0.07)**	0.23 (0.17)
Age squared (std.)	-0.52 (0.08)**	-0.67 (0.09)**	-0.15 (0.16)	-0.49 (0.12)**	-0.56 (0.12)**	-0.46 (0.27)+
Male	0.03 (0.04)	0.15 (0.04)**	0.38 (0.08)**	0.03 (0.06)	0.14 (0.06)*	0.36 (0.14)*
Education: high school	0.18 (0.06)**	0.20 (0.07)**	-0.10 (0.12)	0.18 (0.08)*	0.26 (0.09)**	-0.22 (0.18)
Education: college	0.16 (0.08)*	0.36 (0.08)**	0.07 (0.14)	0.30 (0.11)**	0.45 (0.11)**	-0.03 (0.24)
Larger settlement (std.)	-0.08 (0.04)+	0.11 (0.04)*	-0.02 (0.08)	-0.17 (0.06)**	0.06 (0.06)	-0.02 (0.15)
Lower class	0.32 (0.07)**	0.40 (0.07)**	0.45 (0.13)**	0.29 (0.10)**	0.32 (0.10)**	0.38 (0.25)
Middle class	0.17 (0.06)**	0.23 (0.06)**	0.14 (0.12)	0.12 (0.09)	0.13 (0.10)	-0.05 (0.25)
Direction of Russia bad	0.67 (0.05)**	1.21 (0.05)**	1.34 (0.08)**	0.55 (0.07)**	0.95 (0.07)**	1.03 (0.14)**
Communist sympathizer				0.65 (0.12)**	0.89 (0.12)**	2.42 (0.34)**
Democrat sympathizer				0.27 (0.10)**	0.34 (0.11)**	0.64 (0.41)
Nationalist sympathizer				0.56 (0.18)**	0.98 (0.18)**	2.16 (0.43)**
Sympathizer of other centrist party				0.09 (0.27)	0.49 (0.27)+	1.30 (0.70)+
Sympathizer of other party				0.20 (0.24)	0.88 (0.23)**	0.16 (1.06)
No party sympathy				0.56 (0.08)**	0.92 (0.09)**	1.78 (0.33)**
Constant	-0.41 (0.12)**	-1.10 (0.13)**	-3.13 (0.27)**	-0.79 (0.15)**	-1.23 (0.16)**	-4.22 (0.45)**
Survey fixed effects	YES			YES		
Observations	16306			7965		
Log-likelihood	-19212.8			-9030.3		

Note: Logit coefficients with robust standard errors in parentheses
+ $p < 0.10$, * $p < 0.05$, ** $p < 0.01$

TABLE 9.A.2 } Multinomial Logit Estimates of Responses to the Question "Are There, in Your Opinion, Situations in Our Nation When the People Need a Strong and Imperious Leader, a 'Strong Hand'?" ("Our People Always Need a Strong Hand" Response as Base Category)

	"There are situations (such as now), when you have to concentrate all power in the same hands"	"In no case it should be allowed that all power is put into the hands of one person"	"Hard to say"
Age (std.)	0.01 (0.21)	-0.00 (0.28)	-0.87 (0.39)*
Age squared (std.)	0.14 (0.43)	-0.15 (0.53)	-0.14 (0.84)
Male	0.00 (0.20)	0.04 (0.26)	-0.45 (0.35)
Education: high school	0.01 (0.46)	-0.42 (0.58)	-0.49 (0.70)
Education: college	-0.15 (0.51)	-0.56 (0.63)	-0.47 (0.75)
Middle class	0.68 (0.31)*	0.40 (0.41)	1.31 (0.63)*
Upper class	0.98 (0.35)**	0.94 (0.45)*	1.78 (0.70)*
Moscow resident	1.05 (0.51)*	1.45 (0.58)*	-0.83 (1.15)
Larger settlement (std.)	-0.03 (0.25)	0.15 (0.31)	-0.58 (0.40)
Direction of Russia bad	0.54 (0.27)*	0.78 (0.31)*	0.30 (0.49)
Constant	-0.48 (0.55)	-1.12 (0.57)+	-2.29 (0.87)**
Observations	791		
Log-likelihood	-911.8		

Note: Logit coefficients with robust standard errors in parentheses
$^+ p < 0.10$, $^* p < 0.05$, $^{**} p < 0.01$

10 }

Legitimacy, Resilience, and Political Education in Russia and China

LEARNING TO BE LOYAL

Karrie J. Koesel

All states use their educational systems to build popular support for the nation and the regime. Contemporary Russia and China are no exception to this generalization. What better investment in the survival of authoritarian rule and rulers is there than instilling in the young a strong appreciation of their country, its political and economic systems, and its leaders? Such policies are particularly important for two reasons. One is historical. In both Russia and China, building communism meant using the state in general—and the educational system in particular—to create obedient socialist citizens. The other is practical, returning us to the emphasis on preemptive politics in Chapter 1 of this volume. Young people are often a problem for authoritarian regimes, as indicated by their willingness to rise up against dictators—as the color revolutions (1998–2005), the Arab Spring (2011–2012), Tiananmen Square (1989), and protests in Hong Kong and Moscow (2019) remind us.

The purpose of this chapter is to compare how the Russian and Chinese regimes attempt to educate students to be loyal citizens. Specifically, this study analyzes government-recommended political and patriotic education materials in order to identify the themes used to teach regime allegiance and bolster popular support. Political and patriotic education materials provide insight into how the regime understands and articulates legitimacy in its own words, as civics and social studies textbooks, teachers' pedagogical manuals, and examination questions are written and vetted by regime representatives. The materials thus reflect the issues and political orientations that the regime deems as most important *and* wants to communicate to its younger generations. A comparative study of political and patriotic education in Russia and China is further instructive because it contributes to ongoing debates about the resilience of authoritarian rule—that is, it helps us identify and analyze the preemptive measures authoritarian leaders take to protect themselves and the regimes they lead (Silitski 2005; Koesel and Bunce 2013); provides insight into how autocrats attempt to cultivate an aura of invincibility and signal strength to their publics (Magaloni 2006; Huang 2015, 2018); indicates when and why they turn to ideology and economic growth, as opposed to nationalism and ethnicity, to foster national unity; and whether these strategies free those in power from the need to rely so heavily on coercion.

This chapter develops in several steps. The first provides a brief overview of political and patriotic education as a long-term strategy for regime maintenance. The second section analyzes political and patriotic education materials in Russia and China and how they attempt to socialize youth into loyal stakeholders. This includes three decades of government-recommended civics and social studies textbooks and teachers' methodology handbooks used in Russian secondary schools. In China, the empirical focus is on six decades of the politics subject test of the National College Entrance Examination (NCEE). This is a nationwide, standardized examination that high school seniors must take to gain admission to universities. This comparison identifies a number of similarities and differences between Russia and China, including shared themes of legitimation around ideology, political institutions, and rule of law, as well as different foci on economic performance, cultural traditions, and the personalization of power. The chapter concludes with a brief discussion of general trends in political education in China and Russia and implications for authoritarian resilience.

What Is Political and Patriotic Education?

Political philosophers from Plato and Aristotle to Rawls all recognized the importance of education in cementing and sustaining support for those who rule, because what is learned early on in life is often difficult to displace (Easton and Hess 1962). In modern, liberal democracies support for the political system is typically fostered in civic education courses in schools, which teach students about government processes and institutions, provide guidelines for political awareness and behavior, and set the parameters of what it means to be an engaged and active citizen (Almond and Verba 1963; Easton and Dennis 1969; Campbell et al. 2012; on schools and nation-building, see also Weber 1976; Tilly 1975; Hobsbawm 1990). Although it has long been understood that schools are the key arena in which to cultivate regime support, there is little comparative work that evaluates the role of civic education in authoritarian political systems (see vom Hau 2009 as an important exception).

In authoritarian regimes, civic education courses are also integral components of the education system but tend to fall under the heading of political or patriotic education. These courses are often colorfully dismissed as indoctrination, propaganda, or brainwashing, but they play a role similar to civics courses in democracies. Patriotic education is intended to develop the building blocks of political knowledge and the skill set for responsible citizenship, but it focuses less on encouraging young people to vote and more on raising their ideological consciousness or stressing obedience to the regime (e.g., Fairbrother 2003; Rosen 2010; Law 2011).[1] I argue that political and patriotic education is a preemptive strategy of authoritarian resilience. It is the day-to-day process of learning where young people are taught to recognize the political authority of the regime and its leadership; it is a systematic approach to communicate the expectations and obligations of citizenship; it is designed to cultivate student-citizens who are supportive of both the nation and the regime and can reproduce the worldview of those in power; and it is a strategy for constructing and maintaining an aura of invincibility.

Political education cultivates diffuse support for the regime by socializing students around shared political orientations that legitimize the authority of ruling elites and builds linkages across generations (Easton and Dennis 1969, 25–65). Although the content of political education is often repackaged over time, each generation is taught to recognize the authority of the regime—that is, political education constructs vertical linkages across disparate generations, while also building horizontal ties within a generation by molding a shared political consciousness (Vickers 2009). In this way, the mechanism behind political education is socialization. Political education socializes students within and across generations into regime stakeholders, which permits those in power not only to preempt the volume and type of demands stemming from society but also to hedge against external threats and stresses. What distinguishes political education from other preemptive tactics authoritarian leaders use to manage threats, such as diffusion-proofing (Koesel and Bunce 2013), coup-proofing (Quinlivan 1999), or deploying economic resources to buy off or limit opposition forces (Bueno de Mesquita and Downs 2005; Silitski 2005), is that political socialization does not necessarily depend on an existing crisis or strong economic performance to be effective. Political education, put simply, is the insurance policy that is expected to kick in when other measures fail.

Russia and China are instructive for a comparative study of political and patriotic education because they share long and rich traditions of political socialization. A key part of the communist political project was to build socialist citizens. The Russian roots of patriotic and political education date back to the years following the October Revolution, when Lenin sought to transform schools from a weapon of the ruling class into a tool for bringing about a communist metamorphosis of Russian society. For Lenin, "the school not only must be a leader of communist principles in general but also a guide of ideological, organizational and educational influence of the proletariat" (quoted in Zajda 1980, 11). Chinese political education was integrated into schools shortly after the Communist Party came to power with the goal of guiding "students to develop correct political orientation and [the] correct outlook on life and way of thinking" (Outline on Secondary School Moral Education [1995] 2006, 27; Law 2011).

However, it is not only the shared experience of political socialization that makes this comparison fruitful, but also that the leadership of both countries has recently reinvigorated political and patriotic education. Since coming to power in 2000, Vladimir Putin has launched several initiatives to reinstate patriotic education in Russian schools to combat external, and presumably hostile, forces (Putin 2012).[2] These initiatives have sought to restore patriotic education in schools, something that was phased out in the early 1990s and discredited as propaganda to prop up totalitarian rule (see, e.g., Sanina 2017; Bagdasarjan et al. 2009; Golunov 2012; Rapaport 2009; Elkof 2005; Semenova 2004). One of the primary drivers behind Putin's new patriotic programming is the values vacuum that emerged in post-Soviet Russia. The 2001–2005 Initiative on the Patriotic Education of Citizens, for example, calls on patriotic education to counter "events of recent times," including "economic disintegration, social differentiation of the society and the devaluation of spiritual (moral) values" and to combat growing "apathy, selfishness, individualism, cynicism [and] unmotivated aggressiveness" within the public consciousness (*Pravitel'stvo RF* 2001, 1). The plans further aim to develop a "sense of loyalty to the Fatherland, readiness to perform their civic duty, and constitutional duty to protect the interests of the Fatherland" (Ministry of Education and Sciences in Russia 2015; see also Tsilulina 2009; Omelchenko et al. 2015; and Sherlock 2016).[3] Although patriotic education has not yet reached the same levels as during the Soviet era—approximately 20 percent of Russian youth participate in patriotic education clubs now, compared to the 90 percent who participated in Pioneers or Komsomol—there nevertheless has been an authoritative return of patriotic education under Putin (*Pravitel'stvo RF* 2015; Riordan 1989, 22; Yurchak 2005).

In China, renewed emphasis was given to patriotic education in the 1990s, in the wake of the Tiananmen Square protests and the global collapse of communist regimes. At this time, Deng Xiaoping declared, "During the last 10 years our biggest mistake was made in the field of education, primarily in ideological and political education—not just of students but of the people in general. We did not tell them enough about the need for hard struggle, about what China was like in the old days and what kind of country it will become. That was a serious error on our part."[4] Following Deng's remarks, the Chinese government launched an elaborate patriotic education campaign that included significant changes to the national curriculum as well as the construction of hundreds of patriotic education sites and museums in the 1990s (Action Plan for Patriotic Education [1994] 2006; Liu and Ma 2018; Yan 2014; Vickers 2009; Zhao 1998; Hayhoe 1992, 1993). Similar to Russia, political education courses should "systematically educate students in ideology, moral character, general knowledge of Marxism-Leninism and Mao Zedong Thought, and the theory of socialism with Chinese characteristics" in order to "nurture the entire body of students as citizens who love the socialist motherland; who have social morality and civilized behavior; and who observe discipline and obey the law" (Outline on Secondary School Moral Education [1995] 2006, 22, 27).[5] Patriotic education, in other words, seeks to unify political thinking around the ideological pillars of the party-state.

Under President Xi Jinping new prominence has been assigned to patriotic education, reaffirming that "China's higher education institutions are under the leadership of the CPC, and are socialist colleges with Chinese characteristics, so higher education must be guided by Marxism, and the Party's policies in education must be fully carried out" (Xinhua 2016). Thus, political and patriotic education in Russia and China permits us not only to compare the major strategies of legitimation articulated by those in power but also to understand patterns of continuity and change in how authoritarian regimes socialize youth (and future elite) to be supportive.

Political and Patriotic Education Materials

To compare how Russia and China engender popular support among youth, it is necessary to turn to patriotic and political education materials. These materials are written or vetted by regime representatives and thus reflect the political orientations those in power deem most important. In Russia, I examine twelve civics and social studies textbooks published between 1991 and 2014. These textbooks were selected based on two criteria: they are government recommended and represent the highest level available for the subject (ninth through eleventh grades). To complement Russian textbooks, I also evaluate thirteen teachers' methodology handbooks, which include supplementary lesson plans and classroom activities. The teachers' handbooks advise instructors on how to best engage students, integrate patriotic content, and display their personal patriotic sentiments in the classroom. As one handbook advises, "A student-patriot can only be brought up by a teacher-patriot" (Golev 1996, 54). This totals twenty-five course materials for political education instruction.

In China, I draw on the politics subject test of the National College Entrance Exam (NCEE; Putong Gaodeng Xuexiao Zhaosheng Quanguo Tongyi Kaoshi), commonly called the Gaokao. This is the nationwide, standardized exam that is somewhat equivalent to the U.S.-based SAT and ACT or the Japanese National College Entrance Examination (Luo and Wendel 1999, 62).[6] The examination spans two days each June; questions include essay, multiple choice, short an-swer, and fill-in-the-blank, and the exam tests knowledge of mathematics, Chinese language, foreign languages, physics, chemistry, biology, geography, history, and politics.[7]

I analyze the politics subject test of fifty-four NCEE exams over six decades (1952–2018), which yields a total of 1,199 questions (Beijing tian li kaoshi xinxi wang 2010).[8] On the politics subject test, students weigh in on topics of Marxism-Leninism and socialism as well as provide correct interpretations of current and sensitive political events. As one government document outlines, "The political education test lets students express the right emotions, attitudes, and values they should have; and at the same time, should also focus on checking how much students know about basic [political] knowledge and skills, and their capacity to use this knowledge to analyze and solve questions."[9] In practice, the politics subject test evaluates a student's command of socialist ideology, knowledge of political institutions and specific government policies and laws, and awareness of contemporary events—all subjects covered in po-litical education curricula (see, e.g., Law 2011; Cantoni et al. 2017).[10] The test also evaluates how well a student can interpret political events in line with the regime's worldview—that is, many questions require a correct and measured response. The examination is *not* intended to be a reflection of a student's cre-ativity and individuality in thinking; rather, it is an opportunity for students to demonstrate their "good political thinking" as the party-state understands it.

The combination of the two types of sources in Russia and China—the Russian textbooks and the politics subject test of China's NCEE—offers dis-tinctive advantages in analyzing how regimes socialize young people. The NCEE has been in place since 1952 and the examination questions are written and revised annually. In this way, the exam questions provide a finely tuned analysis of political socialization in China and allow us to identify which themes have the most staying power over time. The Russian textbooks have the advantage of providing a deeper discussion and contextualizing the political knowledge the regime deems as important, whereas the teachers' handbooks, which are published at more regular intervals than textbooks, help identify patterns of continuity and change in Russian political and patriotic educa-tion. The teachers' handbooks also provide insight into how patriotic content should be integrated into classrooms.

This comparison reveals that Russian and Chinese patriotic education materials socialize students along several common dimensions, including ideology, political institutions, and rule of law. These shared pillars of legit-imacy resonate in both countries but vary in terms of how they attempt to bolster regime support. We also find that the Chinese give special emphasis to economics and culture to reinforce the authority of the party-state, whereas Russian textbooks instruct students about the negative and positive aspects of democracy and underscore the importance of strong, centralized leadership.

Legitimation in Russia: Patriotism and Democracy

Contemporary Russian patriotic education materials converge on two ideological fronts: patriotism and democracy. Patriotism is a dominant theme and depicted as the moral and spiritual belief that unites and binds Russians together. One teachers' handbook recommends that teachers should define patriotism in the classroom as "normal behavior," suggesting that "every normal person loves their Motherland . . . a normal person treats their Motherland as they would their own mother." The handbook advises educators to reinforce this emotional point by identifying the shared root of the words "Motherland" (*Rodina*), "to give birth" (*rodit'*), and "parents" (*roditeli*), as well as to underscore that patriotism is one of the highest moral principles, akin to belief in God (Bykov and Lutovinov 2008, 238–245). A 2008 social studies textbook teaches that patriotism means to value your homeland and love your Motherland and nation (Bogolyubov, Lazebnikova, and Smirnova 2008, 299). Another describes patriotism as honest work for the homeland, including having deep knowledge of Russian history, culture, and traditions and striving to ensure unity to protect the land and nature. The same textbook further instructs that civic patriotism is a strategic principle of national politics—that is, a person, recognizing their ethnonational belonging, must first and foremost feel like a citizen of Russia (Bogolyubov, Lazebnikova, and Litvinov 2014, 170–171).

Elsewhere, patriotism is depicted as one of the most important orienting values (*tsennostnyy oriyentir*) tied to citizenship, with a patriotic person being someone who is committed to national traditions, the social and political system, and the language and faith of their nation (Bogolyubov, Lazebnikova, and Telyukina 2014, 112–113). A 1991 textbook, for instance, outlines the expectations of citizen-patriots in the following way:

> A citizen must empathize with the pain and difficulties of his homeland, as if these were his own problems. A citizen cannot just watch as the environment is degrading. He protests and participates in ecological meetings . . . he protests against the destruction of cultural heritage . . . he protests against theft and asks his authorities to make order . . . [A] citizen cannot watch as his nation is dying because of vodka . . . [A] citizen is someone whose thinking and action serve the homeland and its people. (Nikitin and Sokolov 1991, 12–13)

The textbooks are quick to point out that patriotism not only is an emotion or value linked to citizenship but also should be understood as a call to action (Bykov and Lutovinov 2008, 7). Here the idea is that patriotism will combat the litany of challenges facing post-Soviet Russia, including organized crime, corruption, a declining population, immigration, terrorism, nationalism, Nazism, globalization, and even the "McDonaldization" of national culture (Bogolyubov, Lazebnikova, and Litvinov 2014; Bogolyubov, Lazebnikova, and

Smirnova 2008, 31, 390). One 2008 teachers' handbook contends that patriotism will help Russian youth combat the devaluation of traditional values, lack of spirituality, and creeping Westernization (Bykov and Lutovinov 2008, 7). It also reminds teachers of their duty to inspire state patriotism as an alternative to liberal democratic ideology (Bykov and Lutovinov 2008, 16–17).

The course materials adopt varied approaches to teaching the value of patriotism. Frequently, historical examples of Russians who defended or advanced the influence of the Motherland are used to illustrate the importance of patriotism. One teachers' handbook recommends that patriotism should be cultivated not by encouraging students to negatively judge the Soviet past but by studying the past to gain wisdom and learn from the patriotism of their ancestors (Golev 1996, 6–9). Other materials recommend that patriotism should be taught through traditional state symbols. A suggested exercise divides students into small groups to discuss the continuity between the tsarist and post-Soviet coat of arms. Teachers are encouraged to help students draw connections between the two state symbols and give special attention to the shared religious imagery (Tislenkova 2007, 33–42). The exercise concludes with students collaborating on a coat of arms for their school to mirror patriotic symbols at a local level.

Other materials incorporate short vignettes about famous Russians (and Soviets) to demonstrate pride in the homeland. Consider the following examples from social studies textbooks published in 2008 and 2014. The passage tells of Mikhail Koryakov, a student at a military-engineering school in the 1940s. One afternoon Mikhail serendipitously finds himself in the library of a monastery, where he picks out a random book from the shelf and opens it. By chance, the opened page displays "The Song of Igor's Campaign," a twelfth-century poem that pleads for national unity in the face of growing threats from the East. As Cadet Koryakov reads the poem, he is deeply moved by the long tradition of national unity: "I am not a politician and Russia is always for me, regardless of its government. Whatever happens, we should not spare ourselves, but put bandages over the wounds of our nation and ease her suffering" (Bogolyubov, Lazebnikova, and Litvinov 2014, 166; Bogolyubov, Lazebnikova, and Smirnova 2008, 300). This vignette appears in two Russian textbooks and is curious for the number of coincidences—that is, a military cadet in the 1940s is browsing a library located in an Orthodox monastery (ignoring the fact that most monasteries were closed in the 1940s), and he casually selects a book and opens it to one of the most well-known and patriotic poems of Russian history. These unlikeliest of coincidences give the impression of patriotic destiny for young Russians.

Another social studies textbook illustrates the long tradition of patriotism through the story of Ivan Pavlov, a famous Soviet scientist known for the conditioning of dogs. The text tells of Professor Pavlov's lectures and his fondness for saying: "All of my achievements . . . are connected to the dignity and interests of my Motherland [*Rodina*]. I am, was, and will be a Russian person [*Russkiy chelovek*], son of my homeland. I am primarily interested in her [Russia's] life, I live by her interests and strengthen my dignity with her dignity" (Bogolyubov, Lazebnikova, and Smirnova 2008, 300). In this way, the lesson seeks to remind students that some of the country's most influential scientists are also deeply patriotic.

Other materials require students to reflect on their own patriotic sentiments. A 2011 teachers' handbook outlines the following activity to help students understand their duty as Russian citizens. Students must read the following poem by Pavel Kogan, a World War II veteran who placed Russia above all else.

> I am a patriot. I love the air,
> the land of Russia.
> I believe that nowhere in the world
> One can find another land with the same breezes at dawn,
> With the same smoky wind over the sands . . .
> And where you can find
> such birch trees as there are in my country!
> I would die like a dog from nostalgia
> In any coconut palm paradise.

After reading the poem, students must complete the following three sentences: "I consider myself a citizen of Russia because _____; As a citizen of Russia, I worry about _____; As a citizen of Russia, I am proud of _____" (Rozhkov 2011, 15–16).

It is also important to note that the course materials occasionally include misinformation in order to cultivate pride in the homeland. Although Russia is facing a declining population and some estimates indicate that 1.6 to 2 million have emigrated since Putin came to power (Wemer 2019), the course materials nevertheless indicate that Russia is an attractive destination to immigrants and that it is increasingly common for foreigners to apply for Russian citizenship. To support this argument, one textbook includes survey results asking where young people would like to live. The textbook reports, "Thankfully in each grade there were groups of people who firmly stated that it is better at home in Russia." The textbook also warns that if this was not the case, "they [Westerners] will be running to us soon" (Sokolov and Prutchenkov 2000, 26). Thus, the lesson is that Russia is a highly desirable destination and students should stay in their home country. Of course, another implicit lesson is that emigrants are not patriots.

DEMOCRACY

Democracy is a second touchstone in government-recommended materials; however, its portrayal is far from straightforward. In support of democracy, a 1991 civics textbook instructs that "the masses are awakened, people do not want to be gadgets in a state machine," and "dictatorial governments are part of the past" (Nikitin and Sokolov 1991, 3, 41). Textbooks explain that true democracy represents everyone, including all nations and nationalities (Bogolyubov, Lazebnikova, and Matveev 2014, 6), and that the most important characteristics of a democratic political system are human dignity, freedom, and equality for all (Voskresenskaya and Davletshina 1997, 8–9).

The textbooks largely define Russia as a democracy or democratic regime, and there is no mention of the rise of competitive authoritarianism. Rather, a 2014 textbook teaches that Russian national politics is based on "democratic principles," affirming that democracy is the "most important achievement of humanity" (Bogolyubov, Lazebnikova, and Litvinov 2014, 169, 235–236). Others teach that "Russia chose a very democratic way" in the 1990s and that the country is "on the path to democracy" and should be considered democratic (Sokolov and Prutchenkov 2000, 29; Nikitin and Sokolov 1991, 41; Volodina, Polievktova, and Spasskaya 2010, 144).

Elsewhere, course materials highlight democratic practices in Russian history. A 2008 textbook, for example, teaches of long parliamentary and social traditions in Russian history dating back to imperial times, including the Zemsky Sobor under Ivan the Terrible, the Senate under Peter the Great, and the Congress of the People's Deputies of the USSR (Bogolyubov, Lazebnikova, and Smirnova 2008, 162–169). Other materials draw attention to democratic values in Russian political thought, such as the writings of Dostoevsky and Tolstoy (Bogolyubov, Lazebnikova, and Smirnova 2007, 38, 42). One teachers' handbook reminds instructors to identify the Russian Federation in class as a "democratic republic," where citizens have rights and share democratic values (Bykov and Lutovinov 2008, 234–235).

These same government-approved textbooks, however, often suggest that democracy is not always "ideal" and is rife with "weaknesses" and "contradictions," including political parties and social movements that crowd out the rights of citizens; incubate corruption and a lack of transparency in bureaucracies; and wield unfair influence in campaign financing and candidate selection for elections (Bogolyubov, Lazebnikova, and Litvinov 2014, 235–236; Bogolyubov, Lazebnikova, and Smirnova 2008, 170). A 1997 civics textbook, for example, instructs students to differentiate between democratic ideals and practices, arguing there are many contradictions and challenges that society cannot overcome to achieve an ideal democracy (Voskresenskaya and Davletshina 1997, 9).

The textbooks also range from ambivalent to highly critical of Russia's democratic transition, maintaining that democratic values have been slow to take hold and that nostalgia for the Soviet past has returned (Bogolyubov, Lazebnikova, and Litvinov 2014, 236; Bogolyubov, Lazebnikova, and Smirnova 2008, 282). The lesson here is that democratization and the shift to a market economy dramatically increased citizens' expectations but yielded a long list of indicators that demonstrate failure, including the decline of living standards, economic disappointment, the capture of state resources by oligarchs, and the loss of prestige for entire professions, such as workers on collective farms (*kolkhozniki*) (Bogolyubov, Lazebnikova, and Smirnova 2008, 282). Put simply, students are taught that democratic ideals and Russia's transition have resulted in concrete disappointment.

Beyond a disappointing democratic transition, contemporary textbooks present the consolidation of Russian democracy as weak. The course materials are generally optimistic that the challenges for democratic consolidation will be overcome so long as political institutions remain open, reflect the majority of the population's interests, and protect democratic values (Bogolyubov, Lazebnikova, and Litvinov 2014, 237; Bogolyubov Lazebnikova, and Smirnova 2008, 283). However, the course materials are quick to place blame for the failure of Russian democracy on anything but the Kremlin. One common target is the Russian people. Some materials draw on the writings of Russian philosopher Nikolai Berdyaev to suggest that "the people [*narod*] might not believe in a democratic setup and might not have a democratic mindset" (Bogolyubov, Lazebnikova, and Smirnova 2007, 141–142). Still others blame Russians' lack of experience with democratic values and practices (Bogolyubov, Lazebnikova, and Litvinov 2014, 236; Bogolyubov, Lazebnikova, and Smirnova 2008, 282). This last argument is a bit surprising considering that these same books also teach of a long democratic tradition in Russian history (Bogolyubov, Lazebnikova, and Smirnova 2008, 162–169).

Other targets include Soviet legacies and local authorities. The blame here is attributed to the "Russian mentality," formed under absolute monarchy and totalitarianism, which is incompatible with the mentality needed for democratic traditions to flourish (Voskresenskaya and Davletshina 1997, 111–112). Another textbook points to authoritarian legacies from the Soviet period that are still visible at the local and regional levels. The result is a hybrid political system that possesses a more democratic political center with autocratic tendencies at the regional level (Bogolyubov, Lazebnikova, and Smirnova 2008, 283). Moreover, the materials instruct that democratic consolidation may remain out of reach in Russia until local authorities take human rights, criminality, and corruption more seriously (Bogolyubov, Lazebnikova, and Matveev 2014, 51). As one civics textbook appropriately concludes, "Democratic methods to rule are a lot more difficult than dictatorial ones" (Voskresenskaya and Davletshina 1997, 18). Thus, young people should temper their expectations about Russian democracy and expect democratic consolidation to be a lengthy process.

Institutions

Institutions make up another core theme in textbooks, which highlight the political institutions the regime deems most important and often reinforce the legitimacy of those in power. Social studies textbooks write of the evolution of political institutions in the twentieth century, including parliamentarism, multiparty systems, and the presidency (Bogolyubov, Lazebnikova, and Telyukina 2014, 25). Among these topics, the course materials prioritize discussions of political parties, but do so in uneven ways. Political parties are introduced as expressing and protecting the interests of social groups, but they have yet to fully develop in Russia (Bogolyubov, Lazebnikova, and Litvinov 2014, 220–221). The 1990s are described by a proliferation of parties that created a weak party system with limited social foundations, poor organization, and undefined platforms. As a result, new laws were introduced to tighten the restrictions on parties and help develop a more meaningful and robust party system (Bogolyubov, Lazebnikova, and Litvinov 2014, 220–221, 267–268). However, because political parties remain weak, meaningful political authority lies in the strong leadership of the state (Bogolyubov, Lazebnikova, and Smirnova 2008, 245). More importantly, the lesson is that Russian parties will only mature under strong, centralized leadership.

Another textbook reinforces the authority of the central government by including a poll reporting that 66 percent of Russians have a preference for strong and energetic leaders over effective laws and political programs. The survey reports that a majority believe the "president should be an all-powerful 'lord' of the country" and that "authority must be feared in Russia" (Bogolyubov, Lazebnikova, and Matveev 2014, 7). Another textbook justifies the submission to authority in the following way: "Russian people [*Russkiy narod*] have always had a different attitude toward power than Europeans. They never fought authority and, importantly, never participated in it" (Voskresenskaya and Davletshina 1997, 112). The importance of authority is also developed in another civics textbook, which incorporates a chapter titled "Men in Society" with the message that men play a leading role in social and political life because "nature endowed men with strength" (Sokolov and Prutchenkov 2000, 243–246). The corresponding chapter "Women in Society and the Family" further warns that if women want to be equal to men and earn equal pay, they will not be able to do housework, "for which they are valued so much," and thus risk destroying the whole idea of a family (Sokolov and Prutchenkov 2000, 236). These overtly gendered chapters set up the discussion of strong, centralized, and male leadership.

Although the textbooks advocate for the importance of a powerful leader and give special attention to the president, it is rare for them to name Putin or other political elites. Instead, they present the idea that Russia has a long history of strong, centralized leadership and that this tradition should continue. One textbook, for example, notes that the orders of the president occupy the highest position in the hierarchy of the laws (Bogolyubov, Lazebnikova, and Telyukina 2014, 200). The role of the president is further developed in chapters on political leadership. A chapter cites evidence that strong leadership has always been one of the most important factors for political development in Russia, citing reports that the majority of the population agrees that a strong national leader guarantees national stability (Bogolyubov, Lazebnikova, and Litvinov 2014, 280). Elsewhere, the same textbook affirms the importance of centralized political authority and suggests that it is necessary for the flourishing of society (Bogolyubov, Lazebnikova, and Litvinov 2014, 230). Still other course materials include discussions of the qualities of Russian leaders. A teachers' handbook recommends an exercise to help students understand the important role of the president. The best president is described as decent, healthy, patriotic, competent, and educated. The lesson recommends that teachers identify the "ideal" qualities of a president as understanding the people, being determined and firm, and having a good sense of humor (Tislenkova 2007, 52–57). These are all qualities the Kremlin PR machine has cultivated about Putin, along with the more dominant narrative that the president is needed to bring stability to the chaotic political arena. Another textbook includes a vignette of a son asking his mother if he could be an important person in Russia, like a government deputy or even Putin. The mother responds yes to all, but adds that her son cannot become Putin but can aim to emulate the Russian president, the most important person in the country (Volodina, Polievktova, and Spasskaya 2010, 215). In this way, Putin is set apart as a role model for Russian students.

The discussions of political institutions in contemporary texts suggest two observations. First, what is missing? Contemporary Russian textbooks provide a very limited discussion of elections, electoral processes, and the responsibility of youth to vote or become politically active. Only one of the teachers' handbooks surveyed incorporates a lesson plan about voting. Here, students are encouraged to elect a parliament to help with school governance, including organizing roundtables to inform students of their rights and duties, a press club to report on activities, and social monitoring systems to both observe elections and prevent "asocial behavior" (Malinin et al. 2009, 31–35). The lesson plan does not elaborate on how to develop a social monitoring system or what is considered asocial behavior, but one could speculate that it has more to do with election manipulation than monitoring.

A second observation relates to how the textbooks discuss various political regimes and their legacies. Russia is classified as a democratic political system in spite of its weak political party system or unconsolidated institutions, and the Soviet Union is frequently identified as totalitarian alongside other despotic regimes, such as Germany under Hitler. However, the course materials say very little about the nature of totalitarianism in the Soviet Union and are quick to recommend that Soviet history should be taught in a patriotic way to help formulate a shared political culture and understanding of the hardships endured by earlier generations, especially the World War II generation (Bykov and Lutovinov 2008, 48–55). Teachers are encouraged to prioritize events and incorporate works that paint a positive image of the Soviet Union as a working and victorious nation whose achievements in economics, science, and culture are without equal. As one handbook advises, this is important because "without encouraging young people to love, respect, and glorify our ancestors, there will be no citizen or patriot" (Bykov and Lutovinov 2008, 174, 255).

The Rule of Law

Laws and rights make up a final common theme in Russian patriotic education materials, but individual rights are depicted as less important than a citizen's duties and responsibilities to the regime. Young people are taught to respect the law and the hierarchy of laws, including defending the homeland, fulfilling their military obligations, paying taxes, and protecting the environment, but there is only limited discussion of freedom of speech, association, religion, or movement (Bogolyubov, Lazebnikova, and Matveev 2014, 16; Volodina, Polievktova, and Spasskaya 2010, 103–117, 234; Bykov and Melnichenko 2007, 125; Golev 1996, 54).

Contemporary textbooks further highlight the constitutional foundations of the Russian Federation and how this promotes patriotic feelings and interethnic harmony, and emphasize that political authorities and government organs are not above the law (Bogolyubov, Lazebnikova, and Smirnova 2008, 141, 92–93). At the same time, the textbooks are fairly critical of the development of Russian legal culture, suggesting it falls short of the ideals outlined in the constitution. One textbook instructs, "Russian legal nihilism has also been strong . . . [There are] unfinished legal reforms, ineffective working government organs, the breaking of laws, corruption and problems in the fight against criminality," and calls for greater legal education (Bogolyubov, Lazebnikova, and Telyukina 2014, 223). Another passage provides an example of a lawless young man who received his invitation for military service but ignored it and left to visit relatives. The young man was then fined for not fulfilling his constitutional duty (Bogolyubov, Lazebnikova, and Matveev 2014, 36). To address lawlessness in Russian society, a civics textbook asks students to consider the following question: "Do you think Russia should be an authoritarian country to end criminality?" opening the space for students to consider the advantages of a strong, authoritarian government (Sokolov and Prutchenkov 2000, 143).

This brief survey of Russian textbooks elicits a number of observations. First, the textbooks highlight the political issues and ideological orientations the Kremlin deems most important and wants to transmit to its young people. The course materials share an emphasis on the importance of patriotic upbringing and the state as the defender and protector of rights, but also on the duty of citizens to submit to the rules of the regime—that is, law is a duty to be followed but is not a guarantor of rights. Second, the course materials firmly place Russia in the democratic camp but suggest that democratic values and practices have yet to take hold. The materials also warn that democratic processes are easily undermined and democratic institutions, from political parties to the legal system, lack coherence and discipline. All of this helps explain the absence of democratic consolidation in contemporary Russia and the nihilist legal culture that has developed. The explicit lesson that emerges from these materials is that only the combination of patriotism and strong, centralized leadership can protect Russia from the threats at home and abroad. Only patriotism can fill the ideological vacuum and inspire young people to defend the Motherland. Only an authoritative leader can discipline weak or unruly democratic institutions and provide order and stability to minimize the uncertainty of Russia's democratic transition. As we will see, many of these same themes of legitimation play a prominent role in the Chinese case.

Legitimation in China: Ideology

The politics questions on the NCEE bear a resemblance to those in Russia—that is, contemporary Chinese political education courses place heavy emphasis on ideology, institutions and law, but also introduce economics and cultural life to help build support for the party-state.[11] To understand how these themes seek to foster legitimacy for the regime, it is necessary to turn to the questions themselves.

MARXISM-LENINISM

One of the main goals of the politics subject test is to assess a student's fluency with regime ideology. Questions that touch on political ideology more generally, and Marxism-Leninism specifically, account for roughly 30 percent of the exam since the 1990s and made up a significantly larger portion of the exam in earlier decades (Koesel 2017). These questions play upon the revolutionary and foundational myths of the Chinese Communist Party (CCP), the benefits of socialism, and the failures of other ideologies and political systems. Ideologically oriented questions are striking in the first decade of the NCEE because they require students to answer how the new regime is far superior to the previous one. The 1952 exam, for example, asks candidates to complete the following sentence about what China was like before the CCP came to power: "Old China was a _____ and _____ society, whose ruling class at that time was _____, _____, and _____." Here, the correct responses are "semi-colonial and semi-feudal" and "imperialist, feudal, and bureaucratic-bourgeois" (Question 6, 1952). During the 1990s, students had to identify the shortcomings of democratic capitalist countries in the following two questions:

There exists a contradiction within democratic capitalist countries between equality-in-form and inequality-in-fact. The basic reason for this is that:

A. The constitution was established by the bourgeoisie
B. The principles of democracy are disconnected from practice
C. Working people cannot participate in the management of state power
D. The realization of democratic rights is restricted by private ownership (Question 10, 1995)

Lenin said capitalist democracy, "from the global perspective of social development, is a huge progress." He also pointed out that capitalist democracy "is always limited by the narrow framework of capitalist exploitation, and is thus always going to be a democracy enjoyed by the minority, the bourgeoisie and the wealthy." From the above quotes, Lenin analyzed capitalist democracy by using the methods of:

A. Comparative analysis and dialectical analysis
B. Historical analysis and comparative analysis
C. Class analysis and comparative analysis
D. Historical analysis and class analysis (Question 7, 1997)

For both questions, the expected answer is D—capitalist democracies restrict private ownership and Lenin used historical and class analysis to point out the failures of capitalism.

Ideological questions also evaluate a student's comprehension of Marxism-Leninism and how these ideas can be applied to understanding contemporary China. Questions may require students to apply Marxist concepts, such as "Use the principle of Marxist materialism to explain why it is necessary for socialist construction to be based on the conditions of our country" (Question 16, 1981) or "Use dialectic knowledge to analyze" the negative aspects of the internet, such as false information and pornography (Question 38, 2001). In this way, a student must both demonstrate mastery of the ideology that legitimizes Communist Party rule and apply it to explain public policy.

Over the years, questions on ideology regularly highlight class conflict and class struggle. Earlier exams, for example, ask students to identify the "three major forms of class conflict" within China (Question 10, 1952; Question 5, 1964; Question 13, 1979). However, by 1993 the exam suggests that class struggle is no longer the main source of societal conflict in the country. Instead, students need to explain why and how class struggle had been solved. Here, the correct response is because "the socialist system in China has already been established" (Question, 19, 1993). Thus, the message is that socialism solved class conflict and class struggle, which, of course, overlooks the growing social stratification and inequality of the 1990s or the fact that China's Gini coefficient (a measure of income disparity) had increased from 0.28 in the early 1980s to 0.42 in 1993.

INSTITUTIONS

Like the Russian textbooks, the politics subject test requires students to demonstrate broad knowledge of institutions, both domestic and international. While these questions assess general understanding of political institutions, they also often stress the superior nature of Chinese institutions over other political systems. During the 1950s, for example, students had to explain "Why is the National People's Congress the state body with the highest power in our country?" (Question 5, 1955) and describe "the superior nature of our People's Congress system" (Question 5, 1956). Other questions place importance on the democratic and participatory nature of Chinese institutions, such as a 2009 question that notes "members of democratic parties have 40 people holding provincial-level leadership positions in central and local government departments" (Question 39, 2009).

Still other questions tap into China's leadership in global institutions, such as the Shanghai Cooperation Organization (SCO). In 2003, one question (Question 31) suggests that the newly minted SCO charter reaffirms mutual respect between China and Russia and asks students to weigh in on what respect for diverse civilizations means in this context:

> At this meeting, the Chinese and Russian heads of state signed the Charter for the Shanghai Cooperation Organization [which] reaffirmed "mutual trust, mutual benefit, equality, consultation, respect for diverse civilizations and seeking common development." The meaning of "respect for diverse civilizations" refers to needing to:
>
> 1. Respect the different models of development of different countries
> 2. Respect the different cultural traditions of different countries
> 3. Affirm the historical and current policies of different countries
> 4. Respect the social systems selected by different countries
> A. 1, 2, & 3
> B. 1, 2, & 4
> C. 1, 3, & 4
> D. 2, 3, & 4

The correct response is B; in spite of different pathways in the 1990s, China and Russia continue to cooperate and respect each other's different models of development, cultural traditions, and social systems.

The CCP also has a prominent institutional presence on the examination. It is hardly surprising that the expected answers are far from neutral, instead highlighting the leadership and accomplishments of the ruling party. In 1980, one essay asks students: "Refute the following fallacy: 'Our country can realize the four modernizations without the leadership of the Communist Party'" (Question 14, 1980). In 1997, students need to understand why the "Party is key" "in constructing a socialist spiritual civilization" (Question 8, 1997). In 2013, another essay requires young people to use their "knowledge of political life to explain the leadership role of the CCP in the process of building a socialist and culturally powerful China" (Question 13, 2013). Another essay asks students to explain how the spirit of patriotism, independence, and self-reliance was developed under the leadership of the CCP (Question 53, 1990). Other questions ask students to weigh in on how the CCP "led the Chinese people in overthrowing the three big mountains," a reference to imperialism, feudalism, and bureaucratic capitalism (Question 18, 1991), or led numerous soldiers and civilians to fight back floods and produce historic bumper crops (Question 29, 1992).

By way of another example, the 2000 exam includes a statement from President Jiang Zemin about the invincibility of the CCP. Jiang is quoted as saying: "To make China great, the key point lies in our Party. As long as our Party always represents a force for China's advanced social development, a progressive course for China's advanced culture, and faithfully represents the Chinese people's fundamental interests, our Party will always be invincible, always have the wholehearted support of people of all nationalities, and continue to lead the people forward." Students are then asked whether the quotation demonstrates:

1. The nature of the CCP is advanced
2. The establishment of the CCP leadership is the inevitable result of the development of the Chinese revolution
3. The CCP is the core leadership for socialism in China
4. Only in strengthening the Party's leadership can we improve the Party's leadership

Here the correct answers are both 1 and 3—the CCP is both advanced *and* the leader of socialism (Question 12, 2000). This question is revealing in that it uses the remarks of a standing president to signal the authority of the Party above all else.

As a point of contrast between the two countries, the Russian materials depict a weak party system in favor of strong, centralized leadership, whereas the Chinese materials put the authority of the Communist Party above any individual leader. The CCP is depicted as united and strong, and it is credited for the country's progress. As one question declares, "In the past 80 years . . . the CCP has always represented the development of China's advanced social productivity, the direction of China's advanced cultural progress and the fundamental interest of China's people" (Question 34, 2001). While other Chinese leaders do make appearances on the exam—most notably Mao Zedong in the 1950 and 1960s—it is the Party that plays the dominant role. Yet there is some reason to suggest that this may be changing under President Xi. In 2017, for example, 20 percent of questions on the politics subject test mention Comrade Xi as the core of the Communist Party Central Committee or praise his policies (Question 15, 2017; Question 16, 2017; Question 23, 2017). In 2018, the proportion of Xi-related questions increased to 26 percent, a number on par with only one other Chinese leader—Mao. This is a noticeable change, but it is too early to tell if Xi's personalization of power will fundamentally shift how students are taught to view the authority of the Party over the president.

THE RULE OF LAW

Laws and rights make up a third theme to help legitimize the authority of the party-state. Laws and rights tend to be outlined in the Chinese constitution and defended (or enforced) by the CCP. This is strikingly similar to the discussions of the Russian constitution in textbooks that focus less on individual rights in favor of one's duty to obey the law. To illustrate how this narrative is shared with Chinese students, we can turn to the exams following the Tiananmen Square uprising. One month after tanks cleared the square, test takers were required to complete the following paragraph:

> In our constitution, "citizens of the PRC enjoy the freedom of assembly, of the press, of association, of procession, and of demonstration." Simultaneously, "The exercise by citizens of the PRC of their freedoms and rights may not infringe upon the interests of _____, of society, and of the collective, or upon the lawful freedoms and rights of other citizens." (Question 38, 1989)

The correct response is "the state," which underscores the unlawful nature of dissent and that individual freedoms should not infringe on state interests. The 1989 exam also asks students to identify which "unlawful acts" are violations of criminal law: stealing someone's motor vehicle; unlawfully manufacturing and carrying a dagger or other restricted knife; violating regulations by destroying grass fields, flowering plants, and trees; or majorly disrupting social order to such an extent that work, production, business, and education can no longer continue as the country and society suffer massive loss (Question 17, 1989). The correct response is "majorly disrupting social order," which was precisely what the 1989 student protests accomplished.

The 1990 exam resumes themes of law and order by requiring students to complete the following: "Article 55 of the Constitution stipulates: it is the honorable duty of citizens of the PRC to perform _____ and join the militia in accordance with the law" (Question 47, 1990). The correct response is "military service." Again, this question is relevant in the post-Tiananmen context because part of the punishment for some incoming university students in

Beijing was to spend their first academic year in military service rather than in classes.[12] Before this time, compulsory military service for university students ranged from one to three months. The question, therefore, strengthens the legitimacy of the Party's decision to extend military service for incoming students. The legal questions not only illustrate the regime's emphasis on order but also include indirect references to the Tiananmen Square uprisings and the need for students to place blame on hostile external forces. In 1990, for example, students were asked to reflect on the previous year's "counterrevolutionary rebellion." The exam stated:

> During the spring and summer of 1989, our country experienced unrest and there, in fact, occurred a counterrevolutionary rebellion in Beijing. While vigorously strengthening the country's social management functions and taking hold of socialist modernization, we must not weaken the functions of the country's dictatorship. This is because:
>
> A. Our country's economic and cultural backwardness is unlikely to change in the short term
> B. To a certain extent, class struggle will continue to exist long-term in our country
> C. The ideology of the exploiting class will continue to exist long-term in our country
> D. The bourgeois international monopoly has never given up its desire to destroy us

The expected answers are B and D (Question 29, 1990)—that is, class struggle will continue in China so long as hostile international forces are determined to undermine the country's development.[13] The wording of the question is further instructive, specifically the labeling of the 1989 student movement as a "counterrevolutionary rebellion," because it signals how students should interpret the student movement and places blame for the events outside of China.

ECONOMICS

Economics is another theme on the politics subject test that provides opportunities to highlight how the party-state has delivered prosperity. Often, economically oriented questions have socialist overtones, such as "Why is a state-owned economy an economy with socialist characteristics? Why must the state-owned economy function as the leader over other parts of the economy?" (Question 9, 1953), or ask students to reflect on the "essence of capital," with the correct response being "the capitalist's exploitation of workers" (Question 5, 1985). In 2005, for instance, test takers needed to elaborate on the economic benefits of "Red tourism," the official policy for promoting socioeconomic development of revolutionary bases and promoting patriotism (Question 40, 2005).

As the Chinese economy transformed during opening and reform, so did the content of economic questions. The 1994 exam asks students to justify China's shift to a market-based capitalism based on a passage from Richard Nixon's *Seize the Moment*. The passage notes, "Today, as we celebrate the defeat of communism in Eastern Europe and the Soviet Union . . . many deeds remain to be done abroad and at home. . . . While we should celebrate the current turn of events, we should not give into euphoria . . . Today, China has arrived at a critical moment in its evolution . . . It therefore becomes doubly important that the United States and the West maintain economic contacts with Chinese society in order to nurture the growth of peaceful change" (Question 39, 1994).

Although many economic questions also have ideological overtones, others test general knowledge of the principles of economics. More neutral economic questions, for example, may require students to explain "how the market price of commodities are decided"(Question 2, 1982); the "causes of currency inflation" (Question 10, 1986); how a rise in the dollar impacts RMB-dollar exchange rates (Question 15, 2015); and the role of China's central bank (Question 27, 2006). These more neutral questions, however, also tend to highlight how the party-state has solved various economic challenges, including reducing the income gap between urban and rural residents (Question 39, 1999) and "resolutely adopt[ing] a series of active fiscal policies and maintain[ing] the stability of the RMB exchange rate" in the face of "massive assaults from the Asian financial crisis" (Question 7, 1999), or how the Chinese government likewise successfully limited inflation (Question 1, 1997). The explicit lesson is that the party-state has delivered growth and economic stability in the presence of significant adversity, especially when other regimes' economies have weakened. In some questions, the prosperity delivered by the CCP is astonishing. In the late 1990s, students weighed in on China's exceptional grain and steel production as well as foreign currency reserves:

> 1996 was the first year of the Ninth Five-Year Plan, and, in this year, our country's economic construction and social development achieved inspiring, grand success as we not only maintained the rapid growth of our national economy but also effectively controlled currency inflation. The total grain production for the year reached _____ million kilograms, which was once again a historic high; the steel production reached _____ tons, which makes it the _____ rank in the world; foreign reserves broke through 100 billion dollars and the overall strength of the country was further strengthened.

A. 4600, 120 million, #1
B. 4500, 100 million, #2
C. 4800, 100 million, #1
D. 5000, 80 million, #3

The expected answer is C, which ranks China first in the world for steel production. This line of questioning aligns with broader observations about performance-based indicators of support. Stanley Rosen (2010, 170), for instance, argues, "In the aftermath of Tiananmen in 1989, Chinese leaders realized that they had to find a solution to their legitimacy crisis, particularly among rebellious youth. In moving even further from a legitimacy based on ideological criteria to a legitimacy based on performance indicators." Thus, delivering economic prosperity has become as important for the legitimacy of the CCP as ideology.

CULTURE

A final and growing area in political education materials is cultural. In the mid-2000s, the context of political education expanded with the issuance of a new core textbook called *Cultural Life*. This textbook identifies many of the cultural accomplishments of China, the Chinese nation, and highlights traditional Chinese values. Topics range from the invention of the compass, gunpowder, and movable type to filial piety and achievement in athletics and technology. This shift to culture to bolster regime support dovetails with other political trends. Elizabeth Perry (2013, 2) notes that the collapse of communist regimes in Eastern Europe prompted the Chinese leadership to lean "heavily upon cultural governance, or the deployment of symbolic resources as an instrument of political authority." The argument here is that to better distance itself from the Soviet collapse, the CCP now stresses the "distinctively 'Chinese' character of the political system" (Perry 2013, 2; also see Guo 2004). Thus, we also find culture included in the politics subject test to illustrate the cultural strength of China.

Questions tap into traditional culture by asking students to identify important heritage sites, such as the Forbidden City, the fossils of Peking Man at Zhoukoudian, the mausoleum of Qin Shihuang (first emperor of the Qin Dynasty), the terra-cotta warriors of Xi'an, the Great Wall, and the Dunhuang Mogao grottos (Question 9, 1998). At the same time, cultural legitimation may also be reinforced from abroad. A 2004 question suggests that China's successful bid for the 2008 Olympic Games "directly and clearly conveys the beauty and magnificent spiritual strength of the Chinese people and culture" (Question 25, 2004). Two questions from the 2018 exam ask students to reflect on the cultural significance of the spread of traditional Chinese medicine around the globe (Question 20, 2018) or the diffusion of Chinese words in foreign countries, such as "qi gong," "Alipay," and "One Belt, One Road" (Question 19, 2018). These questions signal to young people China's growing global cultural footprint, a theme that the CCP is pleased to promote as it reinforces the influence of its rule.

Conclusions

The purpose of this chapter has been to explore how authoritarian regimes attempt to promote political allegiance among their younger generations. I compared the trajectories of political and patriotic education in Russia and China to identify the political knowledge these regimes view as most important and want to transmit to their youth, and how this cultivates an image of regime invincibility. This included three decades of Russian patriotic education materials and six decades of the politics subject test of the NCEE in China. When compared side by side, the political and patriotic education materials in these two important authoritarian regimes reveal strikingly similar patterns of political socialization around themes of legitimacy: ideology, institutions, and rule of law. These similarities are important because in spite of dramatically different pathways since the 1990s, diverse regime types (single-party authoritarian vs. competitive authoritarian), and distinctive political cultures, the Russians and Chinese are socializing students in similar multidimensional ways. As we discovered, political and patriotic education has given rise to a sophisticated narrative where the leadership of the regime—whether it is the CCP or the Kremlin—is the custodian of values and bringer of progress, prosperity, and order. The course materials paint an image of very accomplished authoritarians.

The political and patriotic education materials also teach young people that without the current leadership—Putin or the CCP—it would be very difficult for Russia or China to endure crises at home or defend against hostile threats from abroad. Therefore, students should respect, if not idealize, political authority and understand how their regimes, leaders, and institutions are superior to those of competitors, especially in the West. Moreover, the materials send a strong message that young people should submit to political authority. Those who rise up are labeled as counterrevolutionaries; those who emigrate are cast as traitors to the nation. All of this imprints on students that the current political system and rulers are worth defending.

This comparison also reveals important differences in political socialization. The Chinese regime has turned to economic and cultural success to build support, with the implicit understanding that China's global status and economic accomplishments have been possible only because of the guidance of the party-state. At least for now, young people are taught that the Communist Party is the key to a prosperous and powerful China. In contrast, Russian materials are both supportive and subversive in their discussions of democracy. Patriotic education materials portray democracy as an ideal, but something that is still largely out of reach in contemporary Russia. There are at least two ways to reflect on these critical discussions of democracy. One is that there is room for critical self-reflection as young people grapple with both the positive and negative aspects of Russian democracy—that is, there is a somewhat open discussion about the nature of competitive authoritarianism in Russia. The other, far less optimistic interpretation is that the criticisms leveled at democracy are used as a thin veil to reinforce autocratic rule. Recall, for instance, the Russian textbooks that teach the importance of having a strong central authority for the flourishing and stability of the country; the statistics of Russians preferring strong leaders to effective public policies; and lessons that the president should be an "all-powerful 'lord' of the country." These textbooks signal that democracy is flawed, that it may not be a suitable import for Russia or Russians, and that there is a longer tradition of centralized rule—whether tsarist or Soviet—that may ultimately be necessary to maintain order and stability. Put simply, autocracy may be unavoidable.

These findings have important implications, first, for our understanding of the strategic interaction between authoritarian regimes and their societies. The chapter unpacks society to focus specifically on how the regime seeks to influence its younger and potentially more contentious generations. This is important not only because young people tend to be at the forefront of challenging authoritarian rule but also because today's youth are more globally minded and connected than generations in the past. Second, the findings contribute to our understanding of authoritarian resilience. They demonstrate that authoritarian rulers worry about challenges to their power and take extensive action to cultivate favorable feelings toward themselves and the regimes they rule. They also draw attention to political education as an understudied instrument in the authoritarian tool kit and detail how autocrats use it to hedge against potential threats. In this way, the chapter provides insight into the politics of preemption, a central theme of the volume.

Political education is a preemptive strategy, a long-term approach that begins in students' formative years; it is a proactive measure to shape the kind of political actors young people (and future elite) will become. Political socialization is intended to work as the regime's insurance policy. Autocrats pay political socialization premiums to ensure that they are fully covered for when times get tough. This is significant because other preemptive measures, such as the use of rents or repression, often depend on strong economic performance or disciplined security forces to be effective. Political socialization, however, does not. The power of political socialization lies in its ability to persuade.

Notes

The author thanks the participants of the Citizens and the State Workshops held at Cornell University and the University of Notre Dame for their valuable feedback, and Katya Dunajeva, Yizhi Hu, Joshua Pine, Jessica Saeli, Flora Tang, Zhuo Li, Meian Chen, and Boyang Chen for research assistance.

1. Patriotic education is also present in democracies. See Estrin 2018; Hoisington 2017.

2. The state initiatives include State Program on the Patriotic Education of Citizens of the Russian Federation, 2001–2005; Conceptions of Patriotic Education of the Citizens

of the Russian Federation State Program, 2003; State Program on the Patriotic Education of the Citizens of the Russian Federation, 2006–2010; State Program on the Patriotic Education of the Citizens of the Russian Federation, 2011–2015; and State Program on the Patriotic Education of the Citizens of the Russian Federation, 2016–2020. For commentary on growing Nazism in Ukraine and foreign funding for Russian textbooks, see Vladimir Putin, "Patrioticheskoye vospitaniye dolzhno stat' organichnoy chast'yu zhizni nashego obshchestva" [Patriotic education must become an organic part of our society], Channel 1, 2016, https://www.1tv.ru/news/2016-04-05/299813-v_putin_patrioticheskoe_vospitanie_dolzhno_stat_organichnoy_chastyu_zhizni_nashego_obschestva; "Patrioticheskoye vospitaniye dolzhno vernut'sya v shkoly—Putin" [Patriotic education must return to schools—Putin], December 8, 2014, http://www.edu.ru/news/education/24976; RBK, "Putin poruchil zanyat'sya rannim patrioticheskim vospitaniyem molodezhi" [Putin ordered the early patriotic upbringing of the youth], April 6, 2015, http://www.rbc.ru/rbcfreenews/55229d7e9a79474c838a998a.

3. See also "Vstrecha s predstavitelyami obshchestvennosti po voprosam patrioticheskogo vospitaniya molodyozhi" [Meeting with members of the public on the issues of patriotic education of youth], President of Russian Federation, December 12, 2012, http://news.kremlin.ru/news/16470.

4. Deng Xiaoping, June 9, 1989.

5. These ideals are widely expressed in government reports on patriotic and moral education; see, for example, Ministry of Education 1980; Ministry of Education 2004; Action Plan for Patriotic Education 2006 [1994].

6. The NCEE was centralized in 1952 and is supervised by the Chinese Ministry of Education. The exam was suspended during the Cultural Revolution (1966–1976), when universities were closed and top leaders saw "the entrance exam as the 'flaw' in the 'revolution' of the cultural and educational spheres" (Zheng [2007] 2010, 17). Since 1977, the NCEE has been offered each summer and serves as the gatekeeper of higher education.

7. Before 2003 the NCEE was offered in July; in earlier decades it spanned three days. It is important to note that not all students test in each subject. Students seeking to major in the arts and humanities (*wenke*) will have a slightly different exam than those pursuing the sciences (*like*). The humanities track tests only one of the three sciences covered on the exam (biology, chemistry, and physics).

8. This includes NCEE exams from 1952–1957, 1959–1965, and 1977–2018.

9. See, for example, "2013 Nian gaokao wen zong kaoshi dang gang (xin ke biao)" [2013 outline for the college entrance examination in humanities], http://edu.qq.com/a/20130302/000097.htm#p=1.

10. See Law 2011 for a survey of political education curricula reforms in China since the 1950s.

11. These themes were identified using a number of primary sources, including the New Course Standard for Full-Time High School Political Education (2004), Course Standard for Full-Time High School Political Education (1996), and Outline of the NCEE, distributed by the Chinese Ministry of Education.

12. For example, Beida and Qinghua Universities required incoming students to spend a year in military training.

13. It is interesting to note that one exam compendium referenced in this study listed this question on the Tiananmen uprisings as "missing," indicating that it has since been censored (Beijing tian li kaoshi xinxi wang 2010, 368).

References

Action Plan for Patriotic Education. [1994] 2006. "Aiguozhuyi jianyu shishi gangyao." Reprinted in *Chinese Education and Society* 39, no. 2 (March–April): 7–18.

Almond, Gabriel A., and Sidney Verba. 1963. *The Civic Culture*. Princeton: Princeton University Press.

Bagdasarjan, V. Je., Je. N. Abdulaev, V. M. Klychnikov, A. Je. Larionov, and A. Ju. Morozov. 2009. *Shkol'nyy uchebnik istorii i gosudarstvennaya politika* [School history textbook and public policy]. Moscow: Direct Media.

Beijing tian li kaoshi xinxi wang. 2010. *Zhongguo gaokao zhenti quan bian 1978–2010* [Collection of Gaokao questions 1978–2010]. Beijing: Xizhang renmin chuban she.

Bogolyubov, L. N., A. Yu. Lazebnikova, and V. A. Litvinov. 2014. *Obshchestvoznaniye, 11y klass* [Social studies, 11th grade]. Moscow: Izdatel'stvo Prosveshcheniye.

Bogolyubov, L. N., A. Yu. Lazebnikova, and A. I. Matveev. 2014. *Obshchestvoznaniye, 9y klass* [Social studies, 9th grade]. Moscow: Izdatel'stvo Prosveshcheniye.

Bogolyubov, L. N., A. Yu. Lazebnikova, and N. M. Smirnova. 2007. *Obshchestvoznaniye, 10y klass* [Social studies, 10th grade]. Moscow: Izdatel'stvo Prosveshcheniye.

Bogolyubov, L. N., A. Yu. Lazebnikova, and N. M. Smirnova. 2008. *Obshchestvoznaniye praktikum, 11y klass* [Social studies, 11th grade]. Moscow: Izdatel'stvo Prosveshcheniye.

Bogolyubov, L. N., A. Yu. Lazebnikova, and M. V. Telyukina. 2014. *Obshchestvoznaniye, 10y klass* [Social studies, 10th grade]. Moscow: Izdatel'stvo Prosveshcheniye.

Bueno de Mesquita, Bruce, and George W. Downs. 2005. "Development and Democracy." *Foreign Affairs* 84, no. 5: 77–86.

Bykov, A. K., and V. I. Lutovinov. 2008. *Patrioticheskoye vospitaniye* [Patriotic upbringing]. Moscow: Moscow Textbooks and Cartography.

Bykov, A. K., and I. I. Melnichenko. 2007. *Patrioticheskoye vospitaniye shkol'nikov v uchebnom protsesse. Metodicheskoye posobiye* [Patriotic upbringing of students in the educational process. Methodological supplement]. Moscow: Tvorcheski Center.

Campbell, David E., Meira Levinson, and Frederick M. Hess. 2012. *Making Civics Count: Citizenship Education for a New Generation*. Cambridge, MA: Harvard University Press.

Cantoni Davide, Yuyu Chen, David Y. Yang, Noam Yuchtman, and Y. Jane Zhang. 2017. "Curriculum and Ideology." *Journal of Political Economy* 125, no. 2: 338–392.

Easton, David, and Jack Dennis. 1969. *Children in the Political System: Origins of Political Legitimacy*. New York: McGraw-Hill.

Easton, David, and Robert Hess. 1962. "The Child's Political World." *Midwestern Journal of Political Science* 6, no. 3 (August): 229–246.

Elkof, Ben. 2005. *Education Reform in Post-Soviet Russia*. New York: Routledge.

Estrin, James. 2018. "Coming of Age amid Patriotic Training." *New York Times*, February 22.

Fairbrother, Gregory. P. 2003. *Toward Critical Patriotism: Student Resistance to Political Education in Hong Kong and China*. Hong Kong: Hong Kong University Press.

Golev, A. G. 1996. *Vospitaniye patriotizma i kul'tury mezhnatsional'nykh otnosheniy u starsheklassnikov* [The education of patriotism and culture of internationalism among high school students]. Pyatigorsk: Pyatigorskogo gosudarstvennogo lingvisticheskogo universiteta.

Golunov, S. V. 2012. "Patrioticheskoye vospitaniye v Rossii: za i protiv" [Patriotic education in Russia: for and against]. *Educational Studies* 3: 258–273.

Guo, Yingjie. 2004. *Cultural Nationalism in Contemporary China*. New York: Routledge.

Hayhoe, Ruth. 1992. "Moral-Political Education and Modernization." In *Education and Modernization: The Chinese Experience*, 211–238. Oxford: Pergamon Press.

Hayhoe, Ruth. 1993. "Political Texts in Chinese Universities Before and After Tiananmen." *Pacific Affairs* 66, no. 1: 21–43.

Hobsbawm, E. J. 1990. *Nations and Nationalism Since 1780: Programme, Myth, Reality.* Cambridge: Cambridge University Press.

Hoisington, Sam. 2017. "College of the Ozarks Now Requires Course in 'Patriotic Education and Fitness.'" *Chronicle of Higher Education*, October 27.

Huang, Haifeng. 2015. "Propaganda as Signaling." *Comparative Politics* 47, no. 4: 419–436.

Huang, Haifeng. 2018. "The Pathology of Hard Propaganda." *Journal of Politics* 80, no. 3: 1034–1038.

Koesel, Karrie. 2017. "Learning to Be Loyal: Political and Patriotic Education in Russia and China." Paper presented at the annual meeting of the Association for Slavic, East European, and Eurasian Studies, October 9–12, 2017, Chicago.

Koesel, Karrie J., and Valerie J. Bunce. 2013. "Diffusion-Proofing: Russian and Chinese Responses to Waves of Popular Mobilizations Against Authoritarian Rulers." *Perspectives on Politics* 11, no. 3 (September): 753–768.

Kravchenko, A. I., and E. A. Pevtsova. 2011. *Obshchestvoznaniye, 9y klass* [Social studies, 9th grade]. Moscow: Russkoe Slovo.

Kumitskaya, T. M., and O. E. Zhirenko. 2009. *Otechestvo: grazhdanskoye i patrioticheskoye vospitaniye, 5–11 klassy* [Fatherland: civil and patriotic education, grades 5–11]. Moscow: VAKO.

Kurbatov, V. I. 2006. *Obshchestvoznaniye* [Social studies]. Rostov-on-Don: Izdatel'stvo Feniks.

Law, Wing-Wah. 2011. *Citizenship and Citizenship Education in a Global Age: Politics, Politics and Practices in China.* New York: Peter Lang.

Liu, Chuyu, and Xiao Ma. 2018. "Popular Threats and Nationalistic Propaganda: Political Logic of China's Patriotic Campaign." *Security Studies* 27, no. 4, 633–664.

Luo, Jiali, and Frederick C. Wendel. 1999. "Preparing for College: Senior High School Education in China." *NAASP Bulletin*, October, 57–86.

Magaloni, Beatriz. 2006. *Voting for Autocracy: Hegemonic Party Survival and Its Demise in Mexico.* New York: Cambridge University Press.

Malinin, V. A., E. M. Tyuntyaeva, N. I. Sergeevskaya, and M. S. Grishina. 2009. *Grazhdanin, patriot, sem'yanin novogo veka* [Citizen, patriot, family man of the new century]. Nizhny Novgorod: ZUM.

Mikryukov, V. Yu. 2009. *Voyenno-patrioticheskoye vospitaniye v shkole, 1–11 klassy* [Military-patriotic education in schools, grades 1–11]. Moscow: VAKO.

Ministry of Education. 1980. "Gaijin he jiaqiang zhongxue zhengzhi ke de yijian de tongzhi" [Notice on improving and strengthening middle school political opinions]. http://www.cbe21.com/subject/politics/html/060301/20012/200122_197.html.

Ministry of Education. 2004. "Putong gaozhong sixiang zhengzhi kecheng biaozhun (shiyan)" [Notice on general high school ideological and political education standards (experimental)]. http://www.moe.edu.cn/publicfiles/business/htmlfiles/moe/moe_711/201001/78375.html.

Ministry of Education and Sciences in Russia. 2015. "O gosudarstvennoy programme 'Patrioticheskoye vospitaniye grazhdan Rossiyskoy Federatsii na 2016–2020 gody'" [On the state program "Patriotic Education of Citizens of the Russian Federation in 2016–2020"]. http://government.ru/media/files/8qqYUwwzHUxzVkH1jsKAErrx2dE4qows.pdf.

Nikitin, A. F., and Ya. V. Sokolov. 1991. *Grazhdanovedeniye I II, 5–9y klass* [Civic Education, 5th–9th grade]. Moscow: Izdatel'stvo Pravleniya Obshchestva Znaniya.

Omelchenko, Daria, Svetlan Maximova, Galina Avdeeva, Natalia Goncharova, Oksana Noyanzina, and Olga Surtaeva. 2015. "Patriotic Education and Civic Culture of Youth in Russia: Sociological Perspective." *Procedia: Social and Behavioral Sciences* 190: 364–371.

Outline on Secondary School Moral Education. [1995] 2006. "Zhongxue deyu dadang" [Outline on Secondary School Moral Education]. Reprinted in *Chinese Education and Society* 39, no. 2: 21–36.

Perry, Elizabeth J. 2013. "Cultural Governance in Contemporary China: 'Re-orienting' Party Propaganda." Harvard–Yenching Institute Working Paper Series.

Pravitel'stvo RF. 2001. "O gosudarstvennoy programme "Patrioticheskoye vospitaniye grazhdan Rossiyskoy Federatsii na 2001–2005 gody." Postanovleniye Pravitel'stva RF of 16 febralya 2001 g, no. 122, http://base.garant.ru/1584972/#friends

Pravitel'stvo RF. 2015. "O gosudarstvennoy programme "Patrioticheskoye vospitaniye grazhdan Rossiyskoy Federatsii na 2016–2020 gody." Postanovleniye Pravitel'stva RF ot 30 dekabrya 2015 g., no. 1493. http://www.garant.ru/products/ipo/prime/doc/71196398/

Putin, Vladimir. 2012. "Vstrecha s predstavitelyami obshhestvennosti po voprosam patrioticheskogo vospitaniya molodyozhi" [Meeting with members of the public on the patriotic education of youth]. September 12. http://news.kremlin.ru/news/16470.

Quinlivan, James T. 1999. "Coup-Proofing: Its Practice and Consequences in the Middle East." *International Security* 24, no. 2 (Fall): 131–165.

Rapaport, Anatoli. 2009. "Patriotic Education in Russia: Stylistic Move or a Sign of Substantive Counter-Reform?" *Educational Forum* 73, no. 2: 141–152.

Riordan, Jim, ed. 1989. *Soviet Youth Culture*. Houndmills: Macmillan.

Rosen, Stanley. 2010. "Chinese Youth and State-Society Relations." In *Chinese Politics: State, Society and the Market*, ed. Peter Hays Gries and Stanley Rosen, 160–178. London: Routledge.

Rozhkov, M.I. 2011. *Vospitaniye grazhdanina: uroki sotsial'nosti, 10–11 klassy* [Civic education: lessons of sociality, grades 10–11]. Moscow: Vladoc.

Sanina, Anna. 2017. *Patriotic Education in Contemporary Russia: Sociological Studies in the Making of the Post-Soviet Citizen*. Stuttgart: Ibidem-Verlag.

Semenova, N. E. 2004. "Vospitaniye patriotizma uchashchikhsya sredney obshcheobrazovatel'noy shkoly sredstvami dopolnitel'nogo obrazovaniya" [Education of patriotism of pupils of secondary school by means of additional education]. Ph.D. dissertation. State Academy of Postgraduate Pedagogical Education, Moscow.

Sherlock, Thomas. 2016. "Russian Politics and the Soviet Past: Reassessing Stalin and Stalinism Under Vladimir Putin." *Communist and Post-Communist Studies* 49: 45–49.

Silitski, Vitali. 2005. "Preempting Democracy: The Case of Belarus." *Journal of Democracy* 16, no. 4 (October): 83–97.

Sokolov, Ya. V., and E. S. Korolkova. 1991. *Grazhdanovedeniye* [Civic education], vol. II. Moscow: Izdatel'stvo Znaniye.

Sokolov, Ya. V., and A. S. Prutchenkov. 2000. *Grazhdanovedeniye, 9y klass* [Civic education, 9th grade]. Moscow: NVTs Grazhdanin.

Tilly, Charles, ed. 1975. *The Formation of National States in Western Europe.* Princeton: Princeton University Press.

Tislenkova, I. A. 2007. *Grazhdansko-patrioticheskoye vospitaniye v 6 i 7 klassakh* [Civic and patriotic education in grades 6–7]. Volgograd: Uchitel'.

Tsilulina, M. V. 2009. "Patrioticheskogo vospitaniya molodezhi v usloviyakh sovremennoy shkoly" [Model of patriotic education of the youth in the context of modern school]. *Mir nauki, kul'tury, obrazovaniya* [The world of science, culture and education] 7, no. 19: 276–278.

Vickers, Edward. 2009. "Selling 'Socialism with Chinese Characteristics': 'Thought and Politics' and the Legitimisation of China's Development Strategy." *International Journal of Educational Development* 29: 523–531.

Volodina, S. I., A. M. Polievktova, and V. V. Spasskaya. 2010. *Obshchestvoznaniye 8–9 klass* [Social studies grades 8–9], 2 vols. Moscow: Akademkniga/Uchebnik.

vom Hau, Matthias. 2009. "Unpacking the Schools: Textbooks, Teachers and the Construction of Nationhood in Mexico, Argentina, and Peru." *Latin American Research Review* 44, no. 3: 127–154.

Voskresenskaya, N. M., and N. V. Davletshina. 1997. *Grazhdanovedeniye. Demokratiya: Gosudarstvo i obshchestvo, 10–11k* [Civic education. Democracy: government and society, 10th–11th grades]. Moscow: Drofa.

Weber, Eugen. 1976. *Peasants into Frenchmen: The Modernization of Rural France, 1870–1914.* Stanford, CA: Stanford University Press.

Wemer, David A. 2019. "More and More Russians Are Fleeing Oppression in Russia." Atlantic Council. February 21. https://www.atlanticcouncil.org/blogs/new-atlanticist/more-and-more-russians-are-fleeing-oppression-in-russia.

Xinhua. 2016. "Xi Calls for Strengthened Ideological Work in Colleges." December 9. http://news.xinhuanet.com/english/2016-12/09/c_135891337.htm.

Yan, Xiaojun. 2014. "Engineering Stability: Authoritarian Political Control over University Students in Post-Deng China." *China Quarterly* 218: 493–513.

Yurchak, Alexei. 2005. *Everything Was Forever, Until It Was No More: The Last Soviet Generation.* Princeton: Princeton University Press.

Zajda, Joseph I. 1980. *Education in the USSR.* Oxford: Pergamon Press.

Zhao, Suisheng. 1998. "A State-Led Nationalism: The Patriotic Education Campaign in Post-Tiananmen China." *Communist and Post-Communist Studies* 31, no. 3: 287–302.

Zheng, Ruoling. [2007] 2010. "'Ju Guo Da Kao' de heli xing—Gaokao de shehui jichu gongneng yu yingxinang zhi fenxi" [On the rationality of the college entrance examination: analysis of its social foundations, functions, and influences]. Reprinted in *Chinese Education and Society* 43, no. 4: 11–21.

11 }

Going Public

CHOOSING TO WORK FOR THE RUSSIAN STATE

Bryn Rosenfeld

The preceding chapters have studied the strategic interaction between authoritarian regimes and their societies from a variety of angles. An important part of this strategic interaction in both Russia and China is these regimes' ability to secure support by doling out patronage jobs in the public sector. As discussed in Chapter 1, these jobs may be attractive not just to regime supporters but may also help to blunt opposition from would-be challengers. This chapter asks: Who seeks out a career as a public official, making and implementing policy in a non-democratic regime? Who desires to join the ranks of the civil service, to educate citizens on the state's behalf, to work in state enterprises, and to maintain social order in support of the regime? More precisely, what kinds of people elect these types of careers in a country such as Russia? These questions are especially important in autocracies, where officials are less constrained and accountable to citizens than in democracies. They are also of specific importance in Russia, where state control over the economy has expanded since 2000 under Vladimir Putin.

More than twenty-five years after the collapse of communism and the demise of central planning, the share of state employment in Russia's economy remains substantial. While the 1990s are often remembered as a decade of state downsizing, between 1990 and 1998 the share of total employment in the public sector actually increased. The number of teachers in state schools rose, as did the number of academic staff in state higher education and the number of employees in healthcare, social protection, and sport (Gimpelson and Treisman 2002).[1] Employment in public administration grew by 45 percent, or approximately 900,000 employees.

By 2005, roughly half (48 percent) of all full-time employees in Russia worked in the government sector, according to data from the International Social Survey Programme (Houston 2014, 851). OECD figures from 2011 give the rate of public employment in Russia's labor force as 31 percent. Since the labor force includes both unemployed and part-time workers employed at least one hour a week, this figure significantly understates the real weight of government employment in the Russian economy. Much as the institution of universal state employment served as an important instrument of social control in the communist period, so does an extensive state sector help to mobilize regime support and ensure political stability in Russia today.

This chapter investigates the political orientations and career aspirations of students who intend to join Russia's public sector. The analysis focuses on whether and how Russia's future public servants differ from others in terms of their motivations, networks, values, and background. While I examine a range of factors highlighted by existing cross-national research on public employment in established democracies and developing states, I also extend these frameworks by examining whether prospective government workers differ in their political attitudes, a set of variables less frequently studied in the extant public administration literature.

In what follows, I study prospective Russian public servants' views on the importance of political freedom, order, national security, and strong economic performance. I also probe whether democratic values, both in the abstract and in terms of support for specific democratic institutions, are tied to the preference for public employment. The analysis sheds light on whether Russia's autocratic institutions are in part sustained by the self-sorting of autocratic types into public service or whether these institutions must cultivate in their workforces the political values conducive to regime stability.

I find that students who choose public sector careers begin with political attitudes very similar to those of students who choose other fields, but with somewhat different backgrounds and motivations. Rather than make career choices on the basis of political orientations, I find that the single most important factor shaping public sector career preferences is preexisting networks—having a parent who works in the public sector or attending a university with a strong alumni network in government. It is the availability of these informal networks, rather than ideology, that shapes who is most likely to serve the Russian state.

Working for the State in Comparative Perspective

In both Russia and China, as in other developing autocracies, many young people aspire to work for the state. Lee and Zhang (2013) report that government employment has consistently been the most preferred career option among Chinese university graduates (1504). This preference for public employment extends also to Chinese elites. According to the Beijing Colleges Panel Survey of nearly five thousand students enrolled at fifteen elite universities in China, government entities ranked as the third-most-desirable type of organization to work for upon graduation. Only private-sector entities with foreign investment and state-owned enterprises were more popular.

Similarly, the World Bank reports that across the Middle East and North Africa, a majority of young people aspire to public sector positions (cited in Behar and Mok 2013, 13). In Indonesia, civil service jobs are so desirable that they are bought and sold (Kristiansen and Ramli 2006). In Kazakhstan, Nurmagambetov (2010) finds that survey respondents at all levels of educational attainment saw state jobs as a source of greater opportunity than either working for a private company or starting one's own business. In Russia, the popularity of majoring in state administration has increased alongside economics and business over the post-Soviet period.

Although autocracy often goes hand in hand with a large public sector (Greene 2010), few studies have directly examined what makes public sector positions desirable in these contexts and how those who take government jobs differ from their peers.[2] As a starting point, scholars studying these questions in other settings often focus on extrinsic motivations such as salary or, in the high-corruption context of new democracies, opportunities to earn informal rents. However, existing cross-national research has reached mixed conclusions on the importance of financial incentives for public sector recruitment (e.g., Dal Bo, Finan, and Ross 2013; Lewis and Frank 2002; Karl and Sutton 1998; Krueger 1988). Some studies find that those who prioritize high income are more likely to seek government employment (Lewis and Frank 2002), while others find that private sector workers place a higher value on good wages (Karl and Sutton 1998). Still others find that there is little difference (Gabris and Simo 1995).

Sharunina (2013) notes that public sector wage premiums are generally higher in less developed countries, especially where there is a large informal economy. Yet in Russia she documents a sizable public sector wage gap. Looking at the period from 2000 to 2010, Sharunina finds that public employees are paid 30 percent less than private sector employees, even after accounting for workers' observed and unobserved characteristics.

While low official salaries may drive qualified candidates out of the public sector, state jobs may also provide lucrative opportunities to earn informal rents. Indeed, in high-corruption contexts, government workers can offset low official salaries by exploiting their official positions. Gorodnichenko and Peter (2007), for example, show that state employees in Ukraine hide a substantial proportion of their total income, which the authors attribute to bribes and other informal payments. Gerber and Schaefer (2004, 46), meanwhile, find that a degree in state administration yields among the highest returns of any major in contemporary Russia (together with economics and business). Thus, if workers are drawn to Russia's public sector by the promise of financial gain, they are probably motivated by informal benefits rather than high official salaries. Here again, however, the evidence from existing work, even in high-corruption contexts, is mixed. Some studies based on experimental games suggest that corrupt types are more likely to pursue public employment (Banerjee, Baul, and Rosenblat 2015; Hanna and Wang 2017), while others suggest that they are less likely (Gans-Morse et al. 2017), and still others suggest that there is no relationship between dishonesty and the preference for a state career (Alatas et al. 2009).

Alongside the literature on extrinsic financial motivations, a large body of research in the field of public administration focuses on intrinsic motivations for public service. This literature hypothesizes that individuals with a high level of public service motivation are drawn to, and will self-select into, jobs that meet these needs (Houston 2014, 856). Indeed, research in the developed democracies consistently finds that aspirants to public service display higher levels of altruism and a stronger desire to be useful to society than those who seek private sector careers (e.g., Lewis and Frank 2002; Barfort et al. 2015). Similarly, using experiments embedded in an online survey in Russia, Gans-Morse et al. (2017) show that students who prefer public employment are more altruistic than their peers. Attitudinal evidence from the same survey further suggests that the desire to help others is closely associated with a preference for the public sector. Still, as Houston (2014) finds, such intrinsic motives may not be uniformly important beyond the Western democracies, especially in places where public administration is not as clearly rooted in a strong public service ethos.

A third body of scholarship focuses on the role of networks in shaping the public sector workforce. On the supply side, scholars have long studied how social networks and influential relationships affect the allocation of valuable commodities, including jobs, in communist systems. Considerable evidence documents the importance of *guanxi* in communist China and *blat* in Soviet-era Russia—that is, personal connections and informal networks of exchange—for obtaining opportunities within the state (e.g., Bian 1994). More specifically, in post-communist Russia, the importance of family ties and personal connections for establishing one's career has been tied to low intergenerational social mobility (Yastrebov 2011).

Access to networks impacts the demand for government jobs by shaping individuals' strategic considerations.[3] Along these lines, Liu and Wang (2017) offer evidence from a natural experiment in China that students who perceive their universities as having strong alumni networks in government are more likely to pursue government careers. Comparing students just above and just below the threshold for admission on the nationwide university entrance exam, they find that attending one of China's three most selective universities increases the probability of joining the civil service by 25 percent. Having a network in the public sector, whether through school or family ties, should heighten the expectation of a successful career.

Drawing on these bodies of literature, this study asks what motivates those who enter public service in an autocratic country, such as Russia. In terms of character and ambition, how do future public servants compare with their peers? In what ways do their aspirations differ? Does career stability, greed, prestige, or a strong public service motivation animate those who intend to take up public sector professions?

A second important set of questions, which extends existing research agendas, concerns whether those who elect to work for the state hold different political values from their peers. Do they differ in how much they value freedom, political order, global influence, and economic growth? Do they differ in their views of the type of political system that is best able to deliver on these goals? In short, how different are they from their peers in terms of what they want from their government?

Finally, a third important set of questions regards the background of public servants. Are their political and economic experiences similar to or different from those of their peers? Were their families more likely to be winners or losers in the transition from communism? What kind of educational and occupational profile do the parents have? These are critical questions given the lasting impact of adolescent socialization, the importance of networks, and the role of familial ties for enhancing perceived public sector career prospects.

Who Goes Public? Motivation, Networks, Values, and Background

Though there is limited empirical evidence beyond the developed democracies on what makes public sector positions desirable and how public officials differ from their peers, extant studies suggest several relevant variables. First, there is a large body of work on patronage and clientelism, which implies that the primary motivation for seeking state employment in a developing non-democracy is personal enrichment. Even if formal salaries are low, official positions are often a lucrative source of informal rents. Working for the state may provide the chance to solicit bribes, gain access to state resources, or obtain preferential treatment. Indeed, an emerging line of research considers whether corrupt types self-select into the government sector where corruption is widespread (Gans-Morse et al. 2017; Hanna and Wang 2017; Banerjee, Baul, and Rosenblat 2015). If material incentives drive the decision to enter the public sector, we would expect students who prioritize a high salary or other benefits to express a stronger preference for state employment. This leads us to predict that:

Hypothesis 1: The preference for public employment will be stronger among students who prioritize financial gain.

Second, students may make occupational choices in response to their perceived career prospects, choosing to go into jobs and organizations where they are likely to benefit from preexisting networks (Liu and Wang 2017). Such networks may be essential to accessing public sector opportunities when recruitment is not strictly meritocratic and jobs are doled out as a form of patronage in exchange for political loyalty. Even where recruitment is meritocratic, preexisting networks may facilitate access to preferable posts and career advancement.

Networks can come from several sources. As Liu and Wang (2017) show, attending a school with a strong alumni network in government may encourage students to pursue government careers. Elite universities often supply such networks. Another source of network-based recruitment is family ties. Children who follow their parents into the same profession may benefit from their parents' professional contacts and connections. A parent who works for the state can make introductions, provide know-how, or influence colleagues and acquaintances, enhancing their child's career prospects in the government sector.[4] In sum, preexisting networks open opportunities that may enhance the motivation for choosing a public sector career. If networks are an important factor in the choice of state employment, we would expect that:

> Hypothesis 2: Attending a school with a strong alumni network in government will increase the likelihood of a public sector career.

> Hypothesis 3: Having a parent who works in the public sector will increase the likelihood of a public sector career.

Third, a variety of studies have shown that political attitudes affect economic behavior (e.g., Gerber and Huber 2009; McConnell et al. 2018). For example, recent experimental evidence suggests that reservation wages are lower when a prospective employer shares a subject's partisan identity, implying the preference to work for co-partisans (McConnell et al. 2018). Yet much of the literature on how politics shape economic behavior focuses on partisanship, an especially strong form of political identity. We have less evidence on the extent to which other political attitudes and orientations influence employment choices.

One possibility is that political values shape the choice of career path. More concretely, students who elect public service in an autocratic system such as Russia's may have systematically different views on the importance of political freedom, economic growth, order, and their country's global influence than others. Another possibility is that they differ from their peers on what type of political system they believe is best suited to achieving these objectives.

In recent years, Russia's political system has become increasingly autocratic. Key democratic institutions have been eroded and political competition has been stamped out. As political freedom has declined, the Kremlin has aimed to secure legitimacy through economic growth, political stability, and rising global influence. Are young Russians' political values, and especially their views on democracy, as compelling a factor in the choice of employment as partisanship is in the United States? While partisan affiliations are a key component of social identity in the United States, there are reasons to doubt that political values are as central to identity or as powerful in determining economic behavior in Russia. For one, apoliticism and even political apathy have long been a mode of survival under autocratic rule. In the late communist period, opportunism rather than ideology more often motivated the choice to join the Communist Party. In short, Russian students may prefer to work for an employer who shares their political values, or they may give political values and ideology relatively low priority next to personal, pragmatic concerns.

With these points in mind, if political preferences are an important selection criterion in the choice of government employment, we would predict the following:

Hypothesis 4: The preference for public employment will be stronger among students who hold more authoritarian values.

Fourth, the case-specific literature on Russia has long emphasized differences between those who see themselves as winners in the transition from communism and those who see themselves as losers (Tucker, Pacek, and Berinsky 2002; Tucker 2006). The collapse of communism brought radical changes in the social status of various groups. While some groups gained, other groups lost in Russia's dramatic economic and political transformation. For those whose families benefited from free market reforms, private sector opportunities may be more attractive than for those whose families were harmed by the reforms. Conversely, losers from the transition may be more likely to seek the security of state employment. I therefore expect that:

Hypothesis 5: The preference for public employment will be stronger among students whose families were losers in the transition from communism.

Another possibility that has received scant attention but is likely important (and not only in Russia) is that the structure of the labor market constrains the choice of public employment. Simply put, in many cases, there is no (or virtually no) opportunity to pursue certain careers in the private sector. This is the case almost universally with regard to the military, police, and other occupations associated with maintaining public order. In the Russian economy, this is also true of occupations in the fields of public health, research, and education. Younger workers may be especially affected by a lack of private sector opportunities if they have a strong desire for a particular occupational profile upon entering the labor market. If these structural constraints are significant, we would expect that:

Hypothesis 6: The preference for public employment will be stronger among students who prioritize their chosen profession as compared with students whose employment preferences are less closely tied to their majors.

Several other factors have been cited as drivers of public employment across other contexts. In many places, public employment is prestigious. In China, for example, scholars have often noted that a government job adds to personal and family status (Li and Wang 2017; Lee and Zhang 2013). Public sector jobs are also frequently viewed as more stable than private sector jobs, with a lower probability of being laid off. This argument implies that public employment will appeal most to students who are risk averse and place a high value on job security (Lewis and Frank 2002; Dong 2014; Houston 2014; though see also Gabris and Simo 1995). In addition, the preference for flexibility is an important job value for many students entering the labor market (Karl and Sutton 1998). If students perceive part-time and flexible work arrangements as more prevalent in the private sector, it may drive them out of public employment. Finally, we would expect a strong public service motivation—defined here as placing a high value on serving one's country—to be associated straightforwardly with a preference for public employment (Lewis and Frank 2002; Houston 2014). I control for each of the factors just mentioned in subsequent analyses.

Data and Measures

To test these hypotheses, I draw on a survey I designed in collaboration with researchers at the Higher School of Economics in Moscow. The survey was conducted in late 2014 among 1,399 undergraduate students at three elite Russian universities: the Higher School of Economics (HSE, N = 540), Moscow State University (MSU, N = 496), and the Moscow State Institute for International Relations (MGIMO, N = 363). The survey included detailed information about students' career plans, political values, family backgrounds, and personal characteristics.

Although students at these three institutions are not representative of students pursuing higher education in Russia as a whole, they are indicative of the group that already is part of, or stands the best chance to join, the Russian political and economic elite. These three institutions are consistently ranked among Russia's top universities and are widely considered its most prestigious. Accordingly, their alumni are well represented in elite government circles. In the year following the survey, the schools' alumni held five of eight deputy prime minister positions in the Russian government. MGIMO is run by the Russian Ministry of Foreign Affairs and has traditionally trained Russia's diplomatic core. Approximately 45 percent of the HSE's alumni in the social sciences begin their professional careers in the state administration. Moscow State University is one of the country's oldest universities and is much larger than the other two, with a broader educational mission in the natural sciences. It remains at the top of several university rankings in Russia and sends many of its graduates to public sector institutions and organizations.

The primary dependent variable in subsequent analyses is the preference for state employment. However, in view of the differences between working in public administration and other government structures, I also separately analyze the group that intends to directly serve the state. In total, approximately one-third of the full sample say that upon finishing university they are most likely to work in the public sector. Of these, 7 percent report that they are most likely to work in public administration. Another 7 percent say that they are most likely to work in a state-owned enterprise, and 17 percent say that they are most likely to work in a public medical, educational, or research institution. The full distribution of responses to the survey's post-graduation employment question is presented in Table 11.1.

Next, I measure job values and motivations with a battery of fourteen items. For each item, respondents are asked to evaluate the importance to them personally of various job characteristics on a four-point scale ranging from not important (1) to very important (4). Figure 11.1 shows the average response for each of these items. The questions on salary and

benefits tap extrinsic financial motivations, while the question on the importance of finding work that is directly related to one's major taps the extent to which the respondent's job preferences are a function of his or her commitment to pursuing a career in a particular field over other considerations. In addition, the item on prestige captures the importance of social esteem, while the items on risk of being fired and the desire to do something novel/risky capture the extent to which respondents prioritize job security. I also measure the importance of flexible hours, and I tap public service motivation with a question on the importance of serving one's country. Additional items measure the importance of opportunities for career advancement, work-life balance, the chance to make contacts, specialization vs. broad professional skills, and the ability to work independently. I include the last five items, which are standard in the literature, as controls.

To capture political preferences and orientations, I use several items that measure these attitudes in different ways. First, I use a question that asks

TABLE 11.1 } Distribution of Anticipated Careers

Public sector medical, educational, research	0.17
Public administration	0.07
State-owned enterprise	0.07
Military, police, law enforcement	0.01
Private sector/corporate	0.42
Self-employment	0.08
Journalism	0.08
Other	0.02
Difficult to say	0.08

Note: Share of all respondents.

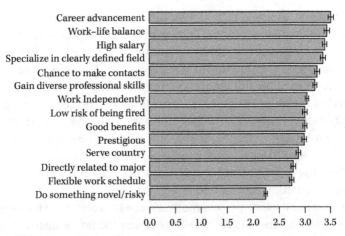

FIGURE 11.1 Job Values and Motivations

Notes: This figure presents the average response and 95% confidence intervals for survey questions measuring the importance of different job characteristics. The response options were: not important (1), rather unimportant (2), rather important (3), and very important (4).

whether democracy is always preferable, treating democracy as an abstract concept. Second, I use an index consisting of the average of seven items measuring respondents' views more concretely on the importance of particular democratic institutions: free and fair elections, independent courts, equality before the law, freedom of speech, an independent press, minority rights, and a strong political opposition.[5] Given Russia's democratic retrenchment over the Putin years, if political preferences affect employment choices, I expect that the preference for public employment will be weaker among students who give greater importance to democracy and democratic institutions.

Third, I measure authoritarian attitudes by examining the trade-offs that respondents are willing to accept. Specifically, the question asks which of the following respondents consider most important: freedom, stability, economic growth, the absence of corruption, a fair chance to succeed, or redistribution from rich to poor. I then use this item to investigate whether the preference for public service is stronger among students who prioritize things like order and economic growth over political freedom.

In addition to ranking national priorities, survey respondents were asked whether democracy or autocracy is better at providing freedom, stability, economic growth, low levels of corruption, equality of opportunity, and redistribution. Based on a comparison of these two items, I coded an indicator for whether the respondent believes that an autocratic system is best suited to delivering on his/her top national priority. I use this measure to test whether the preference for public employment is stronger among students who believe that autocracies are better at providing for the things they prioritize.

Besides looking at these explicit measures of the preference for autocratic political institutions and the willingness to trade off democracy for political stability and growth, I am also able to leverage several indirect measures of authoritarianism. A first set of items taps chauvinistic political values such as the belief that Russia will be respected only if it is feared and the conviction that one's own country is better than all others. A second set of items taps the willingness to accept hierarchy at home and at work as well as the belief that those in power should be feared. Again, if authoritarian dispositions affect employment choices, I expect the preference for public employment to be stronger among students who express more xenophobic values and a greater acceptance of hierarchy in different facets of their lives.

Next, as indicators of the role that networks play in the decision to enter government service, I focus on two items. The first captures whether having a parent who works in the public sector increases the likelihood of a government job. For the second, I include a dummy variable for each university. If alumni networks matter, I expect that the preference for government service will be stronger among students of MGIMO, which is connected to the Ministry of Foreign Affairs and has long served a central role in training Russia's diplomatic core. Of the three institutions, the HSE has the strongest network in the private sector. I would thus expect the link with public employment to be weakest there, though much stronger than at other Russian universities.

Finally, I measure transition experience using an item that asks whether the respondent's family is better off now or was better off before the collapse of communism. I code as winners those who say that their families live better today and as losers those who say that their families lived better in Soviet times.

I also control for several background characteristics: gender, Orthodox religion, the type of settlement where the respondent's family lives, a proxy for family income, parents' education and occupation, and the respondent's field (social sciences and humanities vs. natural sciences) and class year. I control for gender, since previous research has found that men are more likely to take up careers in the state administration, military, and law enforcement, while women are more likely to major in education, medicine, and science (Gerber and Schaefer 2004). I control for religion given the state's close association with the Russian Orthodox Church in recent years (Anderson 2007). I include settlement type as well as various proxies for income and social status, since state employment often provides upward mobility (or "social lift") for those who are less well off or from the provinces.

Empirical Results

I test these propositions for public sector employment as a whole and then separately for the state administration. Across all analyses, I estimate logistic regression models suitable for predicting employment choice as a dichotomous variable. Because the hypothesized correlates of this choice—background, networks, job motivations, and values—lie at different points in the causal chain, I estimate my main models in four steps. In each step, I include factors that lie at the same or prior stages of the causal chain. Thus in the first column of Table 11.2, I include only background characteristics: gender, religion, settlement type, family income, transition experience, parents' education and occupation, whether a parent is employed in the public sector, university, class year, and field.

Model 1 suggests that proximity to public sector networks and transition experiences have a significant impact on the likelihood of entering the public sector. Students at MGIMO and MGU are much more likely than students at HSE to plan public sector careers. This is consistent with MGIMO's strong ties to the state administration and MGU's influential network in public education and research. By contrast, HSE has the strongest private sector alumni network of the three institutions, and more of its students appear to gravitate in that direction. Likewise, students who have a parent working in the public sector are more likely than others to make the same career choice. This is true controlling for both parental education and occupation, suggesting that parents' informal networks matter more than intergenerational transmission of human capital. Finally, those whose families lost during the post-communist transition are more likely to choose the public sector, perhaps because they feel their prospects in the private sector are limited or because they seek the security of government employment.

Model 2 adds the additional items on career motivations. Each of the findings from the first model holds, and the coefficients remain remarkably stable. At the same time, the results imply that a strong public service motivation also drives the choice of government employment. In addition, the model lends modest support to the notion that a lack of private sector options in one's chosen career may push otherwise similar students into the public sector. The desire for a career that is closely related to one's major is positive, as expected, though only marginally statistically significant ($p < 0.1$). Finally, the results suggest that public sector jobs are more appealing to those who are willing to sacrifice flexibility. This makes sense given that part-time and informal employment arrangements are concentrated in the private sector. There is also, however, some evidence that future public employees are less ambitious, or at least anticipate less career growth (perhaps because professional jobs in, for example, education and medicine imply a less hierarchical career ladder than positions in large private sector organizations). Notably, neither the value placed on salary and benefits nor that placed on job stability clearly separates future public from private sector workers.

In model 3, I consider the impact of political values on career choice. If people with more authoritarian values self-select into the state sector, it would help to explain the persistence of autocratic institutions. However, the results in column 3 confirm that neither the belief that democracy is preferable to other political systems nor the preference for democratic institutions is significantly

TABLE 11.2 } Models Predicting Public Sector Employment

	Background	Motivation	Political Values	Political Values and Priorities
	(1)	(2)	(3)	(4)
Prioritizes stability				0.215 (0.365)
Prioritizes economy				-0.147 (0.312)
Prioritizes corruption				0.096 (0.316)
Prioritizes equality				-0.242 (0.334)
Prioritizes redistribution				-1.111 (0.611)
Autocracy delivers				0.097 (0.208)
Democracy preferable			0.098 (0.206)	0.111 (0.212)
Democratic institutions index		-0.158 (0.148)	-0.080 (0.142)	-0.051 (0.147)
Salary			-0.166 (0.151)	-0.173 (0.153)
Benefits		0.037 (0.115)	0.033 (0.116)	0.034 (0.118)
Serve my country		0.317** (0.098)	0.321** (0.099)	0.321* (0.101)
Prestige		-0.113 (0.115)	-0.106 (0.115)	-0.117 (0.118)
Stability		0.095 (0.109)	0.097 (0.109)	0.073 (0.111)
Independence		-0.069 (0.118)	-0.036 (0.120)	0.002 (0.123)
Related to major		0.162 (0.096)	0.150 (0.096)	0.168 (0.098)
Broad skills		0.008 (0.113)	0.006 (0.115)	-0.003 (0.116)
Specialization		0.025 (0.123)	0.027 (0.124)	0.043 (0.126)
Career growth		-0.386* (0.159)	-0.334* (0.161)	-0.351* (0.164)
Risky/novel		0.186 (0.107)	0.181 (0.108)	0.183 (0.109)
Flexible		-0.236* (0.106)	-0.246* (0.107)	-0.248* (0.108)
Work/life balance		-0.055 (0.124)	-0.035 (0.127)	-0.034 (0.128)
Make contacts		0.125 (0.118)	0.122 (0.120)	0.122 (0.122)
Public sector parent	0.307* (0.149)	0.372* (0.179)	0.367* (0.180)	0.366* (0.182)
MGIMO	0.418* (0.189)	0.609** (0.224)	0.605** (0.227)	0.611** (0.230)
MGU	0.997*** (0.172)	0.910*** (0.204)	0.916*** (0.204)	0.931*** (0.208)
Transition loser	0.688*** (0.198)	0.705** (0.240)	0.727** (0.242)	0.779** (0.246)
Male	-0.254 (0.148)	-0.387* (0.179)	-0.383* (0.181)	-0.436* (0.184)
Urbanicity	-0.051 (0.037)	-0.063 (0.044)	-0.063 (0.044)	-0.075 (0.045)
Orthodox	-0.286 (0.149)	-0.442* (0.184)	-0.442* (0.186)	-0.507** (0.190)

(Continued)

TABLE 11.2 *Continued*

	Background	Motivation	Political Values	Political Values and Priorities
	(1)	(2)	(3)	(4)
Parents' education	0.126 (0.146)	0.144 (0.171)	0.155 (0.172)	0.171 (0.173)
Parents' occupation	-0.194 (0.184)	-0.308 (0.221)	-0.325 (0.221)	-0.363 (0.225)
Income	0.036 (0.053)	0.031 (0.065)	0.025 (0.066)	0.022 (0.066)
Constant	-0.969 (0.562)	-0.170 (1.006)	-0.359 (1.017)	-0.285 (1.042)
Observations	938	717	711	707
Log likelihood	-576.007	-422.298	-417.849	-411.247
Akaike inf. crit.	1,178.015	898.595	893.698	892.495

Note: $* p < 0.05$; $** p < 0.01$; $*** p < 0.001$. Logistic regressions predicting public sector employment. All models include dummies for class year and field. The reference category is "freedom" for the question on priorities and the HSE for university.

related to the likelihood of a public sector career. Both coefficients are close to zero and statistically insignificant. This implies that people choose state employment for other reasons, and thus that the state must work to secure their loyalty through incentives and/or socialization.

Model 4 probes this null relationship further. The results suggest that in addition, the preference for government employment is not significantly related to prioritizing things like stability, economic growth, transparency, equality, or redistribution over political freedom. In fact, as Figure 11.2 shows descriptively, the same priorities are widely held among students who intend to pursue careers both in and outside of government. Additionally, I find no evidence that students who believe that autocracies are better able to deliver on the things they prioritize are more likely to want a public sector career. Again, the coefficient is close to zero and statistically insignificant.

I next repeat these tests only for the group that is most likely to pursue a career in the state administration. The results in column 1 of Table 11.3 are broadly similar to the results in column 1 of Table 11.2. Access both to parental and university networks appears to be a strong driver of employment in the state administration. The main difference from preceding models is that being a "transition loser" loses statistical significance. That is, transition winners and transition losers have about the same probability of pursuing a position working directly for the state in public administration. I also find that the relative size of the coefficients for the universities changes, consistent with the fact that MGIMO has the stronger alumni network in public administration.

Model 2 again adds the additional items on career motivations. While the coefficients on the variables in column 1 remain very similar, several new patterns emerge in comparing the job motivations of those entering the public

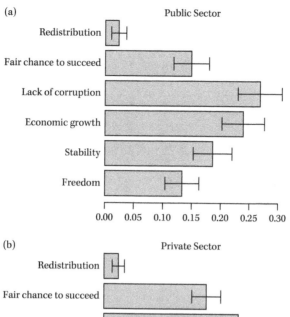

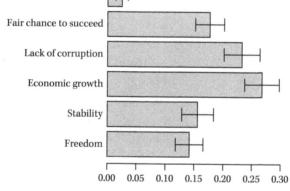

FIGURE 11.2(a) Private Sector; (b) Public Sector

Notes: The figure shows that students planning to enter the public sector from elite universities share similar views on national priorities. Economic growth and combatting corruption are viewed as top priorities among both future public servants and others. The bars are 95% confidence intervals.

sector as a whole to the motivations of those entering public administration. In particular, I find that the public service motivation of those who intend to join the state administration is weaker (though the coefficient is still positive, it loses significance), as is the desire to work independently ($p < .05$). Additionally, the choice of major less clearly dictates a career in the state administration, consistent with the skills necessary to succeed in this area being more easily transferable to other white-collar positions. There is also no evidence that students who plan to work for the state administration are less ambitious than their peers, as seemed to be the case for other public sector professions. The coefficient on career growth is close to zero and statistically

TABLE 11.3 } Models Predicting Employment in State Administration

	Background	Motivation	Political Values	Political Values and Priorities
	(1)	(2)	(3)	(4)
Prioritizes stability				0.364 (0.382)
Prioritizes economy				0.912 (0.752)
Prioritizes corruption				0.340 (0.714)
Prioritizes equality				0.232 (0.725)
Autocracy delivers			-0.015 (0.410)	0.546 (0.746)
Democracy preferable				0.123 (0.430)
Democratic institutions index		-0.320 (0.262)	-0.336 (0.238)	-0.267 (0.254)
Salary			-0.354 (0.266)	-0.371 (0.275)
Benefits		0.030 (0.232)	0.071 (0.236)	0.060 (0.242)
Serve my country		0.340 (0.202)	0.263 (0.203)	0.213 (0.209)
Prestige		0.286 (0.227)	0.266 (0.227)	0.232 (0.231)
Stability		0.198 (0.203)	0.202 (0.203)	0.155 (0.207)
Independence		-0.463* (0.209)	-0.425* (0.212)	-0.327 (0.225)
Related to major		0.197 (0.188)	0.217 (0.190)	0.304 (0.199)
Broad skills		0.110 (0.216)	0.129 (0.217)	0.124 (0.222)
Specialization		0.002 (0.240)	0.023 (0.241)	0.074 (0.252)
Career growth		-0.096 (0.310)	-0.056 (0.316)	-0.084 (0.328)
Risky/novel		0.374 (0.202)	0.362 (0.207)	0.381 (0.211)
Flexible		-0.597 (0.201)	-0.564** (0.204)	-0.597** (0.210)
Work/life balance		-0.095 (0.231)	-0.089 (0.240)	-0.113 (0.247)
Make contacts		0.159 (0.228)	0.173 (0.231)	0.155 (0.233)
Public sector parent	0.979*** (0.286)	0.849* (0.334)	0.842* (0.335)	0.763* (0.343)
MGIMO	1.350*** (0.340)	1.662*** (0.418)	1.658*** (0.421)	1.609*** (0.428)
MGU	0.787* (0.381)	1.184** (0.450)	1.217** (0.452)	1.248** (0.461)
Transition loser	0.479 (0.356)	0.207 (0.430)	0.124 (0.443)	0.168 (0.452)
Male	0.649* (0.271)	0.521 (0.324)	0.491 (0.331)	0.412 (0.342)
Urbanicity	-0.004 (0.072)	0.025 (0.081)	0.017 (0.082)	0.001 (0.083)
Orthodox	0.306 (0.270)	0.036 (0.329)	0.064 (0.332)	-0.012 (0.345)
Parents' education	-0.228 (0.245)	-0.270 (0.291)	-0.265 (0.301)	-0.268 (0.306)
Parents' occupation	-0.514 (0.311)	-0.601 (0.388)	-0.577 (0.393)	-0.647 (0.403)
Income	0.125 (0.099)	0.026 (0.121)	0.034 (0.123)	0.029 (0.124)
Constant	-5.886*** (1.175)	-6.408** (2.083)	-6.355** (2.090)	-6.697** (2.169)

(Continued)

TABLE 11.3 *Continued*

	Background	Motivation	Political Values	Political Values and Priorities
	(1)	(2)	(3)	(4)
Observations	938	717	711	687
Log likelihood	-207.740	-149.800	-147.864	-142.688
Akaike inf. crit.	441.479	353.599	353.729	353.375

Note: * $p < 0.05$; ** $p < 0.01$; *** $p < 0.001$. Logistic regressions predicting employment in public administration. All models include dummies for class year and field. The reference category is "freedom" for the question on priorities and the HSE for university.

insignificant, and the sign of the coefficient on prestige flips, becoming positive, though it does not reach conventional levels of significance. As with other public sector professionals, however, I find that students planning to pursue careers in the state administration prioritize flexibility less than their private sector counterparts.

Next, if the state administration is more highly politicized than educational or medical institutions, political values may play a more prominent role in the choice to serve the government directly than in the preference for a budget-sector position. In model 3 I explore this possibility but find only weak evidence in its favor. The notion that democracy is preferable to other systems is, as before, unrelated to the choice of a career in the state administration. While the preference for democratic institutions leans negative and the coefficient is somewhat larger than before, it is imprecisely estimated ($p > 0.1$). Adding the additional items on national priorities in column 4 further confirms that political values are at best weakly related to the choice to join the state administration. By contrast, attending a university with a strong alumni network or having a parent in the public sector are far stronger predictors.

Table 11.4 tests the robustness of these results. As a first step, I disaggregate the democratic institutions index into its component parts: views on the importance of elections, free speech, a free press, independent courts, equality before the law, minority rights, and a strong opposition. Also, because one might be concerned about the causal order of political values and job motivations or the overall number of parameters estimated in the preceding models, I estimate these models with only the controls for background characteristics. The model in column 1 predicts employment in any part of the public sector. The results are broadly consistent with the preceding models. Only one of the democratic institutions items is significant, minority rights, and it is signed positive, meaning that those who favor minority rights are more likely to seek state employment than others. Meanwhile, as before, networks and being a loser in the post-communist transition remain clear drivers of the choice of

TABLE 11.4 } Robustness Tests

	Dependent Variable			
	State Employment		Public Administration	
	(1)	(2)	(3)	(4)
Elections	-0.118 (0.108)		-0.272 (0.175)	
Free speech	-0.011 (0.122)		0.116 (0.215)	
Free press	-0.081 (0.108)		-0.319 (0.185)	
Independent courts	-0.053 (0.128)		-0.022 (0.213)	
Equality before the law	-0.011 (0.139)		0.135 (0.230)	
Minority rights	0.170 (0.079)		0.070 (0.138)	
Strong opposition	-0.134 (0.082)		0.054 (0.149)	
Democracy preferable	0.141 (0.186)		-0.282 (0.378)	
Our country should be feared		0.050 (0.091)		0.089 (0.171)
Our country better		-0.143 (0.082)		0.145 (0.171)
Hierarchy at home		-0.065 (0.168)		0.471 (0.348)
Hierarchy at work		0.041 (0.168)		0.294 (0.318)
Authorities should be feared	-	0.088 (0.097)		0.115 (0.181)
Public sector parent	0.280 (0.161)	0.386* (0.166)	1.003** (0.310)	1.084** (0.330)
MGIMO	0.368 (0.205)	0.423 (0.219)	1.375*** (0.364)	1.115** (0.378)
MGU	0.972*** (0.187)	0.936*** (0.188)	0.651 (0.408)	0.488 (0.411)
Transition loser	0.822*** (0.218)	0.700** (0.219)	0.462 (0.386)	0.564 (0.388)
Male	-0.225(0.163)	0.712* (0.299)	0.605 (0.313)	-0.230 (0.166)
Urbanicity	-0.080* (0.040)-	-0.023 (0.075)	0.053 (0.082)	-0.033 (0.041)
Orthodox	-0.280 (0.162)	-0.298 (0.169)	0.276 (0.289)	0.133 (0.314)
Parents' education	0.138 (0.159)	0.069 (0.161)	-0.155 (0.267)	-0.334 (0.273)
Parents' occupation	-0.222 (0.200)	-0.204 (0.202)	-0.431 (0.337)	-0.452 (0.350)
Income	0.022 (0.058)	0.047 (0.061)	0.134 (0.106)	-0.001 (0.120)
Constant	0.346(0.652)	-0.415 (0.664)	-5.544 (1.298)	-6.133 (1.331)
Observations	823	766	823	766
Log likelihood	-497.065	-467.104	-182.792	162.281
Akaike inf. crit.	1,036.130	970.207	407.584	360.561

Note: * $p < 0.05$; ** $p < 0.01$; *** $p < 0.001$. Logistic regressions. All models include dummies for class year and field. HSE is the reference category for university.

public employment, though attending MGIMO ($p = .07$) and having a parent who works in the public sector ($p = .08$) are just shy of the conventional $p = .05$ threshold.

Next, in column 2, I investigate whether more autocratic types show a preference for state employment, using several implicit measures. Rather than measure the preference for democracy directly, I here exploit items that tap chauvinism and deference to authority as indirect measures of anti-democratic tendencies. None of these five items is significantly related to state employment. Indeed, the coefficients are small and the signs inconsistent. As a whole, these tests roundly confirm the importance of networks and transition experience over political self-sorting.

In columns 3 and 4, I perform the same tests for employment in the state administration. Again, there is little evidence of political self-selection. The signs on the individual democratic institutions items are mixed and none of the coefficients is statistically significant. Similarly, there is no clear relationship between implicit authoritarianism and the likelihood of entering public administration. These models also reinforce the finding in Table 11.3 regarding networks. Once more, strong networks that enhance career prospects (i.e., attending a university with many alumni in government or having a parent working in the public sector) are the clearest predictors of a civil service career.

Discussion and Conclusion

Put succinctly, opportunism (and, for some, the desire to serve) rather than ideology drives career choice among students in Russia's elite universities today. Although I did not find evidence consistent with hypothesis 1, that the preference for public employment will be stronger among students who prioritize financial gain, I found clear, consistent support for hypotheses 2 and 3.[6] Both attending a school with a strong alumni network in government and having a parent who works in the public sector significantly increased the likelihood of a public sector career. Consistent with hypothesis 2, being a student at MGIMO was a strong predictor of joining the state administration. Similarly, having a parent working in the public sector significantly increased the likelihood that a student believed she would obtain a potentially lucrative spot in the bureaucracy. The latter finding echoes existing work that demonstrates strong intergenerational effects in Russia's labor market (Borisov and Pissarides 2016; Yastrebov 2011). It underscores the importance of informal networks for securing positions in the public sector among those with similar backgrounds and elite educations. Indeed, the importance of having a parent who works in the public sector held even after controlling for parental education and occupation (which were not significant predictors of a public sector career), suggesting that its effect is due primarily to networks and nepotism rather than intergenerational transmission of human capital.

By contrast, I find very little support for hypothesis 4, that the preference for public employment will be stronger among students who hold more authoritarian values. Across all models, I find no significant differences between future state and private sector workers in their preference for democracy, their attitudes toward the importance of democratic institutions, the way that they rank political freedom compared with other priorities like economic growth and stability, or the view that autocracies are better at delivering on these priorities. They are also similar in their views of specific democratic institutions. What is more, I find little evidence to suggest that students who implicitly hold more authoritarian attitudes self-select into government employment. Clearly some do gravitate toward government employment for ideological reasons. However, even for those entering the state administration, such considerations appear rarely to be paramount.

In terms of hypothesis 5, the results provide mixed evidence on whether transition losers are more likely to prefer careers in the state sector. In short, the answer appears to vary across the different parts of the public sector. While the relationship between post-communist transition experiences and employment choice is weak for the state administration, it is robust for the state sector as a whole. This suggests that transition losers are more likely to take budget sector positions, which are less prestigious and less well remunerated, while winners and losers alike chose positions in the state administration.

Finally, there is some evidence consistent with hypothesis 6 that the preference for public employment is stronger among students who prioritize their chosen profession as compared with students whose employment preferences are less closely tied to their majors. Having a strong desire for a particular occupational profile related to one's major was a marginally significant predictor of state employment in models 2 and 4 of Table 11.2 ($p < 0.1$). It was not, however, significantly associated with the likelihood of employment in the state administration. The results thus imply that at least one reason students with certain majors expect to have government jobs is that their alternatives are limited. While the skill set for a position in a research, medical, or educational institution is highly specialized, the skills required for a position in the state administration are more readily employed in other white-collar and managerial positions, whether in the public or private sector. Thus skill specificity and the structure of the labor market compel students in certain fields to take up jobs in the public sector.

These findings largely echo Houston (2014, 851), who concludes that the public service motivation remains weak across the government sector in Russia and five other former communist-bloc countries, but stronger in the budget sector than in public administration.[7] Like Houston, I find that the similarities between public and private sector workers in Russia are more pronounced than the differences with regard to extrinsic motivations such as salary and benefits. Both sets of findings cast doubt on the notion that the public and private sectors attract very different types of people.

The evidence thus suggests that insofar as public and private sector workers hold different attitudes and engage in different political behaviors (Rosenfeld 2017; Smyth, Sobolev, and Soboleva 2013), these differences primarily emerge only later. They are incentivized and socialized through the workplace and arise as a function of the employment setting (Frye, Reuter, and Szakonyi 2014, 2018). With regard to bribe-taking and other illicit behavior, Gans-Morse et al. (2017, 5) conclude similarly that "corruption in Russia results more from the transformation of bureaucrats' behavior and attitudes after joining the civil service, rather than from a process of corrupt self-selection." In sum, then, this evidence is consistent with the view that Russia's large public sector still serves, as did universal state employment under communism (Kornai 1992; Rona-Tas 1997), as an important tool for managing the economic self-interest and loyalty of citizens.

Notes

I wish to thank Mark Beissinger, Mark Urnov, Valeria Kasamara, and Marina Maksimenkova as well as the Laboratory for Political Studies at the National Research University Higher School of Economics in Moscow for their collaboration on the survey used in this project. I am grateful also to Jordan Gans-Morse for helpful comments and Fiza Kahn for excellent research assistance.

1. Contrary to these trends, the absolute number employed in science and research declined dramatically.

2. Exceptions dealing directly with autocratic contexts include Gans-Morse et al. 2017 on Russia and Liu and Wang 2017 on China.

3. See, e.g., Fox and Lawless 2005 for a similar argument.

4. It is beyond the present study to definitively parse the effect of family ties that runs through networks from the effect of family ties that runs through human capital transfers, or transfers of knowledge that heighten the probability of success in securing a government job. However, after controlling for parental education and occupation, most of any additional effect of having a parent who works in the public sector can plausibly be attributed to nepotism and networks. See, e.g., Lentz and Leband 1989.

5. The resulting measure ranges from -2 to 2, with -2 indicating "not at all important" and 2 indicating "very important." An index consisting of the average of these responses was chosen over an additive index in order to preserve observations for which at least one item was missing. The results are similar using either approach.

6. Measuring financial incentives in terms of salary and benefits has obvious drawbacks. Students entering the government in Russia can expect to make lower salaries than their counterparts in the private sector. Still, opportunities to exploit one's official position (for informal benefits that the available survey questions may not have fully captured) could, alternatively, explain the preference for a public sector profession. In a closely related study also among students at the HSE, however, Gans-Morse et al. (2017) find that those who are willing to cheat and bribe self-select out of state careers.

7. Gans-Morse et al. (2017) are more optimistic about the role of public service motivation in Russia, though much of its effect again appears concentrated in the budget sector.

References

Alatas, Vivi, Lisa Cameron, Ananish Chaudhuri, Nisvan Erkal, and Lata Gangadharan. 2009. "Subject Pool Effects in a Corruption Experiment: A Comparison of Indonesian Public Servants and Indonesian Students." *Experimental Economics* 12, no. 1: 113–132.

Anderson, John. 2007. "Putin and the Russian Orthodox Church: Asymmetric Symphonia?" *Journal of International Affairs* 61, no. 1: 185–201.

Banerjee, Ritwik, Tushi Baul, and Tanya Rosenblat. 2015. "On Self Selection of the Corrupt into the Public Sector." *Economics Letters* 127: 43–46.

Barfort, Sebastian, Nikolaj Harmon, Frederik Hjorth, and Asmus Leth Olsen. 2015. "Dishonesty and Selection into Public Service in Denmark: Who Runs the World's Least Corrupt Public Sector?" Working paper, University of Copenhagen, Department of Economics. http://www.econ.ku.dk/english/research/publications/wp/dp_2015/1512.pdf.

Behar, Alberto, and Junghwan Mok. 2013. "Does Public-Sector Employment Fully Crowd Out Private-Sector Employment?" IMF Working Paper WP/13/146, June. http://www.imf.org/external/pubs/ft/wp/2013/wp13146.pdf.

Bian, Yanjie. 1994. "Guanxi and the Allocation of Urban Jobs in China." *China Quarterly* 140: 971–999.

Borisov, Gleb V., and Christopher A. Pissarides. 2016. "The Intergenerational Transmission of Human Capital and Earnings in Contemporary Russia." IZA Discussion Paper No. 10300. http://ftp.iza.org/dp10300.pdf.

Dal Bo, Ernesto, Frederico Finan, and Martin A. Ross. 2013. "Strengthening State Capabilities: The Role of Financial Incentives in the Call to Public Service." *Quarterly Journal of Economics* 128, no. 3: 1169–1218.

Dong, Hsiang-Kai Dennis. 2014. "Individual Risk Preference and Sector Choice: Are Risk-Averse Individuals More Likely to Choose Careers in the Public Sector?" *Administration and Society* 49, no. 8: 1121–1142.

Fox, Richard L., and Jennifer L. Lawless. 2005. "To Run or Not to Run for Office: Explaining Nascent Political Ambition." *American Journal of Political Science* 49, no. 3: 642–659.

Frye, Timothy, Ora John Reuter, and David Szakonyi. 2014. "Political Machines at Work: Voter Mobilization and Electoral Subversion in the Workplace." *World Politics* 66, no. 2: 195–228.

Frye, Timothy, Ora John Reuter, and David Szakonyi. 2018. "Hitting Them with Carrots: Voter Intimidation and Vote Buying in Russia." *British Journal of Political Science* 49, no. 3: 857–881.

Gabris, Gerald T., and Gloria Simo. 1995. "Public Sector Motivation as an Independent Variable Affecting Career Decisions." *Public Personnel Management* 24, no. 1: 33–51.

Gans-Morse, Jordan, Alexander S. Kalgin, Andrei V. Klimenko, and Andrei A. Yakovlev. 2017. "Motivations for Public Service in Corrupt States: Evidence from Post-Soviet Russia." National Research University Higher School of Economics Working Paper No. WP BRP 13/PSP/2017. http://dx.doi.org/10.2139/ssrn.3072181.

Gerber, Alan S., and Gregory A. Huber. 2009. "Partisanship and Economic Behavior: Do Partisan Differences in Economic Forecasts Predict Real Economic Behavior?" *American Political Science Review* 103, no. 3: 407–426.

Gerber, Theodore P., and David R. Schaefer. 2004. "Horizontal Stratification of Higher Education in Russia: Trends, Gender Differences, and Labor Market Outcomes." *Sociology of Education* 77, no. 1: 32–59.

Gimpelson, Vladimir, and Daniel Treisman. 2002. "Fiscal Games and Public Employment: A Theory with Evidence from Russia." *World Politics* 54, no. 2: 145–183.

Gorodnichenko, Yuriy, and Klara Sabirianova Peter. 2007. "Public Sector Pay and Corruption: Measuring Bribery from Micro Data." *Journal of Public Economics* 91, no. 5: 963–991.

Greene, Kenneth F. 2010. "The Political Economy of Authoritarian Single-Party Dominance." *Comparative Political Studies* 43, no. 7: 807–834.

Hanna, Rema, and Sheng-Yi Wang. 2017. "Dishonesty and Selection into Public Service: Evidence from India." *American Economic Journal: Economic Policy* 9, no. 3: 262–290.

Houston, David J. 2014. "Public Service Motivation in the Post-Communist State." *Public Administration* 92, no. 4: 843–860.

Karl, Katherine A., and Cynthia L. Sutton. 1998. "Job Values in Today's Workforce: A Comparison of Public and Private Sector Employees." *Public Personnel Management* 27, no. 4: 515–527.

Kornai, Janos. 1992. *The Socialist System: The Political Economy of Communism.* Oxford: Oxford University Press.

Kristiansen, Stein, and Muhid Ramli. 2006. "Buying an Income: The Market for Civil Service Positions in Indonesia." *Contemporary Southeast Asia* 28, no. 2: 207–233.

Krueger, Alan B. 1988. "The Determinants of Queues for Federal Jobs." *Industrial and Labor Relations Review* 41, no. 4: 567–581.

Lee, Ching Kwan, and Yonghong Zhang. 2013. "The Power of Instability: Unraveling the Microfoundations of Bargained Authoritarianism in China." *American Journal of Sociology* 118, no. 6: 1475–1508.

Lentz, Bernard F., and David N. Leband. 1989. "Why So Many Children of Doctors Become Doctors: Nepotism vs. Human Capital Transfers." *Journal of Human Resources* 24, no. 3: 396–413.

Lewis, Gregory B., and Sue A. Frank. 2002. "Who Wants to Work for the Government?" *Public Administration Review* 62, no. 4: 395–404.

Liu, Hanzhang, and Yuhua Wang. 2017. "Elite School Networks and Working for the Government: Natural Experimental Evidence from China." Unpublished manuscript, Harvard University. http://scholar.harvard.edu/files/yuhuawang/files/vocation.pdf.

McConnell, Christopher, Yotam Margalit, Neil Malhotra, and Matthew Levendusky. 2018. "The Economic Consequences of Partisanship in a Polarized Era." *American Journal of Political Science* 62, no. 1: 5–18.

Nurmagambetov, A. A., and S. K. Azhmetov. 2010. "Rol' formiruemogo srednego klassa v transformat-sii obshchestvennykh otnoshenij i formirovanii grazhdanskogo obshchestva v Kazakhstane." In *Fenomen sotsial'noj inzhenerii: opyt i rekonstruktsiia budushchego. Materialy mezhdunarodoj nauchno-prakticheskoj konferentsii, 21–22 maia 2010,* ed. M. M. Tazhin, 234–239. Almaty, Kazakhstan: Fond Pervogo Prezidenta Respubliki Kazakhstan.

Rona-Tas, Akos. 1997. *The Great Surprise of the Small Transformation: The Demise of Communism and the Rise of the Private Sector in Hungary.* Ann Arbor: University of Michigan Press.

Rosenfeld, Bryn. 2017. "Reevaluating the Middle Class Protest Paradigm: A Case-Control Study of Democratic Protest Coalitions in Russia." *American Political Science Review* 111, no. 4: 637–652.

Sharunina, A. V. 2013. "Iavliaetsia li rossijskij 'budzhetnik' 'neudachnikom'? Analiz mezhsek-tornykh razlichij v oplate truda." *Ekonomicheskij Zhurnal* 17, no. 1: 75–107.

Smyth, Regina, Anton Sobolev, and Irina Soboleva. 2013. "Patterns of Discontent: Identifying the Participant Core in Russian Post-Election Protest." Paper presented at the conference "Russia's Winter of Discontent: Taking Stock of Changing State-Society Relationships," Uppsala University, September 6–7. https://www.ires.uu.se/digitalAssets/254/c_254668-l_3-k_discontentconfsmythpatternsofdiscontent.pdf.

Tucker, Joshua. 2006. *Regional Economic Voting: Russia, Poland, Hungary, Slovakia and the Czech Republic, 1990–1999*. Cambridge: Cambridge University Press.

Tucker, Joshua A., Alexander C. Pacek, and Adam J. Berinsky. 2002. "Transitional Winners and Losers: Attitudes Toward EU Membership in Post-Communist Countries." *American Journal of Political Science* 46, no. 3: 557–571.

Yastrebov, G. A. 2011. "Kharakter strati katsii rossijskogo obshchestva v sravnitel'nom kontekste." *Vestnik Obshchestvennogo Mneniia* 4, no. 110: 15–27.

12 }

Conclusion

CHINA, RUSSIA, AND THE AUTHORITARIAN EMBRACE
OF GLOBALIZATION

Mark R. Beissinger

Russia and China are exceptional in many regards. Their size, power, and ambition on the world stage alone place them in a different category from most states. Size presents special challenges for rulers; it complicates penetration of populations, renders integration of government activity more difficult, raises problems with enforcement of laws and rules and the protection of borders, and helps to foster regionalism and separatism. All these issues are substantial in both Russia and China. Yet despite being two of the world's largest states, China and Russia are relatively strong states compared to the states run by most authoritarian regimes. Hanson and Sigman (2013) use a large number of variables to capture three dimensions of state capacity (extractive, coercive, and administrative). The global average for all states in the 2000s for 162 countries was .12, while the global average for all non-democracies in the 2000s (6 or less on the Polity scale) was -.41. Russia and China in the 2000s scored .45 and .54, respectively (Hanson and Sigman 2013).[1] Moreover, China and Russia are not merely large and relatively strong states. They are globally powerful states that exert influence far beyond their borders. In 2018 China accounted for 19 percent of the world's GDP—behind only the United States. Russia's economic power pales before that of China (approximately 2 percent of global GDP). But Russian military capabilities are second only to American military power.

  Yet, as the authors in this volume have demonstrated, a great deal about authoritarian politics can be learned from these two exceptional and extremely powerful non-democracies. Russian and Chinese regimes face many of the same challenges in maintaining their power and control over increasingly educated, diverse, and globally connected populations as other non-democratic regimes. However, as these chapters detail, they have managed these challenges through distinct strategies. Russia has a form of electoral authoritarianism, with its rhythms largely revolving around its managed electoral cycles. By contrast, China continues to have a non-competitive authoritarianism, with the Communist Party playing the key role of ensuring integration, control, and implementation of the leadership's directives. Its rhythms tend to revolve around moments of reform and retrenchment, as well as around unpredictable leadership succession crises. The essays in this volume provide us with a clear sense of the differences between these two forms of authoritarian rule. As the authors also show, China and Russia represent different models when it comes to the roles of institutions and personal relations as ways of binding individuals to the state. Whereas the Putin regime relies heavily on patronage and personal ties to manage state-society relations, China's communist regime relies heavily on rules and institutions. As Valerie Bunce, Karrie Koesel, and Jessica Chen Weiss put it (Chapter 1), China's regime "is committed to building rule of law as a key way to create a more predictable and therefore more stable political environment," seeking to "maximize certainty," while the Putin regime "is best described as preferring rule without law," aiming instead to "manipulate uncertainty" to its advantage.

This is a key insight into the nature of modern authoritarianism, and these divergent approaches to authoritarian rule and their limits are well exemplified in many of this volume's chapters. Maria Repnikova (Chapter 5) illustrates the very different ways in which Chinese and Russian regimes manage the media (through the certainty of law and institutions or the manipulation of uncertainty). Diana Fu and Greg Distelhorst (Chapter 3) show how China's participatory institutions continue to function to channel participation even as possibilities for contentious politics have grown more constricted under Xi. Bryn Rosenfeld (Chapter 11) elucidates how the staffing practices of Russia's bureaucracies reinforce the personalist character of the regime even at an early age, as recruitment into the civil service occurs largely on the basis of parental connections and alumni networks. And Manfred Elstrom's study of government responses to labor unrest in China (Chapter 8) reveals that the Chinese government's policies are still shaped in critical ways by its socialist legitimation—particularly its fear that worker unrest in the state sector might fundamentally challenge its rule.

The differences between Chinese and Russian approaches to authoritarian rule are rooted in their divergent histories over the last forty years—and particularly in the great divide of the 1980s. There was a time when the study of Russian politics closely resembled the study of Chinese politics—so much so that scholars of Soviet and Chinese politics spoke in identical analytical languages and referenced the same theories of totalitarianism, modernization, and bureaucratic politics to frame the phenomena that they studied. While Chinese communism and Soviet communism were on divergent paths by the

1960s, for both regimes the 1980s—the Soviet collapse and the disorders of Tiananmen—proved to be the conjuncture that continues to weigh heavily on the trajectory of politics in both states. As Aleksandar Matovski notes (Chapter 9), the Soviet collapse and the disorders that followed constitute the main reference point for Russian citizens in evaluating politics; they have functioned as a key justification for Putin's personalist and recentralizing rule—though as Bunce, Koesel, and Weiss observe, Russia still retains elements of its experiment with democracy in the 1990s, even if in perverted form. By contrast, the example of Soviet dissolution and the disorders of Tiananmen led to a decades-long effort in China to revitalize one-party rule by creating channels for popular participation, allowing contained forms of contentious politics, and reining in corruption and abuses by local officials—even while cracking down harshly on dissident opposition.

Despite these differences, Bunce, Koesel, and Weiss emphasize the common dilemma that authoritarian rulers face in the trade-off between compliance and information. As they put it, "Getting good information can undercut popular compliance, yet maximizing compliance often means forfeiting good information." Jeremy Wallace (Chapter 2), for instance, points to the serious problems of subterfuge that the Chinese regime encountered in relying excessively on quantitative measures of performance (the ultimate bureaucratic dream). Xi has instead reverted to less formalized modes of evaluation, but these too contain the potential for abuse through the personalism that they may inject into administrative relationships. In Russia clientelism pervades the administrative apparatus, leading to the mushrooming of venal behaviors and a fundamental unaccountability of officialdom at all levels. Not only has this severely held back efforts at economic modernization, but as Matovski details, it also presented challenges for regime legitimation, playing a key role in instigating the mobilizational waves that emerged from Russia's middle class during the 2011–2012 electoral cycle. Ultimately, there is no definitive solution to the trade-off between information and compliance in authoritarian regimes. The cycling behaviors to which it gives rise long plagued Chinese and Soviet communism and continue to plague their contemporary heirs.

But while Russia and China represent different forms of authoritarian rule, there is another dimension to the great divide of the 1980s that has rendered Chinese and Russian authoritarianisms increasingly similar to each other: their embrace of globalization (defined here simply as intensified interactions across state borders).[2] Until the 1980s, Russia and China remained largely fenced off from the rest of the world, constituting some of the most isolated countries on the planet. This isolation had strongly negative effects for both Russian and Chinese economic development. Cut off from international technological change and from market pressures for greater quality, productivity, and efficiency, the largely autarkic centrally planned economies of Soviet and Chinese communism were, by the late 1970s, incapable of adapting to late twentieth-century economic and military competition. In 1985, at a time when 19 percent of the world's GDP consisted of foreign trade, foreign trade (according to the CIA) constituted only 10 percent of Soviet GDP, and half of this was trade with countries in the Council for Mutual Economic Assistance (Hanson 2003, 119–120). According to the World Bank, only 9 percent of China's GDP in 1985 came from foreign trade—having recovered from a low of 3 to 4 percent at the time of the Cultural Revolution. Prior to the 1980s, communist regimes discouraged citizens from all personal contact and personal relationships with the outside world. Indeed, under Stalin marrying a foreigner was considered an act of treason, and even after the annulment of this law under Khrushchev, Soviet citizens who dated or married foreigners were subject to harassment. Analogous constraints existed in China as well. The right to travel abroad was nonexistent in communist countries. A limited number of lucky Soviet citizens could vacation in Warsaw Pact countries, but in general foreign travel was impossible for most. Visits by foreigners to China were severely constricted; indeed, from 1961 to 1978 only 6,400 foreigners worked in all of China (Brady 2003, 3). Moreover, Chinese foreign travel abroad during this period was minimal. Like the Soviet Union, communist China developed a set of specialized organizations for dealing with and controlling foreigners and subjected all interactions with foreigners to high levels of surveillance. Foreign media were banned, and massive efforts were made to block infiltration of uncensored information from the outside world.

Communist polities were extreme in their attempts to control their citizens' interactions with the outside world. But they reflected a certain dimension of authoritarian politics that has been relatively poorly theorized—that is, in general non-democracies have lagged significantly behind democracies in the extent to which their economies and their citizens are connected abroad. Certainly part of this has to do with the lower level of economic development in non-democracies. But even controlling for the effect of GDP per capita on levels of globalization as measured by the KOF Index of Globalization (a composite benchmark created by the Swiss Economic Institute to gauge the economic, social, and political dimensions of globalization along twenty-three variables for 187 countries), non-democracies are significantly less globalized than democracies (Gygli, Haelg, and Strum 2018; Dreher 2008).[3] Thus, in a cross-national time-series regression over the 1970–2014 period that controlled for the effect of GDP per capita and for both fixed country and year effects, non-democracies score 3.5 points lower than democracies on the KOF Index of Globalization across the entire period.[4] But the price of isolation for non-democracies has been high, and as the democratic world globalized, so too have non-democracies. If the average score for non-democracies on the KOF Index of Globalization in 1990 was 34.0, by 2014 it had risen to 50.7. As can be seen in Figure 12.1, the late 1990s was a period of growing disparity between democracies and non-democracies in terms of global integration. However, by the 2000s the gap between democracies and non-democracies

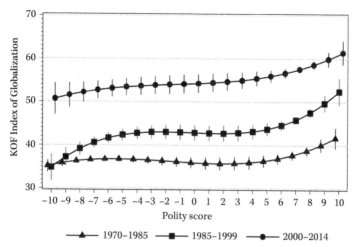

FIGURE 12.1 Globalization and Political Openness, by Time Period

had narrowed considerably—especially among more autocratic regimes like China and Russia.[5] This non-democratic embrace of globalization in the 2000s is an important story that has been largely ignored in conventional studies of authoritarianism—though it is increasingly evident that it can no longer be overlooked.

Of course, globalization has long been thought to have a fraught relationship with democracy. Critics argue that it undermines the sovereignty of political communities over key economic processes within their territories, leads to uncontrolled flows of capital across borders, constrains political choice and shifts the costs of business onto public coffers, greatly exacerbates social inequalities, and threatens cultural distinctiveness through massive migrations and the homogenization of values and ways of life.[6]

But what happens when non-democracies globalize? Clearly, globalization involves similar threats of elusive control over economic processes, assaults on cultural distinctiveness, and increased social inequality in non-democracies as in democracies. But for non-democracies globalization has involved additional risks. Isolated citizenries are more easily controlled. They lack opportunities for exit, have difficulty using external states as leverage to enhance voice, and are more easily influenced by propaganda aimed at ensuring their loyalty. This was why communist regimes imposed such extreme restrictions on their citizens in the first place. There are good reasons non-democracies have lagged in terms of globalization compared to democracies, since, in addition to challenging state sovereignty, globalization contains within it processes that potentially reduce the ability of regimes to dominate their citizens. This is why globalization was long thought to have promoted democratization (see, for instance, Eichengreen and Leblang 2007. For a contrary finding, see Milner and Mukherjee 2009). The political challenges of globalization for non-democracies are precisely those that communist regimes long feared—that exposure to the outside world might infect citizens with foreign ideas, undermining regime control through increased information flows and providing citizens with opportunities to leverage their influence through connections abroad. Indeed, as a result of globalization there is no such thing anymore as a purely domestic political opposition; almost all oppositions take inspiration from foreign examples, are influenced by global events, connect with foreign NGOs or diasporas abroad, or attempt to leverage their influence through engagement with international actors (Tarrow 2005).

Russia and China are on the cutting edge of the non-democratic embrace of globalization and therefore have much to teach us about how globalization has interfaced with authoritarian rule. According to the KOF Index of Globalization, Russia and China are significantly above average compared to all other states in the extent to which they are engaged with the outside world (ranking 48th and 70th, respectively, out of 184 countries) and are among the most globalized of authoritarian states (ranking 9th and 16th among 78 non-democracies). As opposed to democratic regimes, Russia and China have created a statist version of globalization that differs qualitatively from the globalization pursued by democratic states (Harris 2009). In Russia, for instance, economic growth has been fueled by exports under the control of state-owned corporations or corporations owned by oligarchs closely connected with the Putin regime. In China state-owned banks control 60 percent of the country's cross-border investments. Large sovereign wealth funds controlled by governments in both countries cushion the impact of global economic fluctuations. China and Russia have engaged in significant protectionism to preserve the state's commanding position over the economy. State control over foreign investment opportunities has curbed the potential power of large multinational corporations to extract concessions in Russia and China, tipping the balance of power in favor of the state as opposed to business.

Figure 12.2 provides data for Russia and China from the KOF Index of Globalization for four components of the index—economic flows, trade restrictiveness, personal contacts, and information flows—for 1970, 1990, and 2014, with average scores for all states and all non-democracies. While Russia is somewhat more dependent than China on foreign trade and investment relative to its economy as a whole, China is more permissive than Russia in terms of tariffs, taxes, and restrictions on foreign accounts. The growth of economic globalization in both states has left them potentially exposed to influence from abroad in the guise of the large foreign presence on their soil and the leverage that foreign states potentially have through economic ties. One sees this, for instance, in the impact of sanctions on the Russian economy in the wake of Russia's 2014 invasion of Crimea. In the 2000s Russia became deeply integrated into global supply chains in its hydrocarbon and metals industries and highly dependent on European and American capital markets. After the

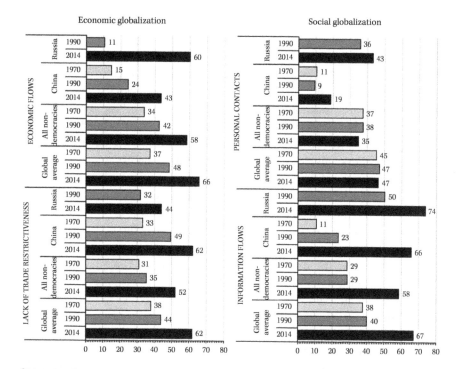

[a]KOF Index of Globalization (Gygli, Haelg, and Sturm 2018, Dreher 2008). Trade flow scores are based on trade as a percent of GDP, foreign direct investment as a percent of GDP, portfolio investment as a percent of GDP, and income payments to foreign nationals as a percent of GDP. Trade restrictiveness scores are based on information on hidden import barriers, mean tariff rates, taxes on international trade as a percent of current revenue, and capital account restrictions. Personal contact scores are based on telephone traffic, transfers as a percent of GDP, international tourism figures, foreign population as a percent of total population, and international letters per capita. Information flows scores are based on internet users per 1000 population, televisions per 1000 population, and trade in newspapers as a percent of GDP. Data for Russia for 1970 are missing.

FIGURE 12.2   Indicators of Economic and Social Globalization, Russia and China (1970, 1990, and 2014)[a]

Russian invasion of Crimea, Western sanctions targeted this vulnerability and, along with a dramatic drop in oil prices, helped to foster a significant contraction of the Russian economy.

In terms of information flows with the outside world, both China and Russia significantly exceed the average for all non-democracies, with Russia in particular well above the global average. Thus, in both countries citizens are potentially exposed to foreign information in ways that were absolutely unthinkable in earlier Russian and Chinese regimes. In the late 2000s many middle-income and upper-middle-income non-democracies like Russia experienced an explosion of internet and cellphone usage that opened up new information spaces that helped to fuel waves of instability. In the Russian case, this rapid growth of social media facilitated the organization of opposition, helping to give rise to the 2011–2012 electoral protests (Lynch 2012; Beissinger 2017). Russia and China differ in the level of personal contacts that citizens enjoy with the outside world. According to the KOF measures, the average level of personal contacts for all countries has remained relatively stable over the last fifty years (and has even slightly contracted for non-democracies). But for both Russia and China, personal contact by citizens with the outside world increased tremendously during this period. Russia approaches the global average (with a large portion of Russians traveling and working abroad for extended periods of time), while China still lags significantly below the average for non-democracies (despite the large numbers of Chinese students studying abroad and Chinese tourists visiting foreign countries). One assumes that this is in part a function of China's lower level of development and sheer size. But the Chinese state has also attempted to mediate the foreign contacts of its citizens in ways that Russia, at least until recently, has not.

A number of the essays in this volume detail the potential dangers that emerged to Chinese and Russian regimes as a result of this heightened global exposure, as well as the strategies that these regimes have adopted to counter them. Karrie Koesel and Valerie Bunce (Chapter 4), for instance, point to the steps that both Chinese and Russian regimes took to counter the threats posed by the spread of transnational waves of contention—what they call "diffusion-proofing" (i.e., "strategies that seek to discourage their citizens from modeling their behavior on the rebellious precedents set by their counterparts elsewhere") (Koesel and Bunce 2013, 754). They show how Russia and China deployed similar strategies of "diffusion-proofing" against different transnational waves of contention by framing and manipulating information about these waves, introducing sophisticated constraints on civil society associations and political opposition in order to weaken their ability to mount challenges, and engaging in "active measures" such as creating countermovements in order to marginalize challenges and control the public sphere. In this respect, as globalization has increased threats to instability, Chinese and Russian authoritarianisms have grown increasingly repressive in similar ways through their attempts to contain the fallout.

If communist regimes monopolized means of communication and traditionally engaged in massive efforts to socialize citizens and to censor information in order to control the beliefs of citizens, globalized authoritarian regimes like contemporary Russia and China operate in a fundamentally different information environment in which information from and about the outside world is readily available to their citizens—either through the internet or through legally operating international or domestic media. Nevertheless, both regimes still spend considerable energy trying to control how citizens think and generating support within their societies, though the tools by which they do so have changed. In the wake of the enormous growth of the internet, China's censorship practices have shifted to allow criticism of the state to be expressed, using it as a way of tracking and monitoring dissent—even while blocking content aimed at mobilizing citizens in collective action (King, Pan, and Roberts 2013). Russia's response to the growth of the internet had been looser, but beginning in 2012, in the wake of waves of internet-organized protests, it introduced a series of laws blacklisting "extremist" content. As Tomila Lankina, Kohei Watanabe, and Yulia Netesova (Chapter 6) demonstrate through the example of media coverage of the 2011–2012 protests in Russia, increasingly sophisticated framing efforts have become an important tool by which the Putin regime has sought to marginalize opponents—especially on widely watched state-run television. As they note, authoritarian rulers have come to recognize that "to keep viewers' and readers' attention and to discourage citizens from turning to independent media, the information projected on state television screens or in newspapers has to reflect political reality at least to some extent." Elizabeth Plantan (Chapter 7) documents how, in the face of the growth of civil society in Russia and China and foreign democracy-promotion efforts in the 2000s, Russia and China enacted strikingly similar legislation aimed at cutting off civil society associations from external sources of support and tightening regulations on the activities of foreign NGOs. Both regimes introduced novel forms of legal regulation of the interface between civil society and the outside world in the face of the potential threat of increased connections. Wallace points to how the Xi regime has shifted away from technocratic rule in favor of more politicized and ideological strategies of control—due in part to the increased threat to political stability emerging from China's global integration. And as Karrie Koesel shows (Chapter 10), in the face of increased connectivity and personal contacts among citizens with the outside world, both countries have reinvigorated efforts to foster political loyalty among youth through patriotic education. In their socialization efforts both states have come to emphasize nationalism and the defense of traditional values against the threat of liberal ideas and social mores imported from abroad.

Thus, while globalization has posed significant risks to Chinese and Russian authoritarianism, the statist strategies of both regimes have buffered its constraining effects while also leading to new forms of repression, pushing these regimes in surprisingly similar directions. But China and Russia have done more than simply devise innovative strategies for containing the potential impact of globalization on their regimes; they have devised novel methods for exploiting globalization to their advantage, harnessing it to undermine democratic opponents and to extend their influence around the world. Both countries, for instance, have engaged in massive investments abroad through state-controlled corporations in an effort to corner markets and resources. As China's economy has developed, it has also become one of the world's foremost purveyors of foreign aid and foreign investment to developing countries, multiplying its economic influence (Copper 2016). Both Chinese and Russian companies hold major investments within the United States and Europe. Chinese firms have significant holdings in American hotel, technology, appliance, food processing, newspaper, and entertainment industries (Gandel 2016). And until sanctions began to bite after Russia's invasion of Crimea, Russian investors poured billions of dollars into American real estate, gasoline distribution, steel, and technology companies. By 2018 the Chinese government owned $1.18 trillion of American debt (7.2 percent of total U.S. debt) (Kenny 2018). In short, China and Russia discovered that globalization is a two-way street; their state-directed versions of globalization have been skillful in reversing the flow of influence emerging from greater connectedness, harnessing the very factors of trade, aid, foreign investment, and information that once seemed to threaten their stability and using them to challenge the sovereignty of advanced democracies.

Perhaps nowhere has this been more evident than in the information sphere, where Russia and China long envied Western "soft power." After the color revolutions challenged Russian hegemony in the "near-abroad" in the mid-2000s, the Putin regime created a series of instruments aimed not only at undermining democratization efforts within Russia but also at undermining the entire project of liberal democracy on a global scale. Russia was able to penetrate significantly into the information spheres of advanced democracies, establishing a sophisticated international television broadcasting operation aimed at breaking the monopoly of Western news organizations (Rutland and Kazantsev 2016). It has repeatedly engaged in massive trolling and surreptitious social media campaigns in order to sow division within Western publics. And even as it has limited the activities of Western NGOs within Russia, it has created "think tanks" within Western societies aimed at influencing the media and public opinion. China has engaged in strikingly similar efforts (Shambaugh 2015). As Christopher Walker has put it:

> Today, authoritarian regimes are projecting power beyond their borders. They are targeting crucial democratic institutions, including elections and the media. They use deep economic and business ties to export corrupt practices and insinuate themselves into the politics of democracies, both new and established. They are influencing international public opinion and investing heavily in their own instruments of "soft power" in order to compete with democracy in the realm of ideas. . . . Through authoritarian learning (for example, by adapting or mimicking democratic forms) and by exploiting the opportunities presented by globalization, authoritarian trendsetters have created a modern antidemocratic toolkit that in many ways serves as the mirror image of democratic soft power. (Walker 2016, 49–51)

Indeed, Putin and Xi have become models for emulation among other non-democracies in a form of authoritarian diffusion that has helped to shore up the reversal of democracy in Eastern Europe, the Middle East, and Southeast Asia (see, for instance, Ambrosio 2010, 2012; Weyland 2017; Bader 2014).

In sum, the essays in this volume provide a rich understanding of the forces that have shaped the evolution of non-democracy over the past four decades. As a result of the great divide of the 1980s, Russian and Chinese authoritarianism assumed divergent form—one an electoral authoritarianism relying on personalism and clientelism to bind individuals to the regime, the other a single-party dictatorship deploying rules and institutions to ensure coherence. Many of the challenges that Russian and Chinese regimes face are in significant part the product of these different modes by which authoritarian rule is structured, shaping the strengths and vulnerabilities, openings and closings, and constraints and possibilities of each. But the differences emerging out of the choice between electoral authoritarianism and its alternatives are constrained by the commonalities these regimes share in the ways in which they have managed their shared embrace of globalization. Both have established similar statist versions of globalization that seek to contain the impact of external influences and global fluctuations even while integrating into the global economic system. And both have engaged in strikingly similar efforts to regulate their civil societies, cut them off from external sources of support, inoculate their citizens against foreign ideas, and utilize globalization to their advantage in countering and undermining the project of democracy abroad. In the long run, in their congruent handling of globalization and the challenges and opportunities it poses, Chinese and Russian authoritarianism may in fact be converging toward common forms of domination that render the institutional differences between competitive and non-competitive forms of authoritarianism moot.

Notes

1. The measure roughly ranges between -3 (absent state capacity) and 3 (extremely high state capacity), with an approximate mean of zero. For comparison, the global average for all democracies in the 2000s (greater than 6 on the Polity scale) was .78, while the average score for the United States was 1.98.

2. Anthony Giddens defined globalization as "the intensification of worldwide social relations which link distant localities in such a way that local happenings are shaped by events occurring many miles away and vice versa" (Giddens 1991, 64).

3. Non-democracy is defined here at 6 or lower on the Polity scale.

4. The results were statistically significant at the .001 level, with robust standard errors.

5. The results in Figure 12.1 are based on a cross-national time-series regression, controlling for the effects of GDP per capita and for fixed country effects.

6. For a sampling of some of the voluminous literature on the subject, see Hardt and Negri 2001; Stiglitz 2002; Held, Barnett, and Henderson 2005; Rodrik 2011.

References

Ambrosio, Thomas. 2010. "Constructing a Framework of Authoritarian Diffusion: Concepts, Dynamics, and Future Research." *International Studies Perspectives* 11, no. 4: 375–392.
Ambrosio, Thomas. 2012. "The Rise of the 'China Model' and 'Beijing Consensus': Evidence of Authoritarian Diffusion?" *Contemporary Politics* 18, no. 4: 381–399.

Bader, Max. 2014. "Democracy Promotion and Authoritarian Diffusion: The Foreign Origins of Post-Soviet Election Laws." *Europe-Asia Studies* 66, no. 8: 1350–1370.

Beissinger, Mark R. 2017. "'Conventional' and 'Virtual' Civil Societies in Autocratic Regimes." *Comparative Politics* 49, no. 3: 351–371.

Brady, Anne-Marie. 2003. *Making the Foreign Serve China: Managing Foreigners in the People's Republic.* Lanham, MD: Rowman & Littlefield.

Copper, John F. 2016. *China's Foreign Aid and Investment Diplomacy.* 3 vols. Basingstoke, UK: Springer.

Dreher, Axel. 2006. "Does Globalization Affect Growth? Evidence from a New Index of Globalization." *Applied Economics* 38, no. 10: 1091–1110.

Eichengreen, Barry, and David A. Leblang. 2007. "Democracy and Globalization." Bank for International Settlements Working Paper No. 219. https://papers.ssrn.com/sol3/papers.cfm?abstract_id=1011681.

Gandel, Stephen. 2016. "The Biggest American Companies Now Owned by the Chinese." *Fortune*, March 18.

Giddens, Anthony. 1991. *The Consequences of Modernity.* Cambridge: Polity Press.

Gygli, Savina, Florian Haelg, and Jan-Egbert Sturm. 2018. "The KOF Globalisation Index—Revisited." KOF Working Paper no. 439. Zurich, Switzerland. https://www.research-collection.ethz.ch/bitstream/handle/20.500.11850/238666/7/KOF_Globalisation%20Index_Revisited.pdf.

Hanson, Jonathan K., and Rachel Sigman. 2013. "Leviathan's Latent Dimensions: Measuring State Capacity for Comparative Political Research." Paper presented at the annual meeting of the American Political Science Association.

Hanson, Philip. 2003. *The Rise and Fall of the Soviet Economy: An Economic History of the USSR from 1945.* New York: Routledge.

Hardt, Michael, and Antonio Negri. 2001. *Empire.* Cambridge, MA: Harvard University Press.

Harris, Jerry. 2009. "Statist Globalization in China, Russia and the Gulf States." *Science and Society* 73, no. 1: 6–33.

Held, David, Anthony Barnett, and Casper Henderson, eds. 2005. *Debating Globalization.* Cambridge: Polity.

Kenny, Thomas. 2018. "How Much U.S. Debt Does China Own?" *The Balance*, June 12. https://www.thebalance.com/how-much-u-s-debt-does-china-own-417016.

King, Gary, Jennifer Pan, and Margaret E. Roberts. 2013. "How Censorship in China Allows Government Criticism but Silences Collective Expression." *American Political Science Review* 107, no. 2: 326–343.

Koesel, Karrie J., and Valerie J. Bunce. 2013. "Diffusion-Proofing: Russian and Chinese Responses to Waves of Popular Mobilizations Against Authoritarian Rulers." *Perspectives on Politics* 11, no. 3: 753–768.

Lynch, Marc. 2012. *The Arab Uprising: The Unfinished Revolutions of the New Middle East.* New York: PublicAffairs.

Milner, Helen V., and Bumba Mukherjee. 2009. "Democratization and Economic Globalization." *Annual Review of Political Science* 12: 163–181.

Rodrik, Dani. 2011. *The Globalization Paradox: Democracy and the Future of the World Economy.* New York: W. W. Norton.

Rutland, Peter, and Andrei Kazantsev. 2016. "The Limits of Russia's 'Soft Power.'" *Journal of Political Power* 9, no. 3: 395–413.

Shambaugh, David. 2015. "China's Soft-Power Push." *Foreign Affairs* 94 (July–August): 99–107.

Stiglitz, Joseph E. 2002. *Globalization and its Discontents*. New York: W. W. Norton.

Tarrow, Sidney. 2005. *The New Transnational Activism*. Cambridge: Cambridge University Press.

Walker, Christopher. 2016. "The Hijacking of 'Soft Power.'" *Journal of Democracy* 27, no. 1: 49–63.

Weyland, Kurt. 2017. "Autocratic Diffusion and Cooperation: The Impact of Interests vs. Ideology." *Democratization* 24, no. 7: 1235–1252.

INDEX

For the benefit of digital users, indexed terms that span two pages (e.g., 52–53) may, on occasion, appear on only one of those pages.

Tables and figures are indicated by *t* and *f* following the page number